I N

T H E I R

O W N

V O I C E S

Get on freeway 80
~~towards~~
- Richmond Hercules

- Corcenas
  Carquinez bridge

$4y

Straight

    exit Venetia Martinez

        go straight, Shell
        station by starbucks

IN THEIR OWN VOICES

Transracial Adoptees Tell Their Stories

Rita J. Simon

and

Rhonda M. Roorda

COLUMBIA UNIVERSITY PRESS

NEW YORK

COLUMBIA UNIVERSITY PRESS

Publishers Since 1893
New York   Chichester, West Sussex
Copyright © 2000 Columbia University Press
All rights reserved
Library of Congress Cataloging-in-Publication Data
Simon, Rita James.
  In their own voices : transracial adoptees tell their stories / Rita J. Simon and
  Rhonda M. Roorda.
    p. cm.
  ISBN 0–231–11828–7 (cloth : alk. paper) — ISBN 0–231–11829–5 (pbk : alk.
  paper)
  [1. Interracial adoption—United States.] I. Roorda, Rhonda. II. Title.

HV875.64.S5576 2000
362.73′4′0973—DC21
                                                                99–055040

Casebound editions of Columbia University Press books are printed on permanent
and durable acid-free paper.
Printed in the United States of America
c 10 9 8 7 6 5 4 3 2 1
p 10 9 8 7 6 5 4

In Their Own Voices is dedicated to the black and biracial men and women who participated in this study and who possess the courage to fulfill their purpose in life and who have the understanding to bring down racial barriers. Thank you for your inspiration and your contribution to this work.

Also, we dedicate this work in loving memory to Jeltje Christina Roorda-Miedema.

Contents

*pseudonym

*pseudonym

Acknowledgments

In Their Own Voices could not have happened without the participation of those who recognized the value and timeliness of this project. This book moves across racial and ethnic lines and exemplifies the collective efforts of adoptive mothers and fathers, educators, playwrites, ministers, grass-roots organizations, politicians, adoption agencies, foster care children, and family and friends. Thank you for your support!

To the following people listed below, thank you especially for bringing forth the "voices" in this book . . . the Simon family, the Roorda family, the Pippin family, the Goode family, the Gray family, Rita Bernhard, Joyce Coninx Wright, and . . .

Dr. Henry Allen
Dr. Charles Atkin
Amanda Baden
Esther Baker
Rachel Ban
Susan Bernbaum
Reynard Blake
Nancy Brazee
Floyd J. and Flora Brumfield
Floyd J. Brumfield Jr.
William C. Campbell
Shelly Campo
Elsa Claveria
Fred Cunningham and Marge Mooney
Barbara Davidson
Thomas and Sydni Dreher
Ron and Nancy Erickson

Amy Espuet
Jeff Febus
Ruby Frazier
Former Mayor W. Wilson Goode
George Grant
Mark Hoeksema
Henry Hofstra
Ruth and Dennis Hoover
Vernon Jarrett
Rev. Dr. Melvin T. Jones
Dan Joranko
Vonja Kirkland
James D. Korf
Rex LaMore
Attorney Ron Landeck
Chuck and Mugs Mast
Rev. Ruth B. Maness

John Melcher
Rev. Dr. Michael C. Murphy
John Nassivera
Arnie A. Parish Jr.
Rev. Rodney S. Patterson
Dr. Mitchell B. Pearlstein
Cyril and Barbara Pinder
Leo and Elaine Pinson
Joseph Rhoiney
Dr. William D. Romanowski
Clarence Schuler
Kathy Smith
Rev. Henry and Effie Soles
Dr. Carl S. Taylor

Dr. June and Richard Thomas
Don and Carol Triezenberg
Dan and Cindy VanderKodde
Gary and Siyroush Visscher
Mike Wall
Eulada P. Watt
Alvin Whitfield and Denise Quarles
Kim and Brian Whitfield
Dr. Gilbert Williams
Keith Williams
J. D. Wilson
Thomas Woods
Michael Worsley
Tyrone and Sharon Wrice

About the Authors

Rita J. Simon is a sociologist who earned her doctorate at the University of Chicago in 1957. Before coming to American University in 1983 to serve as dean of the School of Justice, she was a member of the faculty at the University of Illinois, at the Hebrew University in Jerusalem, and at the University of Chicago. She is currently a "University Professor" in the School of Public Affairs and the Washington College of Law at American University.

Professor Simon has authored twenty-two books and edited thirteen, including: *The Impact of Social Science Data on Supreme Court Decisions* (University of Illinois, 1998); *In the Golden Land: A Century of Russian and Soviet Jewish Immigration* (Praeger, 1997); *The Ambivalent Welcome: Media Coverage of American Immigration* (with Susan Alexander) (Praeger, 1993); *Women's Movements in America: Their Achievements, Disappointments, and Aspirations* (with Gloria Danzinger) (Praeger, 1991); *International Migration: The Female Experience* (with Caroline Brettell) (Rowman and Allanheld, 1986); *Rabbis, Lawyers, Immigrants, Thieves: Women's Roles in America* (Praeger, 1993); *Continuity and Change: A Study of Two Ethnic Communities in Israel* (Cambridge University Press, 1978); *The Crimes Women Commit, the Punishments They Receive* (with Jean Landis) (Lexington, Mass., 1991); *Adoption, Race, and Identity* (with Howard Altstein) (Praeger, 1992); *The Case for Transracial Adoption* (with Howard Altstein and Marygold Melli) (American University Press, 1994).

She is currently editor of *Gender Issues*. From 1978 to 1981 she served as editor of *The American Sociological Review*, and from 1983 to 1986 as editor of *Justice Quarterly*. In 1966 she received a Guggenheim Fellowship.

Rhonda Roorda was born in Rochester, New York, in 1969. She was adopted two years later into a white family and was raised in the Washington, D.C., metropolitan area with her brother, Christopher, and sister, Jean. In 1992 she graduated from Calvin College with a bachelor of arts degree in telecommunications with an emphasis in Spanish and sociology. Her interests in learning about human stories became paramount as an intern in 1991 at WLS-TV, Chicago. In subsequent years she expanded her experiences in the media. From 1991 to 1996 she held intern positions at WOOD-TV and WLHT-Radio, Grand Rapids, and WILX-TV, Lansing. From 1992 to 1994 Ms. Roorda served as program associate to the Council for Christian Colleges and Universities in Washington, D.C., where she concentrated on racial and ethnic issues in higher education. She returned to Michigan to pursue graduate studies. During this time she became the managing editor of *Community News and Views,* a statewide newsletter published by the Michigan Partnership for Economic Development Assistance and the Community and Economic Development Program at Michigan State University. In 1996 she earned her master's degree in Communication-Urban Studies at Michigan State University.

Currently she is working as coordinator of financial and support services at an educational advocacy organization in Lansing, Michigan.

Introduction

Beginning in the late 1960s studies were conducted of white families who adopted American black, Korean, Native American, and other children whose racial and ethnic backgrounds were different from those of their adoptive parents. Part 1 briefly describes those studies and reports their major findings. It also summarizes the ongoing debate between those who support and those who oppose transracial adoption (TRA). The latter claim that black children who are reared in white homes grow up confused about their racial identity and uncomfortable with or alienated from the black community. The supporters of transracial adoption claim that black children reared in white homes grow up aware of and comfortable with their black racial identity and committed to their white adoptive families.

In Their Own Voices does not take an ideological stand on transracial adoption. Rather, its major thrust is to provide a forum for black and mixed-race adults who were transracially adopted and who lived all their childhood and adolescence in white homes to tell their stories in their own words. What was it like to have white parents and siblings, to be the only black person in extended family gatherings, to have their white parents show up at their schools, their sporting events, their social gatherings? What was their relationship with their white siblings during childhood and adolescence-and now, when they are adults? Who were their close friends in primary and high school, whom did they date, how did their black classmates relate to them? As adults who no longer live with their white families, what kinds of relations do they have their adoptive families? Who are their closest friends today? If they are married, did they choose a black spouse? Do they have a clear sense of their racial identity, or are they confused? These are some of the questions the transracial adoptees answer in part 2 of this book. But in the course of the two-to-four-hour interviews conducted with each of the respondents, they tell us a lot more about their experiences and emotions as they were growing up and about how they perceive themselves today. Most of them talk at length about their ties to the black community after they moved out of their parental homes. Many of them also offer advice to white families who are considering adopting a child of a different race, and they state their position on the transracial adoption debate.

All the interviews, save one, were conducted by coauthor Rhonda Roorda, who is a transracial adoptee, and she was interviewed by Rita Simon. Respondents became involved in this project in several ways: Some were referred by friends, or friends of friends; some answered an ad the authors placed in *Interrace* magazine; others were contacted via the Internet; still others contacted Rita Simon, wanting to talk about their experiences;and, finally, in a few instances respondents were well-known personalities the authors sought out for interviews. Eighteen interviews were conducted over the phone and six were done in person. Each interview lasted at least two hours. The interviews were taped, transcribed, and then sent to the respondent for his or her approval. Participants were asked how they wanted to be identified, and the wishes of each respondent were honored. Some preferred to be identified by a pseudonym, others requested that only their first name be given, and still others wanted their real first and last names to be used.

Part 3 compares the respondents' experiences, examining their similarities and differences during various periods of their lives. This final part also compares the respondents' experiences to the major research findings described in part 1 of the book in an effort to see whether the essence of the respondents' feelings and experiences are indeed captured by the surveys and whether their stories match the portraits that emerge based on the survey data.

IN
THEIR
OWN
VOICES

PART I

Argument, Rhetoric, and Data
for and Against Transracial Adoption

Legal Status, History, and Review of Empirical Work

Legal Status of Transracial Adoption

Adoption is a legal process in which a child's legal rights and duties toward his natural parents are terminated and similar rights and duties are created toward the child's adoptive parents. Unknown in common law, adoption was first created in the United States through an 1851 Massachusetts statute. By 1931 every state in the union had passed adoption statutes.

Adoption, like other family law issues, is the province of the states; therefore the law of the state in which the adoption takes place controls the arrangements. The legal structure for adoption consists of the adoption statutes, case law interpreting those statutes, and—perhaps most important—the placement practices of the public and private adoption agencies whose role it is, first, to provide services to parents who wish to place children for adoption and, second, to choose adoptive homes in which those children will be placed. This legal structure shares the common objective of seeking adoptions that are in the child's best interest.

Federal Legislation

Before the United States Congress passed the Multi Ethnic Placement Act (MEPA) in 1994 and the Adoption and Safe Families Act in 1996, transracial adoptions were also governed by the same laws as other adoptions. The purpose of both these acts was to prohibit the use of race "to delay or deny the placement of a child for adoption or foster care on the basis of race, color, or national origin in the adoptive or foster parent or child involved."

While the major supporters of the 1994 act had the above objectives as their goals, the act also contained the following language: "An agency may consider the cultural, ethnic, or racial background of the child and the capacity of the prospective foster or adoptive parents to meet the needs of the child of this background as one of a number of factors used to determine the best interests of the child." That statement thwarted the act's original intention to remove race as a consideration and in fact freed agencies and states to continue to consider a child's racial background in determining placement. It took three more years for the passage of the 1996 act that clearly prohibited the use of race to delay or deny placements.

States found to be in violation would have their quarterly federal funds reduced by 2 percent for the first violation, by 5 percent for the second, and by 10 percent for the third or subsequent violations. Private entities found to be in violation for one quarter would be required to return to the secretary all federal funds received from the state during the quarter. In addition, any individual who is harmed by a violation of this proviso may seek redress in any United States District Court.

Before the intervention of the federal government in 1994 and 1996, twenty states included race as a consideration in the adoption process. Ten of those states simply stated that the race of one or more of the parties directly affected by the adoption was to be included in the petition for adoption. But their statutes were silent as to how the information should be used by those in a position to make final decisions concerning adoption. Arkansas and Minnesota had laws specifically requiring that preference be given to adoption within the same racial group. New Jersey and California statutes provided that an agency may not discriminate with regard to the selection of adoptive parents on the basis of race, but then provided that race might be considered in determining the child's best interest. Kentucky statutes claimed that agencies may not deny placement based on race unless the biological parents express a clear desire to so discriminate, in which case their wishes must be respected.

At the time this book went to press there were no data indicating the effectiveness of the 1996 Adoption and Safe Families Act in moving minority children out of institutions and foster care into adoptive homes. Were the states finding ways of ignoring the intent of the act and doing business as usual? The answer to this question is a very important one. Unfortunately it must await greater efforts at determining what is actually happening.

Adoption Statistics

Transracial adoption (TRA) began with the activities of the Children's Service Center and a group of parents in Montreal, Canada, who in 1960 founded the Open Door Society. The Children's Service Center sought placement for black children among Canada's black community. It worked with black community leaders and the mass media in its efforts to find black homes for these children. It was unsuccessful. The center then turned to its list of white adoptive parents, and the first transracial adoptions were made. Between 1951 and 1963 five black and sixty-six biracial Canadian children were transracially adopted by white families.

In the United States 1961 marked the founding in Minnesota of Parents to Adopt Minority Youngsters (PAMY). PAMY was one of the first groups to be formed in this country along the lines of Canada's Open Door Society. It provided similar referral, recruitment, and public relations functions. PAMY's involvement with transracial adoption, like that of the Open Door Society, came as an unexpected by-product of its original unsuccessful attempt to secure black adoptive homes for black children. From 1962 through 1965 approximately twenty black children in Minnesota were adopted by white families through the efforts of PAMY. By 1969 forty-seven organizations similar to the Open Door Society were operating in the United States.

The federal government began collecting national adoption figures in 1944 and stopped doing so in 1975. In that year the Children's Bureau reported that there were 129,000 adoptions, of which 831 were transracial.

In 1982 a statistician at the Administration for Children, Youth, and Families wrote, "There are no reliable national statistics available on virtually all . . . aspects of adoption. To remedy the situation, Congress mandated the government to resume collecting national figures on adoption by October 1991. In December 1995 the U.S. Department of Health and Human Services published final rules implementing the Adoption and Foster Care Analysis and Reporting System. The rules require states to collect data on all adopted children who were placed by the state child welfare agency or private agencies under contract with the public child welfare agency. But as of the time this book went to press, national adoption data are still not available.

The following are approximate 1996 figures relevant to TRA:

1. There are anywhere from 450,000 to 500,000 children in America's foster care system, about 40 percent of whom are black.[1]

2. There are about 50,000 legally free-for-adoption children, many of whom have special needs (physically/emotionally disabled, sibling groups, older, nonwhite). This figure rises to about 85,000 children if the formula used by many states is taken into account, namely, that

Table 1   Number of Adoptions by Year and Percent Change

Year	1987	1990	1992	% Change 1987–90	% Change 1990–92
Number of adoptions	117,585	118,779	128,000*	+1.0	+7.7

Source: "Adoption Statistics by State," Victor Eugene Flango and Carol R. Flango, *Child Welfare,* CWLA, 52, no. 3 (May–June 1993): 311–19.
*Interview with staffer, U.S. House of Representatives, Ways and Means Committee

about 20 percent of all foster care children eventually have adoption as a casework goal.[2]

3. Table 1 represents all adoptions in 1987, 1990, and 1992 and indicates the changes in percentage. Adoptions are not classified as related (those involving stepparents and relatives) or unrelated (those involving non-relatives). In most years these are approximately equally divided. For example, in 1986 related adoptions accounted for 50.9 percent of all adoptions; unrelated adoptions equaled the remainder, 49.1 percent.[3]

4. TRA figures are extremely hard to come by. Most would agree that actual numbers are very small. For example, in analyzing 1987 data it was found that "92 percent of all adoptions involve an adoptive mother and child of the same race. . . . In only 8 percent of all adoptions are the parents and children of different races."[4]

But this does not mean that 8 percent of all adoptions in the United States were TRAs. Included in this figure are thousands of intercountry adoptions. In fact the 1987 TRA figure, where a black child was adopted by a white family, may be as low as 1.2 percent. There is no reason to believe that this figure is any different in 1999.

Opposition to Transracial Adoption

Organized opposition to transracial adoption began in the early part of the 1970s and was formidable enough by 1975 to bring about a reversal in policy on the part of major adoption agencies in most states throughout the country. The opposition was led and organized primarily by the National Association of Black Social Workers (NABSW) and by leaders of black political organizations, who saw in the practice an insidious scheme for depriving the black community of its most valuable future resource: its children.

Opposition also came from some of the leaders of Native American groups, who labeled transracial adoption "genocide" and also accused white society of perpetuating its most malevolent scheme, that of seeking to deny the Native Americans their future by taking away their children.

Both the black and Native American groups who were opposed to transracial adoption agreed that it would be impossible for white parents to rear black or Indian children in an environment that would permit the children to retain or develop a black or Indian identity. Even if some white parents might want their adopted children to grow up Indian or black, they would lack the skills, insight, and experience necessary to accomplish such a task.

At its national conference in 1971 the president of the NABSW, William T. Merritt, announced, "Black children should be placed only with black families, whether in foster care or for adoption."[5] The following excerpt establishes the flavor of the speech:

> Black children should be placed only with Black families, whether in foster care or adoption. Black children belong physically, psychologically, and culturally in Black families in order that they receive the total sense of themselves and develop a sound projection of their future. . . . Black children in white homes are cut off from the healthy development of themselves as Black people. The socialization process for every child begins at birth. Included in the socialization process is that child's cultural heritage which is an important segment of the total process. This must begin at the earliest moment; otherwise our children will not have the background and knowledge which is necessary to survive in a racist society. This is impossible if the child is placed with white parents in a white environment. . . .
>
> We [the members of the NABSW] have committed ourselves to go back to our communities and work to end this particular form of genocide [transracial adoption].[6]

In his testimony before a Senate committee on 25 June 1985 Merritt reiterated the NABSW position:

> We are opposed to transracial adoption as a solution to permanent placement for Black children. We have an ethnic, moral, and professional obligation to oppose transracial adoption. We are therefore *legally* justified in our efforts to pro-

tect the right of Black children, Black families, and the Black community. We view the placement of Black children in White homes as a hostile act against our community. It is a blatant form of race and cultural genocide.[7]

In addition, Merritt made the following claims:

- Black children who grow up in white families suffer severe identity problems. On the one hand, the white community has not fully accepted them; and on the other hand, they have no significant contact with Black people.
- Black children adopted transracially often do not develop the coping mechanisms necessary to function in a society that is inherently racist against African Americans.
- Transracial adoptions, in the long term, often end in disruption; and the Black children are returned to foster care.

In 1974, the Black Caucus of the North American Conference on Adoptable Children recommended "support [for] the consciousness development movement of all groups" and "that every possible attempt should be made to place black and other minority children in a cultural and racial setting similar to their original group."[8] In May 1975 the dean of the Howard University School of Social Work and president of the NABSW stated that "black children who grow up in white homes end up with white psyches."[9]

In 1972 Leon Chestang posed a series of critical questions for white parents who had adopted or were considering adopting a black child:

The central focus of concern in biracial adoption should be the prospective adoptive parents. Are they aware of what they are getting into? Do they view their act as purely humanitarian, divorced from its social consequences? Such a response leaves the adoptive parents open to an overwhelming shock when friends and family reject and condemn them. Are they interested in building world brotherhood without recognizing the personal consequences for the child placed in such circumstances? Such people are likely to be well meaning but unable to relate to the child's individual needs. Are the applicants attempting to solve a personal or social problem through biracial adoption? Such individuals are likely to place an undue burden on the child in resolving their problems.[10]

And, Chestang also wondered, what of the implications for the adoptive family itself of living with a child of another race? Are negative societal traits attributed to blacks likely to be passed on to the adoptive family, thereby subjecting the family to insults, racial slurs, and ostracism?

> The white family that adopts a black child is no longer a "white family." In the eyes of the community, its members become traitors, nigger-lovers, do-gooders, rebels, oddballs, and, most significantly, ruiners of the community. Unusual psychological armaments are required to shield oneself from the behavioral and emotional onslaught of these epithets.[11]

But Chestang concluded his piece on a more optimistic note than most critics of transracial adoption: "Who knows what problems will confront the black child reared by a white family and what the outcome will be?" he asked. "But these children, if they survive, have the potential for becoming catalysts for society in general."[12]

Most writers who are opposed to transracial adoption have challenged two main hypotheses: first, that there are insufficient black adoptive parents willing to adopt black children; and, second, that the benefits a black child would receive in a white family surpass those the child would receive in an institution. They have observed that many potential nonwhite adoptive parents are disqualified because of adoption agencies' widespread use of white middle-class criteria selection. They also noted that blacks historically have adopted informally, preferring not to rely on agencies and courts for sanction. And they claimed that no longitudinal outcome data were available to show that transracial adoption of black children outweighed the known disadvantages of an institution or foster care. They predicted family and personal problems as the children grew into preadolescence and adolescence. A leading black organization pointed to transracially adopted black children who were being returned to foster care because the adoption was not "working out" or were being placed in residential treatment by their white adoptive parents who could not manage them.

One of the most prevalent arguments against transracial adoption is that white families—no matter how liberal or well-intended—cannot teach a black child how to survive in an essentially racist society. Many of those opposed to transracial adoption insist that because white adoptive parents are not black and cannot experience minority black status they will rear a psychologically defenseless individual, incapable of understanding and dealing with the racism that exists in our society. Amuzie Chimuzie articulated this position when he emphasized the fear of black social workers and other experts in the child-rearing field that black children reared in white homes will not develop the characteristics needed to survive and flourish in a predominantly white society. After first observing that children tend to acquire most of the psychological and social characteristics of the families and communities in which they are reared, Chimuzie added, "it is therefore possible that black children reared in white families and communities will develop antiblack psychological and social characteristics."[13]

Some black professionals argue that there is a major bottleneck in the placement of black children in black adoptive homes because child welfare agencies are staffed mainly by white social workers who exercise control over adoptions. That these white agencies are in the position of recruiting and approving black families for adoption causes some blacks to argue that there is institutional racism on the part of the whites. In contrast, there have been several instances where concerted efforts by black child welfare agencies to locate and approve adoptive black families resulted in the adoption of comparatively large numbers of parentless black children.

The above position was strongly argued by Evelyn Moore, executive director of the National Black Child Development Institute.[14] In an extensive interview on the child welfare system, published by the National Association of Social Workers (NASW) in April 1984—a significant portion of which dealt either directly or indirectly with TRA—Moore said that 83 percent of all child welfare workers in the United States are white, whereas 30–40 percent of their cases deal with black families. This skewed ratio, she contends, is one of the reasons there are so few cases of black inracial adoption (IRA). "The adoption system in this country was established to provide white children to white families. As a result, most people who work in the system know very little about black culture or the black community."[15]

Moore also argued that "white middle-class standards" are largely responsible for the rejection of lower-class and working-class black families as potential adopters; instead, they are encouraged to become foster parents: "while black children under the age of 19 represent only 14 percent of the children not living with their birth parents" (e.g., in foster care or institutionalized.)[16]

Two studies conducted by the National Urban League in 1984 are cited by those opposed to transracial adoption as further evidence of the likelihood that institutional racism is one of the primary reasons that more black children are not given to prospective black adoptive families.[17] These studies reported that of eight hundred black families applying for adoptive parental status, only two families were approved—0.25 compared to a national average of 10 percent. Another study concluded that 40–50 percent of the black families sampled would consider adoption. An acceptance rate of 0.25 percent becomes somewhat more dramatic when compared to black inracial adoption rates of eighteen per ten thousand families. (The figures for whites and Hispanics are four and three per ten thousand families, respectively.)

In a 1987 *Ebony* article entitled "Should Whites Adopt Black Children?" the president of the NABSW was quoted as saying: "Our position is that the African-American family should be maintained and its integrity preserved. We see the lateral transfer of black children to white families as contradictory to our preservation efforts."[18]

In 1986 the founder of Homes for Black Children—a successful black adoption agency in Detroit—issued the following statement:

> I believe it was the convergence of these two diverse movements, the transracial adoption movement and the one on the part of Black people to affirm our ability to care for ourselves and our children . . . that resulted in the clash. . . . For those of us who are Black, the pain has been the fear of losing control of our own destiny through the loss of our children. . . . There is real fear, in the hearts of some of us who are Black, as to whether a child who is Black can be protected in this society, without the protection of families who are most like him . . . [A] Black child is especially endangered when agencies or programs that are successful in finding Black families are not available to meet his need.[19]

The winter 1989 newsletter of Homes for Black Children carried a response to the above statement, written by a member of an Ohio organization called Adopting Older Kids: "Nowhere in this statement is there acknowledgment of the adoptive parents whose love transcends racial boundaries. . . . Nor are there suggestions about the future of those minority children, already waiting for families, who will be denied loving homes because agencies refuse to consider transracial placements."[20]

How can one explain the discrepancy between the apparently widespread desire to adopt among blacks and the dearth of approved black homes for adoption? First, blacks have not adopted in the expected numbers because child welfare agencies have not actively recruited in black communities—using community resources, the black media, and churches. Second, there is a historic suspicion of public agencies among many blacks, the consequence of which is that many restrict their involvement with them. Third, many blacks feel that no matter how close they come to fulfilling the criteria established for adoption, the fact that many reside in less affluent areas makes the likelihood of their being approved slight.

In 1987 the Council for a Black Economic Agenda—a group dedicated to advancing social welfare policies relevant to the black community—met with President Ronald Reagan to discuss what they and other black groups see as unfair practices on the part of adoption agencies. Urging that eligibility criteria for adoption such as marital status, income, and adoption fees be reexamined with an eye toward more black-oriented standards, they said, "The kind of standards that are being applied by these traditional agencies discriminate against Black parents."[21]

At the annual meeting of the Black Adoption Committee for Kids on 8 November 1991 another former president of the National Association of Black Social Workers, Morris Jeff Jr., stated: "Placing African-American children in white European-American homes is an overt hostility, the ultimate insult to black heritage. It is the creation of a race of children with African faces and European minds. It is a simple answer to a complex situation. It causes more problems than it solves."[22]

The Child Welfare League of America (CWLA) holds the position expressed in its "Standards for Adoption Service," which states:

> Children in need of adoption have a right to be placed into a family that reflects their ethnicity or race. Children should not have their adoption denied or significantly delayed, however, when adoptive parents of other ethnic or racial groups are available.
>
> . . . In any adoption plan, however, the best interest of the child should be paramount. If aggressive, ongoing recruitment efforts are unsuccessful in finding families of the same ethnicity or culture, other families should be considered.[23]

Another example in which transracial adoption is the second choice to inracial placement appears in a statement made by Father George Clements, a noted black clergyman and founder of "One Church, One Child," a national plan whereby one family from each black church would adopt a black child. After stating that inracial adoptions were preferable to transracial adoptions, Father Clements added, "But you cannot always have the ideal, and in lieu of the ideal, I certainly would opt for an Anglo couple, or whatever nationality, taking a child in."[24]

By the end of the 1990s the major arguments against TRA by those opposed to it are (1) that more than sufficient numbers of black families would be waiting to adopt all available black children were it not for racist adoption practices that prevent them from doing so; and (2) that black children adopted by white parents would develop into racially confused adults, no matter how sincere their white adoptive parents were, no matter how hard they tried to instill in their adopted children a sense of black pride, and no matter what research said to the contrary.

It also appears that the major child welfare and adoption organizations remain strongly committed to the idea of recruiting minority adoptive parents for similar children. Organizations such as the National Association of Black Social Workers continue to argue that race should be the primary determinant of a child's placement, even if the child has already been placed with and integrated into a family of another race.

The arguments supporting transracial adoptions are based primarily on the results of empirical work that have been conducted over more than thirty years. Those studies are summarized in the next section.

Review of Empirical Studies

The work of Lucille Grow and Deborah Shapiro of the Child Welfare League represents one of the earliest studies of transracial adoption. Published in 1974, the major purpose of *Black Children, White Parents* was to assess the success of transracial adoptions.[25] Their respondents consisted of 125 families.

Based on the children's scores on the California Test of Personality (which purports to measure social and personal adjustment), Grow and Shapiro concluded that the children in their study made about as successful an adjustment in their adoptive homes as other nonwhite children had in prior studies. They claimed that 77 percent of their children had adjusted successfully and that this percentage was similar to that reported in other studies. Grow and Shapiro also compared the scores of transracially adopted children with those of adopted white children on the California Test of Personality. A score below the twentieth percentile was defined as reflecting poor adjustment, and a score above the fiftieth percentile was defined as indicating good adjustment. They found that the scores of the transracially adopted children and those of white adopted children matched very closely.

In 1977 Joyce Ladner—using the membership lists of the Open Door Society and the Council on Adoptable Children (COAC) as her sample frames—conducted in-depth interviews with 136 parents in Georgia, Missouri, Washington, D.C., Maryland, Virginia, Connecticut, and Minnesota. Before reporting her findings, she introduced a personal note:

> This research brought with it many self-discoveries. My initial feelings were mixed. I felt some trepidation about studying white people, a new undertaking for me. Intellectual curiosity notwithstanding, I had the gnawing sensation that I shouldn't delve too deeply because the findings might be too controversial. I wondered too if couples I intended to interview would tell me the truth. Would some lie in order to coverup their mistakes and disappointments with the adoption? How much would they leave unsaid? Would some refuse to be interviewed because of their preconceived notions about my motives? Would they stereotype me as a hostile black sociologist who wanted to "prove" that these adoptions would produce unhealthy children?[26]

By the end of the study, Ladner was convinced that "there are whites who are capable of rearing emotionally healthy black children." Such parents, Ladner continued, "must be idealistic about the future but also realistic about the society in which they now live."[27]

To deny racial, ethnic, and social class polarization exists, and to deny that their child is going to be considered a "black child," regardless of how light his or her complexion, how sharp their features, or how straight their hair, means that these parents are unable to deal with reality as negative as they may perceive that reality to be. On the other hand, it is equally important for parents to recognize that no matter how immersed they become in the black experience, they can never become black. Keeping this in mind, they should avoid the pitfalls of trying to practice an all-black lifestyle, for it, too, is unrealistic in the long run, since their family includes blacks and whites and should therefore be part of the larger black and white society.

Charles Zastrow's doctoral dissertation, published in 1977, compared the reactions of forty-one white couples who had adopted a black child to a matched sample of forty-one white couples who had adopted a white child.[28] All the families lived in Wisconsin. The two groups were matched on the age of the adopted child and on the socioeconomic status of the adoptive parents. All the children in the study were preschoolers. The overall findings indicated that the outcomes of the transracial placements were as successful as the inracial placements. Zastrow commented:

> One of the most notable findings is that TRA parents
> reported [that] considerable fewer problems related to the
> care of the child have arisen than they anticipated prior to the
> adoption. . . . Many of the TRA couples mentioned that they
> became "color-blind" shortly after adoption; i.e., they
> stopped seeing the child as a black, and came to perceive the
> child as an individual who is a member of their family.[29]

When the parents were asked to rate their overall satisfaction with the adoptive experience, 99 percent of the TRA parents and 100 percent of the IRA parents checked "extremely satisfying" or "more satisfying than dissatisfying."

And on another measure of satisfaction—one in which the parents rated their degree of satisfaction with certain aspects of their adoptive experience—out of a possible maximum of 98 points, the mean score of the TRA parents was 92.1 and that of the IRA parents was 92.0.

Using a mail survey in 1981, William Feigelman and Arnold Silverman compared the adjustment of fifty-six black children adopted by white families to ninety-seven white children adopted by white families. The parents were asked to assess their child's overall adjustment and to indicate the frequency with which their child demonstrated emotional and physical problems. Silverman and Feigelman concluded that the child's age—not the transracial adoption—had the most significant impact on development and adjustment. The older the child, the greater the problems. They found no relationship between the adjustment and racial identity.[30]

W. M. Womak and W. Fulton's study of transracial adoptees and nonadopted black preschool children found no significant differences in racial attitudes between the two groups of children.[31]

In 1983 Ruth McRoy and Louis Zurcher reported the findings of their study of thirty black adolescents who had been transracially adopted and thirty black adolescents who had been adopted by black parents.[32] In the concluding chapter of their book, McRoy and Zurcher wrote: "The transracial and inracial adoptees in the authors' study were physically healthy and exhibited typical adolescent relationships with their parents, siblings, teachers, and peers. Similarly, regardless of the race of their adoptive parents, they reflected positive feelings of self-regard."[33]

Throughout the book the authors emphasized that the quality of parenting was more important than whether the black child had been inracially or transracially adopted: "Most certainly, transracial adoptive parents experience some challenges different from inracial adoptive parents, but in this study all the parents successfully met the challenges."[34]

In 1988 Joan Shireman and Penny Johnson described the results of their study involving twenty-six inracial (black) and twenty-six transracial adoptive families in Chicago. They reported very few differences between the two groups of 8-year-old adoptees. Using the Clark and Clark Doll Test to establish racial identity, 73 percent of the transracially adopted identified themselves as black compared to 80 percent for the inracially adopted black children. The authors concluded that 75 percent of the transracial adoptees and 80 percent of the inracial adoptees appeared to be doing quite well. They also commented that the transracial adoptees had developed pride in being black and were comfortable in their interactions with both black and white races.[35]

In 1988 Richard Barth reported that transracial placements were no more likely to be disruptive than other types of adoptions.[36] The fact that transracial placements were as stable as other, more traditional adoptive arrangements was reinforced by data presented in 1988 at a meeting of the North American Council on Adoptable Children (NACAC) focusing on adoption disruption. There it was reported that the rate of adoption disruptions averaged about 15 percent. Disruptions, they reported, did not appear to be influenced by the adoptees' race or gender or by the fact that they were placed as a sibling group.

In 1993 Christopher Bagley compared a group of twenty-seven transracial adoptees to a group of twenty-five inracially adopted whites. Both sets of adoptees were approximately 19 years old and were, on average, about 2 years old when adopted. Bagley concluded his study with the following statement: "The findings of the present study underscore those from previous American research on transracial adoption. Transracial adoption . . .

appears to meet the psychosocial and developmental needs of the large majority of the children involved, and can be just as successful as inracial adoption."[37]

In 1994 the Search Institute published *Growing Up Adopted,* a report that describes the results of interviews with 715 families who adopted infants between 1974 and 1980. When the survey was conducted in 1992–93, the adoptees' ages ranged from 12 to 18. A total of 881 adopted children, 1,262 parents, and 78 nonadopted siblings participated in the study.[38] Among the 881 adoptees, 289 were transracially adopted, of which the largest single group comprised 199 Koreans, who made up 23 percent of the total sample. The Search study reported that 81 percent of the "same-race" adoptees and 84 percent of the TRAs (of whom 68 percent were Korean) said, "I'm glad my parents adopted me."

Various "tests" of "mental health," "self-esteem," and "well-being" were given to the inracial adoptees and the TRAs. The results are shown in Tables 2 and 3.

On attachment to their families, the Search study found that transracial adoptees are more likely than same-race adoptees to be attached to their parents: 65 percent for Asians, 62 percent for all TRAs, and 52 percent for same-race adoptees.

In the words of Elizabeth Bartholet:

> The evidence from empirical studies indicates uniformly that transracial adoptees do as well on measures of psychological and social adjustment as black children raised inracially in relatively similar socio-economic circumstances. The evidence also indicates that transracial adoptees develop comparably strong senses of black identity. They see themselves as black

Table 2   Percent of Adolescents with High Self-Esteem

	Boys	*Girls*
National sample*	51%	39%
All transracial adoptees	55	51
Asian TRAs	53	53
Same-race adoptees	63	53

*National sample of public school adolescents; N = 46,799.

Table 3   Four Measures of Psychological Health for Transracial and Same-Race Adoptions

Measure of Psychological Health	Range	Scale Average		Scale Average (in comparison to same-race group)	
Index of well-being Asian	0–16 11.40	All TRA No difference		11.23	No difference
		Same-race	11.08		
At-risk behavior	0–20	All TRA	1.80		No difference
		Asian	1.55		No difference
		Same-race	1.78		
Self-rated mental health	1–5	All TRA	4.10		No difference
		Asian	4.07		No difference
		Same-race	4.11		
Achenbach	1–120	All TRA	44.63		No difference
		Asian	43.94		No difference
		Same-race	42.29		

and they think well of blackness. The difference is that they feel more comfortable with the white community than blacks raised inracially. This evidence provides no basis for concluding that, for the children involved, there are any problems inherent in transracial placement.[39]

The Simon-Altstein Longitudinal Survey

In 1971–72, as part of the Simon-Altstein Longitudinal Survey, Rita Simon contacted 206 families living in the five cities in the Midwest who were members of the Open Door Society and the Council on Adoptable Children and asked whether she could interview them about their decision to adopt nonwhite children.[40] All the families but two (which declined for reasons unrelated to the adoption) agreed to participate in the study. The parents allowed a team of two graduate students, one male and one female, to interview them in their homes for sixty to ninety minutes at the same time that each of their children, who were between 4 and 7 years old, was being interviewed for about thirty minutes. A total of 204 parents and 366 children were interviewed.

The number of children per family ranged from one to seven; this included birth children as well as those who were adopted. Nineteen percent of the parents did not have any birth children. All those families reported that they were unable to bear children.

Sixty-nine percent of the first-child adoptions were of children less than 1 year old, compared to 80 percent of the second-child adoptions. One explanation for the greater proportion of younger adoptions the second time around is that adoption agencies were more likely to provide such families—who had already proved themselves by their successful first adoption—with their most desirable and sought-after children than they were to place such children in untried homes.

In 1972 only a minority of the families had considered adopting a nonwhite child initially. Most of them said they had wanted a healthy baby. When they found they could not have a healthy white baby, they sought to adopt a healthy black, Indian, or Korean baby—rather than an older white child or a physically or mentally handicapped white child or baby. They preferred a child of another race to a child whose physical or mental disabilities might cause considerable financial drain or emotional strain. About 40 percent of the families intended or wanted to adopt nonwhite children because of their own involvement in the civil rights movement and as a reflection of their general sociopolitical views.

During the first encounter with the children in 1972 (adopted and birth) they were given a series of projective tests including the Kenneth Clark doll tests, puzzles, pictures, and so on, that sought to assess racial awareness, attitudes, and identity. Unlike all other previous doll studies, our respondents did not favor the white doll. It was not considered smarter, prettier, nicer, and so forth, than the black doll either by white or black children. Nor did any of the other tests reveal preferences for white or negative reactions to black. Yet the black and white children in our study accurately identified themselves as white or black on those same tests. Indeed, the most important finding that emerged from our first encounter with the families in 1971–72 was the absence of a white racial preference or bias on the part of white birth children and the nonwhite adopted children.

Over the years we continued to ask about and measure racial attitudes, racial awareness, and racial identity among the adopted and birth children. We also questioned the parents during the first three phases of the study about the activities, if any, in which they, as a family, engaged to enhance their transracial adoptee's racial awareness and racial identity. We heard about dinnertime conversations involving race issues, watching the TV series *Roots*, joining black churches, seeking black godparents, preparing Korean food, traveling to Native American festivals, and related initiatives. As the years progressed, especially during adolescence, it was the children, rather than the parents, who were more likely to want to call a halt to some of these activities. "Not every dinner conversation has to be a lesson in black history" or "We are more interested in the next basketball or football game than in ceremonial dances" were comments we heard frequently from transracial adoptees as they were growing up.

In the 1983–84 phase, all the children were asked to complete a "self-esteem scale," which essentially measures how much respect a respondent has for her- or himself. A person is characterized as having high self-esteem if she or he considers her- or himself to be a person of worth. Low self-esteem means that the individual lacks self-respect. Because we wanted to make the best possible comparison among our respondents, we examined the scores of our black TRAs separately from those of the other TRAs and from those of the white birth and white adopted children. As shown in Table 4, the scores for all four groups were virtually the same. No one group of respondents manifested higher or lower self-esteem than the others.

As shown in Table 5, the lack of differences among our adolescents' responses was again dramatically exemplified in our findings on the "family integration scale," which included such items as the following: "People in our family trust one another"; "My parents know what I am really like as a person"; "I enjoy family life." The hypothesis was that adopted children would feel less integrated than children born into the families. But the scores reported by our four groups of respondents (black TRAs, other TRAs, white birth children, and white adopted children) showed no significant differences; indeed, the three largest categories were almost identical: 15.4, 15.2, and 15.4.

Table 4   Self-Esteem Scores

Categories of Respondents	N	Median	Mean	Standard Deviation
Black TRAs	86	17.8	18.1	3.49
Other TRAs	17	18.0	18.3	3.66
Birth children	83	18.1	18.0	3.91
White/adopted	15	18.0	18.5	3.16

Table 5   Family Integration Scores

Categories of Respondents	N	Median	Mean	Standard Deviation
Black TRAs	86	15.4	15.4	3.66
Other TRAs	22	15.3	15.2	4.27
Birth children	83	14.7	15.4	3.17
White/adopted	15	15.5	16.7	4.00

In 1983 we had asked the respondents to identify by race their three closest friends; 73 percent of the TRAs reported that their closest friend was white. Among the birth children, 89, 80, and 72 percent reported, respectively, that their first, second, and third closest friends were white. In 1991, 53 percent of the TRAs said that their closest friend was white, and 70 percent said their second and third closest friends were white. For the birth children, more than 90 percent said that their three closest friends were white. A comparison of the two sets of responses—those reported in 1983 and those given in 1991—shows that TRAs had shifted their close friendships from white to nonwhite and a higher percentage of the birth respondents had moved into a white world.

The next portion of the interview focused on a comparison of the respondents' perceptions of their relationship with their parents at the present time and when they were living at home during adolescence; on their reactions to their childhoods; and—for the TRAs—on how they felt about growing up in a white family.

Respondents were asked the following question: "When you were an adolescent—and at the present time—how would you describe your relationship with your mother and with your father?" The data indicate that, for both the adopted and birth children, relations with both parents improved between adolescence and young adulthood. During adolescence the TRAs had a more distant relationship with their mothers and fathers than did the birth children; but in their young adult years more than 80 percent of both the TRAs and the birth children described their relationship to their mothers and fathers as very close or fairly close.

We asked the TRAs a series of questions about their relationships to family members during their childhood and adolescence, many of which focused on racial differences. The first such question was this: "Do you remember when you first realized that you looked different from your parents?" to which 75 percent answered that they did not remember. The others mentioned events such as "at family gatherings," "when my parents first came to school," "on vacations," or "when we were doing out-of-the-ordinary activities," and "immediately, at the time of adoption." The latter response was made by children who were not infants at the time of their adoption.

The next question was this: "How do you think the fact that you had a different racial background from your birth brother(s) and/or sister(s) affected your relationship with them as you were growing up?" Almost 90 percent of those who had siblings said it made little or no difference. The few others were divided among those who said that it had a positive effect, a negative effect, or that they were not sure what, if any, effect it had.

We continued with this question: "Was being of a different race from your adoptive family easier or harder during various stages of your life?" Forty percent responded that they rarely found it difficult; 8 percent said they found early childhood the easiest; and another 8 percent said that they had a difficult time throughout their childhood and adolescence. Twenty-nine percent said that people of the same racial background as their own reacted "very negatively" or "negatively" toward them during their adolescence. The other responses ranged from "neutral" (37 percent) to "positive" (10 percent) and "very positive" (15 percent).

We asked the birth children how they felt about living in a family with a sibling of a different race. Only one respondent reported having "somewhat negative" feelings, and this same respondent felt that his parents had made a mistake in their decision to adopt a black child. Thirty percent acknowledged that at times during their childhood they felt out of place in their families—for example, when their families participated in "ethnic ceremonies" or attended black churches. But when asked, "How do you think being white by birth but having nonwhite siblings affected how you perceive yourself today?" all but 13 percent answered that the experience "had no effect." The others cited positive effects such as "it broadened my understanding" or it "made me think of myself as part of the human race rather than part of any special racial category."

Among those children whose parents lived in the same community, all the TRAs and birth children said that they saw their parents at least two or three times a month; most saw them almost every day or a couple of times a week.

On the 1983 survey we asked the children a modified version of the following question: "If you had a serious personal problem (involving your marriage, your children, your health, etc.), who is the first person you would turn to, the second person, the third?" Two other problems were posed: that concerning money and trouble with the law. In 1983, 46.8 percent of the TRAs chose a parent or a sibling; 45 percent of the birth children chose a parent or sibling; and 25 percent of the white adoptees chose a parent or a sibling.

In 1991—eight years later—we again asked the children who would be the first, second, and third person they would turn to with a serious personal problem. Again we found no evidence that TRAs were less integrated into their families than the white children. The TRAs were as likely, or more likely, to turn to parents and siblings as were the birth children or white adopted children. In almost all instances, however, children in all three categories said that they would first turn to their adopted parents or birth parents. For the TRAs, a sibling was named as the next person. For the birth children, spouses and/or girlfriends or boyfriends constituted the second likely choice. The birth children and the white adoptees were older than the TRAs (a median age, respectively, of 26 and 25 versus 22), and this may explain why they were less likely to turn to their parents for help or advice.

We believe that one of the important measures of the parents' unselfish love and concern for their adopted children may be found in their responses to the question about the children's birth parents. In 1983 approximately 40 percent of the parents told us that their children expressed interest in learning about their birth parents. Of those, 7 percent also wanted to locate and meet one or both of their birth parents; an additional 10 percent of the parents had already provided their adopted children with whatever information they had—even before, or in the absence of, the children's request. Of the 40 percent whose children asked about their birth parents, only three parents were sufficiently threatened by the child's interest to refuse to provide the information they had.

Looking at the issue from the adoptees' perspective, we found that 38 percent of the TRAs had already tried or were planning to try to locate their birth parents. The others said that they had not decided or did not plan to try to find them. The most typical response was: "I am happy with my family. My other parents gave me up." Most of the adoptees did not have deeply rooted feelings about their reasons for wanting to locate their birth parents; curiosity seemed to characterize most of their feelings. Many said, "I would like to see what I will look like when I'm older." Those for whom the issue was more traumatic were children who were adopted when they were three or more years of age, had some memory of a mother, and felt a sense of abandonment or betrayal. They expressed their feelings in this rather muted phrase: "I'll feel incomplete until I do."

In the 1991 phase of the study the transracial adoptees, who, by this time, were young adults, were asked how they felt about the practice of placing nonwhite—especially black—children in white homes, what recommendations they might have about adoption practices, and what advice they might offer white parents who are considering transracial adoption. We also asked the respondents to evaluate their own experiences with transracial adoption.

We opened the topic by stating, "You have probably heard of the position taken by the National Association of Black Social Workers and by several councils of Native Americans strongly opposing transracial adoption. Do you agree or disagree with their position? Eighty percent of the adoptees and 70 percent of the birth children disagreed with the NABSW position. Among the latter, 17 percent agreed and 13 percent were not sure. Only 5 percent of the transracial adoptees agreed with the NABSW position. Others were not sure how they felt about the issue. The reasons most often given for why they disagreed were that "racial differences are not crucial," "TRA is the best practical alternative," and "having a loving, secure, relationship in a family setting is all-important."

One black male adoptee said, "My parents have never been racist. They took shit for adopting two black kids. I'm proud of them for it. The Black Social Workers' Association promotes a separatist ideology."

Another black female commented, "It's a crock—it's just ridiculous. They [the NABSW] should be happy to get families for these children—period. My parents made sure we grew up in a racially diverse neighborhood. Now I am fully comfortable with who I am."

Another commented, "I feel lucky to have been adopted when I was very young [24 days old]. I was brought up to be self-confident—to be the best I can. I was raised in an honest environment.

In response to the question, "Would you urge social workers and adoption agencies to place nonwhite children in white homes?" 70 percent of the TRAs and 67 percent of the birth children said yes without qualifications or stipulations. Almost all the others made some stipulations, most commonly that it should not be the placement of first choice, that a search should be made to find appropriate families of the same racial background as the children. The second most frequently mentioned stipulation was that the children should be placed with those white families who are "willing to make a commitment to exposing the child to his or her native culture."

We then shifted to a more personal note and asked, "How do you think being black (or Korean or Native American) and raised by white parents has affected how you perceive yourself today?" One-third of the TRAs thought the adoption had a positive effect on their self-image, one-third thought it had no effect, and one-third did not know what effect the adoption had on their self-image.

One male adoptee said, "Multicultural attitudes develop better children. I was brought up without prejudice. The experience is fulfilling and enriching for parents and children."

Our next question was this: "All things considered, would you have preferred to have been adopted by parents whose racial background was the same as yours?" Seven percent said yes; 67 percent said no; 4 percent said they were not sure or did not know; and 22 percent did not answer. When asked why they held the position they did, most said, in essence, "My life has worked out very well"; "My parents love me"; or "Race is not that important."

One female black adoptee believed that she "got the best of both worlds. I can be myself and have black and white friends. I don't look at people for their race."

Another said, "The transracial adoption experience gives us an open view of the world. Prejudice comes from ignorance."

When asked what advice they would give to parents who have the opportunity to adopt a young child of "your racial background," and about how she or he should be reared, 91 percent largely advised that such parents be sensitive to racial issues; 9 percent advised that they reconsider.

One of the transracial adoptees who agrees with the position of the NABSW said, "I feel that I missed out on black culture. I can sit and read a book about Martin Luther King, but it is not the same." His advice to white parents who adopt black children is this: "Make sure they [the TRAs] have the influence of blacks in their lives; even if you have to go out and make friends with black families. It's a must—otherwise you are cheating them [the TRAs] of something valuable."

Notes

1. Ellen Goodman, "The Orphanage Option," *Washington Post*, 24 April 1994, C6; and "Who Has the Rights to Black Children," *Baltimore Sun*, 7 December 1993, 19A.

2. Packard Foundation, *The Future of Children: Adoption* 3, no. 1 (spring 1993): 63.

3. Ibid.

4. Ibid., 29.

5. William T. Merritt, Speech presented to the National Association of Black Social Workers National Conference, Washington, D.C., 1971.

6. Ibid.

7. U.S. Senate, Committee on Labor and Human Resources, Excerpt from testimony by William T. Merritt, president of the National Association of Black Social Workers, June 25, 1985.

8. North American Council on Adoptable Children, "Barriers to Same Race Placement," (St. Paul, Minn., 1991).

9. Sandy Barnesky, "The Question: Is It Bad for Black Children to Be Adopted by Whites?" *Baltimore Sun*, 28 May 1975, B1.

10. Leon Chestang, "The Dilemma of Bi-racial Adoption," *Social Work* (May 1972): 100–105.

11. Ibid., 103.

12. Ibid., 105.

13. Amuzie Chimuzie, "Transracial Adoption of Black Children," *Social Work* (July 1975): 296–301.

14. Evelyn Moore, "Black Children Facing Adoption Barriers," *NASW News* (April 1984): 9.

15. Ibid.

16. Ibid., 10.

17. Ibid., 11.

18. Morris Jeff Jr., "Should Whites Adopt Black Children?" *Ebony* (September 1987): 78.

19. Homes for Black Children, Statement in *Homes for Black Children*, newsletter, Detroit, Mich., 1986.

20. *Homes for Black Children* (winter 1989).

21. Council for a Black Economic Agenda, Press release on meeting with President Ronald Reagan, Washington, D.C., 1987.

22. Morris Jeff Jr., "Interracial Adoptions Wrong, Says Official," *St. Louis Post Dispatch*, 9 November 1991.

23. Child Welfare League of America, *Standards for Adoption Service* (New York, 1988).

24. "Statement of Father George Clements," *The National Adoption Report* 10, no. 3 (Washington, D.C., May–June 1989).

25. Lucille J. Grow and Deborah Shapiro, *Black Children, White Parents: A Study of Transracial Adoption* (New York: Child Welfare League of America, 1974).

26. Joyce Ladner, *Mixed Families* (New York: Archer, 1977).

27. Ibid., xii.

28. Charles H. Zastrow, *Outcome of Black Children-White Parents Transracial Adoptions* (San Francisco: R&E Research Associates, 1977).

29. Ibid., 81

30. William Feigelman and Arnold Silverman, *Chosen Child: New Patterns of Adoptive Relationships* (New York: Praeger, 1983).

31. W. M. Womack and W. Fulton, "Transracial Adoption and the Black Preschool Child," *Journal of American Academy of Child Psychiatry* 20 (1981): 712–24.

32. Ruth McRoy and Louis A. Zurcher, *Transracial and Inracial Adoptees* (Springfield, Ill.: Charles C. Thomas, 1983).

33. Ibid., 130

34. Ibid., 138

35. Joan Shireman and Penny Johnson, *Growing Up Adopted* (Chicago: Chicago Child Care Society, 1988).

36. Richard P. Barth and Marian Berry, *Adoption and Disruption* (New York: Aldine de Bruyter, 1988), 3–35.

37. Christopher Bagley, "Transracial Adoptions in Britain: A Follow Up Study," *Child Welfare* (June 1993): 149.

38. Peter L. Benson, Anu R. Sharma, and Eugene Roehlkerparrain, *Growing Up Adopted: A Portrait of Adolescents and Their Families* (Minneapolis, Minn.: Search Institute, 1994).

39. Elizabeth Bartholet, "Where Do Black Children Belong? Politics of Race Matching in Adoption," 139 *University of Pennsylvania Law Review* 1163 (1991).

40. Rita J. Simon and Howard Altstein, *Adoption, Race, and Identity: From Infancy Through Adolescence* (New York: Praeger, 1992); and Rita J. Simon, Howard Altstein, and Marygold S. Melli, *The Case for Transracial Adoption* (Washington, D.C.: The American University Press, 1994).

PART II

Transracial Adoptees Tell Their Stories

Introduction

Each of the following twenty-four interviews lasted between two and four hours. All were conducted over the phone except six, three females and three males, who were interviewed in person. The names of the interviewees that appear in these transcripts were those they wished to be identified by. The names of relatives, places of birth and childhood homes, and names of schools attended are also those the interviewees agreed could be identified. In cases where interviewees preferred using a pseudonym, that is so indicated in the transcript.

Female respondents range in age from 22 to 28 years. The men's ages range from 23 to 31, with one outlier, who is 57 years old. Sixteen of the respondents were adopted when they were 6 months old or younger. All except one were adopted by the time they were 6 years old. They were born and/or raised on the East and West Coasts and in the Midwest. The farthest south any of them was born or reared was southern Virginia. All but one of the women have, or were working toward completing, their bachelor's degree. Among the men, eight hold at least a bachelor's degree.

How did these respondents come to appear in this book? Coauthor Rhonda Roorda called Rita Simon after reading Rita's work and suggested that transracial adoptees (TRAs), including herself, have stories that should be told. Rita readily agreed, indeed commented that she had long been thinking about contacting adult TRAs and having them describe their experiences in depth. Other respondents came as a result of an ad we placed in *Interrace Magazine*, from TRAs who knew of Rita's studies and wanted to talk with her about what was happening in their lives, from friends of friends of Rhonda's and a relative of Rita's. Three of the participants were contacted personally: "Pete," after he was profiled in *American Demographics*; Dan O'Brien, after his story was publicized during the 1996 Olympics, in which he won the decathalon gold medal; and Chantel Tremitiere, because of her status as a professional basketball player and as the founder of Assist One, a nonprofit organization that helps find children permanent homes. Of course we cannot and do not claim that our respondents are a "representative" sample of all young adult TRAs. We do believe, however, that given their geographic spread, the types of families they were adopted into and the stories they tell about their childhood and adolescence capture the essence of the transracial adoption experience.

The interviewees were given an opportunity to review their transcripts before the transcripts were sent to the publisher. Any deletions or additions they made were noted and included. None of the persons who initially agreed to participate in this study changed their minds and refused to have their interviews included. All of them believe, as we do, that their stories are important and worth telling. All of them hope that their experiences will help other transracial adoptees better understand themselves and their relationship to their families, have a clearer image of their racial and social identities, and live richer and happier lives.

Donna Francis

ILLINOIS
AUGUST 1997

*We [transracial adoptees] have a unique perspective on race issues
as long as kids are not ashamed of their blackness and embrace it.
I think we have a unique experience because we are black in a
society that does not value blackness and we live with white
people. My family has provided me with a resource. We talk
very candidly about race where a lot of people don't. Race has
been hypersensitized in our home. I have discussions on race that
I don't think a lot of people have in their homes. They have
to go to school to take a class on race, whereas it was a reality
in my home. We learned to deal with it and freely discuss it.
We don't always agree, but we are comfortable in expressing our
opinions.*

Donna Francis was born in Illinois. In 1971 she was adopted at
4 weeks old and raised in a middle-class family in a Chicago suburb. After
Donna Francis's first two years with her family, society's harshness reared
its ugly head. Within the racially isolated neighborhood where her family
lived, the community, in revolt against a black child living in a white family, set a cross burning on her family's lawn. Subsequently hate mail began
arriving at their home, escalating to a national level. Although this incident
occurred when Donna Francis was young, through accountings of the event
and clippings of articles she still holds, her perspective on race and interracial adoption was significantly influenced.

Donna Francis earned her B.S. in psychology and speech communications. Interested in black American education, and also having a desire to
determine her own identity as a black woman, in 1998 she earned her
Ph.D. in the history of American education. Donna Francis's commitment
as an educator, and as one who has embraced the experiences of living in
a white family, centers on her close relationship with her family.

Growing up, Donna Francis was not only exposed to her ethnic heritage, but she felt comfortable talking with her parents about race issues
regularly. Regarding the extent of her parents love for her, Donna Francis says, "In so many ways my parents stepped back when I started inves-

tigating who I was and my identity and my blackness. . . . They never worried about whether I would doubt my love for them or turn on them because they are white. They stepped back and let me do what I had to do to understand who I was as a black woman living in the U.S.A."

Donna Francis, to begin, tell me what you are currently doing professionally?

I am a graduate student getting a Ph.D. in the history of American education.

What did you major in as an undergraduate?

I double-majored in psychology and speech communications.

When were you adopted?

In May 1971. I was 4 weeks old at the time.

Do you have any siblings who are biologically related to your adoptive parents?

Yes. I have a sister who is now 25.

Did you and your sister get along growing up?

Well, as much as teenagers can get along with each other. . . . We get along better now. We have the standard sibling relationship. I consider her a very good friend.

Where was your family living when you were adopted?

We lived in a suburb of Chicago until I was 4 years old. Then we moved to another suburb of Chicago and have lived there ever since.

Did you recognize early on in your life that you were physically different from your parents?

Yes. Very early on.

Did your parents talk to you about these physical differences, or was that not important to them?

No. They talked about it.

Was it something that you brought up, or did they initiate the conversations?

I am sure it was a combination.

What were some of the things you and your parents discussed?

I don't really remember. I just knew that I was adopted. I have always known that I was black. I have always had black dolls. We went to see black shows put on in Chicago. My blackness has just been a constant part of my life. So I don't necessarily remember any discussions specifically about it.

In the first suburb where you lived was the community there mixed or predominately black or white?

It was primarily white. In the other suburb where I grew up, it was primarily white but the school I went to was mixed.

What values did your family instill in you as you were growing up?

Education was very important. Family was very important. My family made a conscious decision to enroll me in a public school where I would be around other black children and my sister would be around children who were nonwhite. I guess compassion and sensitivity were other important values.

Your sister is closely related to you, agewise. Did you and she talk about issues pertaining to race and culture growing up?

No.

Did you feel isolated or lonely growing up? . . . Did you know that you had someone to talk with when you were experiencing any type of challenges?

Yes. You have to remember that teenagers talk to teenagers. Teenagers don't talk to their parents. So I had friends to talk to and when I felt like talking with my parents I could always feel comfortable doing so. My sister and I, we didn't discuss those kinds of things at that time in our lives.

Was race an issue for you and your family?

It was definitely an issue because race is an issue in the larger society and I was a black child living in a white family—so race was an issue.

In what way?

In the sense that we were opposite—they were white and I was black. Race was not something we discussed all the time. We accepted it. Just because we didn't discuss it all the time didn't mean we ignored it.

In your neighborhood and among your friends, was race a reality?

When I reached middle school I identified and claimed friends with persons of color. Two of my best friends that I still have, one is Puerto Rican and one is black, we all met in seventh grade. Since about then I have had black friends primarily, in addition to white friends in high school. And then in college I didn't have any white friends. In the black circles I associated with, you didn't necessarily discuss race; it was a given. I went over to my black friend's house and we ate black food . . .

What is "black food"?

Greens. Cornbread. The way my friend's mother cooks her spaghetti was different than the way my mom cooked her spaghetti. Also, my friend grew up in a different way than I did. Her parents related to her differently. It wasn't uncomfortable for me. Again, I never felt out of place there, just like she did not feel out of place at my home.

Racially, how do you identify yourself?

Black.

What does being black mean to you?

By looking at me you could tell I am black—at least in America. In other places I might be considered Dominican. We are so dichotomized here in America with black versus white. I remember when I went to New York, they did not know what I was. In Illinois everybody thinks I am black. I have black features. The way I talk is black. My friends are black. The issues facing the black community I consider my own issues. The bottom line is that not only is my pigment black, but my thoughts and the way I relate to other people and the way I talk and dance and socialize are black.

Talk about how your "blackness" evolved within a white family.

My parents did as much as they could for me as a white family. I had black dolls. My parents made a conscious effort to enroll me in a public school and move to a suburb where there were other black people. They took me to black plays in Chicago and made me feel comfortable in discussing racial issues. Obviously they could not do everything because they are not black, but they made sure I had access to other people who would be able to teach or demonstrate other facets of the black culture.

Then did you intentionally seek out black people?

I wouldn't say I consciously sought out black people. I'm at a predominantly white institution. It is a very segregated campus, and I naturally fell into relationships with other black people. They do what I like to do socially and are more receptive to friendships.

Some would ask you how, coming out of a white family, you gained the tools needed to build relationships with black people?

Just because I came out of a white family doesn't make me white.

Have people questioned you on your "blackness" or authenticity?

No. I didn't go around screaming that my parents were white, but I never hid it either. All through undergraduate school my parents came down to my college to watch me in a lot of all-black productions I was in. On campus, people obviously saw they were white but I never received any flack for it or questions about my authenticity. People have told me they never would believe I was raised in a white family. To them I acted like every other black person on campus. I have had a few ignorant people make ignorant comments, but I ignore them. Other people have a much harder time than I do reconciling the fact that I think and act the way I do and that I have white parents.

I am going to rephrase my question: How did your self-identity as a black woman in America develop in the midst of a white family?

I did not take my blackness for granted as many black people do. They don't think about greens and cornbread, about the way they raise their families or socialize, how they talk and walk. I never took blackness for granted because I was the opposite of everyone related to me. I had a heightened awareness of my blackness. I never had a problem being black and never wished I was white. At the same time I did not explore that part of my identity until I became an adult.

Is it uncomfortable for you to confront the fact that you are physically different than your family?

Never within my family have I felt uncomfortable or out of place or not fully their daughter.

What about community? Has the community treated you differently or unfairly because of your color?

Yes. In the first suburb where I lived, people within the community burned a cross on our lawn. My family received hate mail because of me. At that time we had recently moved into a predominately white cul de sac in the suburbs, and the community did not want my family living there. I have newspaper clippings of this incident.

How did your parents explain to you why a cross was burned on your lawn?

They kept a scrapbook filled with newspaper clippings describing what took place and waited to show me until I was old enough to understand. This event made national news. We received newspaper clippings from Hawaii, Seattle, California, etc.

What kinds of newspaper clippings were kept in this album?

They were extensive and included both hate mail and positive mail that we received from people throughout the country. My parents actually gave me the album.

Describe some of the mail you received.

There were letters of support, people saying this was a horrible thing to happen to a family, that they would welcome us into their own neighborhoods, that it's too bad the world is so racist.

What did the hate mail that you received say?

One piece said that blacks and whites shouldn't mix, told us to go back to the southside, Chicago jungle.

This incident took place in the early 1970s. Within this context do you believe that the National Association of Black Social Workers and other groups who are opposed to transracial adoption have reason to be concerned about black children being adopted into white families?

I believe that a black child should, if possible, be placed with a black family or a black single mother or a black single father as long as it is a stable household. But if there are no black adults willing or able to adopt, then I would rather have that child with a family who loves the child rather than in foster care. I do think that if a black child is placed with a white family, the family needs to go through more than the typical steps in the adoption process. They are taking on much more of a responsibility than if they were adopting a white child.

White parents need to understand that they cannot treat a black child like a white child. They need to expose the child to his or her culture. These families need extra training. I have seen a lot of kids who have been transracially adopted, and they are very confused. These kids do not like being black, they don't know what it means . . . they would rather be white.

Why is it that an African American child would not like being black, even in a white family?

Part of it is because of society—black is not positive. You see this on television. For example, if all you see on the news are blacks who are welfare mothers or sexual objects, and if you don't have a black mother or a black aunt or a black sister so that you know this isn't true, that all black women aren't this way, then it's very difficult for a child to develop a positive self-image.

Knowing the negative portrayal of black people through the media, is it possible to raise a black child in a white family and have the child gain a positive self-image? And is it in the best interest of the black child to be raised in a white family?

It is best for a black child to be raised in a black family. But if that's not possible, that child should be raised in a loving family. Actually black people are adopting kids all the time. We just don't call it adoption. We are raised by our aunts or our grandparents. But these adoption agencies all have different standards and criteria for suitable parents. So black people who would be good parents are being turned away. I believe that potential black parents are not being recruited effectively or given any incentive to adopt formally.

Can transracially adopted individuals offer an understanding about race based on our life experiences?

We have a unique perspective as long as we are not ashamed of our blackness and embrace it. Our experience is unique because we are black in a society that does not value blackness, and we live with white people. My family has provided me with a resource. We talk very candidly about race where a lot of people don't. Race has been hypersensitized in our home. I have discussions on race that I don't think a lot of people have in their homes. They have to go to school to take a class on race, whereas it was a reality in my home. We learned to deal with it and freely discuss it. We don't always agree, but we are comfortable in expressing our opinions.

What discussions have your parents had with you about your adoption?

We've talked about the black social workers' stand on transracial adoption. My parents know I would like to see black children placed in black homes. At the same time I believe I came out all right. My dad and I discuss whether we, as a society, are more stratified by race or by class. He believes class; I believe race. We both believe in an intersection of the two and that they cannot be divided. My dad is a professor, so we discuss things other people may not discuss in their families.

How does race play out in your personal, professional, and educational pursuits, if at all?

In undergraduate school I majored in psychology and speech communications. I still didn't know what I wanted to do. Then I did a summer research opportunity program for black and Latino students on my campus. There I met a black professor in education and found the nerve to ask him to be my adviser for the summer. After that summer I decided I wanted to be a professor just like him in the history of education. I am especially interested in black education in America.

Race has always been a factor in my education. I am interested in studying my ethnicity. Most of my friends are black. My friends who aren't black are Puerto Rican. There is no white person I consider a friend.

Why have you selected primarily black friends?

I like the friends I have. This is an incredibly segregated campus. There are no social functions on the campus that are mixed. The things I like to do are the things black people want to do. I don't want to go to bars and get drunk (not that all white people like to get drunk). I would rather dance. At the black functions there is a combination of dancing and drinking so I stay away from the drinks and concentrate on the dancing. Conversely, at the white functions I've seen, talking and socializing often revolve around drinking.

Do you find yourself not wanting to interact with white people because the campus is so segregated?

No. I had a white roommate my freshman year. She said a few ignorant things but for the most part we got along fine. We just didn't keep in touch. I like the way my black friends relate to me. We have similar thoughts and concerns and problems. You socialize with people like you, so that's what I do.

At the university you are now attending, in your opinion is the institution addressing its social climate, specifically focusing on racial and ethnic matters?

I don't know because the events that most of the students attend are sponsored by student organizations. If the student organization is all black or if the student organization is all white, then they are appealing to their own clientele. Each organization advertises differently and to different groups. I'm sure the university recognizes that the campus is segregated. And I'm sure they're trying to address segregation issues on campus. But if you really want to get down to it, we still have a Native American as our school symbol—which is racist.

What is the mascot?

A Native American Chief. At football games and basketball games, a white man in a Native American outfit does a sacred dance. There is no respect or regard for another group's beliefs. As long as the university maintains that mascot, they are sending a negative signal to all people of color. It's all about money. It's a marketable symbol, and they are making a lot of money from it so they don't want to give it up.

How can a person of color attending a university or college transcend the visible symbols etched on the buildings, incorporated in the curriculum, and exhorted by the faculty so that they can also find meaning and value in their own ethnic or cultural traditions?

Social and academic groups help. For example, joining a black graduate student association or some kind of social group provides people to talk to who have similar concerns. You don't have to come to the table and explain every little issue. We understand one another because we've had similar experiences—we're starting from a common base.

In general, do you think society should be integrated or segregated?

Ultimately, integrated. But I don't see it as a reality in my lifetime. I think we are getting more and more segregated and that class is playing a bigger and bigger role in segregation. I think you can't have a successful capitalist country without oppression; it's only a matter of who is going to be oppressed. Ultimately, I would love to have an integrated society.

What about the philosophy that transracial adoption works because we are in a color-blind society or are part of a "melting pot"?

I think that's an incredibly stupid reason to adopt a child because we do not live in a melting pot. People who don't recognize race as a reality shouldn't adopt black children. They are going to do more damage to the child than good! We don't live in a color-blind society. We don't live in a melting pot. Race is our reality. It defines our interaction. It needs to be accepted.

Does culture even matter? I was giving a speech about transracial adoption and a young lady asked why ethnicity should be taught to a child when what is most important is that the child is placed in a loving, nurturing American family.

I've heard that argument, too. That's that whole melting pot crap. I think culture is very important. I don't think you can understand who I am and how I think unless you know me. And you need to know me as a black woman to appreciate me. Therefore if we erase who we are . . . understand, that is a very Eurocentric way of thinking. Just because many white people don't practice their Polish heritage or their German heritage and just consider themselves "white" doesn't mean I should consider myself without culture just because they do.

But is culture relevant to one's identity?

I think it's very relevant. Look at different groups who have been fighting over the years—the Palestinians, the Jews. They take their culture and their religions very seriously, and I think rightfully so. Whether I think that they should be "warring" over it is another question. I don't believe we should all shed our culture just because it would be more convenient. It would not solve any problems. I don't see anything wrong with my culture, so why should I shed it? Am I the only one who has to shed my culture?

Why not talk to white people about shedding their culture. Do Puerto Ricans have to shed their heritage? Mexicans forget they're Mexican? Mexican means something, and they should be proud to be Mexican. That does not mean they can't interact and be productive people in American society.

Can a person be too focused on identifying solely with his or her culture, that is, clothes, foods, behaviors? For example, what are your views on Afrocentricity?

Afrocentricity does not bother me. As long as those who strongly identify with their cultural and ancestral heritage aren't harming anyone else, there is nothing wrong with embracing your past. Jews do the same thing, and no one asks why they don't let go of their Jewish culture and heritage.

Can someone get to the point of being so Afrocentric that it prevents him or her from recognizing other people's culture, strengths, and contributions to society?

There are all different levels of Afrocentricity. As long as those who identify with it don't infringe on anybody's rights to be as German as he or she wants to be or as Polish or as Puerto Rican, then I don't think it's a negative thing. Whether a person can get along completely by using only products owned and operated by his or her ethnic group is another question.

I don't see Afrocentrism as unhealthy if people don't take it to an extreme, talking about white devils or denigrating the Jews. But that is not necessarily Afrocentricity; that's anti-Semitism or anti-white.

You're saying, then, that you can be Afrocentrist and not be anti-white?

Yes. You are pro-black, not "anti" anything else. Just because you're pro-black doesn't make you anti-white.

Does the question about race and white people in general come up when you talk with your black friends?

Oh yes. All the time.

How do you feel about that as a black person living in a white family?

Again, they are my family and I love them, but I am black. I have to deal with my reality as a black woman. Therefore I never feel uncomfortable. I guess my discussions on race are not affected by my parents being white because I am not white. I am black.

Viewing it from the angle of the little child who was nurtured and dependent for a significant period of time on parents who happen to be white, does that reality ever conflict with the conversations you may have with friends about whites or society?

No. Anything I say to my friends about white people, I can say to my parents—and have said. This may be helpful in explaining my point: I know my parents are white, but they are my mother and father. They live in a different reality than I do. They have enjoyed certain privileges because of their skin color. I am not ever going to enjoy those same privileges.

How do you feel if and when black people make rude and prejudicial comments about white people in general?

I have never felt badly that they might be talking about my parents. When people say ignorant things, I usually just walk away. If they say things that make sense, like white people having enjoyed a privilege whether they think so or not, then I stay and listen because I completely agree. But if they are being ignorant, I "cuss" them out or just walk away—not because of any allegiance to my parents but because they are being ignorant.

Are you lonely living in two different worlds—one white and one black—where the two worlds don't truly know each other?

I don't feel any kind of "pull and tug." I really don't feel like I'm living in two different worlds. That has much to do with my parents. They didn't keep saying, "You're black, you're black, remember you're black . . ." They didn't have to. In so many ways my parents stepped back when I started investigating my identity, my "blackness." They never worried about whether I would doubt my love for them or turn on them because they are white. They simply stepped back and let me do what I had to to understand who I was as a black woman living in America in 1997. They listened to me when I talked, and we talked about race and gender.

When my parents moved to another state, I wrote them a letter thanking them for encouraging me to investigate my blackness. They could have felt threatened by it but they didn't. They supported me when I participated in a black talent show, when I went through the black graduation ceremony. They know black is who I am. They have let me know that my race and ethnicity have no bearing on their love for me, just as it has no bearing on my love for them.

Growing up, did your parents have friends from different ethnic groups?

I don't think so.

Did your parents attend church or organizations where there was some diversity?

I think their churches were all white. I think they grew up in all-white communities and went to all-white schools. My parents were born in the 1930s and grew up in the 1940s and 1950s. We're still not integrated now, but back then we were completely segregated. I don't believe there were ethnic minorities where they grew up, except for Native Americans and they were run out of town when the sun went down.

Given the homogeneous background, ethnically speaking, in which your parents were raised, why do you believe they chose to adopt transracially?

I'm not sure if they went to the adoption agency saying they wanted a black child. I think they just said they wanted a child. I'm sure they told me but I forget. They both began as very religious people, always interested in social causes. I was not their first brush with social reality. They are both open-minded and accepting people. I think they did an amazing job considering they didn't have black friends to take me to and ask how to do my hair. My mom didn't have anyone to go to.

Some people would still say that because your parents were not exposed to the black community they did you a disservice.

They sought exposure when they adopted me, but when it was just the two of them they hadn't sought out black people. When they were adults, though, they were around black people. My mother worked at a place for children who were wards of the state, which means there were a lot of black kids there. So when they became adults and could make their own choices, they were exposed to other people. Then came me. They didn't do me a disservice by not moving around black people because they did when they got me. When we moved to the second suburb it was a conscious effort on their part for me to attend a school with a diverse mix of students. They were going to put me in a Catholic school but only one other black student was in that school, and they decided not to put their daughter in that situation. The operative phrase here is "conscious effort," particularly when it relates to exposing transracial adoptees to their own culture.

I think white people generally take things for granted. They can move wherever they want to. They don't think about it. Having a black child, my parents had to think: O.K., we want to make sure we live where she is exposed to different kinds of people. They wanted that for my sister, too. Just because she's white doesn't mean they didn't want to expose her to other people also. So they made a conscious effort to move into an integrated community.

How did your grandparents respond to your adoption?

I have never felt a tinge of anything but love from them. We never got any flack from any member of my family—whether cousins, aunts, uncles, etc. I'm the only black person at family reunions and functions, but I have never been treated differently.

How do you feel when you are the only black person at a white family gathering?

Nobody treats me poorly because I am black nor do I get any preferential treatment. I have never felt different. I have explained it to people like this: When you are the only black person, all you see is white. So you don't see racial differences.

Do you then experience a different feeling when you actually see yourself in the picture?

Hmmm. Well, I'm 26 and this is all I've ever known. This is my reality. It would be different if I were thrust into this at 26. For me, this is not odd.

What about dating? Was it difficult for you because of the color issue?

In eighth grade my first boyfriend, if you can call him that, was white, and his parents flipped out when they found out we were dating. Now this was eighth-grade dating . . . no chance of children. We held hands and hung out after school. That is what we did. His parents made him break up with me in eighth grade. That was really hard for me to deal with. Right at that time I think I had just found out about the cross burning and the hate mail from the first suburb. Then this white guy and I are dating, and his parents could not accept the fact that he was dating a black girl. That affected me deeply.

You were aware that his parents did not want their son to date you because of the color of your skin?

Yes. They made it very clear.

How clear?

They told him. He didn't have the guts to tell me so he told my best friend, and she came to my house to tell me. I still remember her coming over that day and her telling me and we cried and cried.

This was in the early eighties. So how did you handle that?

He and I started dating behind their backs. I'll never forget one of the last days of school. We had our yearbooks, and he was going around in our drama class whispering to everyone, "Don't write her name in my yearbook." That hurt so much. This was eighth grade, so obviously I didn't expect our relationship to last. But that was really hard. You're already having a hard time in eighth grade and then, when you compound it with hatred . . . and these people had never met me. I think they must have heard from somebody that I was black. They had never seen me before or met me, but that didn't matter.

Who did you go to in working this situation out?

My friends and family.

What were some of the emotions you were feeling at the time?

I was disgusted. I was hurt. I was confused. Like I said, I found out about the cross burning and hate mail about the same time so I was overwhelmed as well.

Why did that incident in the second suburb impact you so strongly even though it occurred when you were still quite young?

When I was 2 years old people hated me enough that they didn't want me living in their neighborhood. Then there was this guy I liked and he liked me . . . and his parents had no idea who I was and they hated me because they heard I was black.

Today, have these experiences affected you? Would you move into an all-white neighborhood?

Oh no, no, no. Never. I like being around black people. I feel more comfortable around black people. When I have children, I want my children to grow up around black people. I wouldn't mind living in an integrated neighborhood, but I wouldn't live in an all-white neighborhood.

Largely because of your experience dating a white guy?

Actually, I dated a couple of white guys in high school. Since I've been in college I've only dated black men. I feel more comfortable with black men and am attracted to them—not all of them, just some of them. Black men are the ones who approach me and who I approach.

Of the black men you've dated, have any of them met your parents?

Oh, yes.

Did any of those men have problems with you having white parents?

I don't choose those kinds of men. If they have a problem with it, then they are not the men I take home. They aren't the men I date.

What are the types of black men you choose to date?

I like black men who like being black men and who feel comfortable enough with their identity that they don't have to shove it down everyone's throat.

You talked about the incident in eighth grade; were there other incidents fueled by race that occurred after that?

I've been in classrooms where we were discussing race. White people in general are uncomfortable discussing race. They'd rather we forget about race and melt together into one Eurocentric melting pot.

What discussion do you think the white community needs to have that is centered on race, understanding that this community is also diverse?

It goes beyond discussion. However, it's essential that there be discussions about race and ethnicity; it's a reality. There's nothing wrong with that. . . . I don't mind if somebody says to me "I am German." Being German is fine just as long as you let me be black. There needs to be interaction between people from different races and ethnicities, whether in the work place or socially, for a greater understanding of each other. The media needs to be responsive and responsible for its promotion of racial tension and stereotypes. I think economic class needs to be recognized as a factor in social stratification. We also need to recognize that class and race intersect. There needs to be an overhaul of America for there to be any meaningful integration.

Mainstream society is integrating . . .

Whites always expect people of color to integrate into them. It's always the one black person in the white neighborhood and never the white person in the black neighborhood. . . . That's why there needs to be an understanding that works both ways before anything meaningful can come out of it.

What are the candid conversations, in your opinion, that the black community needs to have as it relates to the state of black America?

Black people need to talk about gender.

Please explain.

There's a book entitled *All of the Women Are White, All of the Blacks Are Men, and Some of Us Are Brave.* The title is very telling in that when you say women, everybody thinks white. And, unfortunately, when you talk about black, many people associate that with manhood. I think there needs to be some kind of gender discussion within the black community because black women have always gotten the crappy deal and their "blackness" is questioned when they try to bring up their womanhood. Then they are "taking the attention away from our race issues." I am just as much a black as any man, and I am also a woman. So when black men talk about "black," they are talking about black man issues. That is why I believe they tell black women to stay in the background and keep their issues quiet until they get the race thing together. In a nutshell, I don't think gender issues should be pushed to the periphery. I think they need to be understood and discussed within the community. And I think that class needs to be discussed . . . the way we relate to one another . . . what we are doing to one another, like killing one another with guns and drugs and being nonsupportive. . . .

Black people need to take ownership of their own actions. If you are a black drug dealer, you are just as bad as any white drug dealer. I think blacks can do just as much harm to other blacks as whites can. I just don't think they are making as much money as whites; that doesn't matter, it's still killing us. The fact is that blacks need to take ownership in this drug problem; we perpetuate it in the media and in music. The blacks who are perpetuating this frenzy know what they are doing.

Jumping to education, since this is your area of study, what do you think the trend in 1997 is for blacks attending colleges and universities and actually earning their advanced degrees?

I think black colleges and universities will continue to play an important role in educating black people beyond a bachelor's degree. These institutions, however, need bigger libraries and more money for resources and buildings and lab equipment. I don't think black colleges and universities are the only solution to educating black students, but I do think that these institutions are an important ingredient in black education. Universities that have a serious commitment to diversity, not just on paper but in reality, can offer black students a valuable education at their institutions. I think the trend toward not financing education, lack of money or smaller funds, no tuition waivers, is going to have a disproportionate effect on people of color, as well as poor whites, because we aren't going to be able to afford to go to college, much less graduate school.

Regarding the fraction of black people who are opposed to transracial adoption, is there something they can do to address the disproportionate number of black kids in foster care?

They can adopt a child! Even if the child is adopted into a white family, you can provide services for this child. Maybe this child won't feel as comfortable as I did talking with my parents. So maybe providing some kind of facility or services or support or a discussion group—there are all kinds of things that can be done. There are all kinds of reasons why so many black kids are in foster care. It's a huge societal issue. They can try to tackle some of those in their respective cities and counties and encourage some of their friends who want to have children to adopt.

Some social workers, as you may know, have concerns about transracial adoption because of the "discriminatory" adoption policies that are in place, written and unwritten, discouraging black families from adopting because of their income levels, their education, and simply because of bureaucratic chaos . . .

You can't just scream and holler about it. You have to do something. If you think that adoption criteria is wrong, then you need to help rewrite it. You need to work on recruiting more black families to adopt black children. You need to work on incentives for black families to adopt black children. You need to work on lowering the cost of adoption, so more people can participate in adoption. Just because you may not come from an affluent background doesn't mean you can't be a good parent. As long as a parent can provide for a child, I don't see any reason why a child should be kept from a single parent who isn't middle class or upper middle class.

When you say "as long as a parent can provide for a child," what does that entail?

I'm referring to a parent or parents who can offer a child a stable home environment and love. Because a child is expensive, the parent must also be able to afford to take care of the child financially.

If this is what social workers feel, then they need to be active in recruiting efforts, monetary assistance, support groups for these parents who are adopting, and in changing adoption criteria, rules, and mandates.

Contrary to the belief that white parents cannot instill values or tools that a black adult will need in order to be productive and make it in society, you have grown up to be aware of your self-identity and your personal and professional goals. What do you attribute this to?

I really like the person I am, and I attribute that to my parents. They have helped to make me very independent, strong-willed and determined, compassionate and loving, accepting and understanding, all the things parents hope to pass on to their kids. Their "whiteness" had less to do with it than that they were Mom and Dad and loved me completely. I know my parents would do anything for me and my sister.

It is challenging to be white and adopt, in this case, a black child. What are pointers you can speak to that address some of the challenges these parents and potential adoptive parents may face in raising their children?

I think they need to accept their child's ethnicity. In this case, we're talking about a black child and therefore they need to accept the child's "blackness" instead of saying that we are all just human beings. That would be nice if we all thought of ourselves as human beings, but that's just not the reality. I think these adoptive parents do a disservice to the child if they teach them that. For example, if they teach a young black boy that the police are *always* your friend, that's not true for a lot of black men or at least for a disproportionate number of black men. Potential adoptive parents must do some serious soul-searching before they adopt a child outside their ethnicity because of the major task they will be taking on. First, you're taking on parenthood, which is the hardest job created. But not only are you a parent, you're a parent of a minority, which is going to affect your family structure. Your family may not accept it. You have to be prepared for getting crosses burned on your lawn or having your child come home crying because some white boy's parents didn't want you around him. You're dealing with much more than parenthood; there are all kinds of other complications. White people don't think about race as deeply as people of color do. They have to learn to do that and not to see it as wrong. I don't think white people have discussions about race as much as people of color do because it's not their reality. White people are the standard by which all others are judged.

Critics of transracial adoption are genuinely concerned that the child may grow up in an isolated community, stripped of his or her culture and community. Doesn't this concern go beyond whether the family is accepting or not? Doesn't it permeate the mind-set of the community and school system into which the child is "integrated"?

Absolutely. Whether the family is accepting is one question, but what about the community? The kid wants to go to school and have friends. I don't think that white families living in isolated communities should adopt black children. Black children need to be around other black children. Truthfully, I don't think such people would even go to an adoption agency and ask to adopt a black child.

What can be done to minimize the concern or fear of a black child being raised in an isolated community?

It's a real fear and concern and shouldn't be minimized. It's a serious issue and needs to be discussed. You have to think about the child's well-being. This is a sweeping generalization, but chances are black children will have questions later on about their blackness. And who can they talk to about this? They could be completely isolated in the community. Their parents would love them, I would hope, but parents are not your entire life. Children eventually need to function on their own. I think that's a legitimate concern.

Delving deeper into your views on social issues, do you identify with black figures such as Martin Luther King Jr. or Rosa Parks? Do you have black mentors?

Yes, I have black mentors. My adviser, who I consider a wonderful mentor, is a black man. I've looked up to other black people in the past . . . I don't know about the present. There aren't many black national leaders now that I respect.

Why is that?

I don't think they are doing a whole lot. I have problems with Farrakhan. I have some problems with Jesse Jackson and Clarence Thomas.

Why do you believe that the people you mentioned are not the most effective leaders?

I don't think they're leading . . . well, Clarence Thomas is not leading. Farrakhan is leading but I don't think he is leading as many people as he thinks he is. And Jesse Jackson used to lead but he has lost so much respect.

Why do you believe they are not leading? In your opinion, do they understand the issues the black community is currently facing?

I think they speak to the issues—not Clarence Thomas—but I think Farrakhan speaks to the legitimate concerns of the black community, and Jesse Jackson does as well. Jesse Jackson just seems to pop up everywhere there's a popular issue, which is fine because we need all the support we can get and maybe he can mobilize a lot of people in Chicago . . . maybe I don't know what they're doing, so perhaps they are wonderful leaders.

Where do you think the black community needs to go?

I think one of our problems is that we are waiting for a leader. One person cannot represent a whole community, a whole race. I think that's dangerous. I think whites are also looking for the next black Messiah. They pick one of us and put us in the paper. That's what Jesse Jackson is; I wouldn't call him the Messiah, but he is like the appointed "Negro" so whenever something happens they go to him and ask him his opinion. Well, not all of us think like Jesse Jackson. We don't need one leader. We need grass-roots organization.

We need to discuss problems and solutions within our community. I think that somehow we only talk about our problems and don't focus on finding solutions.

Exactly. It's much easier to theorize than actually do something about our problems. I think that starting small, in your own community where you can really make a difference—taking a bite out of a little chunk instead of a big national chunk is where it's at.

Do you believe that we, as a black community, can be truly honest with ourselves? On a national level, are we responsibly assessing what is going on in our communities and what we must do to strengthen them?

I think, for example, that the Million-Man March provoked some dialogue, but again women were told to hold our tongues, that we were being divisive or aligning ourselves with white women when we expressed our misgivings about the march.

I believe we had a great dialogue in addressing the need for black men to be an integral part of black families, but where did we go from there? Or am I missing something?

I don't even know if we had a great dialogue. I tried to have a dialogue on this campus and I got—

With whom?

With black men. I would tell them my opinion, and they would tell me theirs. I respect their opinion, but they just refused to acknowledge another point of view and that perhaps there was a different way to go about the problem. I don't doubt that black men have issues that they need to discuss among themselves. I don't have a problem with that. But if you want to accomplish anything within the black community, you need black men *and* black women. I think that black men are being divisive; they ask why women are being divisive when women ask why they are being excluded.

I'm still struggling with the issue of where we, as a black community, can have a critical dialogue that will foster positive solutions.

I guess at the local YMCA, the local library—

Because somewhere we just stop. For instance, I just came back from West Africa. On my way there I was reading *Out of America* by Keith B. Richburg. The book is about Mr. Richburg's firsthand experiences in Africa as an African American and news correspondent. In the book he talks about the demographics of the countries and communities he reported on and his personal thoughts about what he saw from the perspective of a black American. Now, I believe he's being unfairly criticized, particularly by the black community.

For what?

For not talking as extensively about the "positive" aspects of Africa and its people. "Africa" is a sensitive topic for many people. Maybe African Americans look at what Mr. Richburg says as an indirect threat on who we are as a black people in America. Sadly, very few of us have lived in Africa and experienced what Mr. Richburg has.

I think that black people would love to create a myth of Africa as the perfect place, that only good came out of Africa until white folks arrived. I think that's what a lot of black people want to believe. Of course when colonialism hit, all kinds of crazy stuff went on. Everything wasn't good in Africa. We had our own problems before the Europeans arrived. There have always been ethnic wars in Africa and there probably always will be because Africans are different from one another. I think that black people in America think that Africans are just "African." We see them as monolithic when actually they believe in different religions, speak different languages.

Some of us in America indict white Americans for assuming a similar ideology—believing that black Americans are monolithic in nature.

True, we do the same thing. Some of us say that Africa was a wonderful and beautiful place where men respected women and women respected men, where kids were always valued and we never hurt one another, where we ate fruit and nuts. Well, you know people were killing other people in Africa. Women and men were being abused. All kinds of things happened in Africa. The reality is that people are human beings who are fallible. But, like you said, we are unfortunately prone to create a monolithic picture of Africa.

You have spoken honestly about your views and experiences living in a white and black world, and I know that isn't easy. But are you able to discuss critically some of your vulnerabilities and concerns and still be confident in who you are as Donna Francis who is also a black American?

I studied and questioned. You have to allow people to be human. Martin Luther King Jr. was a great man, but he was only a man. Malcolm X was a great man, but he too was only a man. People are people. That does not mean that Martin Luther King Jr. and Malcolm X should be respected less because they were human beings. People need to recognize that certain shortcomings or faults do not necessarily mean defamation or rejection of some hero . . . or of ourselves. We have some serious problems, and not all our problems have to do with whites. We have other issues we need to discuss that white people have nothing to do with. I think we need to have candid discussions and be open-minded about our place as blacks living in America. We also need to know that there are wonderful things about us, great things, unique things, that people have been copying for centuries because they see the value of who we are whether in Africa or in America. We need to know that we still have a lot of work to do!

On that note, what are your future goals as they relate to your contribution to the strength and identity of the black community?

I want to be a professor and do research on black education because there is a myth that blacks don't value education. We used to die just for the right to go to school. People need to understand that black people have always valued education and still value education today. White people didn't have to die in order to integrate schools. We as black people were so serious about our children having a good education that we sent little children into the enemy camp, and then whites pulled their kids out of these schools. As a professor, I want to focus on the black experience in America, educationally and otherwise, and provide a forum for *informed* discussions on race, cultural diversity, ethnicity, and gender.

Jessica Pelton

WEST RUPERT, VERMONT
DECEMBER 1997

*[It was important for me to learn about my ethnicity because]
I always felt "half-baked." I mean I didn't feel completely done.
It's very much a part of my personality. . . . I wonder how much
it has to do with being black in a white family . . . but I would
strive and strive to get to some point and then I would get there
and think there's so much more I still have to do. There's never
a feeling of accomplishment or achievement or that it's all
coming together for me. The piece that seems to be missing is my
blackness.*

Jessica Pelton, a 24-year-old biracial woman, struggles with
feelings of inadequacy and low self-esteem. Never feeling complete as a
person, Jessica believes the answer to being happy is to find her black identity. Jessica's story documents the pain and frustration of trying to fit into
the "accepted groups" in her life and the need to legitimize herself as a black
woman.

Born in Indianapolis, Indiana, Jessica spent two weeks in foster care
before she was adopted. Jessica's adoptive parents, who were in their early
thirties and college-educated, raised her and their other three children in
their hometown of West Rupert, Vermont. Juxtaposed against the mostly
white community where Jessica was raised, she looked to her biracial sister and Korean brother as a reflection and affirmation of who she was.

In her junior high and high school years, Jessica's desire to be perceived
as part of the group, whether in her family or among peers, became an
obsession. Seemingly, it was through these relationships that she validated
her self-identity. Even with the love and support of her family and friends,
to Jessica, her physical characteristics became the overshadowing and unfor-
giving reminder that she was different.

Devoid of her self-identity, Jessica sought to learn about her African
American heritage. Perhaps she believed that this was the key to unlock-
ing the oppression of racial and ethnic isolation she experienced in her com-

munity, that it would ultimately enable her to accept herself. Through her experiences overseas and at a historically black college, Jessica inevitably became more aware of her ethnic history. She also was exposed to others who looked like her. This interview with Jessica follows a part of her journey to find acceptance within herself. It begs the question: What does it take to love and accept yourself?

Do you have siblings?

I have two older brothers. Peter is 28 and Jay is 26. And I have a sister who is 20. My oldest brother is biologically related to my adoptive parents. Jay is adopted. He is Korean-American. My youngest sister is also adopted and biracial.

Did you discuss with your parents why they chose to adopt transracially, specifically a black child?

I don't remember talking about it when I was younger, except, when I was angry, I would question why they even bothered to adopt me. In recent years, when we have talked about it, my mother told me that they thought if there were children who needed homes, and they were willing and able to provide a stable home to a child, then they should adopt that child. To her, it was extra special to adopt children from another race who possibly would not have had the opportunity to be adopted.

Your parents adopted you in the state of Indiana. What led your parents to live in Vermont?

My parents both grew up in West Rupert, where I grew up. And both of their families had lived here.

Describe West Rupert.

Well, it is in Vermont and borders New York state. Actually, my house is less than a mile from the border of New York state. The town I lived in consists of about six hundred or maybe seven hundred people. There is one store, which is owned by my father. Everything else is just houses. There is a central part to the town—a lot of houses close together—and then there are people who live in the hills and in the woods. There are three churches in the entire town.

What is the racial makeup of the town?

It is an all-white town. There are no black families in West Rupert. When I was a teenager, there was one older black man in Rupert. Now he lives over the border in New York state. But there were no black families there. One family, a couple of houses up the street, adopted a daughter from India. I was probably 10 years old at the time.

Was it awkward for you being black in a white family and also surrounded by an all-white community?

Because the town was so small and close-knit and most of the people knew my family, it was not that bad for me . . . unless it was someone who came from out of town or unless we were in another town or setting . . . that was when I experienced shock or surprise or stares from people. But in our town everyone knew us, and we were accepted.

Why do you think your family was accepted even though they stood out racially?

When I look back and analyze it, I think it was because it was just one family that was different. We had Asian and black in our family. I believe we weren't seen as a big threat to the community because there were so few of us. And we were all contained in one family that was respected.

Did it help you in your development that you had siblings who came from different ethnic groups?

Yes. My sister and I look a lot alike. Again, we don't know my sister's ethnic background for certain like we do mine. But our complexion, hair color, and body type are very similar. We're sometimes mistaken for each other. It's not that "all black people look alike" thing. We really do look alike, and we're not biological sisters. That my sister and I looked alike made me feel good. You know, there's that feeling transracial adoptees have that nobody in their family looks like them. My sister and I were each other's reflections. And Jay, who is also adopted, has our complexion. He's Korean, but I always thought he was mixed with black because his hair is kinky. It definitely helps to have siblings that look like you because basically it's your family or nobody.

As a child did you ask, "Mommy, why do I look different than you?"

I think those questions are kind of stupid, but probably when I was very small I asked that question. Obviously I knew from the beginning that I was brown and my mommy wasn't. Or that my hair was like this. . . . Maybe it was easier because I had brothers and a sister.

What activities did you participate in as a family?

When we were younger we would take trips and vacations to places like Disney World or Niagara Falls. We used to have a camp on a lake near the Canadian border. We would spend a week at the camp in the summers. Around the holidays we would do things with other families. I remember that Jay and Peter would have their activities, and Maria and I would have our activities. Even when my parents went away and we'd stay with our grandparents, Maria and I would go to my mother's parents house and Jay and Peter would go to my father's parents.

Were you accepted by your extended family?

Oh, yes. In recent years I realized that not only is my immediate family white but so is my extended family, my grandparents, aunts and uncles, cousins. That I have no black family member in my extended family either is a new realization for me.

So you did not consciously realize this in your childhood and adolescent years?

I only thought of them as my cousins, my uncles, my grandmother . . .

Does it bother you that you have no black relatives?

I guess the honest answer is yes. I wish I had black relatives. But I love my family, and I accept them just as they accept me. . . . Yet I do wish it because now that I am older and more aware of who I am and my identity is starting to gel and take shape, there are certain things I want to do and share with black people that I could never do with my family. It's not that I feel my family wouldn't be willing to do certain things with me; it just wouldn't feel right to me.

Then who do you do those things with?

With friends. I have created a family of black friends. Of course I have "aunties" who are black.

Before we go into that, I want to ask you about school. Were you exposed to black people in school?

No. From kindergarten through sixth grade, absolutely none. Actually there were two exceptions. When I was in kindergarten there was a little black boy in my class. He was a twin, and his brother was in the class across the hall. I fell in love with him, and we held hands all the time. I wish I knew where he was now. I clung to him. That was amazing to me. I had a great kindergarten teacher. I think she really tried to foster that relationship because we were similar racially. At the time it didn't matter to me what color someone was, black or white.

In second grade there was a little black girl and I clung to her. We were best friends. I fell in love with her older brother. Both these families ended up moving away.

In other words, when black people came into your environment you were attracted to them like a magnet.

Yes. I don't give myself enough credit for that.

Especially considering that you were not exposed to blacks regularly. Since we are on the topic of exploring oneself, in your home

did your parents reinforce the value of the African American heritage?

We talked about black people's contribution. We heard stories about runaway slaves. My mother had a print on the wall of a little black boy. His hair is locked. He is standing with his little hands crossed, and he has this mad look on his face. My mother says she got the picture because it reminded her of me when I would get really mad. She had that print on the wall in our TV room. When we were little my mom tried to bring in whatever she could to expose us to our ethnic heritage. If you look at where we were and what surrounded us, it was not real common that there would be such things as Black History Month, etc., wasn't celebrated around here. My mother never tried to keep me from it, and she would run to it if it was there.

On a practical level, did you struggle to maintain your hair or your skin?

When I was little I could always get by with a close little afro or my mother would put my hair in two little puffs. My mother didn't know how to braid my hair or take care of black hair other than wash it and comb it out . . . which was the worst. I had so many issues with my hair, it's hilarious. We would go to a YMCA nearby and swim. My mother would cut my hair herself at home until I was about thirteen. It was just my natural hair and it was easiest to wear a close cut because when it got too long it was unmanageable. Then I reached a stage where I was actually styling my hair. I no longer wanted just the ordinary cut. So I let my hair grow and grow until it was long. Then I told my mother just to part my hair down the middle, because basically that is all she could do, and then cut one side short and leave the other side long. . . . My mother just stares at me. She doesn't remember this. I remember it because I'd go swimming at the YMCA and would swim lopsided because my hair would push me to the other side. I thought this was the cutest modern hairstyle a black girl could have. I guess it was a time when white girls put their hair to one side, and I just wanted that effect. But I couldn't get all the hair to stay to one side . . . it would just puff back up. I thought, if I cut it low it would stay to one side . . . so my mother cut it that way. She was always game for whatever I wanted to do.

You were definitely creative. Why did you want the long, straight hair?

When I was growing up I had sleepovers, and "everybody does everybody's hair." Nobody did my hair. . . . If they tried they would touch it on top and say it was so bouncy . . . and then be done in a minute. Or they would pin a barrette in it. They would take forever to make me feel good, and then say: Look, your hair is so beautiful. Basically, it was my same hair with a barrette hanging off the side because they couldn't even fasten it.

On the other hand, I could do French braids. I could do the best braids and was so into that hair and it wasn't even mine. But I could not do French braids on my own hair. I was always jealous because of that, I guess. I felt inadequate because there were certain things I couldn't be a part of for anything in the world. That hurt a lot.

How did you use that pain?

I used it to fuel my desire to style my hair even more. I also used it to "work" my clothes. Everything matched to a T, including my socks. No one could say anything about my clothes. If I couldn't do anything with my hair, I was going to look "tight" with my clothes.

How were you dressed when you were younger? Were you into the name-brand clothes?

In ninth or tenth grade I started to get into the name brands. Where I was growing up, not many people wore name-brand clothing. But you had to have the accepted "look," like stone-washed pants and crumpled socks. So I'd definitely work to get those things.

Did you question anything about your color or ethnicity when you saw depictions of African Americans on television?

What I remember most is that somehow the black person on the program or in a movie was singled out and was either made fun of or discriminated against. It would bring a rise out of me. I'm not saying I would protest, but my cheeks would get hot. I'd keep staring at the screen. I didn't want to look around and see if anyone was looking at me.

One time I went to my best friend's house. They always watched the new *Twilight Zone* movies when they came out. In one of them, there was a black guy who was somehow brought back into the past. The Ku Klux Klan was riding around him and crosses were burning and they were yelling "nigger." My friend jumped up and fast-forwarded that part, which made me even more uncomfortable.

Was there a sense of embarrassment when you saw depictions like this that showed blacks being treated unfairly or stereotypically? Did you associate those images with yourself?

Yes. I really took it to heart.

Do you think you would get that same rise if you saw a Korean person treated unfairly or stereotyped?

I would get it for my brother but not for myself. I definitely know how he feels. I'd almost catch myself laughing when I'd see people making fun of an Asian person, and then I would stop laughing and give the person a sympathetic look.

So because you have a brother who is Korean, you are sensitive to racial innuendos targeted to the Asian community as a whole.

Right.

Where could you go to have someone empathize with you, someone who shared a similar ethnic background and experience?

I know how I deal with things now, but looking back I never went to anyone. I kept a journal every year of my life. But when I read through it searching for moments of identity crisis, they just aren't there. My journal is filled with entries detailing what I wore to school, whether I like some boy. I can tell you what I was emotionally going through on any day, but I didn't write anything down about my identity crisis.

I'd bring things to my mom a lot. She definitely listened to me and always comforted me, either physically or with words. She'd try to soothe my hurt. When I was angry at how I or someone I identified with had been treated, my mother naturally wanted to channel my anger into something more positive. I think it's O.K. to be angry. Sometimes it's important to express it and not just pray for world peace.

The healthy attitudes and emotional state of transracial adoptees, from childhood to adolescent years, clearly shows up on surveys that examine these adoptees. In your opinion, why is it that the intense emotions of striving to overcome feelings of inadequacy and pain do not show up?

I don't know. I'd have to know who's doing the surveys, what they're trying to prove or represent to society—basically what their motives are. I think its irresponsible for anyone who cares about what is really going on in the life of a black person adopted by a white family to make a negative report like that. I'm completely happy with my family and love my family. I wouldn't ask for another family, but I think that issue is complex and goes deeper than first impressions.

Did you look to your parents to guide you in nurturing your black self-identity?

No. I've always felt that regarding my identity and ethnic origin, my parents were not the source of information for me. Especially when it came to the black experience. I don't know if that was fair of me. I just know I didn't turn to my parents for that. I felt like I was on my own.

I consider my sister, Maria, black. And she says she's black because there's nothing else she could possibly be. But to me it doesn't sound like she's saying "I'm proud to be black." It sounds more like "I'm resigned to being black." It hurts me that we can't really share the experience of learning as much about our ethnic heritage as possible. So she wasn't my supporter either. No one told me to not find stuff out, but there was no one who was really on my team.

Why was it important to learn about your ethnicity?

I always felt "half-baked." I mean I didn't feel completely done. It's very much a part of my personality. . . . I wonder how much it has to do with being black in a white family . . . but I would strive and strive to get to some point and then I would get there and think there's so much more I still have to do. There's never a feeling of accomplishment or achievement or that it's all coming together for me. The piece that seems to be missing is my blackness. In recent years I've done everything possible to bring that "blackness" to my life. When I was younger, in junior high and high school, I was a cheerleader and had my name put on my jacket. I was "Freddie," just like Freddie of *A Different World*. Looking back, I was trying to identify and to have an identity. Another way I tried to identify with the black culture, besides being outspoken in class, with little or no education on the subject, was by intentionally deciding not to date a white person.

There was one black family in the town in New York state where I went to high school. There were three boys in the family, and one daughter. I went out with at least two of the brothers, if not all three, during my high school career. When my friends and I went to the movies or the mall and saw a black person, we followed that person around all night. I made a conscious choice to identify with blacks.

How did your decision to go to college come about?

I always knew I was going to college. Now I consider myself a scholar, but I was never serious about school. My grades were above average and I loved learning, so I knew I'd go to college. My oldest brother went to college for only a semester, and Jay didn't go to college. I was looked on as the student in the family. I guess it was predetermined that I would go to college.

My family and I looked at schools in upstate New York. When I looked at college catalogues, I'd go right to the racial composition of the campus. If it wasn't more than 18 percent black, I wasn't going there. So I picked a few colleges in upstate New York that fit that description and visited them with my parents and sister. Again, all I saw were white people. I remember feeling uncomfortable about that for the first time.

Why?

Because I'd be outside my close-knit community, people who accepted me as Jessica. There no one knew me. I'd probably be considered " 'Jo

Schmo' black girl," and I didn't feel prepared for that. I don't think I was scared but I was disappointed with my options.

At around the same time I was applying to schools, I also wanted to be an exchange student from my high school. So I applied for that.

What country did you want to go to?

Japan. I knew that learning Japanese would be valuable. I also wanted to go where there were no white people. I've never said this to anybody before. The organization that was sending me abroad didn't exchange to Africa or anywhere like that. My first choice was Japan; my second, India; and my third, France.

What pushed you to think that broadly?

I always had high hopes. I guess because everything was so close-knit, I wanted to have big times. I've always been independent. Travel allowed me to explore, meet new people, learn their language—the outdoors learning experience is what I'd call it. I was really into that. I still am.

My parents had something to do with my global mind-set as well. If they couldn't bring the black culture to me, they did make me aware of other cultures. From the time I was 5 we had foreign exchange students in our house every year. My family always supported going abroad.

What country did you end up going to?

Brazil. I told the district person who was affiliated with the organization that sent me abroad that I wanted to go to Japan, and he said no, no, no. Because I was outspoken, he said I shouldn't go to Japan. He said that in Japan the culture is very traditional. He was talking about stereotypes like women walking behind the men. He was convinced Japan was not the place for me, that Brazil was the place for me.

Because?

People looked more like me there. I took offense at that at first because the organization was sending a lot of white people to Japan. I know he was trying to help me, but I also think he felt I would face more discrimination in Japan.

You were in Brazil for a year?

Yes. I went there when I was 18.

Living in Brazil, did you learn more about yourself as a black person?

Brazil opened my eyes to the dispersion of African people throughout the world and the connection between all of us. I think I actually learned more about African Americans being in Brazil than I did in the United States. In Brazil I was forced to learn because most of the experiences of

Africans in Brazil and in America are closely correlated. So if I was learning the history of a people in Brazil, I'd naturally learn about the history of black people in America. And if anybody found out I was American and had any interest in African American culture, I was perceived as the representative of black Americans.

To me, they couldn't have picked a worse person to report on the culture and history of black Americans. I didn't feel I knew anything about being black. All I knew was what I saw on TV or what mainstream America thinks is the black experience. At that point I had no close contact or interaction with black Americans and their culture.

In America I felt like an outsider, that I had been placed in a culture I couldn't possibly fit into. I had left the United States to get away from that. In Brazil most people thought I was Brazilian. But if they knew I was American, I was *American*. They didn't want to hear about the differences between white Americans and *African Americans*. I was American! And I should be damn proud of it. America the beautiful, etc. . . . I was made to fit into a picture that I had never yet fit into.

How did that make you feel?

I was very angry. In Brazil people would say, "Oh, America!!!" and I'd shake my head and make noises to show them they didn't understand how "America" was to me. I'd communicate with them nonverbally like that, until I learned the Portuguese word for "bad." I also learned the word for "shit." And I applied it all to America, to white people. They couldn't understand. They'd name a TV show familiar to them that they based their perception of America on, like "*90210*". I couldn't get away from that image.

So you came back a year later when you were 20. Is that when you decided which college you'd attend?

I had applied to a historically black college in the south (HBCU) and several other predominately white colleges. The white schools offered me money and were impressed with me academically. They particularly wanted me to be a part of their diversity programs. Interestingly, the HBCU school of my choice put me on their waiting list.

My father had gone to college with a black man named Bob whose daughter now attends HBCU. Later on, Bob became chairman of HBCU, among other things he did. When I was only in tenth grade he'd send a letter or a picture of his family and somehow find a way to promote HBCU for Jessica, like there was no other option. So when all the white schools offered me scholarships and HBCU put me on their waiting list, that was the school I wanted.

In the fall of my senior year, my mother suddenly called me at school and said, "Get your books and tell your teachers we're going down South. We're going to visit HBCU."

How was that experience?

I can visualize the hotel where my mom and I stayed that weekend. We walked all the way to the college along the highway. My mom either wanted to save money by not taking a cab or thought we could see things along the way. I have no idea why we walked such a distance—along the highway, across train tracks, with subways zooming by. It's funny to think of it now.

When we got to the college, my expectations were completely blown out of the water. I decided right off I wanted to go there, so I applied. That's when they put me on their waiting list. So I went to Brazil.

When you say your expectations were blown out of the water, what do you mean?

Before visited HBCU, I thought black people were "a" and I was "b." If black people were "this skin complexion," then I was "that skin complexion." They dressed like this, I dressed like that. They had hair like this, I had hair like that. I looked at myself and at black people as opposites. So I felt that the campus scene would be all these black girls "staring me down" because I was different. I guess all my life I felt I was black and that I dressed black. Going into that situation for the first time, I felt that maybe I don't look black or that they'd stare at me because I'm trying to go to their school and I can't possibly be black.

Of course I had no one to talk to before I visited the college. All my emotions were bottled up inside me. I was with my white mother who has short hair and wears sandals with socks. I love her to death but I just wanted us to look as normal as possible. Looking back to how we looked that day, we didn't resemble anything near normal.

How do you learn to balance the level of comfort for your white parents and yourself, as their black child, in a predominantly black environment?

Today I negotiate every situation by trying to make myself as comfortable as possible. At this point in my life I'm sick of being concerned about always finding a balance for others around me. My feelings in a given situation are my priority now.

Actually, visiting this college with my mom didn't look completely off. Here was this girl who looked mixed, walking with a white person who's her mother. You see that at this college. But my mind-set was that black people came from black people and that they regenerated into a group of black people. I see plenty of girls there who have white parents. A couple of girls I know were adopted into white families. Back then, my reality was that because I was with my mother I couldn't be considered black. I wasn't "black enough." When my parents come to visit me, I love walking on campus with *one* of them. Then the assumption is, "Oh, her father must be black" or "Oh, her mother must be black," depending on which one I'm with. But when I'm with both my parents, I feel that old familiar embarrassment.

Reflecting on this situation now, how did the students treat you when you were walking with your parents on campus?

Probably 75 percent of them paid me no mind. The student who gave us a tour was lighter than my mother. That was the first thing that blew me away. I thought she was just a tour guide. I didn't realize she was a student. When she showed us her dorm room I was shocked. I asked her where she was from. She told me Rhode Island. I couldn't understand why she wanted to go to this school. Probably all the other girls at HBCU thought this, not just me. They grew up in their biological black families but also completely isolated in white environments.

It's so common now for black people to immediately start a conversation on skin tone and skin color. Back then I thought it was so taboo to tell a black person that he or she looked white, especially a black person who has pride in his or her culture.

Everyone has a story about being dropped off at college. I'm sure your experience was quite unique.

My mother, my father, my Korean brother, and my black sister all came along. My sister was dating a white guy at the time and he came, too. On the way we stopped in North Carolina to pick up a "long love affair" friend of mine who is black. I rode with him in his car, and the whole family rode in the Caravan with all my stuff. All the windows in the van except the front ones were tinted.

My parents pulled up first, two white people—and this was the move-in day for black girls attending the college. The college is surrounded by gates, and there are guards. Cars are not normally allowed on campus unless someone is moving or for some other good reason. Anyway, here come two white people who look like they have no business at the school.

My parents had to explain that their daughter was the girl in the car behind theirs. I literally shrank in my seat and covered myself, I was so embarrassed. It seemed like everyone had stopped at the gate to see these two white people. Then they let us through the gates. Most of the families were already under small tents, because it was raining, getting ready to register. We weren't the last ones to arrive but quite a few people were already there. Of course, they were all looking in the direction we were coming from. It seemed like the whole freshman class got a view of me and my family. So I tried to walk with my sister, move her boyfriend away from us, and get mine closer. I talked with somebody else's father who was walking in front of us. I was trying to make it look like I wasn't with my parents. But we got to the tent, my parents were shouting "Jess," calling my name—I was literally trying to get away from my parents. It was the worse scene I've ever been in.

So we move my things into my dorm. It was bad enough that white people were moving me in, but then there's this Korean person. For most black people who have had interactions with Koreans, it was always the Korean store owner; so it was like who is this person in the dorm? My sister is sitting at the end of the hall "smooching" with her white boyfriend and here I am trying to make my debut as "the black girl." It wasn't working at all! Finally, as soon as everything was moved in—and I do mean the very moment—I wanted my parents to leave. They, on the other hand, were excited about meeting the president of the college at a reception the college hosted for students and their families. When my parents expressed their eagerness to meet the president, I became visibly upset. I said if they wanted to go they should go, but that I was not going. I think they were disappointed. Then they asked if, instead, I wanted to go to the college store to get a T-shirt. I told them no, adamantly, and said that I was staying in my room and that I didn't care what they did as long as they got out of my room.

My mother got angry and stormed out of the room. My father said he was going to the college store and would be back to check on me. He really wanted us all to spend time together as a family before they had to leave the following day. My boyfriend had already left. He was the first to leave, and that made it worse because he was my one "black thing" to hold onto. My brother's always been quiet. He doesn't talk about a lot of things. So he gave me a quick hug and left. My sister looked angry. On her face was the question: "How could you do that to our parents?" She'd always been our parents' mainstay. They were always right; I was always wrong. She didn't latch on to why I might be feeling this way. She just didn't understand where I was coming from. When her boyfriend followed her out of the room, I was left in my dorm room alone, having an anxiety attack. I've had them all through college, and that's where they started. This whole experience was a smack in the face when it came to racial relationships.

I want to stand up at graduation and apologize to my parents. I don't know if I ever really apologized to them. I feel like a jerk. I did end up running out to the parking lot just before my parents were to leave and said good-bye to them. But my mother was still hurt, and my father tried to smooth things over. It was terrible. I was leaving home for a long time.

Once everyone left and you were back in your dorm room, what did you do then?

I remember unpacking and trying to find the appropriate clothes to wear. No matter what I put on, I didn't feel like it was right. It was literally like walking into a whole new world. At home I thought I was the cutest thing but at college I felt so behind the times.

I remember sitting alone by the window that overlooks the main campus and intently watching people as they walked by. I had often done that in Brazil. It was a cool way to assimilate into a foreign culture. So I thought, why not apply it to this situation. I watched how people walked, what shoes they wore, how they dressed, their hairstyles, if they wore makeup or not, how they interacted. My goal was to assimilate into this culture.

When you use the word *assimilate*, does it have a negative or positive connotation to you?

I think the word has a negative connotation. But it's been my ticket into the black experience. I think that assimilating into a situation like mine was at college has very positive potential for the black adoptee in a white family who has been raised in an all-white environment. To an extent, I'm still assimilating.

When you hung photographs or pictures in your dorm room, what message were you communicating regarding your views on life and family?

In the beginning I displayed the attitude that we're all one people. I had a pin that had the world on it with the words, "We are all one people." I put pictures up of babies of all different colors. I was representing the world. I had Brazilian art on one wall, and on another friends and family. They were mostly me and white people. Occasionally, like in my pictures from Brazil, there may have been darker-skinned people in some of the photos—I had a really close friend I had met in Brazil who's black. She goes to this college, too. And I had another picture of a black friend. Some of those pictures confirmed I was "down." Of course most of the students had pictures of their moms and dads, and they were all black. And then there were mine. Of course my sister added a little spice. But it was still a wall filled with pictures of white people.

Did any students overtly comment on your having been adopted into a white family?

About three days after I moved in, the issue came up in conversation. A girl named Donna roomed across the hall from me. She was this grass-roots revolutionary person into "Black Power" and "Back to Africa." I don't want to generalize or convey that this is necessarily negative, particularly since I support it, but I had an initial perception of her as a militant person. Her roommate, Stephanie, was from Washington, D.C., and to me was the epitome of a black girl. Donna would play music from Arrested Development and Bob Marley, and Stephanie listened to Hip Hop and Go Go. My roommate was from Mississippi and had her own issues.

It was Donna who came into my room—she wore her hair natural and very close to her head—anyway, we were chatting and she asked me where I came from. I told her I was adopted and that my parents were white. She said she'd noticed that I had had the whole United Nations helping me move in, and she asked me, "What was that about?" At that moment I felt apprehensive. Today I recognize that it was just a type of verbal interaction, but back then I saw it as an affront. Oh God, I thought, she's going to "call me out" and punch me.

What did you say when she asked you that question?

I said they were my family, and she asked me what that was like for me. Then we started to talk about race in general and what brought us to this school. I told her about my preconceptions of the college, about how, when I got here, I fit in more at this college than I had anywhere else in my life.

What made you feel like you fit in at this college?

The students are predominately black, and we're all women. Nobody looked the same, yet there was an underlying commonality or bond that everyone latched onto.

For a lot of black women, this college is a place to discover more about our heritage and history. Considering where I came from and who raised me and how little I thought I knew about my ethnicity, it's interesting that I was actually at the same point in searching for my identity as others who had been raised in completely black areas and had gone to black high schools. We all basically had the same understanding when it came to our political views and what "African American" really means, what our struggle is and the complexities of race relations. In my classes I definitely had a handle on many things other students didn't comprehend.

Based on your personal experience and expertise in transracial adoption, would you argue that transracial adoption doesn't limit a child from developing into a positive contributor to society?

I haven't come to a decision about that. That's partly why I'm struggling with that subject in my thesis. For me, it's been a positive experience. But, to be honest, I don't look fondly upon white people adopting nonwhite children. Even though I feel like I came out O.K., a lot of different factors in my favor may not be there for another child. And I'm still struggling.

What are some of your major struggles?

Right now it's in the social arena. If I go out, which is rare, I feel uncomfortable, actually afraid, in the club setting. My fear comes from my perception of the purpose of the clubs and where I am emotionally in my journey. I view the clubs as a major outlet for black people of my generation to let off steam but also to express themselves through music and dance and verbal communication. The people who go to the clubs interact on a level all their own. It scares me because I don't know if I can do that. I have a good friend who's very much into music. I just don't feel it in me like he does.

Among the priorities in your life, which ones would make it to the top-ten list?

I'm into my art. I'm into myself. This scares me, too, because I feel like I've come through one struggle but that I'm not facing up to the next.

And what would that be?

Being an adult and being black. I feel like my whole college experience is still part of my childhood or weaning away from my parents. I did it, I survived. And I really loved it and had fun. But now I'm at a transition in my life. The question is: Will I grab the next struggle and look it straight in the eyes or will I walk beside it?

The struggle is hard?

It really is. Some time this year I read an article that my mother had left out. It was a story about a white family in Vermont who participated in the Fresh Air Child Program.

What is the Fresh Air Child Program? I'm not familiar with that program.

It's specifically set up to bring an inner-city child to a rural family during the summer for three to five weeks. They say "inner-city child," but they're really talking about a black child. My family had a Fresh Air child when I was younger. It scares me because of how white people conceptualize what it is they are doing. True, you are exposing a child to new and different things. That's always a positive thing. It's a way a person gains knowledge and experience and cultivates his or her likes and dislikes. To me, though, too many white people who support this program are convinced that it is 1 oo percent positive.

What are some of the repercussions with a program like this?

A child visits you in your comfortable and cozy ten-bedroom house. There are horses and land and clean water. There is food on the table every night. The child goes to parks and to the mall where he gets clothes and toys and so on. Then this child has to go back to where he's from, where he doesn't experience any of those things.

I don't know if that's the best thing for a child or if it's done in the best way. I'm not comparing the experience of transracial adoption to this, but in a sense both are carried out in a humanitarian, charitable way; but then after eighteen years, whether you still live in the same home or not, you're an adult and are left to survive without any debriefing. I don't know if that's healthy. I actually know of some cases where the adoptee became schizophrenic. I escaped that. And I say escaped because it's so easy to become that way.

Finally, what does the term *transracial adoption* bring to mind?

Difference. Self-identity. Frustration. Anger. Loneliness.

Andrea

PORTAGE, MICHIGAN
MARCH 1997

What you look like is not who you are. Self-identity is based on the degree of confidence you have in yourself, on what you do, your accomplishments, the goals you set for yourself and achieve—this is what shows on the outside. If you want to know about your ethnic background, go to the library, read books, hang out with people of your same race.

Andrea, 23, is biracial. She was born in Grand Rapids, Michigan, but spent her early childhood years with her adoptive family in Washington, D.C. Her family then moved briefly to London, England, before returning to Michigan, this time to Big Rapids, a largely white, semirural community, where she spent her teen years.

Like many adoptees in interracial families, Andrea faced the dilemma of living in a divided world. On the one hand, she was raised by white parents whom she knew loved her. Yet her familial security was juxtaposed against a larger society that judged her solely on the basis of her ethnic identity. Between these two extremes, Andrea has risen to levels of confidence that easier circumstances might never have revealed. This inner strength has kept her worlds from colliding and fueled her hopes for future success.

Andrea was taught "to respect people for who they are." She was encouraged by her parents to set high goals and to develop a plan to accomplish those goals, whether in athletics or academics. While she agrees that learning about one's heritage is important, Andrea believes that a greater determinant of an individual's self-identity comes from his or her own achievements.

In 1993, while attending Ferris State University in Michigan, Andrea made the conscious decision to participate in the African American community. Many of Andrea's friends felt comfortable talking with her about the social issues and everyday realities confronting them. Through these interactions, Andrea recognized that there were important differences in perspectives and experiences between her black and white friends. Still, given those differences, she has been able to transcend skin color and other barriers in order to embrace the spirit of the individual.

Today, as Andrea reflects on her life, she feels especially thankful to have been adopted into her family. She has learned to accept the visible differences and appreciate the commonalities the members of her family share with one another including love, support, trust, and stability. The taping of this interview finds her balancing her time between raising her three-year-old son, Latrelle, teaching swimming, and completing her medical assistant degree. Andrea has two brothers, Jamie (26) and Daniel (19), both of whom are adopted and biracial. Her parents, Jim and Alice, are instructors at Ferris State University.

Months after this interview, Andrea and Antonio were married. They live in the Detroit area with their two sons, Antonio Jr. and Latrelle.

Where did you live the first five years of your life?
Washington, D.C.
Please describe the community you lived in.
It was multicultural. There were blacks, whites, maybe Hispanics.
Did you identify with the children in this community?
I played with everybody. There wasn't any one race I associated with. My best friend was a black boy. He was my neighbor. I don't remember his name.
You are not the only adopted child in your family. Tell me about your other siblings.
I have two brothers, Jamie and Daniel. Both are adopted, and both are mixed—black and white.
Looking back at your relationships with your siblings, do you think it was important to you that they were from similar ethnic backgrounds?
It didn't phase me.
You mentioned that the community you were raised in your early childhood was multicultural? Was it important to you to be part of a diverse community?
No. At that age I didn't think about that.
At what point did you begin thinking about racial differences?
Real seriously? I would say in college—

We'll talk about that shortly. First I want to ask whether your parents talked with you about your own cultural heritage when you were growing up?

No.

Did they discuss with you issues about adoption in general?

Not to my knowledge, not until I got older and asked them questions about my adoption. I'd say I began asking them questions in junior high.

It seems I'm always asked, "When did you realize you were adopted?"

I don't know. I knew there was a difference but I can't think of the moment when I said, "Mommy, why am I a different color than you?"

Did your parents discuss with you why they adopted you?

We talked about it. They adopted us because they just wanted to adopt. They didn't care—male, female, black, white, Asian, whatever. They just wanted three babies.

In conversations with your parents, did they make it a point to discuss with you the importance of interacting with the African American community?

No. But if I had questions they would answer them.

Did you confront people who questioned whether you belonged in your family? In other words, did anyone come right out and ask, "Why are you, a black, living in a white family?"

Not really. What usually happens is that people see me with my mom and don't know it's my mom right away. They wonder. Then when they find out she's actually my mom, it's a whole different look they give me.

What is that look?

A surprised look. It's like, "Oh?!" Because my parents are white, I seem to get a little more respect. For example, when I was living in England, some boy gave me problems. He always picked on me, not that he said racial things blatantly to my face. He'd make some racial comments but was generally just mean to me. One day I told him that he'd really be surprised when he saw my mom. I'd never said anything about her being white. So when that moment came, he was very shocked. Things were different after that. His behavior changed.

When you were in England, did people in your surroundings notice a difference between black and white?

Sure. But in England I was accepted. I was cool because I was an American, not because I was black. People noticed my accent and that I was from a different country.

Race wasn't an issue. It didn't even phase them. The first day of school the teacher asked me where I wanted to sit. Everyone who had an open seat nearby raised his or her hand for me to sit by them. When I sat down, a kid came up to me and asked me to say hello—just to hear my accent. And at the first recess, everybody swarmed around me. Again, it was because I was from another country, not because of my race.

You were in fifth grade when you lived in England. A year later, when you returned from England to the United States with your family, did you see a difference in the way Americans treated you?

No. The biggest thing I realized when I came back and started school was that I was so far ahead of my classmates. Having been in England for one year, I was ahead of the game. I thought Americans were kind of stupid and slow. As far as my friends were concerned, I didn't experience any difference because of my race. They were all the same friends that I had when I left for England.

When you came back to the states, you were about eleven years old. Where did your family end up living?

In Big Rapids, Michigan.

Was this also a multicultural community?

It was predominately white.

Do you remember the ethnic makeup of the school you attended in Big Rapids?

It was mostly white. I was the only black person who graduated from my grade. When I was in high school there were probably eight or nine blacks in the school.

At any point in high school did you question your racial identity?

No.

Did you have experiences that made you confront who Andrea is as a black person?

No.

With whom do you identify the most, the white or the black community?

I don't know. As far as race is concerned, I don't even think about it because all that does is cause problems. I don't want to waste my time. When people confront me with stuff like that, I don't even deal with it. It's childish if a person can't accept another person for who they are regardless of race. That's their problem. As a rule, I don't get involved with that. I'll listen to a person's point if it's relevant, but I don't get into racial debates or arguments because I think that it's stupid.

I respect people more who live for themselves, who can give people their space and accept people for who they are.

Thinking back to the values your parents taught you, what main value or values left the biggest impression in your life?

They taught me to love people and to learn to respect people for who they are. I try to live that way in my life. Loving one another is more important to me than identifying only with the African American community.

To a certain extent I'm part of the African American community, but I'm not just associated with the African community. Because I'm mixed, I accept all sides of myself. I don't try to live just the "African American way." I admit that I've never done much research into my heritage, and I haven't looked into my background at all.

Is that because you don't want to know about your heritage?

It's because my "heritage" isn't as important to me as people make it out to be. I know about the problems that have existed in the black community historically. I know that blacks prefer certain foods, certain music, etc. Some of the stuff I like, some I don't. As far as whites go, I know what they've done in the past. I know the foods they eat, how they talk.

With what race classification do you identify yourself?

I consider myself a Mulatto, a person of mixed culture, half-white and half-black.

In your opinion, does society treat you as a white person or as a black person?

Society treats me as an African American. Society treats me based on what they see. I look African American so society, including African Americans, think I'm black. For example, if I'm among a bunch of African Americans and they make comments or jokes about white people, they think I'll go right along with what they're saying, that I have no problem with it.

Personally, I've never had a confrontation with white people treating me badly, but I know there are differences. I just can't be specific.

Do you associate with both blacks and whites?

Yes, I think I do.

Do you see a difference in the way both groups generally work and function?

Oh, yeah. Both groups have their own style, like different foods, different music, different ways of raising a family. What is most important to each group is also different. Simple living conditions are different. What's fun to white people in the summer, what's fun to black people in the summer—it's all different.

What you just said signifies that you are aware of the lifestyles and values of both groups. Who guided you in your life's journey to the point that you can distinguish between two different groups?

It wasn't a matter of someone guiding me. I just went through it. When I started attending Ferris University in Big Rapids, I began hanging around with a lot of black people, mainly guys.

Did you intentionally choose to hang out with black guys?

No, I didn't choose to. I just started talking with guys who were black. Most of my girlfriends were white. For me, it's a whole different issue when it comes to girls or guys.

Did it bother you that white guys didn't ask you out on dates?

No.

Your male friends are predominately black. Was it a conscious decision to interact with and date black men?

No, it just happened. Growing up I've always been a "Tom Boy." I always had more male friends than female friends. The boys I liked best in high school were mostly white. But a couple of black guys started coming to the school. I knew one of the black guys and we started dating. The black guys, as opposed to the white guys, were interested in me as a girlfriend, so I guess that's why I spent more time with black guys.

In college, did your mom talk to you about race?

No.

Did anyone in the African American community take the time to invest in your life for the long term?

No.

Now, do you have a good relationship with your siblings, so that you can talk to them about personal issues?

Yes. We have always been close.

What is the most difficult challenge that you've encountered in your life?

Raising my son by myself.

Is your son, Latrelle, African American?

He is both black and white.

Your son is still quite young, but have you begun teaching him about his cultural heritage?

How would you describe "teaching"?

By "teaching," I mean identifying for your son experiences and culture that make up an aspect of the African American story.

I haven't yet, no.

Do you think it's important that Latrelle know and appreciate his heritage?

Yes, but it's not a huge deal. I don't want him to be naive and not experience or know about his cultural heritage, but it's not real important.

Some would say that African American males today are facing a crisis. Too many are incarcerated, on drugs, or unemployed. While I believe a significant number of black males are gainfully employed, educated, and raising their kids, the statistics speak to unfortunate challenges that are facing black males. Are you concerned about Latrelle's future and safety as a visibly African American male?

Oh yes, it scares me. It's not just black males. It's the community at large. There's so much crime and violence going on—that's what I'm afraid of. I can't guarantee that Latrelle won't fall into that . . . I'm afraid of it. At some point in my life I hadn't wanted to bring a child into the world because it's so screwed up.

What are your views on transracial adoption?

If the child is exposed to his or her ethnic community and has a loving and supportive family, I don't see any problem with transracial adoption. The only thing I regret about my childhood is that I wasn't raised in a multicultural area. The community was predominately white.

Why do you think that it's important for a child who is adopted transracially to be raised in a multicultural community?

So the child can learn to handle differences. Even though I was raised in a predominately white community, people make such a big deal about the importance of one's heritage that I feel like I'm supposed to know about my black heritage. On the other hand, knowing my heritage isn't as important to me because I wasn't raised with that. I believe I'm an intelligent person. I'm very secure with myself.

Where do you get your security from?

From my parents. They loved me and respected me and gave me my individualism. They didn't tie me down to one thing but were open to what I wanted to do . . . they let me explore. I knew my parents were there for me even when I did something bad.

Andrea, you talk about the value of having love and support, letting a child explore who he or she is. Groups like the National Association of Black Social Workers (NABSW) have stated in the past that a black child living in a white family will not be able to develop as a total person, appreciative of his or her ethnicity and

culture. **Do you think that it's possible to become a "total person" living in a white family as a black American?**

My only statement to the NABSW is this: If transracial adoption is such a problem for them, then they need to go out and adopt all those kids who aren't getting adopted. I have a big problem with people who talk like that but aren't doing enough to give children homes. What are we going to do about the children?

I don't believe that heritage and race are all that's needed to make a person complete. How does knowing one's heritage ensure a child's best interest? A child may know that he's black but still be locked up in a foster home, not loved or cared for in long term.

Then once a black child is in a nurturing and loving white family, how does that child also develop a black self-identity?

Eventually those black individuals need to find out about their cultural heritage, live in a black community and have friends in that community.

What you are describing isn't easy. I think that's where the arguments opposing transracial adoption come in. My two questions to you are these: First, at what point does a person understand that it is desirable to be exposed to her ethnic community? And, second, who directs the individual to these places and experiences?

I think that the groups and experiences need to be accessible to the person.

Let me rephrase the question. How can the black and the white communities provide access to the adoptee?

By working together. Both black and white communities need to stop being segregated for the sake of the children. If a black child is in a white family and it is important for the child to know his cultural heritage, then both communities need to come together and set up a program with the adoptee and have people at both areas meet regularly. In that way, not only will the adoptee understand her own heritage but those supporting the child in that quest will also understand the adoptee's environment.

People generally have their own views on this issue but don't act on them. If it is important to expose a black child to her cultural heritage, then the black community needs to ensure that the child has this opportunity. How do you come together? You just do it!

Both the white and black communities need to accept their differences, put them aside, and then focus on the child.

Why is the concept of a multicultural community attractive? What can this kind of community teach?

That people are different but are also the same. Everyone is human but we all have different ways of growing up. If a person is around different people all the time, then one doesn't think about the differences. I grew up around white people and now it doesn't bother me to be around them.

Clearly you have been able to go beyond race and develop into a confident person. How does the "I" in you become so strong and confident in a society that is defined so much by race?

Religion. God doesn't see people in terms of race or color. God is focused on loving your neighbor as yourself, and He is the main true judge. He created us and has the power to destroy us at any time. That's my one answer. I try living the way He wants us to live, respecting others and loving everyone, not just my own race.

The fact that a black child is living in a white family presents tension. People in the black community truly believe that placing a black child into a white family is an act of "cultural genocide" and a direct attack on the black family. What do you think about that perception?

They need to ask themselves, "Why is it so important to me that this child is being supposedly 'stripped from his or her community'?" They need to worry about themselves first, then deal with other things.

To me, blacks focus more on race than whites do. Maybe this is how I see it because blacks don't have a problem telling me their feelings about white people since they think I'm African American. I think that they are too focused on race and not focused enough on loving each other and getting themselves straight.

This brings me to my next question. In your opinion, what are three areas that the black community, understanding we are diverse, need to work on?

Loving each other. They should quit making excuses because of the "white man" and learn to respect themselves. If the black community wants a better life, then they need to do it themselves. I understand it's tough and that there are real issues this community confronts, but the black community brings a lot of stuff on themselves.

What about the white community? How do they learn how to respect and love someone from a different racial and ethnic background?

The white community needs to make it a priority to understand the cultural values and style of communication of people from different backgrounds. The community needs to learn to look at the inner person and talk with that person rather than rely on stereotypes based on race. It's all about being human. People need to have the "balls," so to speak, to talk with someone who is different and find out that person's interests.

What you are saying is hard to hear, but I believe there is definitely validity in it. To be honest, though, I am confident some people are hearing this and questioning your authenticity as a black person, questioning your credibility to speak on aspects of the black community.

I am authentic. I'm me, Andrea. I don't have to prove to anybody where I came from. If someone can't accept me for who I am, then that's his problem. I'm not worried about that because there are people who accept me for who I am, and I like who I am.

Society has a way of perpetuating stereotypes and false expectations—of black people in particular. One sees this in the media, in schools, in communities, and in politics. While I believe that we, as a nation, are slowly making strides to rectify these inaccuracies, what has enabled you to transcend these real obstacles and progress as an individual?

I just do. I've always been focused on what I want. I'm not caught up in political issues. Race is political. It's stupid if people let their race limit them based on what other people say. We as adults make things complex when they need to be simple.

The plight facing black children in foster care is political. Currently, there is a disproportionate number of black children in foster care in America. Race and politics collide right there. What do we do about that?

Politics, race, and reality have to come together. Nothing can be done until each person decides that everyone is his brother or sister. As the saying goes, "You can lead a horse to water, but you can't make it drink." If people truly want to provide homes to the disproportionate number of black children in foster care, they're going to do it!

Andrea, you are in a unique position because of your experiences in two apparently different worlds. What is the secret of being able to communicate with people?

I genuinely interact with people everyday. When I meet someone, I give that person the benefit of the doubt. I talk with people and see how they respond to me. If someone is rude to me and doesn't want me around, I won't be around. And if someone is nice to me, then I'm very polite. I always start off being polite and open-minded.

On the subject of dating, how have black males responded when they found out your parents are white?
No problems.

Do you find yourself explaining that your parents are white?
Yes.

Why?
Because they ask me, "How do you talk so proper" or see the things I see. Or they ask to see pictures. Then I tell them I'm adopted and that both my parents are white.

Has that made any of them take a second look at whether they want to date you?
No.

How did these individuals relate to your parents?
They didn't know how to. I don't think they felt comfortable around them. I know one of them didn't.

What was his behavior like?
Fake. I think he felt uncomfortable. Maybe he had so made up his mind that whites were not a positive thing that they automatically were seen as negative.

Did he tell you specifically why he may have been uncomfortable?
Not really. The only time it came up was when we broke up. When I broke up with him—and he is my baby's father—he proceeded to tell me I was brainwashed by them—not even knowing who "them" were—that my parents were fake and that they didn't like blacks.

Were you hurt by what he said to you?
No. It was stupid thinking on his part. He made excuses for himself because he needed something to make him feel better.

This may be an unfair question. Where does the intimidation that some African Americans show toward whites come from? Or does it even exist?
I don't know. But I do understand. Black males have said to me that they were intimidated by me because of the way I talk—that was it. When they first met me and I spoke, they were intimidated by me.

Is it lonely for you to be in the middle of two different communities that do not necessarily get along?

No. Why should I be lonely?

Do you have African American friends who listen to you, especially when discussing feelings about dating and self-identity?

I've never talked to anybody about my experiences in depth like this before.

To children and adolescents who are black and adopted into white families, what key issues can you tell them about, based on your experiences, to help them make it through?

Worry about your internal self, that's what is most important. Feel secure about who you are. What you look like is not who you are. Self-identity is based on the degree of confidence you have in yourself, on what you do, your accomplishments, the goals you set for yourself and achieve—this is what shows on the outside. If you want to know about your ethnic background, go to the library, read books, hang out with people of your same race.

Looking around your house, I see pictures of your family and friends. I see CDs with African American faces on them. Tell me about the CDs.

I bought these CDs because I like the music. African Americans who are confident in themselves bring to society their strong inner self. I think they are very strong inner beings, and that is very important.

What allowed them to possess this inner strength you speak about?

I assume it was their strong belief in and love for who they are and for each other. Family, I believe, is important to them. For those who are true to that, then that is one of their riches.

Was there a time in your life when you tried to forget you were black?

No.

Is education important to you?

Very, very important. If you don't know anything, you can't grow and you won't get anywhere.

What are the primary values you are going to teach your son, Latrelle?

To love one another, to respect himself and others. I want him to know that material things are not that important, that what is most important is to know God.

What is your purpose in life?

To help people. And to have a positive impact on people—black, white, Korean, whoever.

What is the highlight of your life?

My son. He's a part of me. I have such an influence in his life. I can make or break this child. My son is what I live for.

Do you expose him to the African American community?

Yes. The day care center he goes to is multicultural. The director is African American, and there are a lot of African American kids. There are also white children, and some of the teachers are white.

Why do you believe that this will have a positive impact on your son?

My son is exposed to diversity. He is with people who look like him and with those who don't. The philosophy of this day care center is a model of the way that I want my son to be raised. The people there are Christian, loving and yet stern.

The current state of America shows that we, as a society, need to do more for kids. What do you suggest can be done for the welfare of children?

We must get involved in the lives of children and love them. Adoption is a wonderful option. If people choose to adopt older children, they need to be patient with them. These kids have probably been on their own more than not, and have not no one to love them. So the parents need to give these kids extra love. I think family and love is the best thing. When I get older and have a more established income, I want to adopt.

Why?

Because I was adopted, and because there are a lot of kids who need to be adopted. I don't want to adopt a baby. I want to adopt a child around three years of age. Babies are always getting adopted, and there are so many children in foster care who people forget about. Foster care is meant to be temporary. When you are adopted into a family, you are part of that family. It's not even a question of adoption. It's just family.

Do you support same-race adoptions? Case in point: Do you think a black child should be raised in a black family, as opposed to a white family?

If the black and white families are both of equal status, then sure, adopt the child into the black family—so the child can see who he is. Personally, I don't feel I have a problem because I was adopted into a white family and I wonder how many black kids feel they have problems because of that. So that's why I believe that if both black and white families are the same economically and one family shows more love and compassion to the child, then I would want the family that shows love and compassion to adopt the child.

Why did you decide to be interviewed for this book?

I don't think there are many books or much information available to people who are actually going through this experience. I think readers will get a lot of insight from this book. And here are my last words: *I feel very, very, very blessed to be adopted!*

Kimberly Stapert

GRAND RAPIDS, MICHIGAN
MARCH 1997

I still believe that transracial adoption should be considered for the permanency of all abandoned children. But more attention should be given to training agencies to improve their work with parents before the adoption in order to prepare them to adopt transracially.

A social worker by profession, Kimberly Stapert was born and raised in Grand Rapids, Michigan. In 1970, six months after remaining in foster care, Kimberly was adopted through a private adoption agency located in Grand Rapids. According to Kimberly, the Staperts, who were both in their mid-twenties and wanting to build their family, found themselves looking at transracial adoption as a viable option. They became aware of the disproportionate number of black and biracial children who needed permanent homes, and they believed they could provide a child with a stable and loving home. What began for them as opening their home to one child turned into extending their family to include six more children, all biracial.

Influenced largely by her own transracial adoption experience and the interactions with foster care children under her supervision, Kimberly maintains that children need to be expeditiously placed in a stable and permanent home. Too often children are lost in the foster care system or placed in multiple foster care homes, causing their lives to become fragmented. In a significant number of her cases, Kimberly witnesses children deteriorating emotionally in the system, waiting for their biological parents to become rehabilitated. Kimberly asserts that "the courts are giving the biological parents unreasonable amounts of time and opportunities to do what they need to do to get their kids back." She believes strongly that the courts and the adoption agencies must be held accountable to ensure that the well-being of the child is a priority.

Kimberly Stapert benefited from the stability, love, and permanency of her family. Through her relationships with her parents and siblings, Kimberly learned the value of responsibility, education, and the appreciation of people from different ethnic backgrounds. The foundation she gained from her upbringing has helped her through personal struggles and has given her the strength to accomplish the goals she set for herself. Yet Kimberly maintains that transracial adoptions should be considered on a case-by-case basis. In situations where the potential adoptive parents are not prepared to address the child's cultural difference, Kimberly believes they should not adopt transracially.

While this interview includes Kimberly's insights on adoption from the perspective of a social worker, she speaks primarily as an adoptee who has contended with identity issues, and as a mother who is raising her two sons.

What were some of your fondest memories growing up with your parents?

Mom and I always had a close relationship. We would go shopping, get a cookie, or go out to lunch. Most of my fondest memories are of all of us together as a family because we rarely did things individually with our parents. It was family-oriented. We went on a lot of family trips during spring break. We did a lot of stuff with my mom's parents, like going to the beach. We still have a cottage today that we go to for a week every summer.

Did your mom tell you in a very clear way that she loved you?

Oh, yes. Constantly. My mom is very expressive, open, and loving. My mom and dad always told us they loved us. They were both very demonstrative, especially my mom. She wasn't working at the time, so when we came home from school she'd have warm cookies and a good snack. She'd ask how our day was and would tuck us in at night. I had a very loving home.

You were adopted at a very young age—six months. When did your parents actually tell you that you were adopted?

I've been asked that question before and have tried hard to think about the actual moment I knew. I can't think of one big event where it just hit me. My parents were open about it all along. Obviously, my adoption was something you can't hide because physically I didn't look like them. So they always were talking about it, just like you'd talk about other things growing up, like who your grandmother is, etc.

We each had a special day that was celebrated like our birthday. My day is September 4. On that day we would sit down with our parents at night and go through our baby book. They would tell us our adoption story. Our baby books start with pictures from the time they were visiting us at the adoption agency—and then the birth announcement that said, "We've adopted." Following the announcement were the cards people sent to my parents after they adopted us. The baby book also included pictures of the party they had when they first took us home. So we'd look through that book and they would tell us the story. We also got to pick what we had for dinner that night, and we got a small present that was usually a special book, not a major toy.

Your parents made the gift of adoption a very natural part of your experience.

Yes, it was very natural. It wasn't something hidden, it was just a part of who I was. It was something I always knew. My parents still continue this important event today, even though I'm an adult. I don't get to pick the meal, but they still send me a special card and a special gift on my placement day, and they phone me.

What encouraged your parents to choose adoption, specifically transracial adoption?

At first, for the same reason many people do. Infertility. They went to the adoption agency initially with general questions about adoption. They found out there was a long waiting period and lots of red tape to adopt a white child. The agency introduced transracial adoption as an alternative. My parents realized that if these kids need homes and are waiting and available right now, why should they wait for a white child. So after much thinking, they decided to adopt transracially.

Have your parents, since the time they've adopted, sought out support groups to assist them with raising kids outside of their cultural group?

They've attended family support groups periodically over the years through the agency. They even organized a couple of informal networks among parents in the same situation. It's ironic because a lot of other families adopted transracially where we live, specifically through our church. Just in my own grade, I went to school with two other girls who were also mixed and had been adopted into white families. These families were close with my family. And through our church, there were also several other families. So that, too, provided informal support.

Did your parents have African American friends they could talk to regularly on how to raise a black child?

The neighborhood we lived in was quite diverse. There were black families, white families, and the two adopted families I mentioned. My mom has a very close friend who is of mixed race, black and white. She's married to a black man and grew up in a black home. My mom is very close to both her and her husband. My siblings and I call them auntie and uncle, even though they aren't related to us by blood or legally. We did things with them as families. He'd dress up like Santa and be the black Santa.

We also had a couple of African American babysitters quite regularly, who were from the neighborhood, and others through our church. My mom has reached out to the African American community because she teaches kindergarten in the inner city. I guess the primary connection with other African Americans is the couple who are our aunt and uncle.

You've mentioned you have siblings. How many brothers and sisters do you have?

Three brothers and three sisters. I'm the oldest.

The ages of the "children" in your family range from twenty-seven to nine. Are your siblings biologically related to your parents?

They're all adopted. None of us are blood siblings. Many people ask that question. We were all adopted as infants, except for my sister Melissa who was adopted at two and a half. We are all mixed, black and white, except for one brother who I think has Hispanic in him as well.

Growing up in a white family, did you see your siblings as a support system?

Having siblings with similar ethnic backgrounds helped me a lot. My mom and dad would joke and say we were like a black family because the kids canceled my parents out. We outnumbered them seven to two. My siblings definitely helped because I didn't feel different compared to someone else I know who was the only black child adopted into her family. It was positive to see my whole family together and know I wasn't the one that stood out in the crowd.

What values did your parents instill in you?

I was raised in a Christian home and taught the love of God, treating people the way God would want us to treat others. My parents also instilled in me the value of respecting people regardless of race, economic background, or disabilities. Some of my brothers and sisters have special needs. One brother wears hearing aids; one of my younger sisters has learning disabilities and special educational needs. My parents taught me to respect people regardless of external things.

Probably because I'm the oldest sibling, being responsible was a value I picked up. Education was also an important value, particularly because both my parents come from an educational background.

Were your parents able to teach you about who you are as a black person in this society?

Yes. My parents taught me that I was brown. We had a book that I now read to my son. Its called, *Black, Is Brown, Is Tan*. My mom likes to think along this spectrum. Right now she's reading *The Color of Water*, which describes people as being light-skinned or darker-skinned—not simply black and white. If you look at people, nobody is totally black or totally white.

I clearly remember filling out a form, at a relatively young age, for some activity I wanted to participate in with my dad. I had to check off my race on the form. I asked my dad what to fill in since none of the boxes said "brown." He said to check the box that said black because that's how people in society see me. So still there were both heritages but also the message that society saw me as black and that I should look at my ethnicity as positive. I considered those who had problems with my skin color—and I had experiences with that—the ones with the problem and that I still should feel good about who I was. But the differences were not denied by my parents.

As a family, did you discuss the important contributions of the African American community and appreciate the richness of the African American culture?

When I was a child, we went to a couple of African American festivals in a park near our home. Other than that, we didn't go to many ethnic activities when I was younger.

My parents had a phonograph record about Martin Luther King Jr. They played the record a couple of times a year, close to Martin Luther King's birthday and during Black History Month. I distinctly remember his "I Have A Dream" speech.

What were your images as a child of Martin Luther King Jr. and what he symbolized?

He was a good man. I remember a line from one of his well-known speeches, that people shouldn't be "judged by the color of their skin but by the content of their character . . ."

In your own experience, did race play a part in your life? Did people seem to judge you because of your skin color without regard to your person or character?

Once my three oldest siblings and I were in a restaurant with my parents in Iowa. We overheard someone near us whisper, " I wonder where they got those children from." They seemed disgusted that my parents were with us. My mom, who is quite forceful, stood up and said, confidently, "If you're wondering, we got these children from God." A lot of people stared. That was hard to accept. My parents would remind me that it was the people who were rude who had the problem. Still, it's hard. It makes me feel like a freak.

My husband Brian, who is white, and I have experienced overt racism. We stopped in Fowlerville, Michigan, at a McDonald's on our way to Ann Arbor. That's the time somebody gave me the most direct and hateful look ever. This person craned her neck all around to stare at us. It was one of the most ill and intense feelings I've ever experienced—the hatred of it.

I think Brian's friends made comments when we first started dating. Then when we actually became serious, a couple of his friends questioned, rhetorically: "Was Brian really gonna get serious with me?" I was just somebody to fool around with, somebody who would be fun, but that I was not the person Brian should marry or have a legitimate relationship with. That was the feeling I got.

When did you first feel "different"?

When I was six or seven. I was playing with some neighborhood kids who were white. There was dog poop on the ground and they said I was the color of poop, that black people are the color of poop. That was really, really hurtful. I remember feeling small and ashamed. Before that experience I remember thinking that when a mommy had a child sometimes it popped out white, sometimes black. I didn't think about race as a stigmatizing feature.

Did you speak with anyone about this isolating experience?

I always felt comfortable talking with my parents about racism and experiences like this one. They would be open and not minimize it or think the experience was in my head. In fact, I had trouble with a teacher in junior high school. I felt that he was discriminating against me and also had a problem with the other black students in the class. Again, my mom went to the school and told this teacher, in effect, that she had a problem with him and that I thought he was racist, and that, according to what I'd told her, it seemed he was having a problem with the black kids in his class.

My mom was a real advocate for me and got me out of the class. She was a model for not accepting ignorant behavior and letting things go by just because it was the most comfortable thing to do.

You grew up in a very diverse community. Did you find that your community was a strong support?

Yes. It was a good place to live. There weren't a lot of tensions, one way or the other.

Was the high school you attended diverse?

No. I went to Christian schools throughout my life. The middle school and grade school were ethnically diverse. I'd say 50-50. But the high school I went to was mostly white, much more upper class.

I think high school is a very difficult time. It was for me. High school is difficult for a lot of adopted kids because that's when you're facing identity issues, trying to figure out who you are and where you fit in. For adopted kids, it's doubly hard, and for kids who are adopted transracially it's even harder. Someone who is adopted can't say to her parents, "I know I got this from you," and use that in her formulation of her identity. The questions "Who am I, and where did I come from?" aren't answered.

You've been raised with a lot of love, care, and commitment from your family and church. Was the support enough to carry you through your experiences in high school, when the color line, black and white, was threatening at times?

During that time I continued to have, and still do, a strong relationship with my parents. I probably wouldn't have made it through high school if it hadn't been for my mom. My mom and I were very open and I could tell her things I was getting into.

My self-esteem at that time was very, very low. I didn't feel like I fit in anywhere. There was a small core group of the few African American's in the school; they all hung out together. Then there were subgroups among the many whites. I didn't feel like I fit in with any of the white groups or the black groups. Grade school didn't have racial divisions or cliques to the same degree.

As a black person, why didn't you feel you could get along with the other black students in your class?

Some of it was because of me, but some of it were the messages I was getting from the black students. I knew there were differences between us. I didn't grow up in the inner city so my language was different, as were my experiences in terms of what I ate and the activities I participated in. I guess that's why I felt uncomfortable. Some of them also told me I talked too white. Some called me "yellow girl" because my skin was somewhat lighter.

What made your self-esteem remain low?

I didn't know who I was. I couldn't figure this out because I didn't have the other piece—namely, where I came from.

In light of the contrast between these two groups, was there another group in your high school that attracted you?

I got into a group where I could establish a commonality or identity in terms of drinking and smoking pot and partying all the time. This group was mainly white. I also had a core group of black friends that ran track with me. I felt more accepted by them because this sport was our common bond and the basis of our friendship.

As with most people, being accepted is important. This reality becomes more intense for someone adopted transracially. How did partying tie into your wanting to be accepted?

I did stupid things, like having poor relationships with guys because of wanting to be accepted and loved. These types of relationships were destructive to me. I remember writing in my diary at the time that no man would ever want me to be his wife. I'll end up being somebody's mistress or whore for the rest of my life. That's where the drinking and partying was coming from. At one point we were partying at the beach, and I got so drunk I passed out. When I woke up I realized I had been raped. I didn't know what happened until the next morning. A lot of people at the school knew. I was getting this negative reputation. It was very painful. Looking back, I can see that I didn't know who I was and I was looking to fit in by changing my personality.

Race and identity play a part in this whole experience of "not fitting in." Was there anyone in the black community at this time who reached out to you?

I don't think so. All my teachers were white. I was quite isolated. I didn't hang out with the white group anymore, and I didn't feel connected with anyone outside my family. There weren't any role models from the black community who were my mentors at this time.

In college, what was the racial and ethnic makeup?

It was more white than in high school. The college was more conservative, and there was a strong Christian emphasis on higher learning. Again, I didn't feel like I fit in anywhere. I put a shell around myself. I was very distrustful of people, especially men. I was hardened in a sense. I just went to school and chose not to interact with other people. I don't think I gave other people much of a chance to interact with me because of my assumptions of the way people were—close-minded.

Here, at this college, did you come in contact with black friends or faculty members you could talk with?

I had a really good professor in social work who I really enjoyed. I don't know if we developed a close relationship but I felt she was a good role model. She had a family and had achieved a degree. I admired her as a person and as a teacher.

For one semester I was a mentor and had the opportunity to work with a black student and to help undergraduate students get a sense of community. As a group we went on outings in the community, and then met one on one with the kids assigned to us and worked with them. That was a good experience and perhaps the first time I did anything with a community, black or white, at this college. Still, my defenses were always up. I didn't want to be rejected, so I wouldn't give anybody the chance to reject me. I still felt uncomfortable with each culture, that I didn't fit in anywhere.

This campus has a somewhat cohesive African American presence. How did you respond to this group of students and were you ever fearful of these students approaching you?

I don't think I was afraid of that. Maybe another part of me felt I didn't need that, that I was above needing to bond with other black students.

I wasn't scared of black people. I felt they might reject me or that I wouldn't feel a part of the group. My perception of this group on campus was that other people who were having troubles adjusting needed them but that I could deal with those problems myself.

Speaking from personal experience, in college I was continuously confronted with being the only black person in a classroom and having most questions regarding race, economics, and culture directed at me. I imagine you had similar experiences. Can you describe these?

People joked that there would be one black person in every class and that they wouldn't let any more blacks in. You'd be sitting right in the middle, laughing, because of the truth of this scenario. That was my mental picture of the situation and it always seemed to be true—that the black person is in the middle and everyone else is swarming around that person like sharks.

I felt uncomfortable. During class discussions about race, I felt as though the students were looking at me. I felt so different from everybody else and totally on the spot.

The experience of being isolated racially in a class setting is not unique to blacks students, especially in higher education across this country. However, most of these students have black parents or extended family members, that is, the community, who are African American and can make the struggle somewhat easier for them. In your situation, you don't have black parents you can talk to or with whom you can identify? How do you deal with this added obstacle?

I don't know if having black parents would have made it easier for me in college or in high school. I had a very open relationship with my parents. My mom is my advocate. I knew she'd do anything for me. I don't think one has to have experienced racism to be a good parent. Certainly my mom has experienced discrimination just because she's a woman. So she had sensitivity in that area she could draw on. We had a close and loving relationship. My mom wouldn't minimize my feelings, so I don't know if I would have had an easier time had my parents been black. Racism sucks and its hard to deal with, but I don't think one has to be black to help somebody deal with the effects of racism.

Based on your background and your professional experience, what is your view on the state of children's welfare today?

In general, it makes me feel sick to see the way children are treated by society. It particularly concerns me that children are viewed as their parents' property, regardless of the way they are treated, and that their needs sometimes seem secondary to a lot of other needs. Case in point: a dog that gets shot gets more hype than kids who are being abused and neglected every day. There needs to be a lot more emphasis on establishing permanency for kids.

Working with "special needs" adoptions, I've seen many kids remain in foster care for years and years, moving from one home to the next. Many of these kids essentially grow up in the system and increasingly experience emotional and behavioral problems. Meanwhile, the courts are giving the biological parents unreasonable amounts of time and opportunities to do what they need to do to get their kids back. Often, based on my experience, these parents do a little bit to appease the judge just to get by, or they do something appropriate right before the next court hearing. It's a joke. They're playing the system because they know they can get away with it.

More emphasis needs to be placed on setting a strict time line—for example, a maximum of one year—for the biological parents to have the opportunity to regain custody of their children. If they can't get their lives together within that time, then the goal must be to move the child into a good home, a permanent home, expediently rather than holding the child in limbo for five or six years waiting for the biological parents to get their act together.

Transracial adoption has been viewed by some as the last resort in giving a child a home. What is your view on transracial adoption?

Transracial adoption should be viewed case by case. I think it can work for a lot of kids and can provide them with a great home and family. But some potential adoptive parents aren't prepared to raise a child from a different culture, and they shouldn't adopt transracially.

I've seen kids remain in the system because they have no home. Agencies could do a whole lot better recruiting families to adopt these children, especially black children.

Some African American families want to adopt black children, but they believe the adoption system discriminates against them, giving more access for white families to adopt. There's a lot of mistrust in the African American community toward these agencies. I believe the agencies have traditionally put up financial barriers and red tape to discourage African American families from adopting. But, still, there aren't enough black families available to adopt black children. So the question is this: Is it better for children to grow up in foster care with no connection to anyone, bounced from one home to the next, or be placed in a family that is prepared to raise them?

The National Association of Black Social Workers has articulated a public and emotional argument in support of same-race adoptions. Do you believe it is valid to question the ability of white families to raise black children in this society?

I'll never join the National Association of Black Social Workers because of how strongly I oppose their position. I believe that their very strong voice has divided people and society on this issue. But I do understand in part where the NABSW is coming from. Much of their concern comes from the mistrust African American families feel toward adoption agencies, which they believe have prevented some black families from adopting. The process can be quite intimidating. Many of the agency people are white. These black families feel that they don't want a white person coming into their home, studying their home, going through their business, and evaluating them. Some of the concern traces back to the slavery days when white people divided black families, when white people stripped slave families of their children.

I think much more can be done with kinship networks, which is an informal way to adopt and an avenue African Americans use regularly. I still believe that transracial adoption should be considered for the permanency of all abandoned children. But more attention should be given to training agencies to improve their work with parents before the adoption in order to prepare them to adopt transracially.

I see black social workers causing a lot of hype around this issue but solving nothing. The fact is that transracial adoptions continue to exist, regardless of the views expressed by NABSW and other groups. Instead of opposing TRA, these groups should focus their efforts, experience, and knowledge on educating people on how to raise children from different cultures so that we can do our best for the children in this situation.

I have placed kids transracially. Much needs to be done in working with these families prior to adoption. A lot of parents assume that it's enough to love these kids without acknowledging their ethnic differences. That is not an educated viewpoint. We need to help parents recognize the real issues their son or daughter will face. Take dating, for example. Is it acceptable to have a white family and still date someone who is black? How will the family react if their son or daughter brings home someone of a different race? It's also helpful for parents to tie in their own experiences with discrimination. How did that experience make them feel? And how would they respond if and when their child is discriminated against? Love isn't going to conquer all.

You've had an eyewitness view of foster care?

Most of the kids I worked with had been removed from their homes when their parents' rights had been terminated because of abuse and neglect. Some of the babies I saw had special physical needs, like birth defects and exposure to cocaine. Other kids were 5 years old and up. Of course they are the ones who have been in foster care for years and years before the parents' rights were terminated. Most of them were over 10.

I visited the foster care homes to see these kids who needed a permanent home. Luckily, foster parents often adopted. We also had a residential facility where kids lived, mainly older kids with severe behavioral and emotional problems who couldn't be handled in a foster home.

Were there behavioral differences between the children who were placed in a permanent home at an early age compared to those who languished in the foster care system?

Definitely. Those who were placed early were closer to "normal," if there is such a thing. These kids were functioning at the normal developmental level. They seemed very happy. On the other hand, the kids living in the residential facility had severe developmental problems. It's so sad to read their histories. Many of them were self-mutilators or had other deviant behaviors. They also had very low self-esteem. Their feelings came from the pain of not belonging to anybody, not having any stability, never having one person to say he or she loved them.

One boy, in particular, was very close to my heart. He was 15 and had been removed from his biological parents at the age of 4. Six years later, at the age of 10, he finally became the ward of the court. Meanwhile, between the ages of 10 and 15, he had been in more than fifteen foster homes, where his foster parents continued the abuse. This kid was continually victimized. Amazingly, he was doing really well in school and wanted to have a family. After many rejections, he still clung to the hope of having a family. He was able to trust, to admit he wanted a home, a mom and a dad, someone to hold onto.

I tried very hard to recruit a family for him. But who wants a 15 year old kid with a history of behavioral problems? Finally I found a home that I hoped would work out for him, but it didn't. Again he was victimized. This had been his last chance, and everyone knew it. He ended up running away.

This should not have happened to him. When he was 4 his mother should have had one year, and I'm being generous with that amount of time, to get her act together. If my kids were in foster care—and I know this because I love them—I would do everything the court told me to do in order to get them back.

This country is racially divided. That was evident in the aftermath of the Los Angeles riots of 1992 and in the O. J. Simpson case. Is it reasonable, then, to believe that a black child can be raised with a sense of self in a white family?

Yes, I believe it's reasonable, if the parents are accepting of the child, like my parents were. Transracial adoption isn't really the problem to me. Rather, it's something that can bring people together and can educate them. Before we were adopted, my mom's parents were skeptical about adopting transracially and had misconceptions. They learned to accept us and love us just as much as they love their other grandchildren. Their attitude changed.

You said that your parents and, to a degree, even your community are accepting of you and the whole concept of transracial adoption. But a significant segment of society doesn't accept blacks integrated into a white family—and vice versa—because society is often polarized legally, politically, and socially. In your opinion, doesn't this create barriers that are almost too high to get over?

No. I disagree. That situation will still exist regardless of a black child being adopted into a white family. If I had grown up in a black family, I'd still have to deal with that issue. The thing that's important is what is inside yourself, how prepared you are to deal with and confront the issue. As I said before, just because my parents haven't experienced racism and aren't black doesn't mean they can't help me personally deal with racism or help me feel pride in myself and feel pride in being black and where I come from. This is a problem for black Americans in general.

The inner city school where my mom teaches is all black, and the kids don't feel pride in being black. Critics of transracial adoption talk about how white people can't do black people's hair. Well, some of these kids in my mom's school come to school with their hair a mess. So being raised in a black family doesn't protect you against prejudice, nor does it necessarily help you feel good about being black.

Clearly you've gotten beyond intimidating obstacles and you have so much to offer to the social work profession, to your family, and to your children. As a transracial adoptee, you have the ability to narrow the gap between black and white. In general, what might you say to the black community based on your own experiences?

What I have to say isn't very popular. The black community needs to realize that racism goes both ways. Often African Americans only perceive themselves as victims, but they need to learn to accept transracial adoptees as well in order to help us feel good about ourselves.

What do you want to say to the white community?

The white community needs to look beyond skin color and look instead at the people themselves and at their experiences. This community needs to be open-minded and not base their views on stereotypes and preconditioned notions. They need to look inside their hearts and see what they can do for kids as well.

For parents interested in adopting a child from a different culture, what advice might you offer to help make this a positive experience for them and the child?

They need to do a lot of soul-searching. They need to ask themselves if they are adopting for the right reasons. Most important, these parents must look at the whole impact of adoption on the child's life. If they haven't done so already, I'd encourage them to develop relationships with other people who have adopted transracially. Above all they must realize that love isn't going to change everything and that there will be problems. They must understand that their child will experience racism and that they need to be the child's advocate. It's also helpful to adopt more than one child transracially so the child doesn't feel alone. For me, it was truly beneficial to have brothers and sisters like me.

I'd tell black youths who are adopted into a white family to feel good about themselves because I know how difficult that is. Know that you are not a freak, like I thought I was at times. I hope that you can find a place to fit in and that you're not caught in the middle like I was. It's important that you stand tall and let your voices be heard. I kept my voice suppressed and turned my emotions inward. Most important, *love yourself*!

Rhonda, that's why I'm so glad you're doing this book. No one has ever consulted us, and that makes no sense. People on both sides, black and white, think they are the experts, but no one talks to us transracial adoptees who *are* the experts, just from our experience.

How are you raising your children, especially being in a mixed marriage?

This has been another awakening for me. I'm interested in African American art, and I want my home to reflect that. But now I'm realizing certain things. My son has been asking why his dad and I are married to each other since we're not the same color. It's rather difficult for my other son, too, because he is much lighter-skinned. Even at their young ages, they are so aware of race. So I can't just forget that. Above all else, I try to give them a healthy sense that they are O.K. just the way they are. As simplistic and fundamental as that is, it's also difficult to achieve because I know my children will experience prejudice. I just want them to know that they are O.K. and will survive it, that it's the other people who have the problem. I know I have to start early.

We now live in a multicultural community, and I look forward to providing positive African American images for my children.

Shecara

*I feel like I'm the go-between for the black and white sides.
I know lots of black people who think white people are a certain
way; I also know white people who believe all blacks are a certain
way. They have stereotypes of white people that do not fit my
experience with white people. The issue is not just black and
white; it extends to people's views about Mexicans and Puerto
Ricans.*

Shecara was born in Indiana in 1970. In that same year she was
adopted into a large family where she was raised in the predominantly white
college town of West Lafayette, Indiana. Her parents were devout Roman
Catholics, but they eventually stopped going to church because of disagreements they had with aspects of the doctrine. Still preserving their
strong morals and values, they raised their eleven children with guidelines
that would help them live a productive and responsible life.

Shecara was the only biracial-adopted child in her family. She had a good
childhood and enjoyed spending time with her older siblings. It was apparent in her teen-age years, however, that her allegiances to the white and
African American communities were divided. Needing, from her point of
view, to be "accepted" by persons who physically resembled her, she pursued relationships primarily with black students in her school and at the
local university. She says that it was "her way of getting in touch with her
blackness." Yet many of the cultural views and traditions she believed in
conflicted with those maintained by her black friends.

The road she took to understanding her ethnicity and to feeling a part
of a group led her to leave college and move to a neighborhood in Indianapolis that was predominately black. Her experience there was tumultuous and potentially dangerous. She returned home to live with her parents. During that period she gave birth to her daughter India (and later to
her son Asante). In 1996 Shecara earned her nursing degree and married
her husband Arsale. Now with a family of her own, Shecara recognizes

the value of exposing her children to their ethnicity but, most important, she also realizes that children need love most of all. That is the lesson she gained from her parents.

You come from a family in which there are eleven children, and you are the only one who is adopted. What compelled your parents to adopt a black child?

I asked my parents why I was adopted. They said they had seen a commercial or a public service announcement about kids in Cambodia, I believe, who needed to be adopted. Apparently, when my parents contacted the child welfare agency about these children, there were no more Cambodian children available through that agency. That's when the child welfare agent asked them if they wanted to adopt a black child. My parents said yes. And that's how I came to live in my family.

Describe the community you were raised in.

I was raised in West Lafayette, Indiana. The community I lived in was middle-class, mostly white. There were 175 students in my high school class and only 10 black or biracial individuals in the school.

I have eight brothers and two sisters. I'm the youngest girl. Seven of my brothers are older than me. One sister is six years older than me and one is ten years older. They are all biologically related to my adoptive parents.

Growing up, would you say you were generally a contented person?

In my younger years I was. Looking back, I remember that one of my first grade teachers was really mean to me but, in my opinion, wasn't mean to the other kids. Recently I asked my mom if she thought that teacher was prejudiced against me because all the kids were white and I was the only minority in class. I don't know the answer. But I know she was mean to me. I look back at situations like that and wonder.

Living in a predominantly white family, was it obvious to you that you were physically different?

I didn't know I was different in elementary school and within my family. I only became aware of that difference in the sixth grade when a little boy called me by the "N" word and also called me a "coon." I came home that day and asked my parents what those words meant and why I was called those names. They sat me down and told me. That's when I understood that I was brown and my family was white. Before that, it wasn't an issue for me.

Once you realized that, did you become aware of those around you who resembled you?

Yes. I don't recall if I asked questions specifically about my cultural heritage, but my parents encouraged me to go to the black cultural center at Purdue University and to join some group that would help me learn more about my ethnicity. I was in a youth group that was all black. That was in seventh and eighth grades.

Returning to your family experience and understanding that your family is quite large, did you do things together, like go camping?

According to my older brothers and sisters, we did go camping but I was too young to remember. As we got older, it was such a hassle that we just stayed around the house. We didn't even go out for dinner. Sometimes we'd go through the drive-through at McDonald's. That was because our family was so big. My older brother, who's 1 year, 9 months, older than me, were buddies. We tried to hang out with each other. But when he got together with one of our older brothers, they'd gang up on me, just because I was their sister.

As a child I enjoyed talking. I rode my bike and loved being around other people. I wasn't a loner. It seemed like I always tried to be accepted, and more so after I found out I was brown. I guess I was trying to find people more like me, so I swayed toward the black side. When I started junior high school—which was mixed with three other middle schools, making for more black kids—I tagged along with one of them and we became good friends. I spent time with her family. That's when I became more exposed to the black experience—or doing the black thing.

And what was the "black thing" you did with this family?

I went down South and visited with her family. I went to the Bahamas with them. I felt really comfortable around them.

Would you say there were cultural differences between your friend's family and your own family?

There were some differences. What stood out most was that this family was around more black people. I think that was one of the reasons why I enjoyed spending time with them. Other than that, they weren't that different from my own family.

What about the values within the families. Were there similarities?

The values of the families were similar overall. But when it came to discipline issues, there was a noticeable difference—literally, a black and white divide between the way the children were punished. In my experience, black families tend to use "material" things to punish their kids, like a belt. Kids got "whooped" and got switches. In my family, I got a hand on the butt. They got switches on the back and the legs.

In addition to the black friends you met in middle school and your interaction with this family, did you continue to seek out the black community?

When I was in seventh and eighth grades I became real close with this black girl. There were probably five of us and one white girl. We would all act "stupid" together. We had lunch together and walked home together. We were a clique. It was my way of getting in touch with my blackness. We also were in the youth group together. We'd go to Indianapolis as a group, predominately the black sections.

In high school I didn't particularly seek out black friends. Guys in general wouldn't ask me out. I never went out with any of the guys, black or white. There was one black guy who may have liked me but I grew up with him and he was like my brother. He lived down the street. So I didn't consider dating him. I started going to campuses where there were blacks from other cities. I was probably sixteen at the time. That's when I met a freshman who was African American and from Ohio.

How did your family react when they recognized that you were interacting regularly with persons who were African American?

They never had a problem with it, as long as I wasn't doing anything they disapproved of—and I never did at that time. I did stuff I usually did with my own family but just with a different family.

When you were in public with your adoptive family, did you feel awkward because they were physically different from you?

I remember going to the children's museum in Indianapolis with my family. We had a big white Ford van with windows all around so people could see in. From the inside of the van, I felt like there were all these white heads and then right in the middle this little brown dot. Essentially I felt like everyone was staring at us. In hindsight, I don't think they were staring at us as intently as I thought at the time. It's true, though, that when people saw me with my family, they'd do a double take. One time my sister, who was a student at Purdue, took me to see her room and introduce me to her roommates. When they saw us, her roommates thought that my sister was babysitting for a neighbor. She had to explain that I was her sister. I was always having to explain. It's an awkward feeling.

After high school, did you go to college?

I went to college and partied too much and took myself out of school. I was partying with this black sorority and wasn't doing what I should. I ended up moving to Indianapolis with a friend. I lived there for a long time. I met my daughter's father there. I also ended up working in Indianapolis for some time.

What type of community did you live in?

I was in a lower-income area. The next-door houses were boarded up. We lived right by a grain elevator.

Was it difficult to go from an upper-middle-class community to a low-income community?

I was fine with it.

You adapt easily, then?

Yes. I believe it's because I had to learn to adapt within my family so I was able to move outside my personal space. I found it really easy to have friends whose parents made less than mine or more than mine. It wasn't a big deal. Apparently, though, I was a bit naive about the area where I lived. One night my boyfriend came home and realized I had just walked the dog. He became alarmed and told me I shouldn't do that here at night. I learned that there's a difference between the inner city and the suburbs, that there you just shouldn't do certain things in the city.

Was your family comfortable about you living in the city?

No. It was stressful for them because I only called home when I had problems. Finally, one of my older brothers came to Indianapolis and told me, "You're going home!" He had brought a truck and dragged me home.

You moved from West Lafayette, a somewhat quiet suburb, to Indianapolis, a busy and at times unruly place. Why?

There just wasn't enough going for me here. I like to keep busy. My mom used to call me a night owl. I liked to stay up really late and party. That's why I went to Indianapolis.

Would you say that you went to the "big city" to explore your black side?

That probably had a lot to do with it. I just wanted to live!

So after you lived this exciting life for a stint and your brother took you back home, were you happy to be back?

Yes. I was ready to get out of Indianapolis. Things were getting hectic there. And according to my boyfriend's parents, I thought I was too good for them. They thought I was "snooty" because I spoke proper English or maybe because they believed I thought of myself as white. I get that reaction from the black side a lot, even in the youth groups I joined. My hair is different from most biracial and black people's hair. It's really straight. Because of that I was told that I wasn't black or that I thought I was superior. I never intended for people to think that. I'm not a snooty person at all.

What was your response to that?

I just figured they were going to say whatever they wanted to say. Even today, people I knew then but didn't associate with will say, "I remember you. You used to be so snobby."

I'm 28, and I'm beginning to think that there are people who just won't let go of their set perceptions of how a black or white person should talk, dress, and behave. That's unfortunate.

Recently I was living in St. Louis. Just walking down the street there, I heard girls comment on how I looked. One time a guy tried to talk to me and some girl with him said, "It's not what you look like on the outside, it's what you have on the inside." I wanted to reply, "Missy, while you're sitting there downing people, I'm a certified nurse." She probably thought I was this "dizzy" little mixed girl with the long hair. I've always had to deal with that.

Once a bunch of my friends were going to Indianapolis to party. One black girl said she didn't want me to go because I got all the guys. What can I do about that? I try to say something positive, to make such people feel better about themselves. That incident happened years ago, but unfortunately this girl still feels the same way. You can't change everyone's mind.

Do you still maintain ties with your girlfriends from earlier days?

There were probably four of us who were close, and three of us were black. We all met in middle school. I was inseparable with the girl whose family I spent time with. The parents of one of the girls were all about money, about how many zeros were at the end of a person's paycheck. She essentially bought into that. I had a child before my career. That wasn't happening in her family or her book. She said I wouldn't amount to anything because I had a child and no husband. So we kind of split. One of the other girls acted the same way. She moved to another state. The other friend has also had a child, and we're still good friends to this day. We have similar challenges, and we support each other.

Currently you are married, but for some time you were a single mother?

I just got married in December 1996. My daughter was born in December 1990. So, yes, I was a single mother for quite some time. (My husband isn't her father.)

My pregnancy hadn't been planned. I met my daughter's dad when I was living in Indianapolis. I came back here and got a job. He'd visit me every weekend.

Was the father supportive of both you and the baby, emotionally and financially?

He didn't have a steady job. Actually, he was in and out of jail. When we first started going out, that wasn't the case. Later on, though, he seemed to be getting into trouble. He drank and smoked—all that "yucky stuff."

So I came back to West Lafayette and gave birth to my daughter. I worked at a day care center and hardly made any money. That's when I decided to stay home with my baby and babysit for other single mothers while they went to school or worked. Then I went to Ivy Tech State College and got a degree to be a medical secretary.

The times I wasn't working I got welfare checks, AFDC [Aid to Families with Dependent Children], and food stamps. After I earned my degree I found a job as a medical secretary but it only paid $6.50 an hour. That wasn't enough to support myself and my daughter and have anything left over. So I left that job to work at a factory, making good money. My jobs were actually quite sporadic because I didn't want factory work to be my career. That's when I decided to go back to school to get my nursing degree, which I did, graduating in December 1996.

Was it difficult for you because you were the first child in your family to have a child out of wedlock?

Yes.

Did that create tension within your family?

I thought it was going to. I was scared to death to tell my parents I was pregnant. I don't know why because my parents are so good. I think I was afraid it would embarrass them. I went into their room around midnight, when I couldn't see their faces, and told them I was pregnant. I was shocked at their reaction. They were calm. I thought they'd want to scream at me. They said, "You'll be all right. You're 21. Maybe you'll grow up and settle down." And so it wasn't really a tragedy for them. I'm sure they may have been disappointed because I wasn't married, but they were really supportive. My dad took me to the hospital when I went into labor. They've been so helpful. When I was going to school and was single, they'd watch my daughter as much as they could.

Have you been in contact with the baby's father recently?

He actually called today for the first time in years. He's had his own problems in his childhood and growing up. I believe he still drinks and smokes a lot. He'll get a job, a check, and then quit. I took my daughter to see him in Indianapolis.

Why?

Because I didn't know my own birth parents. At the time my boyfriend told me that it wasn't my obligation to bring her to Indianapolis to see him. I tried to explain to him that I hadn't known my mom and dad and I didn't want her to grow up not knowing her biological dad. Whenever I could get hold of him, I'd take her to see him.

When you were married, did you continue to bring your daughter to see her biological father?

Once I got into a serious relationship with my current husband, I decided to leave it up to my daughter's father if he wanted to see her. The fact is that he contributes no child support and never did. I don't like that, but he doesn't know any better. He was thrown around within his own family. He didn't have a dad. His dad died when he was young.

Tell me about your husband. Where did you meet him?

He's from St. Louis, Missouri. He played football for Purdue University and graduated from there. We hooked up at that time and dated for a while, but actually I'd met him a long time ago, back in 1991 when my daughter was little. It's funny because my husband is a lot darker than me. He's really dark.

In public, do people give you and your husband double takes because you're lighter than him?

Overall people don't look at us. Once, though, when we were living in St. Louis and went to the mall, other black girls would give us a look that said: "What are you doing with him?" I think I get that reaction from people because they don't know what my ethnic background is. Some people think I'm Puerto Rican or Mexican. Actually, even if these girls thought I was biracial, they'd probably still have a problem seeing me with my husband.

My daughter's dad, who's light-skinned and about the same color as me, also made a comment about my husband. He said, "He is *black*!" So I said, "We're keeping it in the family. It keeps the color going. I can't marry a light-skinned person. The color would just fade out." My son, who is 11 months old, is also dark.

What directed you to the nursing profession?

I've always wanted to be a nurse. On "career days" at school, when you would write about what you'll be when you're older, I always wrote that I'd be a nurse or a social worker. I went to Purdue to be a social worker, but that didn't work out. I don't remember exactly how I came back to nursing. Maybe because I enjoyed working with children. In any case, I love it.

Have you ever thought about finding your biological parents, particularly now that you have children of your own?

Since my son was born, I've stayed home to care for him. I often watched the old talk shows. They'd show these reunions between children and parents, and I'd get emotional watching them. To be honest, I wondered how things would be if I hadn't been adopted; I wondered what my birth parents looked like. Deep down, I've always wanted to find my birth parents but I've never made a serious attempt. I have gotten the paper work done to begin the search. Back in 1988 I was having medical problems and wanted to know my medical history. Unfortunately, in Indiana one can't get that information in my case. That made me angry and strengthened my urge to find my birth parents. Last year Sally Jesse Raphael had a show on the topic. The show provided a 1–800 number for those wanting to find their lost ones. Of course, it cost a lot of money. Then I saw another show that said you could do the search yourself, for little money, by checking out a certain book from the library. I still have the name of the book, but I never checked it out.

Are you concerned about hurting your parents' feelings if you decide to locate your birth parents?

I often make the decision not to betray them. They've told me they don't have a problem with my looking for my birth parents, but I believe they'd be hurt. One time when I was 18 and thinking about finding my birth parents, I wrote my adoptive dad a letter saying that if I ever found my birth parents I didn't want him to be upset or disappointed, that he'd raised me and would always be my dad. I wanted my parents to know that I realized they'd gone through hell on wheels for me and that I'd never forget that. But in the back of my head I want to know my nationality.

The adoption agency told my parents that I was light black, that my birth mom was Caucasian and my dad was light black. Of course my mom took that as meaning I was African American. But when I tell that to people, white people are O.K. with it but black people are hesitant. They ask, "Are you sure you're not Mexican or Puerto Rican?" People ask me what I am about three or four times a week. Why can't they just be happy with my being a human being?

Society is racially divisive. You can see it when you watch TV and literally walking down the street. Are you concerned about this reality as you raise your son who is African American?

Yes. I've become more sensitive to things I believe have a racial twist. In fact, the other night I was watching David Letterman and he said something about the O. J. Simpson case that rubbed me the wrong way and made me think he was racist. I got frustrated and turned off the TV. My black friend was watching the Letterman show last night. When I told him I thought David Letterman was racist, my friend didn't agree. He thought Letterman was just funny. You really have to listen to what Letterman is saying.

Because your experience living in a white and black community is so diverse, do you think you became more aware of certain innuendoes or biases because of race?

Since I've been married and living in St. Louis in a setting where the majority of people are black, I've become more sensitive to racial issues. For example, I was reading a magazine at my parents' house yesterday that referred to the "black thumb of gardening" as doing everything bad in terms of gardening. I said, "Why does it have to be a black thumb?" My brother couldn't believe I'd say that. Once, at dinner, my dad said "black something or other." I said, "What did you say? My daughter and I are black, everyone else is white." My dad responded, "Uh, oh. Discrimination." I'm also offended when people say *nigger rig* this or *nigger rig* that.

I've never heard that term. What does it mean?

When something in your house is broken, you "nigger rig" it—meaning, you don't really fix it, you just put it together as quickly as you can. Sometimes people say it when they really don't even know what they are saying.

I agree. Often it is not until a person is held accountable or questioned about a given word or behavior that he or she is able to alter that viewpoint or at least understand how it comes across to others. That is why reconciliation is needed. On that note, do your parents interact with African Americans?

No. They're typical white people who claim to have black friends. You know how people say, "Well, my best friend is black." My parents say they aren't prejudiced. In the past five years I've noticed that people will say that and at the same time make racially ignorant remarks. White people who haven't interacted with blacks have a preconception of what a black person is like from watching TV. And that's how my parents are sometimes. My daughter was at my sister's house, and she was walking around in her swim suit. My sister said, "Oh, she's definitely black." I asked her what she meant by that. She said, "Well, look at her butt." Supposedly black girls have big "booty's," which isn't true. It's just one of the stereotypes. Stuff like that hurts my feelings, even though it's unintentional. Many of my family members, like many people, find it easier to stay within their own boundaries. They're not going to step outside and learn something new.

In my own experiences with my family, it seemed that I was the one learning about other cultures and views. I was the one consistently stepping out of my comfort zone. Did you experience that as well?

Yes! I feel like I'm the go-between for the black and white sides. I know lots of black people who think white people are a certain way; I also know white people who believe all blacks are a certain way. They have stereotypes of white people that do not fit my experience with white people. The issue is not just black and white; it extends to people's views about Mexicans and Puerto Ricans.

My older brother, who is 39, is awesome to me because he looks past the stereotypes and is interested in learning about people from different cultural and ethnic backgrounds. In fact, he's in Africa right now. He's touring the world, even goes to Third World countries, because he doesn't want to be close-minded. He's so knowledgeable about so many different cultures. Between him and me, my parents are getting the "lowdown" on everything.

I've been around drug dealers and crack heads and I tell them my stories, whether they want to hear them or not. The other day my mom asked me, "Well, do all black people have curly hair?" So I asked her, do all white people have straight hair? The point is, she's trying to understand.

That's how it is in West Lafayette, Indiana. There are very few black people here, so the white people are really close-minded. They know just what they see on TV. While their daughters are going out with black guys, the parents remain extremely prejudiced.

Why do you think they are pursuing black men?

I think it's because they were brought up close-minded and want to know someone who is black for themselves. At one time I was resentful toward white girls who went out with black guys. Because I was adopted myself, I thought the white girls might get pregnant and then give their baby up for adoption because their parents wouldn't want a black baby. I was also resentful toward the white girls because the white boys never asked me out. I believed they were taking something from me. The black guys were dating the white girls and the white guys wouldn't ask me out, so there was no one left for me.

And why didn't the white guys ask you out?

They seemed intimidated when I tried to talk to them. My mom says it was because I was pretty, that they probably wanted to but were scared. The bottom line is, they never did. I guess I'll find out why at my tenth-year reunion.

When I was going with my daughter's dad, he found a white girlfriend when he moved to Lafayette. That she was white made it worse. My daughter would refer to her as "that white girl." I felt so bad that my daughter was putting a color to a person—and it was all because of me.

Based on your experience as a transracial adoptee, is there anything you wished could have been different?

Only that my family and I had been more educated about the "black side." But our history books aren't geared toward that. They stop at slavery. I remember slumping down in my chair when the teacher was talking about slaves. When I was in school we didn't even talk about Martin Luther King Jr. or the NAACP. I wish that white people who plan to adopt biracial children would utilize some group for support and knowledge early on.

How were you able to find ways to educate yourself on the black experience?

I made it an issue to be around other black folks. I was literally the black sheep of my family. I did stuff my brothers and sisters never thought of. I explored. So I consider myself blessed that I was the type of person who was able to seek out what I wanted and needed. Not everyone can do that. Some people I know who are biracial don't know where to go, what to do, or who to talk to about issues of identity. Maybe if they were aware of mentorship programs for biracial or adopted children, that might help. In the youth group I attended, I considered the leader as my mentor. She didn't necessarily give me any information about "being black," but she was always there for me.

Do you consider yourself a confident person now?

Yes.

As an adolescent, did you feel confident?

Not at all. Growing up in seventh and eighth grade I was fine. But beginning in high school my self-esteem dropped. Guys wouldn't ask me out. One time I was getting a drink of water and this little white boy came up to me and said, "You are so damn ugly I can't believe it!" I thought that was how I was. Then I started going out with black guys and they told me I was gorgeous. I didn't believe them. They thought I was just being modest. So I really had a real hard time growing up because no guys would ask me out.

I also didn't have a lot of material things that my peers had. That's not a color issue but it affected my self-esteem. My family was middle-class, like the families of my peers, but my family was so big that my siblings and I had to share clothes. I'd get a lot of "hand-me-downs." I felt like a sore thumb.

When I was 16 I went out with a guy from Purdue for two years. He was my first boyfriend. Then, at 18, I found out he had another girlfriend. I was so upset I tried to take my life. I thought there was something wrong with me.

I really had a hard time growing up. I was in a split world. The white people would say this about me, and the black people would say something different. I didn't always feel comfortable around white people. My white girlfriends would want me to come over. Most of them had boyfriends. Going to the prom was a big thing. No one asked me to the prom or the dances.

Is there a sense that you have missed out on your adolescent years because you were between two seemingly different worlds?

I think I missed out because I didn't take one side. I jumped into the white world and then dove back into the black world. For some reason I couldn't do both at the same time. And that's where I am now. I'm confident as a black person, even though black people still tell me, "You speak so proper."

Don't you think, though, that you reached the point where you were able to determine who you are and who you are going to be internally as opposed to letting other people define you?

I believe that's true. Once I found myself, I decided that this is the way I am. If you like me, you like me. If you don't, you don't. That's my attitude now.

And how do you visualize yourself now?

When I look in the mirror I see what I see. But I don't emphasize that anymore. The way you look doesn't mean as much as a person's internal qualities. When I'm talking, I'm just me. I'm not thinking about accentuating the fact that I'm black. I have straight hair and light skin. A lot of black people would exaggerate those features. Black folks are always telling me how pretty I am—and that my hair is *good*.

One hates to ask the "what if" question. But do you think that if you were adopted into a black family, your self-identity and acceptance would be stronger today?

Maybe if I was in a black family I'd be more confident—probably because of the way I look and how black people would treat me.

Because you are lighter-skinned?

Yes. And also because of my physical features.

How does your husband's family, who is African American, relate to your parents?

I often asked myself what it would be like when I get married. Would half the church be black and the other half white? So when I did get married I made sure that everyone mingled. I didn't have my family on one side and his on the other side.

His mother is awesome. She's a God-fearing Christian woman and has been through a lot herself. She isn't judgmental. I told her about my family and she took the initiative to introduce herself. They've gotten along great. My parents were amazed at how she raised nine children herself, in the black city. My parents are willing to step outside their boundaries and get to know other people and other cultures, so they were happy to meet her. Unfortunately they don't see each other often. Otherwise, I think they'd be good friends.

Are there obvious differences between your parents and your husband's mom?

The one difference is religion. My husband's mother is into her Bible reading. My parents were Roman Catholic, like I said, but because of disagreements with the church we stopped going. My parents still have the morals and values they grew up with, but they aren't as devout in their faith as she is.

You mention the "values your parents grew up with." What values did they instill in you?

For one, I wasn't supposed to have premarital sex. The problem was they just said it once. I think if they pressed the issue, it probably wouldn't have happened with me. I think that the older generation, in general, doesn't talk about things the way we do today. Going back to your question, I acted the way they acted. I didn't "cuss." I never disrespected my mother.

My husband and I see discipline differently. My parents didn't beat us with extension cords and belts. They spanked us. It didn't take a beating to get us to respect them. My husband thinks my daughter is going to be disrespectful and run away because I don't whip her the way he wants me to. We go back and forth on this issue. My mom thinks she has it figured out. She thinks that black people hit their kids with belts and stuff because slaves were beaten if they didn't do what they were told.

Do you find that the difference in discipline isn't only isolated in the family your husband grew up in but that it also happens in other black families?

Yes, I believe it's a cultural difference. From talking with my other black friends, their families used switches and belts. My white friends were spanked and given time out. It shouldn't be a black and white thing, but it seems to be.

In hindsight, do you think you would have wanted to stay in foster care awaiting a black family rather than being placed relatively quickly with a white family?

I'd rather have been adopted as a baby by a white family than have been in long-term foster care until a black family came along to adopt me. I'd rather have been in a family setting, black or white, than in foster care. I know too many people, white and black, who are totally messed up to this day because they didn't have any family background. The bottom line is that race isn't as important to me as being placed in a family. I consider myself blessed that I had the experience of being black and white. It gave me the opportunity and reason to explore who I am. I think I'm a better person for it. I'm willing to go outside of what I'm used to in order to find myself.

Why were you interested in participating in this book?

For me, as a biracial person, it's important to see other people's experiences and learn from them. I hope that when people read about my experiences, they'll realize that they aren't alone in their struggle. I often felt like there was nobody around who understood my journey.

Laurie Goff

HOLLYWOOD, CALIFORNIA
JUNE 1997

*Discriminating against a child because of the color of her skin is dis-
allowing a child a life. I have been more places, done and seen more
things, and received an amazing education more than people twice
my age have done or will ever do because I was adopted into my
family, which happens to be white.*

Laurie Goff was born in Seattle, Washington, in July 1970. That
same year, the Goffs, a Jewish family residing in Seattle with their two biological sons, ages 3 and 5, adopted Laurie. Laurie's parents remained in
Seattle while her father completed his medical internship. Soon after, the
Goffs moved to Sierra Leone, Africa, where her father was a physician with
the Peace Corps and her mother served as a Peace Corps volunteer teaching in the local African school. By the time Laurie was a teenager, she had
lived in countries in the Middle East, Africa, and Central America.

Along with their strong conviction to work toward social justice in the
United States and overseas, the Goffs made it a priority to raise children
of good character. Reared in the Jewish tradition, Laurie learned the value
of family, the importance of cause-oriented work, and the need to appreciate persons from different ethnicities and cultures. Education was also
emphasized within the home. Through reading culturally diverse literature,
Laurie took great pride in the significant contributions African Americans
made to society.

Laurie describes herself as a self-assured, goal-oriented, fun, and "no
nonsense" person. Undoubtedly, her personality was influenced by the love
and commitment of her family. Perhaps the strong foundation her parents
gave her proved to Laurie that she could overcome the hurdles in her life.
As a child she suffered from attention deficit disorder, hyperactivity, and
dyslexia. Plagued with these learning disabilities, Laurie confronted the
ironies of being black and Jewish in a white family, and, at times, in foreign lands. She faced the tension of racial bias in the United States and often

saw where equality was defined in black and white. Refusing to ignore these issues, Laurie fought them head on.

At the time of this interview, Laurie had received her bachelor's degree from Evergreen State College in Olympia, Washington, and was working as a production assistant in animation for Steven Spielberg's Dreamworks Productions. While she enjoys working in cinematography and television, her passion lies in advocating for children. Laurie has previously worked with youths at risk and with the homeless population in Seattle.

Tell me about some of the places where you lived while you were growing up.

First we were in Seattle, Washington where my dad was in private practice or had a medical internship. He decided he wanted to join the Peace Corps. So my family went to Sierra Leone in Africa. I was 18 months old, my brother Adam was 3 years old, and my other brother Mike was 6. There, my dad was the staff officer of the Peace Corps, and my mom was a volunteer.

Do you remember living in Sierra Leone?

Yes. We lived in a huge three-story house. Since my dad was a staff officer, one of the only people who got paid, the Peace Corps volunteers would come over to get checkups and they'd fill up the big house. They'd play chess with my brothers, and Adam, who was 4 at the time, would beat all of them.

Did you learn a different language there?

The first language I learned in Africa was Creole. I spoke the tribal language and English.

Where else did you live?

After leaving Sierra Leone our family went back to the United States, to Seattle, Washington. We were there probably two years. My dad was in private practice. He felt like he was not spending enough time with his family, so, after being recruited by the State Department, he accepted a position.

Our first post was the Ivory Coast on the west coast of Africa. I was around 9. I enjoyed the Ivory Coast and remember my time there. I spoke fluent French. When we lived in foreign countries, my parents didn't allow us to sit home and watch TV. We only had one television that I remember. It was in the playroom and was black and white and it barely worked. All we could really tune in was the *Muppets* in French. In all our posts we had a cook or a butler and a guard, because in the State Department you have to add to the economy by hiring people. We went to Liberia and went on a safari to Kenya. It was fun.

After your father fulfilled his post in Africa, where did you move to?

New Orleans.

How did you adapt to the culture?

Fine. My mother was positively frightened because I was black in a white family in an all-white neighborhood in New Orleans. My mom said she'd wait for me to come home from school. She didn't know if I'd get through the neighborhood.

So there were not many African Americans in your community?

No. We lived in an all-white neighborhood. But I did go to an elementary school that I think was the first integrated elementary school in the south of New Orleans. Most of my friends there were black.

Why was your mom concerned for your safety?

A black child in a white neighborhood in New Orleans?! New Orleans is not one of the most racially mixed places. You have white neighborhoods, and you have black neighborhoods. Whites don't move into the black neighborhoods, and blacks don't move into a white neighborhood. New Orleans is not progressive. It's *really* racist.

What year did you live there?

In the late 1970s.

How did people in your neighborhood respond when they saw you?

I don't remember because it wasn't an issue for me. I was 7, 8, or 9 and didn't care. But my mom told me that that experience was the hardest time she ever had—trying not to show she was afraid, trying to hide her concern for me.

As we continue on your journey, where did you go after New Orleans?

Panama. I hated Panama. That was back in the 1980s when Carter was giving back the Panama Canal. So of course all the Panamanians hated the Americans. Then there were the zone areas, like the militarized zone where all the military people lived. They had bowling alleys, movie theaters, everything. All the schools were in the zone, and you had to go to school. The problem was that if you weren't a "zonie" (or military person) you had the worst time. The military kids would be mean to you. I had the worst time.

After Panama, where did you go?

The State Department sent my dad to Bangledesh. Some people thought that was the worst you could do to somebody, but we actually enjoyed Bangledesh.

What were the people like?

They were fine. Bangledesh has got to be one of the absolutely poorest countries in the world. At the time we were there, there were 90.1 million people living in an area the size of Texas.

How did you relate to the people there?

Fine.

Are the people dark-skinned?

Yes. I remember one incident when I was riding my bike to a friend's house and these Bengalese started calling me "nigger."

They called you what?

"Nigger."

They knew this terminology?

Yes. But they were a bit more educated. I stopped my bike and said, "*Who's talking to who?!*" The Bengalese look like people from India. I was like "whatever." I totally enjoyed Bangladesh.

After living in Bangladesh, you and your family returned to the states, specifically to Washington, D.C.?

Yes. My parents wanted me to go to high school in the United States. I protested profusely because I hated the United States. I hated the kids in the United States because they were small-minded; they didn't get things. Case in point: Our family would go back home for "home leave" every two years, and every other year we'd go to Greece or on a safari or whatever. When you live overseas your life evolves around what is happening in the world.

In my seventh grade class, there were about twenty-four kids and about twenty-two different nationalities represented. We learned American history, world history, and the history of the country we were in. I knew the names and all the capitals of every country in the world. And I learned all about different religions—Buddhism, Islam, Christianity, Judaism.

So when you go back to the United States, these kids don't know anything. It was very hard for me to have a conversation with them. My "homies"—friends who returned to the United States after living overseas—would all get together and we'd talk about our leave or we'd sing commercials since we had TV overseas. But whenever someone had to go home to the United States to live, everyone's greatest fear was interacting with kids in the United States because they were so mean.

Elaborate on the word "mean."

Someone would say something like, "Oh yeah, I remember when I was in Oklahoma with my family . . ." And I'd say, "I remember when I was in Greece . . ." People thought I was showing off, but I wasn't. I was talk-ing about my life. They didn't understand me because they didn't have a worldview.

That was a lonely experience for you?

It was very lonely. I was in a group called AWAL—Around the World in a Lifetime—which was made up of kids whose parents worked with the State Department. I was the new member coordinator. We'd find out who came back from overseas and then we'd contact them to see if they wanted to do things with us just because it was so hard.

What about the role that race played in your life growing up?

When I was younger I had a hard time because I was hyperactive, dyslexic, and had an attention deficit disorder (ADD). My parents sent me to classes for the dyslexia to learn how to read and to keep my dyslexia in the background. Dyslexia makes it difficult to learn because you don't want to read out loud; you don't want to talk because you mispronounce words. I was extremely quiet when I was younger.

I don't think I had a problem with being black because, first of all, my family didn't. It wasn't an issue. And, second, when you're living over-seas, where you're from is more important than the color of your skin. People would say, "I'm from America," and the response would be, "Oooooh" or "I'm from Yugoslavia," and the response would be "Wow!" That was the important thing. Or whose club was better. America was of course the best club, and everybody wanted to be in that club.

Once, when my family and I were at the airport in Sierra Leone, I remember this big, black African guy *staring* at us. I walked up to him and said, in Creole, "I'm adopted. Do you know what that means?" I said that I was adopted into this family and that's why they're a different color than me, and I walked away.

I think people have more problems with race in the states than over-seas. For example, in Bangladesh a friend of mine is Vietnamese, quite dark. She was adopted into a German family, and it wasn't a big thing. Sometimes people who were in a country other than their original coun-try would adopt a child from that country.

A funny story. Once when we were in the American Club in Bangladesh, this guy said to me, "Where is your family?" I pointed to my mother, who was on the tennis court, and to my dad, who was in the pool. This guy looked really confused. I told him, "It's a birthmark. If you look in the *Guinness Book of Records,* you'll see I have the world's biggest birthmark.

Only in my most private places can you tell that I'm white." He said, "Ooh." He actually believed me!

Going back to Washington, D.C., where did you spend your high school years?

My first year I was at a small private school.

Was it primarily a black or white school?

It was white. I hated my school experience there—and the kids. They hated me, too. The students were snobs and had no clue what was going on in the world, and I couldn't comprehend that. There were six black kids in the whole school. We hung out together, whether we liked one another or not. I still stay in contact with one of my friends from that school.

The six students you hung out with, what brought you all together?

We were *black*! Of course the white students thought that anyone who was black and going to this school was on scholarship—which wasn't true! I wasn't on scholarship, nor were most, if not all, of my black friends there.

It was a good school academically, and my mom didn't imagine there would be stupid people there. The minute my parents found out about the other kids' reactions, they asked me if I wanted to leave. Then, my mom looked at other public schools and found the best one for me.

What school did you go to?

The Duke Ellington School of the Arts. I had a difficult time in that school, too. When I came back from overseas I had a British accent. Many of the teachers at the schools I attended overseas were British. And Bangladesh was a British colony. So I spoke very correct English—and I didn't speak "slang." I didn't have to since my parents were diplomats. So people in the school called me "white girl." More than being hurt, I was annoyed at these people who thought how I talk was more important than who I am.

I did have one good friend at this school. She was Puerto Rican and didn't speak English well. One day I saw her crying on the steps of the school. She didn't think she could make it through school because of the challenges she faced. I told her we'd get through school and graduate together—and we did. By the way, I immediately learned how to speak "slang" and roll my "eyes" and snap my fingers.

Why did you choose to do this?

It was easier than calling them stupid every day. It was easier just to blend in. Some students got mad at me because of how I spoke. When we were in speech class they were pissed at me because I spoke English well and didn't say "a-x-ed" meaning "asked." When I wanted to read Shakespeare, I read Shakespeare. I understood what we were learning in class because my parents knew all these things. When you're living overseas, you learn what your parents know—their music, their books, and so on.

Tell me about the role your mother played when you were in high school.

People were afraid of my mother. If they messed with me once, she'd come to school. For three months my school didn't have a world culture teacher or a French teacher. My mother called the principal's office, but he did nothing. Then she wrote letters to the school board and two teachers were hired—two of the best teachers in the school.

In history I ended up getting a grade point average of 5.8 out of 4.0— my teacher let us do extra credit. I did mine on Apartheid. In a school of four hundred students, with only ten of them white, no one knew what Apartheid was. No one.

How did you explain the meaning of Apartheid?

I explained that it was like slavery, that for decades white people came into the country and took it over, that they didn't allow blacks to gather or to keep their family units together. It was legalized slavery. These students didn't know this was going on. I did an assembly for the whole school to clue them in. People told me I was so smart. I said that I read.

My father came to school to give a talk on AIDS since he's a medical doctor. Kids were impressed with my dad. Some people asked me if I ever wanted to meet my *real* parents. My philosophy has always been that a parent is someone who loves you, who takes care of you, who is there for you when you are sick, when you do fabulous things, and when you do stupid things. They'll even bail you out of jail. I told these kids that I *have* my real parents, that if they were referring to my biological parents that I didn't really want to meet them. Some of them didn't understand. They wondered if I felt weird because my parents were white and I was black. I said, "No. The people who feel weird are people like you."

The people who gave me the hardest time because my family is white were black people. But they couldn't explain why. Maybe white people hide their feelings better.

What plays did you participate in during high school?

I was in *MacBeth in Haiti*, the *Taming of the Shrew*, *The Reporter*. I also auditioned for a prestigious art place in New York and made it.

Laurie, your family is Jewish and you identify with the Jewish religion and culture. As a black woman, did this impact other people's perceptions of you?

People were totally confused when I told them I was Jewish. I just let them be confused. I love being Jewish.

What does it mean to be Jewish in your family?

My siblings and I all had a barmitzva. We went to the temple regularly until we were 13. We celebrated the High Holidays and Passover, which commemorates the exodus from Egypt, Hanukkah, etc. My parents gave us our base, which is Judaism, and then let us decide whether we wanted to practice or not.

What beliefs do you take from Judaism?

I don't believe in Jesus Christ or that someone died for my sins. That's one of the great things about Judaism. No one died for "your" sins; you have to deal with your own sins. On Yom Kippur, the Day of Atonement, you can ask God for forgiveness but only for sins you committed against God. If I did something awful to you, I'd have to ask you for forgiveness. I love the fact that you have to take responsibility for yourself, for the person you wronged, and God.

I think I have an edge being Jewish. Because the Jews were persecuted throughout history, they are the one group that can truly identify with the black community. Jews understand what it means to be oppressed because of your looks and your beliefs. People tell me, "You don't 'understand' because you're in a white family." I think I understand in an even larger sense than some black people. I've learned about the persecution of black people, and I know there is another group that has also been persecuted, in some ways more so because it goes on continuously.

How so?

Anti-Semitism is all over the world. Prejudice against African Americans isn't. You can go into any country in the world and find people who hate Jews and would love to destroy them. So from that part of my culture I gained the understanding that not everyone is free. Someone will track you down because of your religion and what you look like.

What are your views on black and Jewish relationships in America?

I'm so angry about that. I think many of the problems come from the black side. I don't think the Jews are perfect, the black community is closed-minded about getting together with the Jews, putting our heads together, and so on. Rarely do you hear Jews say, "Black people are bad." I think the present relationship between blacks and Jews erupted partly because of certain people within the majority who want to make sure these two groups never get together. That is, certain people have cultivated the current relationship between these groups.

In the 1960s the first white people to support Martin Luther King Jr. were Jewish. And they gave money to the cause because they understand about civil rights. Nelson Mandela basically scolded Minister Louis Farrakhan for Farrakhan's statements about Jewish people. Mandela said that in his country Jewish people put their necks on the line for him. The firm that trained him as a lawyer was Jewish.

Granted, Jews have money but I think they're still an easy target in the white community because they have a culture that brings them together and makes them easy to pick out. I think the black community likes to have a scapegoat in the white community for these reasons. It's not productive for the black community. If there's a group who has money and influence and wants to help you, why turn your nose up at them? And they're hated by the same groups who hate you—white supremacists, the Ku Klux Klan. Farrakhan pisses me off. He says, "The Jews are trying to get you." Why would they try to get you? They're trying to stay alive themselves.

I guess I should ask you what your views are toward Louis Farrakhan.

I don't like him. He preaches hate. His idea about black-owned businesses is cool, but you can't overcome the "shit" you have to overcome in this country and preach hate. It's not healthy. If you waste all your energy on hating, you have no energy left to better yourself and move forward.

Farrakhan is wrong. I don't respect him. I think the Million-Man March was a good thing, but unfortunately it was Farrakhan who came up with the idea. That nullified everything the march meant to people because all they saw was Farrakhan. They didn't see a bunch of black men saying it's time to come together and find solutions to our problems and become part of a family.

What are your views on transracial adoption?

People should stop being so stressed about this issue. Kids need to be adopted. There's a six-year waiting list for white children. If you want to adopt a black child or a Hispanic child or any child of color, these kids are ready to be adopted. Because many social workers and others in the community have a problem with transracial adoption, these kids lose out.

For five years, as a social worker, I worked with homeless youths and kids at risk. I had a lot of experience with foster homes and working within the system. Many of the foster homes are run by white people. They try to place black children in homes where at least one parent is black, but sometimes that doesn't happen. So there are a lot of kids growing up in foster homes bouncing from home to home in a white family. So I don't see what the problem is in letting a white family adopt a black child?

Do you think that a black child has a "future" in a white family?

Yes, if the family recognizes that the child is from a different culture and makes a point of actively engaging themselves and the child in that culture. Problems arise when people adopt children from a different race and pretend the child's racial identity is not important.

Don't you think that in many transracial cases that is the problem, that white families across the board who adopt black children don't understand the importance of the child's cultural and ethnic heritage?

The circumstances a child is born into is a "crap shoot." Anybody can give birth to a child. A lot of kids who are first-born generation in this country grow up without a culture and don't know their own language. Transracial adoption could be a problem, but not if people are aware of the challenges and if social workers work with the parents before the adoption.

I am hyperactive, ADD, and dyslexic. If I had been raised in a foster home, I wouldn't speak English today. I'm very glad I was adopted regardless of what color my parents are. I don't think someone should deny a child a right to a happy life just because of the parents' skin color. How dare people assume they have the right to decide what's best for you, namely, growing up in a foster home when you could possibly grow up in a family that wants you, loves you, and will do their damnest to make you happy.

What do you think is in the child's best interest?

Is it in the child's best interest to be put through foster home after foster home or to be adopted into a family that can support and love the child? That's the bottom line. I've seen children who have gone through foster homes. Occasionally a child is placed in a really fabulous foster home, but moving a child after two months or six weeks isn't in the child's best interest. A stable home is in the child's best interest.

Whether you're born into a healthy family is also a "crap shoot." In adoption, you have the opportunity to look at the people who are adopting. Social workers do home visits and make sure the people aren't psycho.

They make sure the child isn't being beaten. That's better than most kids get who are born into psycho families. Discriminating against a child because of the color of her skin is disallowing a child a life. I have been more places, done and seen more things, and received an amazing education more than people twice my age have done or will ever do because I was adopted into my family, which happens to be white.

What lessons have you learned being in your family that you apply in your life today?

That's a really easy question! In Jewish families, a mother is the center of the universe. And for me, my mother was. Men are in charge of religion, and women are in charge of the household. In my family, the women are held in high regard. I learned from my parents that relationships are hard, that everything is a compromise in whatever you do, especially in relationships. My mom always said that finding the person to marry is the easiest thing; staying married is the hardest. My parents were married for thirty-three years. They compromised on everything—jobs, where they lived, everything. They had a healthy, wonderful relationship. They discussed things.

They also taught me the value of family. Both my parents are committed to social issues, like being in the Peace Corps and the State Department. They were active in the sixties. They taught me to be socially conscious and socially responsible. Whatever community I live in, I have to take responsibility for what I do.

Did your parents speak with you specifically about being black in a white family, or was that not emphasized?

I don't remember. My early years are fuzzy for me because of my dyslexia and ADD. For my dyslexia, part of my training was to learn how to color within the lines. All my coloring books were African American oriented. They had titles like "All the Important Black People in America from A to Z." My parents also gave me comic books that were educational stories about African Americans in American history, like George Washington Carver and Adam Samuel. They made a real effort to make sure I knew that being African American was important and something to be proud of and that people from my culture made a huge contribution to this country.

So your family shaped you and gave you a firm foundation. You have developed a strong sense of self. Given this picture, does society impact your views?

Definitely. When I was growing up I thought I was fat because I had a big butt. Everybody called me bubble butt. I couldn't fit into jeans. I have a very small waist and a big butt. I wasn't fat, I was thin. I swam in the mornings and did track. I loved fitness and sports. I just couldn't fit into jeans. I had such a body image problem because of how mean children can be to other children. And I thought I was fat. At such times there's nothing your parents can do but support you and tell you they love you.

What about the hair thing? Society gave me a run for my money on this issue.

I always wanted straight relaxed hair, and my mother hated my hair straight. But being the fabulous mother she was, she and her friend Mona, who is African American, would take me to get my hair straightened. When we were in Africa, my mom had my hair braided. She loved my hair braided or in a short Afro.

One time in Africa my mom had to go away on business for a week. She told my father that all he had to do was take my hair out of the braids and go next door where they would braid my hair again. I'd get my hair braided there every week. Then my mom added that if he couldn't take out the braids, he could just take me next door. Well, in Africa they wrap the end of the braids in a special thread, and my dad neglected to take that out of my hair when he was unbraiding it. I was *screaming!* Then, instead of taking me next door, he took me to a French hotel on the Ivory Coast and got my hair cut off. My hair had been down to my shoulders, and my mom had always arranged it beautifully—and my father cut it off. So my mother comes home and doesn't talk to him for a week. She said, "I told you to take her next door." And he said, "But her hair looks really good."

In college I went from straightening my hair to getting it curled, and in France I got it braided with extensions.

On a more serious note, you recently located your biological father's family. Tell me about that experience.

At the time I was adopted my mother, Ellen Goff, had Jewish Family Services write a letter to me with all the information they had about my biological parents, so that when I was 18 I could call them and they'd give me this letter. I wanted to find my biological parents because I knew I was part Cherokee and I wanted to do public health work on an Indian reservation. It's much easier to get a job on a reservation if you have an Indian number. But the information Jewish Family Services gave me was insufficient to find my birth family.

When my mother got sick, I told her I really wanted to find my biological family because I wanted my health records. I told her I wasn't pursuing this to find my "real" parents, because I wasn't. She said, "Laurie, I know I'm your parent. I was there when you had the chicken pox. I dealt with you in your teens. You'll always be my daughter."

My godbrother, who also found his biological mother, gave me the name of the person who helped him. Her name was Martha, and she charged $325 for everything—finding my birth mother and father and a session with whichever parent I met. She then sent a letter I had written to my birth mother. My birth mother called Martha and told her she'd decided not to meet me, which was fine.

Is your birth mother black or white?

I'm not sure. I think she was mixed. My birth certificate says that my ethnic background is Cherokee, Negro, and Irish—and my birth father isn't Irish.

About a year later Martha found my birth father. First she told me to sit down. Then she told me that she found my birth father through his parole officer because he's in jail. I asked her what he's in jail for? And she said for murder. I said, "Well, isn't that precious." She said that his parole officer thinks there might be some gang involvement and that he's been in jail for sixteen years. She asked me if I wanted her to contact his family through him. I said sure, but I didn't know if I wanted to meet him.

Then I met my birth father's twin sister, Eda, who's 47, in Takoma, Washington. Eda and I have the exact same eye color and our faces are shaped the same. She cried and hugged me. She's a very sweet lady. Eda didn't know much about the family's health history. I'd have to ask the grandmother. But she told me a little bit about Ed, my birth father. Supposedly he hadn't committed the murder. He was twenty at the time, fell in with the wrong people, and robbed a jewelry store. One of the people he was with killed the owner of the jewelry store. Ed was the only person they caught. He wouldn't say who shot the guy, and his whole family was angry at that. Anyway, he spent sixteen years in jail. Then, after he got out, around two years ago, he was sent to jail again for a parole violation for two more years.

My birth father has ten brothers and sisters. And all their children have children, and their children have children. The grandmother is very funny. All the kids live within a mile of her. Basically she's raised her grandchildren and great grandchildren. Everyone drops off their children at the grandmother's house and comes in and out. It's her home and it's fabulous. I met the grandmother first, and I met everybody else at a family picnic. I think I have twenty-four or twenty-five first cousins.

They have a very big family.

Their sense of family is very important. That's why I think that my birth mother didn't want to meet me. She didn't tell Ed I existed. When my birth parents were breaking up, my birth mother was six months pregnant. I was two months premature so when Ed saw her at seven months, she'd already given birth to me. Ed asked what had happened to the baby, and, according to Eda, she told him she lost the baby. So no one in the family even knew I existed. Today the family feels bad because had they known I existed they would have taken care of me. They felt betrayed by this woman, and I think she didn't want to meet me because she had lied to everybody.

I think it's important to emphasize the importance black families place on raising children and that many black families informally adopt children within their own extended families. We need to take time to go through your birth father's family tree. It's amazing how large his family is. I thought my family was extended.

In Ed's family, the oldest brother is James; they don't know how many kids he has because the family hasn't seen him for years. Ed also has a brother named Al. Eda, as I said, is Ed's twin sister. James, Al, Eda and Ed all have one father who died. The rest of the children have another father. James, Al, Eda, and Ed were raised by the second guy, and they call him dad. My biological grandmother ended up kicking him out of the house because he was cheating on her. He begged to come back, but she said "No!" I think grandmother had two houses, and he's paying rent at one. All the kids in the family think it's hysterical. They said, "That's what you get; he not only cheated on her, he cheated on her with a *white* woman."

You have such a big biological family, and we didn't even mention everyone.

I know. I'm sure glad I didn't date any of my "brothers" when I was in Seattle, Washington, because they are a *big* family!

Now you've met a significant part of your biological family and you've made the decision not to meet your biological father.

I was at my biological grandmother's house twice when he called. I didn't talk to him. When my biological father was in jail, his mother and sister paid the rent on his townhouse for two years so that he'd have a nice place to come back to. And because he was a good worker and they like him, his job was also held for him. He's a garbage man and makes bank. Anyway, he was yelling on the phone at his mother and sister because they weren't paying the utility bills on his townhouse. Meanwhile his girlfriend, who doesn't have a job and is an alcoholic, is staying there. She expected *them* to pay her bills. At the time, I was working with juvenile delinquents in a minimum security prison as a counselor. Ed's behavior smacked of the way all the little boys I was working with behaved; they were ungrateful for what their families were doing for them. It really pissed me off.

So I didn't want to see Ed in jail. Then Eda said I should see him in neutral territory. I thought I might do that, but then Ed accused Eda of keeping me from him. That infuriated me and hurt Eda, who was doing her best. Eda was the only reason why I met the family and why I even considered meeting Ed. And this little man sitting in jail was so ungrateful.

I did tell Eda that if Ed wanted to meet me he should set up a meeting with my contact person because I wanted to meet him on neutral grounds. Eda agreed. Ed then tells Eda that if I want to talk to him or if I want anything from him, I have to talk with his lawyer.

His lawyer?

Yes. What could he possibly give me that I don't already have? Nothing. So I told Eda that my mother was dying and I didn't have any energy for this man. I gave Eda my phone number and address and told her that if she wanted to get in touch with me, that would be fine, but not to give this information to Ed. She obliged.

Next topic. What do you think about World Cup golfer Tiger Woods? I know you've been itching to talk about this.

Black people make me mad. This "child," Tiger Woods, is multiracial. His mother is Thai, his father is black, Native American, and white. The black community got angry because Tiger was paying tribute to the other parts of his heritage. Just because this child's skin is dark and his father is black, black people feel he has to be black. They won't accept that he could be multiracial. We do this all the time. For example, actress Halle Berry is also white. Her mother, who raised her, is white. But God forbid if she were to say that in public—because she "looks black." Why should someone have to choose to be black or white? Tiger Woods doesn't have to choose. He made a point of saying he didn't have to choose. In Thailand, being Thai is incredibly important. Yet people in the black community are angry because he's paying tribute to another part of his culture.

Does this mentality have the potential of limiting the breadth of the black community?

The black community puts us in a little box. Yet black people keep screaming that the "man" is putting us in a box. When someone becomes successful who happens to be biracial, you're not allowed to mention it. You have to be black.

What areas do you think the black community as a whole needs to work on?

First, we need to get over the idea that it's the white man's fault. We all know there's racism in this country. No one knows it better than the transracially adopted. We get more shit from the black community than from the white community. How dare someone say we're not "black enough" because we're biracial or adopted into a white family.

What is "black enough"? Does it mean I have to talk Ebonics or slang? Suck my teeth? "Roll" my eyes? Because I speak correct English, I'm not "black enough"? Because I go to college and better myself, I'm not "black enough"? Because part of my family happens to be white, I'm not "black enough"?

Won't I be discriminated against just the same? Won't I be beaten up in the streets because of my skin color? What is "black enough"? The *Cosby Show* wasn't "black enough." You can't have a TV show where black people are doctors and lawyers. They have to "shoot 'em up" outside a house. We stereotype ourselves.

We need to stop hating other people. You can't better yourself as a group if you denigrate other people. Yes, there are whites in this country who don't respect us, but we shouldn't act as they do. They are evil, stupid people. I'm not saying that all blacks do that, but it's something we need to get over as a group.

Third, it's important to teach black children in this country that we were brought here as slaves, that many of us died on the slave ships, and that this was a huge tragedy. Black people have made significant contributions to this society, and we need to focus on that. We don't talk enough about people like Thurgood Marshall and black inventors—not just amazing musicians or athletes. We need to learn more about black people who are into literature. There's a plethora of works black people have created.

What do you think about reparations?

I think that Japanese Americans who were put into detention camps during World War II deserve to get reparations. That was very recent. But giving reparations to all the black people in this country because our great, great, great grandfathers were enslaved—no! That's a little much.

How is it different?

Because when this happened to the Japanese Americans, they owned land; they were a part of this society. Because they were Japanese they were considered spies and everything was taken away from them. It's different because it's like it happened yesterday.

Giving reparations to every black American in this country today is a bit over the top. Reparations should have been given one hundred years after slavery.

So black Americans missed out?

Yes. A reasonable form of reparations would be to add black history to our history books and make it a separate class in high school. Put the accomplishments of black Americans in the history books and make it a part of the American culture!

For me, this is better than money, because it would be taught to everyone and be an acknowledgement in our high schools, in our colleges, of what happened and what our contributions were.

Professionally, you already have a diversity of experiences. You worked as a social worker for some time. What did you do?

I worked at an inner city high school in Seattle with "At Risk Youth." My job was to keep the kids in school and help create a health program. Every year we focused on a different topic. One year we addressed AIDS. Before that, I worked in a security home for boys who had been in jail and were making their way back into society. I counseled boys between 14 and 20 to help them go to high school or get into a GED program and to teach them living and job skills.

What are your views about education in this country for minority kids?

The distribution of money for public schools is way out of kilter, having gone to public schools myself. This country needs to reflect seriously on the structure of education in the United States. For example, I worked at an inner city school in Seattle that was racially and economically mixed. The school didn't have enough books for the kids to take home and do their homework. Classes were overcrowded. So kids were dropped off in my room for a class period because there wasn't any place for them. Some of the best teachers were in this school. They were dedicated teachers, but there weren't enough books!

I'm concerned that this country is becoming more and more divided along social and economic lines. Either you have or you don't have. Either you don't have books, good teachers, or a facility conducive to learning—or you have it all.

You're right. And the division isn't along color lines. It's all about economics. Here in California, a Beverly Hills public high school has it all—books, computers, everything. Then you go to the public schools in Watts and it's drastically different.

Returning to your professional endeavors, you also worked with the homeless?

Yes, I worked in a university district for homeless kids. I was the only black person who worked there.

What came to mind when you saw these kids who had no home? Did you reflect on your own life?

I thanked my parents every day for being so wonderful! So many people think that kids run away from home because they don't like rules. They run away from home because they're molested or abused in other ways. Their parents do drugs. Their parents beat them.

It's a sad situation that we partake of socially, directly and indirectly.

Congress cut funding for "traditional homes," homes where youths can stay for up to eighteen months. They're required to have a job, go to school, and get their stuff together so that ultimately they can contribute to society. Well, because there is no funding, there's not enough available housing for these kids.

Tell me about your job at Dreamworks.

I work in animation. I'm a production assistant, which means I'm lower than low, which means I'm on the bottom of Steven Spielberg's shoe. But it's interesting.

What do you want to do in this field?

To be in live action. But I have great respect for animation. It's amazing. It takes three to four years to make an animated film.

To wrap up this interview, tell me why you agreed to be interviewed for this book?

My experiences having been adopted into a white family have been fabulous. Knowing all about myself, what I started out with, all my deficits, I was incredibly lucky to have been adopted into a family that adores me. That's the bottom line. It doesn't matter what the color of your skin is. What matters is whether the people who adopt you are willing to sacrifice their lives for you. My family picked me. I was chosen.

Transracially adopted kids should feel lucky because so many children out there don't have a family and are so unhappy. Awful things are happening to them. And you have this chance for a family. No one is perfect. No family is perfect . . . except for mine, of course. People should be happy with what they have and not let other people depress them by saying it's bad to be adopted by white people. Saying that is evil and wrong.

Chantel Tremitiere

SACRAMENTO, CALIFORNIA
FEBRUARY 1998

The biggest thing you can give a kid is time. A lot of people are running everywhere, throwing their kids on nannies, raising them on computers and television. Just give them time and love. That's what they need.

Chantel Tremitiere is a player for the Women's National Basketball Association (WNBA) and the founder/CEO of Assist One, an adoption-related foundation currently based in Sacramento, California. She believes that children who are blessed with stable and nurturing homes have a strong shot at a bright future. That is why she has partnered with adoption organizations, community leaders, and celebrities to help encourage adoption in order to provide homes for children who otherwise would be left in foster care or neglected.

Chantel's passion for promoting opportunities for children comes from the fact that she herself benefited from adoption. Born in 1969, Chantel was placed directly into her adoptive home. Bypassing the ethnic differences of her siblings, Chantel says she focused on the laughter within her family. To her, laughter was the force that unified and strengthened the Tremitiere family. Because of the foundation she gained from her parents and siblings, Chantel became self-assured regarding her abilities and skills. In 1991 she earned her bachelor's degree in public relations at Auburn University, taking her further down the road of success.

What is in Chantel's near future? In addition to receiving her college degree and playing professional basketball,* she is venturing into acting. There may be movie deals already in the works. Chantel hopes that one day she will win an Oscar.

---

* [At the time of this interview, Chantel was playing for the Sacramento Monarchs. She has since moved to the Utah Stars.]

Chantel, you are involved in activities that are important to you personally and professionally. To begin, you are the founder of an adoption program in Sacramento, California, where you live.

Yes. The foundation is called Assist One. The foundation assists adoptive parents and kids who need homes. In general, we help the adoption agency get kids adopted in any way we can.

Is Assist One targeted to the Sacramento community specifically, or do you have plans to broaden your market?

At first, yes. Our goal is to eventually go nationwide with the program.

Why did you feel it was important to start a program aimed at helping children find stable homes?

I think there are a lot of negative stigmas attached to adoption. In my opinion, a lot of people don't even know about adoption. Also, I was lucky with my adoption experience so I wanted to be able to give other kids a chance to be adopted. I wanted other kids to have opportunities in life. I see the need for children to have families from both sides. I see it from the perspective of knowing the good experiences I had and also from the perspective of being a guidance counselor and seeing kids who don't have homes. The need for kids to be placed into homes is there.

Describe some of the kids you met.

There are all different kinds of kids starving for attention and starving for permanent homes. I see kids going through ten, fifteen foster homes in a year.

Does your concern for children to have permanent homes include transracial adoption?

Yes.

How is your organization publicizing the need for children to have permanent and stable homes?

We do a lot of public service announcements and actually show the public the children who are waiting for homes. People call our office, and we channel them to the right agencies. Then the agencies take it from there. Assist One is not an adoption agency.

What is the top age of the kids you're trying to find homes for?

Up to 17.

Do these kids tend to be ethnically diverse?

Yes.

Are you finding that most of them are black, white, or Asian?

They come from all those backgrounds.

How is the organization doing?

Great!

Is the community supporting the efforts of the organization?

Definitely. We get a lot of support from the community.

How do people contribute to this cause?

We have volunteer positions. People contribute computers. Accountants and lawyers have contributed their time for free for some of these families. And obviously we've had some donors.

On a personal note, you mentioned that you've had positive experiences in your own adoption process. Can you elaborate on that?

Well, you never know where you'd be if you weren't adopted. All the positive things that have happened to me in my life had to do with my being adopted. I don't know if I would have been able to achieve the things I have if I hadn't been adopted.

You were raised on the East Coast in York, Pennsylvania. What activities did you do as a family that you've held onto?

Like any large group, we tended to have our cliques—you're closer to some than others. One big thing we did was laugh a lot. Laughter can bring anyone together. Just looking at my mom and seeing what she did with all of us makes me glad every day that I was adopted.

Do you have a good relationship with your mom now that you are older?

Yes. It's been better in the past. I'm not the type of person who talks a lot about my feelings. My mom and I were closer when I was younger. I still love her the same. I just don't talk a lot.

Let me ask you this question. Because you grew up in a family where your siblings came from different ethnic backgrounds, were you comfortable in identifying yourself as an African American?

Yes, always.

Was it difficult, having been adopted by white parents, to identify yourself as an African American when you were around them?

No. I didn't even think about it. To me, it was a chance to grow up with a great family. I don't even remember realizing that my mom and dad look different than I do.

In your school or in your community, did anyone overtly call you a name or communicate to you that you were inferior because of the way you looked?

No.

Do you see our current society as racist?

I see people in society who are ignorant. They just don't know any better. People tend to play down or make fun of stuff they don't understand.

How did you get beyond the attitudes of people like that?

One good thing growing up in an ethnically diverse family is that you learn to look past prejudices. I figure that people are always going to say something, and it doesn't matter what they say, good or bad. If they believe something, you can't change it. So there's no sense in getting stressed over what somebody says that might hurt your feelings.

Somehow you were able to understand that and move on. Can you pinpoint what it was that allowed you to do that?

I've always been outgoing, so I'm often around a lot of people. I learned you can't please everybody. You just have to be yourself.

As a child, what did you dream of becoming one day?

One thing—an actress.

Did you believe you could do it?

Yes!

In addition to your commitment to Assist One, you are also a professional basketball player. For starters, what team are you currently on?

I play for the Sacramento Monarchs. I'm the point guard.

Congratulations! What brought you to the WNBA?

The league invited sixty women from around the country to participate in "combines" in Orlando, which are tests of basic athletic ability. Then they held a draft, and I got drafted. The Sacramentos were eighteenth in the draft, and they picked me.

Before that, did you play basketball as a hobby? How did you get invited to Orlando?

I always played basketball. I've played since I was eight. I played in high school and in college. The director of player personnel came to see me play in a tournament in Washington, and she invited me to Orlando. That's how you got to Orlando; you couldn't just go.

Do you find that your experience being black in a white and ethnically diverse family has helped you professionally and in public?

Yes. I think my experience as a transracial adoptee has made me outgoing. I'm not really sure if there's a direct correlation. Race has never really bothered me.

What public African American man or woman do you respect and look up to?

I would say Dr. J. (Julius Erving) because he exhibits so much class on and off the court.

As someone with the potential of making a lot of money, what drives you to discipline yourself to help people who are less fortunate than you?

Society helped me arrive at the point where I am at today. I knew if I was ever in a position to help others, I would.

Do you have a connection with your siblings today? For example, if you ever needed help, would they be there for you—and vice versa?

Yes. If I ever needed help from them, I'd call them. Most of the time we talk on the phone and laugh.

As a black woman, you've been able to adapt in many situations, whether on the basketball court or in an all-white or all-black setting. Given that some people in society are racist, how are you able to be comfortable in adapting to unique situations and manage to accomplish your goals at the same time?

I think I've been able to accomplish my goals successfully because I don't worry about the negativity. I don't worry about any of that stuff. I take care of my business. Like I said, if you get all worked up about how much negativity there is in this world, you won't have time for anything else. You need to focus on the positive and take care of what you need to do.

At the age of 28, what goals do you still have to conquer?

I had three goals in life—to graduate from college, play professional basketball, and win an Oscar—and I've accomplished two out of three. I just have one more to go.

Now that you're living in California, have you been able to build a network of professionals in the movie business?

I've had conversations with some movie and television producers. Eventually the word will get out that Chantel wants to get into movies and television, and then it will go from there. Right now I'm taking it one day at a time.

Chantel, do you think that movies can be a medium to get the word out about the value of transracial adoption?

Oh, yes. I think eventually I'd love to do a movie about that issue.

Focusing on the process a child goes through when he or she is adopted transracially, what would your movie be like?

I'd tell the story of my family. I wouldn't be able to address the negative aspects since I haven't had any. I'd do what you're doing, except I'd put it in a movie.

Some people argue that if you're black and raised by white parents that, without doubt, you'll end up confused. Are you confused

because of the circumstances in which you've been raised? That is, do you have low or high self-esteem?

I don't think a person's self-esteem has anything to do with being black or white. It's all about the individual person. Whether I'm black, white, half and half, or Chinese, I'm the only one who can make my self-esteem go up or down. If you waste your time thinking that you're not good enough for anyone, then sooner or later you'll start believing it. And then when you start believing it, everyone around you will start believing it, too. I don't think I'm better than anybody. I like to think I'm always good enough to at least try to do anything I put my mind to.

I've met several adoptees who clearly struggle with their self-esteem. It seems as though they're waiting for others to determine who they are, whether it's the media, family, peers, or someone who's an "expert" on "how to be black." What is sad is that these individuals are looking for reasons to explain why they can't excel.

My advice is never to second-guess yourself until you've tried something five, ten times. And if that doesn't work you're still not a failure. Use another strategy. People have low self-esteem for a lot of different reasons. You have to look within yourself to solve it. Just like no one can make you have low self-esteem, no one can make you feel good about yourself. You're the only one who can do it.

Often the very same people who boost you up are the first to tear you down. When it comes down to it and you're ready to meet the Big Man upstairs, all the little people won't be there with you.

Can you give me three reasons why potential parents would benefit from adopting a child?

You're giving a kid a chance to love some parents. You're giving yourself a chance to love some kid. You're decreasing a big problem we have in America—all these children without homes.

You've mentioned a couple of times that your experience of being adopted into a white family was positive. What is one aspect that made your experience a good one?

Growing up with so many brothers and sisters and their being diverse made it great!

Let's talk about dating. Do you prefer to date a white man or a black man? Or doesn't it matter?

I've dated both but I'd probably marry a black man. No reason.

Considering the issues that both the black and white communities have, what do think these communities need to do to address the plight of children in our nation?

There are a lot of people, white and black, who are saying that people shouldn't adopt transracially. And I say that those same people, the ones always "bitching" about it, should get out there and adopt these kids. If you're a white family and don't think white children should be with a black family, then get out there and adopt them. The same goes for a black family. It shouldn't be a question of black or white. Black people are putting their children up for adoption. White families are putting their kids up for adoption. So go out and adopt these kids. If you choose not to, then don't say anything.

The bottom line is?

The kids. That's what it comes down to.

So it's the kids, regardless of their ethnicity or whether they have "special needs," who are our future?

Yes. They are all we have for the future. We're not going to be here forever.

Then what do we need to give to these kids?

Time. The biggest thing you can give a kid is time. A lot of people are running everywhere, throwing their kids on nannies, raising them on computers and television. Just give them time and love. That's what they need.

One of your goals was to graduate from college. Did you know at an early age that college was in your future? And was achieving a college degree something your parents instilled in you?

I always knew I wanted to go to college. My parents instilled that desire in me, but I always knew anyway that I wanted to go to college. You know the saying, "Knowledge is power and power is knowledge." I never wanted to be in a situation where I didn't know something. So I went to school.

I remember watching black youths playing basketball on a court in the outskirts of Washington, D.C. If you asked them what they wanted to be when they became older, most would say they wanted to be a professional athlete like Magic Johnson or the boxer Sugar Ray Leonard. It seemed that college didn't enter the picture and certainly didn't enter their conversations. Some of them honestly thought that a major way to get rich was to become a pro.

You can see why kids aren't worried about college since the pros are letting so many high school kids skip college and come right into the pros. Often parents push their kids to play, play, play, and they forget the part about education. You can't go anywhere without an education. Eventually it will catch up with you, whether you're a professional athlete or not.

Even if you make millions?

Even so. Money doesn't make you educated. I don't know anyone who's educated just because they make millions of dollars. A lot of people make millions of dollars *because* they're educated, but it doesn't work the other way around.

To end on a lighter note, and because I need suggestions on a practical hairstyle, tell me how your hairstyle came about?

My momma used to kill my hair with an afro comb and I'd cry until she was done. Growing up, I was playing basketball so much that I didn't care how my hair looked. My brothers and sisters called me "Madame Medusa." It didn't bother me. I could go with a "nappy" head right now.

Do you wear it natural now?

Yes.

Great. I think you'll start a Chantel hair Natural fad. Best of luck in the WNBA and with Assist One.

Nicolle Tremitiere Yates

York, Pennsylvania
December 1997

*I dispelled all the myths and stereotypes of black people. I realized
that I needed to be proud of who I am and stop hiding behind
being biracial. I learned to stand up and say, "I am who I am.
A beautiful black woman. God made me and He 'don't make
junk.' "*

Nicolle Tremitiere Yates's undaunting character and faith in
God are the underpinnings that have given her the liberty to discover who
she really is. She was born in Huntington, Pennsylvania, in 1969, where
she was in foster care for eighteen months before being adopted. Nicolle's
adoptive parents were active supporters in the civil rights movement in the
1960s and believed that children, regardless of race or ethnicity, deserve
stable homes. Within ten years, her parents, in addition to their three biological children, adopted twelve kids from Amerasian, Korean, African
American, and Vietnamese backgrounds.

Nicolle grew up in the city of York, Pennsylvania. Throughout her elementary and high school years, she attended ethnically diverse public
schools. She then went to Kutztown University, where she earned her bachelor's degree in sociology in 1992. She became interested in seeking out her
African American heritage. Certain books, especially *Their Eyes Are Watching
God* by Zora Neale Hurston, helped Nicolle to identify with her inner being.
After graduation, she continued to explore her racial identity and reflect on
her experiences as a transracial adoptee. She says, "I felt strongly that I had
to be very clear as to who I was and where I fit into society."

It was in that process of reconciling her interracial experience with her
black identity that Nicolle regained peace within herself. Nicolle believes
she has been transformed into a confident and grounded wife, mother, and
friend. Today, Nicolle and her husband Jerome are raising their six-year-
old daughter Azariah in York, Pennsylvania. Nicolle currently works at the
YWCA, serving as the director of a program for teen-age mothers. In her

spare time she speaks publicly on transracial adoption issues and is a "listening ear" for other transracial adoptees.

As someone who has been adopted into a white family, what have you learned about the value of love?

I believe that love transcends all racial barriers. I love my parents and my brothers and sisters. Growing up I thought that if the world could feel what my family felt, there would be no racism. My family is a living experiment that race does not have to be a negative issue unless one allows it to be an issue.

You have nine brothers and five sisters, all representing a variety of different ethnic groups including Amerasian, African American, and Vietnamese. Were issues of race and ethnicity emphasized in your family?

Growing up in a family as unique as ours we noticed the color differences but didn't know much about the cultures. But when my sister Laura was adopted she introduced us to the food, taught us some of the language, and showed us some games she learned in the orphanage where she stayed.

The majority of us didn't have much knowledge about our history or culture. For some of us, we were black children in America without anything we could identify with as part of our ethnic culture, including music, dance, language, and clothes. That was something you decided to learn about or you didn't.

I don't believe that race was a focal point, but an effort was made to make us aware. Most of what I learned about race and ethnicity was learned in college. I remember, though, that my parents made us watch *Roots*. Watching *Roots* made me angry because of the injustices slaves had to endure. I also learned a lot about my history, although it wasn't pleasant. My mother had objects around the house that affirmed my race, but when you're a child, that's not the first thing on your mind.

My siblings and I didn't think that we had to learn this or that about our ethnicity or else we'd be lost in the world. As kids, we were concerned about playing and what we'd get for Christmas. Anyway, why would we want to learn about something that our society viewed as inferior or bad? We didn't want to be different. We wanted to be like our parents. So either we hid from it or showed no interest.

Was there a time in your childhood or adolescent years when you acknowledged that you were physically different than your parents?

I knew I was different when I was three years old. I distinctly remember a boy in my nursery school asking me, "Why is your mother white and you're black?" I didn't know how to answer him. All I knew is that when he said black, he said it like a dirty word, and I knew it was something I didn't want to be. So I told him, "I'm not black! What are you talking about?" I remember my mother explaining how I was adopted. I doubt that I truly understood at that age. At the time my family was pretty diverse, so I doubt it phased me.

Describe the neighborhood you grew up in.

The street was predominately white, but soon after you turned the corner there were people of different races.

This is in York, Pennsylvania?

Yes. We lived in the city. We went to public schools. Our school was ethnically diverse. The neighborhoods of some of my friends were very different. Their homes were different. I had a friend whose home was in the projects. Interestingly, her mom was white and her father was black. When I arrived at her home, her mom was in the kitchen making neck bone, greens, and rice. I had my first taste of food that has historically been served in the homes of many African Americans. It "tripped me out" because in my home we never had anything like it.

Can you articulate some other differences between your family and the families of your black friends?

My family was always involved in activities like gymnastics, swimming, ice skating, horseback riding, and camping. We always went on vacations. Maybe it had to do with economics, but my friends didn't talk about things like that. They'd talk about going to the discos. I began to go with them. When I first started going, my parents objected. I wanted to go so badly that I lied to them about it. I'd tell them I was going roller skating and then take my skates with me and drop them off at a friend's house and go to the disco. Except for a few white kids, most of the kids there were black.

Eventually I confessed. I asked my parents, "Why can't I go to the disco? Is it because the people there are black?" I honestly think that my parents realized for the first time that they had fears about certain types of black people. They quickly corrected the problem.

There was a lot of crime where the disco was located. I don't know if my parents' concern was the issue of crime or the people that would live in a crime-infested area. Anyway, they quickly corrected the problem. They decided to let me go to the disco, but they dropped me off and picked me up.

Did your parents tell you why they adopted a child from another culture and race?

They grew up in the 1960s and were very involved in the civil rights movement. They truly believed we wouldn't have to deal with racism as adults. The problem is you can have laws to ban discrimination and promote equality but you can't change people's hearts. My parents believed they could protect us until that time came. They were wrong.

As you continued to grow and identify with the black community and its traditions, did you see your parents' fear increase?

No, I think that was a one-time incident.

In your adolescent years, did race become an issue for you?

It became an obsession. Most of my friends at that time were black. I don't know if that was a conscious choice or not.

What were you confronting then?

The question of where I fit in. Everyone knew I was biracial. They said things like, "She's a half breed, a red bone." I always felt I had to defend myself against one group or another.

Did you ever run from the term "black" when it was used to describe you?

Yes. It was clear as I was growing up that being mixed was somehow better than being black. I felt comfortable with the term mixed. In society, I saw the varying degrees of preferences among lighter-skinned blacks as opposed to darker-skinned blacks. I know people treated me differently because I was lighter-skinned, even the black people. Not until someone asked me why I always said I was mixed did I take inventory of the reasoning behind it.

What propelled you to make the transition from identifying yourself as mixed to calling yourself black?

Dating triggered it, and feeling O.K. with who I was. I constantly felt compelled to settle this quest for identity. My first boyfriend appeared to be black but he actually was black and Latino. At that time I was attracted to Latinos. I was also extremely attracted to black males, but as a young girl I was afraid of their demeanor. They behaved differently from how I was raised. According to my family, there was a way males should treat me. My parents had rules about how a boy is supposed to act around a girl and vice versa. When I was attracted to black males and they didn't have the same rules, it was uncomfortable for me.

What were the black males' rules?

For instance one boy said, "If you like me, let's do something." It wasn't about sex at that point. It was "Let's hang out in the park" or "Let's go to a friend's house." The boy's parents weren't involved in the courtship process. Courtship wasn't even discussed. I was uncomfortable with that.

I watched the courtship process with my older sister. Her boyfriends would come to the house. The boy would sit in the living room and they'd get to know each other. She went out on double dates, and when she was 16 she was allowed to date. That's how I thought it was supposed to be and so that's what I expected. Any deviation didn't seem right.

So for a while I only dated people who played by those rules. From my experience, they were white boys. So in high school most of the males I dated were white. I also began thinking about how I wanted to live. Most of the black boys I was interested in lived in poor neighborhoods. I never thought it may be because of institutional racism that the blacks in our city may not have had equal access to employment or had people invest in their future. So I thought if I wanted to live in a nice neighborhood and have a decent standard of living, I'd have to marry a white man.

Many of my black friends were having sexual relationships with older black men. Some became pregnant. So I assumed that all black men expected sex from their girlfriends. It never occurred to me that white men also expected sex. So in my quest to protect my virginity, I vowed never to give up the "drawers" to anyone. I was fearful of having to explain to my church-going parents that I was having sex before marriage or, worse, being a teen mother. I was very old-fashioned compared to my friends in school.

At the time I was afraid of being automatically stereotyped with the labels white society puts on black people. I always felt I had to break the stereotype. You can't lump everyone together.

Now I understand that much of what my friends experienced had a lot to do with the environment, with poverty, and with racism. Not with color.

Tell me about your college experience.

College was a whole different ballgame. At the time there were few blacks on campus. There may have been three hundred blacks on campus of seven thousand undergraduate students. College was a turning point in my life. I felt strongly about making the choice in determining who I was going to become. By that time I had learned more and more about the lie in the United States. I had seen the way many blacks buy into the self-ful-filling prophecy, feeling ugly and inferior, thinking it's better to be lighter-skinned than darker-skinned. The college I went to was in a small town known for welcoming KKK marches.

How did you go about accepting yourself as a positive black woman?

I dispelled all the myths and stereotypes of black people. I realized I needed to be proud about who I am and stop hiding behind being biracial.

I learned to stand up and say, "I am who I am. A beautiful black woman. God made me and He 'don't make junk.'" I saw that on a plaque in my home. It took me a long time to get it.

Every time I learned a new piece of information about my black heritage I felt more at peace. On the other hand, I was becoming angrier and angrier thinking about why hadn't gotten this history before. Why wasn't it important enough to be taught this at every stage of my education? The history of black people coming into this country is an amazing story and that much of it is left out of our history books really makes me angry.

I had a literature class on "black novels" in college that I found so interesting. We read *Their Eyes Are Watching God*, *The Chennysville Incident*, and others. I was moved by both books.

During my four years in college I got real information about my heritage, and it felt so good. It was a sigh of relief. Thank God.

And isn't that feeling liberating?

It's very liberating because you can easily be in bondage by your own thoughts. For example, if you're a lighter-skinned person, you could find yourself oppressing people because they are darker-skinned than you. Or you might take pride in the fact that white people treat you better than darker-skinned people. Many people won't admit that, but it's the truth. I felt free in that I could celebrate my being a part of culture that is so rich in many areas. For the first time I felt O.K. I still had to deal with junk at the university, like people assuming that all black people on campus were there because of Affirmative Action.

How do you deal with that?

If you let it, it can make you feel rejected or like you don't belong there. I once heard a speaker say that 20 percent of the people aren't going to like you because, let's say, you're black and you wear funky clothes; the other 20 percent *are* going to like you because you're black and you wear funky clothes. The other 60 percent don't care that you're black or that you wear funky clothes; they just like you. I'm learning not to focus on that other 40 percent too much and to stick with the people who don't base a friendship on my clothes or my race. There are people who won't like you for one thing or another. I found that those who don't like me really don't know me, but if they'd take twenty-four hours to get to know me, they'd like me.

Does it irritate you when people say, "You're not black enough"?

It used to, but it doesn't anymore. I try not to focus on things I don't have control over. When people say, "You talk like a white girl," I say,

"No, I speak proper English." I do change my speech according to whom I'm around. A mother talks to her child differently than she does to her husband. I look at it like that.

No matter who you are, it's so vital to communicate with the people who are important to you in different areas of your life. It's called acculturation. I'm able to adapt to the environment that I'm in. I'm comfortable with that. When I'm around my "girls," I speak differently than when I'm in a business meeting or talking to potential funders for the program I run.

What are your views on transracial adoption? Assuming you have the choice to pick the race of your adoptive family, would you prefer living with a white family or a black family?

If I didn't know my parents and love them, I'd choose a black family. That's primarily because of all the time I spent obsessing about my identity and where I fit in. Also, in dealing with racist issues, my adoptive parents couldn't give me a clear perspective from their experiences of how I was to understand what I was feeling. My parents could sympathize with me over what I endured because of my race, but they couldn't empathize with me.

If my parents had been black, they could have told me of their experiences and challenges, explaining how they dealt with people who didn't like them or treated them poorly because they were black. That stuff is hard.

My mom didn't know how to do our hair. To her credit, she asked someone to help us. But for a long time we got the "I can tell you're adopted by white people" look. Interestingly enough, I usually can pick out the black kids who are adopted into white families. There was a girl who attended the same college I did, and I knew she was transracially adopted immediately.

How can you tell the difference?

The hair gives them away. Also, many transracial adoptees only feel comfortable around white people. That's my observation. I refused to have my hair looking crazy, so I learned how to do it myself. It took my sister a little longer, but now she keeps her hair very nicely.

Now that you're married to Jerome, who is African American, does that change your perceptions about race in America?

It confirms my view that we live in a racist society. Jerome is dark-skinned. He's also 6 foot, 2 inches, tall and weighs about 245 pounds. He's a big guy by many standards. I find that his looks intimidate people, his build, the darkness of his skin, the way he dresses. He likes to dress in jeans and baseball caps.

Jerome is a very hardworking man, but he's been stopped by the police because he "fit the description." There's overkill in our police departments. They stop black men with no probable cause, only that they "look suspicious," especially to white policemen. It seems that a disproportionate number of our black men "look suspicious" or "fit the description."

Jerome went through a traffic light and the police saw him do it. They didn't stop him right away. Instead, they followed him for a couple of miles and then stopped him. When they approached, they told him to step out of the car. One of them held a gun in his face and shone a light in his eyes. The other one searched his car, pulling off all his vents and throwing everything from his glove compartment on the ground. They didn't find anything. Then they said they had stopped him for a moving violation.

How did he get over that emotionally?

I'm sure it's hard for him. I don't know if those police officers did anything illegal. The sad thing is that Jerome is so used to that happening to him that I don't think he can afford to care anymore. We talk about it, but he seems to just let it roll off his back. I know it eats him up inside. As his wife, I fear for his life. I'm afraid that because of stereotypes and a general fear of black men that someday my husband will be hurt physically by a police officer.

What's interesting is that after the police officer handcuffed him, Jerome mentioned that his wife was a Tremitiere—a name that's well known and respected in York's community—and the officer suddenly took the handcuffs off and began treating him nicely. Still, it doesn't erase the image they put on him.

Do you believe that children who need permanent homes should be matched up with parents of their same race?

In a racist world, yes. Like it or not, we live in a racist society and, if our eyes are open, we're reminded of it daily. Black kids need to learn coping skills to maneuver successfully in a racist world. Who better to teach them than adults who faced it themselves. There are also little things, like doing black children's hair and celebrating the African-American heritage. I'm not saying that all black people know their history, but there's a feeling of family among blacks in our society that's very unique.

When I was in college I met a young black woman and we became friends. I developed a close relationship with her whole family, and they loved and accepted me. They said they had adopted me. That felt so good. I went to their family reunions, and I learned how to cook traditional African American food. I can cook a certified soul food meal.

Apparently critics of transracial adoption express concern that a black child raised in a white home will inevitably grow up confused.

I think that's true. But there are different outcomes depending on what you do with that confusion, especially when you become an adult. Some choose to stay confused. I've seen some adult transracial adoptees turn to drinking or drugs. Some have low self-esteem or even thoughts of suicide. Then there are those who take the approach that everyone is the same. The fact is we don't live in a color-blind world. I take offense when someone says they don't see me as black. I want to say, "Are you blind?" They say it as if not seeing me as black is a compliment whereas seeing me as black is something to be sorry about.

Other adult transracial adoptees are like me, doing whatever they can to make sure that whatever damage was done or lack of information given that you replace that information, that you uncover the lie and correct it. I felt that journey was important to take before I had children so that my children could feel proud of who they were. I knew I had to be clear as to who I was and where I fit in. My experiences are different, and I realize that.

Are you saying that you are clear about your own black identity?

Yes.

So this was clear to you even being part of a white family?

Yes. But it was a journey I had to take alone, and it was painful. My mom encouraged me to do what I had to. Some transracially adopted kids don't get that kind of support. I shared the information about my heritage with my mom, and we discussed it. But it was something my parents couldn't do for me.

What are the things you teach your daughter Azariah?

She definitely understands that she's African American. Actually she was saying that word since she was three. She also calls people brown. I don't think she cares too much about skin color. If only we all had the minds of our children . . .

She has a prayer book my mother gave her that has black children in its illustrations and talks about being African American. She has a mix of "Barbies"—black, Latino, and white. It appears she prefers the white Barbies. I'm not sure if that's because they are white or that they're simply featured more in the advertisements. Only time will tell. When she gets Barbies, I make it a point that she doesn't just get white ones.

Her school focuses on a diversity of cultures and heritages. She has books with pictures of children who look like her. My family knows that if they get her books that I'd prefer either African American books or books with some diversity. My parents and siblings respect that.

If you walked into our home, you'd assume that people of color live there. Paintings, statues, books, and art work all reflect the lives of African Americans or people of African descent. My brother works for the United Nations. He lived in Haiti for a few years and is currently in Rwanda. He also travels to other parts of Africa. He sends dolls and other items for my collection.

Azariah, at the age of 5, doesn't understand the significance of the things her uncle has given her. But when she becomes a young adult she'll never say she can't remember anything representing her ancestry in her childhood home.

You mentioned that as a child you didn't focus on race. Similarly your daughter, who has two black parents, doesn't see the color of one's skin as a sign of how to treat others.

The color of one's skin doesn't become an issue, either negative or positive, unless somebody makes it an issue. If someone were to say something negative to her and she attributed the comment to her race, then she'd make race an issue.

As an adult, what issues are you "big on"?

Understanding people of different cultures. Diversity.

Why?

I think racism exists in our society and people pretend it doesn't. Just because we're not living in the thirties or forties and people aren't actively being lynched doesn't mean racism isn't a major issue in America. The fact that my husband gets stopped by the police at least once a year is cause for concern. It isn't an accident; it's because of the color of his skin. Other people in my family experience the same type of racism. Racism is an issue, and we need to bring it to the table because it isn't fixed yet.

How can transracial adoptees contribute to this?

That's a hard question. I honestly feel that transracial adoptees who don't have a healthy identification with their race or heritage can't contribute in a positive way to the issue of race because I believe they're confused. I don't fault them for it. Certain personalities will find out about their ethnic heritage no matter what. Others are passive. I see those who are passive as wanting to avoid race as an issue. They feel safe, comfortable, in their "color-blind world." That's not how I want to contribute to my race, a race I feel proud of.

I think some transracial adoptees have racist feelings inside that they'll never overcome. That's precisely why it's important for black children to have black families. I think the confusion transracial adoptees experience is detrimental and a cause of low self-esteem.

The fact is that black children are being raised by white families. How are adoptees able to survive in these families and make their experiences valuable? Is that even possible?

It's possible, but I think it should be considered as a second choice. You have to have a conscientious set of parents who realize that their kids can go one of two ways. They can either be in touch with their ethnic roots and be comfortable with their racial identity, or they could end up feeling ashamed or even racist toward the very people they should be identifying with. They'll choose not to associate with blacks because they themselves feel superior.

Superior?

Yes. Because they have white parents, they see themselves as different from other blacks. They even think it's O.K. to think that or say it.

Would you then say that people have reason to be concerned about the consequences of transracial adoption?

The concern is legitimate. But because the issue of transracial adoption is so strong, groups like the National Association of Black Social Workers refuse to see any other options for raising black children. In that sense, I'd rather someone ended up confused but had the opportunity to grow up in a loving family, regardless of race, than for that child to remain in foster care all his or her childhood. If we had the resources to find black families for black children, then that would be the ideal. But everyone deserves a family.

Would the word "lonely" describe a feeling you had as you went through the process of discovering yourself and the issues that were important to you?

Very much so. I can't say it all had to do with race. Nor do I think it all had to do with my having been adopted. It was largely because my parents didn't look like me. I used to get tired of trying to explain to other people that, yes, those were my parents. It was hard for some people to understand transracial adoption.

Did you try to hide the fact that you had white parents?
No.

It's like you really can't.
I never tried.

For a child who was trying to figure out "her place," did it help you that you had other siblings who were adopted transracially and also were black?

No. My siblings don't have the same views as I do, and that's not the topic of discussion all the time. I viewed my siblings as my friends, and we hung out together. There's a group of us—Monique and Mark, who are twins, and Chantel and I, who graduated together and had classes together. We were very close growing up and still are. Transracial adoption isn't one of the issues we talk about when we get together. We talk about family experiences that happened when we were kids, the same stories over and over again. We laugh a lot.

There was a lot of laughter in my family. In my journey to discover who I was, I made choices and then reflected on them. I learned that first you decide what kind of person you want to be, and then you learn what that includes. For me, my race was definitely something to be included. I needed to see what place race played in defining me as a person.

Talking about different viewpoints, it's important to highlight the point that although your siblings grew up in the same home as you, they hold different views on transracial adoption.

Right. One thing I learned growing up in a diverse family was to respect others' opinions even if they weren't the same as mine. That's the American way.

When it came to developing your own views on race and living in a white family, did it help that you had black siblings?

Yes. I can't imagine not having anyone in my family who didn't look like me. I think that would be more traumatizing. I spoke with two black women I know, both adopted transracially, about our experiences. Both of them felt that no one understood them or their situation. Their worst time was in college where they struggled to feel comfortable as black women. One of them took my mother's sociology class, and in one of her papers she wrote, "People expect me to be this black woman; the problem is, I don't know how." She articulated it well. I felt like that, too. It's a painful process.

It's difficult to push yourself to the point where you are ready and willing to find the answer to that question.

Exactly. It's a process you have to go through if you're ever going to find peace in your life about who you are. We all go through identity struggles, regardless of our race or background. But the process is almost ten times more difficult when you are dealing with the consequences of being transracially adopted.

Transracial adoption is so bold, particularly for the adoptee, that one has to be honest with one's feelings in order to find the peace you were talking about.

Yes. How's this for the title of your book: *Transracial Adoptees, Twice Wronged.* They are wronged by the white folk and wronged by the black folk.

Let's return to the question of how to deal with the loneliness of being adopted transracially?

I can't say that everything I've talked about is entirely in the past. I rise to the occasion and discuss my views and feelings about transracial adoption when it comes up, but right now I'm still learning about myself and my issues.

Is there a major source that helps you address these issues?

I have a deep faith in God. To Him race is not an issue. He is the only place I can go where there is no racism. I look forward to the day when I can spend all my days with Him and know I don't have to be concerned about racism.

Are you overly concerned with the views people generally have about white families adopting black children?

I'm learning that there are things you can change and things you can't. I can't change my life experiences. I can only choose to live my life the best way I know how and not to deny my feelings.

You're saying, then, that religion also plays a part in determining how you've chosen to address the realities that transracial adoption has placed in your life?

Yes.

Does a person really know when they are trying to discover their "blackness"?

I believe there's no hiding the fact. When transracial adoptees go through that search, it can be taken to an extreme. The key is to find a balance you're comfortable with.

What's the bottom line for individuals who are adopted and have no support system where they can verbalize their feelings?

You're on your own. If it's important enough to find your identity, then you'll do it on your own.

Obviously you had the freedom within yourself to pursue your identity.

My mom encouraged me. She definitely understands my feelings.

Who would you reach out to in the African American community if you were looking for godparents?

I used to imagine who I'd want my parents to be. The ones who came to mind as two strong black adults are Oprah Winfrey and James Earl Jones. I always felt that James Earl Jones defined a man who is both knowledgeable and proud of his heritage. He also has a voice for some great bedtime stories. I like Oprah for the same reasons. She, too, understands diversity and the need to respect people who are different.

To bring closure to this conversation, tell me what makes you willing to discuss your experiences as a transracial adoptee with others?

I'm happy to talk with anyone about this issue. My mom asks me to speak to her prospective adoptive parents who may be considering adopting transracially. She knows this is a subject I've thought long and hard about.

What should parents be aware of when it comes to raising adopted children?

When you say something positive to your kids, it empowers them to take charge and grow as a person. The key is always to speak positively so when the time comes for your kids to make decisions on their own about who they are, they'll be prepared and feel confident in their decisions. When parents brush their kids' feelings aside concerning race, that isn't addressing the issue.

Do you think the black community has a responsibility to black adoptees?

I think they do, but they don't seem to understand how their lack of involvement impacts the future of some of these black kids.

When you say the black community should get involved, what are you referring to?

I mean that the black community should get involved in adopting black children and reaching out to black individuals who are adopted into white families.

If producers like Robert Townsend and Spike Lee decided to do a movie based on transracial adoption, what would you want the movie to focus on?

Maybe one or two real-life stories, stories that would include all the elements I spoke about in this interview.

What phrase comes to your mind having to do with parents and adoptees?

Provide the right information for your children in order to prepare them to be a part of the world—the real world, warts and all.

Rachel

Sometimes transracial adoption is a good thing. A lot of children of different ethnic backgrounds are in the foster care system without any possible adoptive homes for them. And if white people want to adopt them, that's great. But I think they need to make sure that the children stay in touch with their roots. It's essential that they know the history and background of their people. I feel as though I've lost touch with who I am.

Rachel is a 22-year-old African American. Born in Chicago, she was raised a few minutes away but worlds apart in the predominantly white, Dutch community of South Holland. Delivered into foster care at birth, she was immediately placed in her adoptive family, a forty-something couple with three biological daughters. The couple ultimately adopted Rachel, making her and her subsequently adopted Lithuanian sister unique exceptions among the thirty-five foster children who have passed through their home in the intervening years.

Rachel and her siblings were raised in the Protestant Dutch Reformed tradition pervasive in that area. Consistent with that tradition, her father worked as a carpenter so her mother could be a full-time homemaker. Neither parent pursued a college education.

In our discussion, Rachel emphasized her difficulty in accepting her dark skin, kinky hair, and African features in the context of being part of a white family within the bastion of white society. How does someone who is black and adopted into a white family decide his or her own worth in our society? This is a question Rachel continues to struggle with today.

Currently Rachel attends a community college near her hometown and augments her studies teaching at a child development center. She is interested in attending a college outside Illinois. Her goal is to earn her bachelor's degree in the social sciences.

Rachel, tell me what you are doing right now.

I go to a community college part-time. I have two classes, chemistry and Spanish. I also work at a child development center. Currently I live in South Holland, Illinois, with my parents.

How long have you lived in South Holland?

For my whole life, twenty-two years and ten months. South Holland used to be a predominately Dutch community—I guess it still is to some extent. It's a small community. A lot of Dutch people settled here when they first came from the Netherlands, in 1877 I believe. The community is changing. There are now more blacks and more people of different ethnic backgrounds living in South Holland.

From this perspective, what are your views on transracial adoption?

Sometimes transracial adoption is a good thing. A lot of children of different ethnic backgrounds are in the foster care system without any possible adoptive homes for them. And if white people want to adopt them, that's great. But I think they need to make sure that the children stay in touch with their roots. It's essential that they know the history and background of their people. I feel as though I've lost touch with who I am.

My heart goes out to you. Maybe talking about your experiences will help you understand more of who you are. Something we have in common is that we are both dark-skinned and were adopted into white families. That dynamic alone underscores some very real issues we confront as black women in this society. Having said that, tell me about your adopted family.

I'm the youngest daughter of five children. My parents have had about thirty-five foster children over the years, and they adopted two of the foster children. My older sister, Kim, is also adopted. She's ten years older than I am and is part Lithuanian. The three other girls are their birth children.

The age gap between you and your siblings is wide?

I have a nephew who is two and a half years younger than I am. My parents are older. They're 68.

Being in a situation where you are physically different and set apart by generations must have been difficult.

It's difficult for anyone to have parents so much older than you are. I wouldn't say I'm a victim but I've had challenges because of their ages, plus they are white. Double whammy.

You were part of this family early in your life. What were things you learned to do with your family?

We're a very close family. I recall when I was 8 . . . 8 is my magic number . . . I think everything happened to me when I was 8 . . . we went to Disney World as a family, all of us except one sister. It was great. Now that everybody is older and their schedules are busier, it's difficult to do something like that again, especially since now I have eleven nieces and nephews.

Because you were a close-knit family, did you take on many of the characteristics of other family members?

We're all very similar, even the two who are adopted. People can tell we're from the same family just by the way we think. My mom's name is Nora, and when I was little people would say about me, "There's little Nora."

Given the bond you say exists between you and your family, was there a time when your color stood out, when you were considered different from your siblings and schoolmates?

When I was 8, again that magic number, I was more aware of things than when I was younger. Around that time I had the chicken pox, and that's when I realized that people were different. The other kids with chicken pox would have these red bumps all over their face; mine were red but not as distinguished against my skin. I realized things were different for me. I was the only black person in my whole school.

How did it affect you, as a black person, living with a white family, going to an all-white school, and residing in an all-white community?

It bothered me. I'd pretend I wasn't black; I'd tell myself I was white. Then I'd look in the mirror and realize I wasn't white, but I'd act it. I'd dress like I was white, that is, like my friends who were white.

Who could you talk to as you went through these experiences?

No one. I believed it was better to leave these things inside.

What was your concern?

I didn't want to make waves. That's how my family is. Things would seem O.K. on the surface yet we could have a lot of problems deep down. If you don't discuss problems, you won't make waves.

That's hard. How did the kids in your grade school treat you?

Since I'd grown up with them, I wasn't an issue. I was just Rachel.

So as long as you don't seek who you are, there's a place for you in your family and your community. Did it ever change?

Right before high school I went through a culture shock. When I was in the sixth grade, a few black families started to move into the community and their kids went to junior high school with me. One of the first black girls other than myself to attend the school came during my second semester. My white friends were mean to her—I think because she was different—and I went along with them. We'd say, "Look at the way she dresses, that's not how we dress," etc. She'd cry because of the way she was treated. That continued into seventh grade, when more black people came to the school. In eighth grade I remember an experience in gym class. One of the black girls was bossy, and I wouldn't do what she did. I didn't fit into her mold of being a "perfect black girl." So she started calling me names.

What did she call you?

She called me "Bitch," "Oreo"—very hurtful names.

What did you feel when you were called these names?

Horrible pain. I went off by myself and cried. And then she started making fun of me because I was crying.

Studies have been done on the impact of transracial adoption on the adoptee beginning in childhood. Although the data show that these adoptees grow up "healthy" overall, I don't believe the research addresses the internal struggle a transracial adoptee faces in a situation like the one you've just described.

And society doesn't accept us. So you have to blend in as best as you can, even though in reality you stick out. I struggled with that. Whenever I'd go anywhere with my parents, I'd be the only little black girl. People would say, "How cute you are."

I've heard the term "cute" so many times in my own experience. It's kind of a pacifying word. People tend to say it when they don't know what else to say.

It's not what they're used to seeing, a black child with a white family, and especially since my sisters had blonde hair and blue eyes. I was different. Many people would touch my hair and comment on it.

The point is that the community was not "used to you," yet they learned to accept you. Did you find it necessary to blend into your family as you did into the community?

My parents just accepted me when I was still little—too little even to understand. I don't remember any problems with that.

Did your parents talk to you about the importance of your African American heritage and of possibly locating your biological parents?

No.

Was your home integrated with things reflective of the African American community?

No.

What about going to cultural events with your family?

There was nothing. All the things I've learned, I've learned on my own, when I was curious about something. I admit there hasn't been that much. In a class in college we were given an assignment to report on an ethnic group other than your own. I indicated that I wanted to do it on African Americans. The teacher told me no, because I was African American. I said that I didn't know anything about the African American community because I didn't live that way, but the teacher didn't feel that was acceptable.

What did you end up doing?

I did something on Poland.

In your own family, what was the conversation like?

I need to give you a little bit of my medical history. I've had a hip problem since I was 1 month old. Therefore my adoption was subsidized through the state. The state paid for any medical bills that had to do with my hip. And I've had a lot of surgeries. So if I wanted to do anything, my mom would say, "Think about your hip . . . you shouldn't be doing that, it's too physical . . . you'll be too tired." It would always be about my hip. I'd say it was my mom's cop-out.

There wasn't much encouragement from your mother to explore opportunities?

No. In my freshman year in high school I had a starring role in a musical production. At the time my parents were on vacation. When they came back and found out I was in the production, they told me not to get involved with it because it was too much. That's what I hear all the time. Not from my dad. He's quiet. It's my mom.

When your mother would say these things to you, what was your reaction?

I've always been the obedient daughter. I'd always accept what she said because I made myself believe she was wiser than me. These past couple of months I've become more independent. I had been teaching Sunday School at my church and decided I didn't want to teach Sunday School anymore. My mom was in charge of the Sunday School department and insisted that I continue to teach Sunday School. Finally I told her that it wasn't what I wanted to do.

How did she respond to that?

She actually accepted it.

Does your mother treat your siblings in a similar way?

Yes. My mom is a very controlling person. She wants it her way or no way.

The life you live seems to be the life your parents are comfortable living. The community, the traditions, and the beliefs are those they uphold. Have they indicated to you why they chose to adopt a black child whose cultural heritage is so different?

Because my mom had so many foster children she can't remember the exact stories. She believes it's because my birth mother wanted to better herself. She wanted to get a degree and "go from there." And she had two or three other children and couldn't do it. Then my mom told me that maybe that wasn't my story.

If my own parents had said that to me, I'd interpret it to mean that they didn't value where I came from. That's hard. Lets go back to the hair issue. Was it indeed an issue for you?

"Hair" was a pain in the neck for me. My mother would put it in two ponytails, and pull and pull and pull. Every morning we'd go through this. She'd pull it so hard, I would cry. I can still remember the pain—it was horrible. When I was in fourth grade she decided to get rid of the ponytails, so we went to a salon and they straightened my hair. They put a perm in it. My hair was long.

Did you like your hair long?

Yes. My mother told me that we were going to cut my hair.

Why did she want it cut?

It would be easier for her to handle. My hair was down to the middle of my back. I've never had hair that long again. It made me so mad.

After the haircut, how did you wear your hair?

Short, to the bottom of my ears. With a curl. It was nice because I could do my hair myself. It had been so tight with curls that I could never do it myself before. But still, my mother had wanted my hair a certain way.

I didn't start having my hair relaxed until I was in college. I would straighten my hair on my own with the blow dryer. Now I realize that was horrible for my hair. When I was in the hospital on one occasion, a black woman told me she did her hair herself, and she gave me some information so I could do my hair myself. My hair was so much better after that.

I know there can be drama trying to find the right beautician, someone who "knows" your hair.

I went to a white beautician who did my mom's hair, too. She'd relax my hair for me but felt she was hurting me. So she referred me to another place.

How did that go?

It was O.K., but I'd constantly get burned every time I would get it relaxed.

Working through my hair issue—kinks and all—was a nightmare. Did your mother consult with anyone in the African American community who might have been able to assist her with your hair?

Not that I know of . . . I don't think she knows anyone who is African American. It was like "feel your way through" the situation.

. . . without any help.

Right. My mother would discuss with her friends, who were white, how my hair should be done. Meanwhile I was the one who was suffering. It was my hair getting more and more damaged.

On another subject, how far is Chicago from where you lived in Illinois?

Fifteen miles.

Did you spend time in the city?

Yes. As a kid I went to museums. My grade school took field trips there. And my parents have taken me to the zoo.

Changing the subject, I'd like to make one more point about my hair. I got braids once because I wanted them, and my parents had a complete fit. My best friend, who is African American, thought that maybe my parents didn't like my braids because it was too ethnic for them. He said that black people would love my braids but a lot of white people wouldn't because it's different, something they're not used to.

And your parents' reaction?

They said, "Why did you do that? We just don't understand. We like the way you did your hair yourself." My dad would look at me and groan. I took the braids out after a month and a half. I'd love to get them back, but the tension I got from my parents drove me nuts.

Readers may question why we are talking so much about hair. Hair, I believe, greatly feeds into a person's identity. Personally, I went through stages where I questioned my identity because my hair wasn't maintained in styles that many of my black peers had.

The odd thing is that my sisters and all my friends liked my braids. Even my parents' friends liked them. But my mom and dad had a big problem with it. Maybe it's because of the way they brought me up.

And how have your parents brought you up? But first, some background information. What are your parents' professions?

My dad is a retired carpenter, and my mom is a homemaker.

Was getting your advanced degree a priority for your parents?

No. I knew I had to get a degree since you can't get anywhere in this world without it today.

How did you learn that?

From experience.

What values did your parents instill in you?

My parents are Christian, and I was raised as a Christian. I'm so thankful for that. When I was little I'd ask myself where I'd be if I weren't living with my family. If I hadn't had God, my life would be even more messed up than it is.

My parents did show me love. They've never been "touchy, feely" people. They're not the type to tell you overtly that they love you. But they show it by the things they do.

Are issues affecting the black community important to you?

I wouldn't say race is very important to me. I check African American on forms that ask your race. But it's not something I think about daily.

There are these black guys who hang out at the college I go to. I don't know if they go to class. They just seem to hang out there. It makes me feel uncomfortable. They haven't approached me or said anything. They're just there . . . and it makes me nervous.

Do these men look at you?

Sometimes. But a lot of guys find me unapproachable. I don't know why. When I was younger people thought I was "stuck up." I'm not. I'm just uncomfortable with a lot of things, so I don't go out of my way to search for those things.

To return to your upbringing, specifically your professional career, did your parents encourage you in this area?

No, not really. My grades weren't very good in college so I came home to bring up my grade point average. My dad kept saying that college isn't for everybody.

What is your parents' level of education?

They both completed high school. My father thought that maybe I could find a bank job instead. He made the situation even worse by saying that if he'd gone to college, he would have done horribly also.

Rachel, how do you define yourself?

I'm just a woman who happens to have darker skin. People would classify me as an African American, but I don't see myself as being African American.

Are you in touch with parts of the black community?

Not really.

Would you say that it's a priority now for you to interact with people in the black community?

I've made it more of a priority because of the way I've been accepted at college. We have a group called the Black Student Association. At first I didn't think it was important for me to attend the meetings. So I never went. Then I got this attitude from people in the group like I thought I was better than them. I think I started going to the meetings to make them happy.

Did you feel accepted in the group?

No. And I didn't feel comfortable with them.

If you don't feel comfortable with this group on campus or with similar groups and you struggle to find a comfort zone in your own family, what emotions are you going through now because of these dynamics?

A lot of confusion. I feel as though I'm a part of a lot of groups but not involved with them. If that makes sense. I feel that way within my church. I'm with a bunch of white people. I'm in the group but I'm just there. I'm not involved. I struggle with that a lot. I spend much of my time alone. I like to be by myself. That's when I feel the most comfortable.

Before we began this interview, you told me that while you were growing up there was an understanding among people in the community that blacks dated blacks and whites dated whites.

Yes.

So where do you fit, given your background? Would you date someone who is black?

I have, and I've also dated one white guy. People find me unapproachable so I don't date often.

Did your boyfriend, who was African American, accept the fact that you were adopted into a white family?

He didn't have a problem with it. But he constantly brought up the issue. He was often concerned about whether something he said offended me.

Referring specifically to issues that affect the black community such as education, police brutality, welfare reform, and so on, do you identify with these concerns because you are part of this community?

Not really.

Would you say that you don't feel a connection to the black community?

No, none at all.

Do you watch the news?

Not very often.

What about your parents?

My mom doesn't watch television at all. My dad watches all the time.

What I'm wondering about is the degree of conversations you and your parents have about social issues in general.

That's just not like my family, to talk about what's actually going on in their lives.

So there isn't a lot of "open honesty" in your family?

No, not really. Or else they talk about superficial things.

How do you survive in your family? How have you made it this far?

I just do what they do. That's how I survive.

Do you enjoy doing that?

It's what I've done. It's what I know.

What is your perception of yourself? Do you find yourself physically attractive?

I have very low self-esteem. I try to joke about the way I look. Some days I recognize that I'm not that bad looking.

Rachel, my heart is heavy listening to your story. You have nowhere to go to express yourself and feel that it's O.K. to blossom into your own person. You don't have a network in place where you can talk about your experiences. Your family has not provided such an outlet. Nor has the black community. Do you think transracial adoption has worked for you?

I think that transracial adoption is a good thing. My experience could have been quite different had my parents done things differently. If a parent is willing to help a child become more aware, it would be so much better for the child. I feel like I was in a box. I worked in South Holland. I went to school in South Holland. I lived in South Holland. I hardly ventured out of South Holland. If a parent is willing to expose a child to his or her background and history, I think the experience of transracial adoption could be very rewarding for the child.

If you were taken out of South Holland and dropped in New York City where you had to fend for yourself, do you think you could have survived?

I really don't know. I've lived a very sheltered life. I'd probably survive but I'd have a lot of difficulties trying to.

Let's say you're out on your own. Do you think that the tools, so to speak, that your parents have given you over time would help you in society?

Probably. I'm looking forward to being independent, living outside my parents' home. Once I survived on my own, I'd be able to thrive and be my own person.

What are your regrets?

I'd want parents to help their child know who they are so they don't lose touch with their identity.

Do you feel that you've lost touch with who you are?

Very much so. Maybe if things had been different, a child would grow up to be my age and not feel part of a lost community. I'm not saying there's no hope, just that they are cut in the middle without any place to go.

It seems to me that you are Rachel, but without an identity.

Yes, definitely. I dated a guy for awhile, and he told me I had to find out who I am. It's been many years since then, and I still don't know who I am. I'm not even closer to finding out who I am. I'm just me.

This is so painful to hear. If there was something the people in the black community could do for you, what would that be?

To accept me even though my upbringing is different from theirs. I'm an African American, *but I haven't been accepted into that community because of how I was raised.* For example, I don't talk like they do. But where have I been exposed to it? Nowhere. If I could be more accepted by someone . . . it doesn't even have to be an African American. If I could just be accepted by anyone.

I also struggle with my weight. A lot of white people want to be "stick thin." And I'm larger. I know I don't accept my body largely because my friends are white and thin.

You've had to deal with stereotypes?

Yes. You are black. You are not going to succeed. I don't fit into the norm of what I'm expected to do because of the color of my skin. People are astonished that I don't fit into the mold of what they expect I should be.

Society can be vicious.

Yes it can.

Where does God fit into all this?

There was a time when I wasn't close to God. I'm slowly coming back but it's a long process. God is awesome. God is the One who will accept me no matter what. God will take me even though I have so many stains and imperfections. God is there.

So true.

He is there!

Iris

Had I gone to a historically white university, I would have remained confused. I would not have known or understood where I fit in. I would not have known about the contributions of many African Americans or biracial Americans. I believe I gained my self-esteem when I went to college. I could not have gotten that from any other place but a historically black university.

Iris, who was born in Long Island, New York, during the early 1970s, identifies with Harlem Renaissance writer Langston Hughes. Although Langston Hughes was not transracially adopted, his struggle to define self-worth as a biracial individual in America paralleled in many ways Iris's struggles living in a white family. Iris appreciates works by Langston Hughes such as *The Negro Speaks of Rivers* and *Cross*. This prose illuminated for her Hughes's pride in the rich legacy of black people and, paradoxically, the pain he suffered because of society's distinction of him as being neither black nor white.

Like Hughes, Iris grew up embittered, never fully accepted by the white or black race. In the South, where she was raised in an ethnically diverse community, she befriended mostly black peers. Yet she believed that the black community did not welcome her. As a youth, she remembers being ostracized by other blacks because of her light skin and curly hair.

Conversely, in high school Iris was one of the few blacks in advanced placement classes. There she experienced the subtle prejudices and insensitivities of her white peers and teachers toward her and other black students. Race not only surfaced in her outside world but also within her own family. It was glaring and something she couldn't avoid. The dissonance of her physical features denoted to her that she did not completely belong in her family. Depressed, confused, and tired of existing in two different worlds, Iris turned to a historically black college for affirmation.

She earned her bachelor's degree in 1992 and went on to complete a master's degree. Today Iris is employed as a professional negotiator. Now an adult, Iris is able to understand herself more. She has discussed her child-hood and adolescent insecurities openly with her parents, particularly as the only biracial and adopted member of her family.

Currently Iris lives on the East Coast with her husband. She says she cherishes three men in her life who have been her strong supports—her grandfather and her father, who are deceased, and her husband. Based on her life thus far and the frail relationship she has with her adoptive brother, who is one year older than she, Iris still believes that the opportunity for children to live in a loving, caring family far outweighs the pain those children will experience because they are "different."

To begin, where were you raised?
Long Island, New York.
Were you in foster care?
No. My parents got me from an adoption agency and had me from the time I was 1 month old, and then they adopted me when I was 2 months old. It took a couple of weeks for the paper work.
Did your parents indicate why they adopted you?
I know they were looking to adopt a child. I have a brother who's their biological son. The adoption agency said they were all out of white babies; would they mind a black baby? It never really occurred to them either way.
After you were adopted, where did your family live? Describe the community.
We lived in Long Island, New York, until I was 7, and then we moved to a medium-sized southern town.
What prompted your parents to move?
We moved primarily because of me. In New York the communities are segregated by ethnic and racial sects. There I grew up in an all-white community, and I was the only black person in the entire school system we were in. My parents felt that by moving into a more diverse area it would benefit me.
Tell me about the community that you moved to in the South.
It was a very interesting community. Actually, the first time I ever saw a black person happened about a week before my eighth birthday. Before that, I thought I was the only person in the world who looked like I did. I didn't know there were other people who were brown like me.

My hometown is probably 45 percent black. And the neighborhood I grew up in is probably the only middle-class, mixed neighborhood in the city.
Did you play with black kids?

Oh, yes. Very early on I played with both black and white children. Once I was in high school I hung out more and more with black people.

As you were growing up and seeing black kids in black families, did it bother you that you were black in a white family?

Absolutely. People would always ask me, when did your parents tell you that you were adopted? As if my parents weren't really white. My mother's family is Irish. You can't get any whiter in complexion than that. You always know. I'm browner. My hair is different. Even though I spoke like them, I looked very different. So I don't ever remember a point where I thought, "You know, you are really different." I was always cognizant of the fact that something didn't quite fit here.

People who are transracially adopted, in my view, deal with race every day. The town we moved to was a very tight-knit community. Everyone there knew my family was white. The white kids never teased me because of it. If they didn't like black people, they just didn't talk to me. But overall I'd have to say that I had the most difficult time with the black community. That really disturbed me.

With the black community? Why do you say that?

Looking back, I can better understand what was going on. At the time I was very alienated.

Did you have black friends then?

My closest friends were black. They were middle-class. Outside of them, there was a lot of hostility toward me. People called me *zebra, mixed-up, oreo*, terms like that. I learned that it wasn't acceptable for me to be in the environment I was in.

Because of the neighborhood you lived in?

No. I wasn't accepted because of my family's racial composition. Either I was hated because I was black or I was hated because my family was white.

Did the teasing affect your self-esteem.

It wasn't until I went to college that I learned an extra step in all this. Because I was so teased, I grew up feeling I was very ugly. So I grew up saying, "I wish I could be beautiful like her . . ."

Was "her" black?

Her was either white or black, but never like me. It wasn't until I went to college—and I went to a historically black college—that I realized why people were treating me this way. My roommate told me that it wasn't because of my family since no one knew I was adopted into a white family; it was because of my light complexion (and I'm not that light) and because of my hair. I have very fine hair.

I recently read an article about the black community's perspective on transracial adoption, written by Alicia Howard, David D. Royse, and John A. Skerl. It suggests that the majority of blacks in their study do not oppose the idea of transracial adoptions and that this option may even be favorable for the child. If that's true, it goes against the grain of what you experienced.

Right. In my view, you can't have it both ways. You can't say you're against transracial adoption—for how many people have you adopted? Generally, none. And you also can't say that you're against transracial adoption because the child will grow up having no cultural skills nor the ability to deal with racism. Those are the very same people who attack transracial adoptees just because of the experience the adoptees are living. I know that for a fact. I went through a period in middle school when I was beaten up every day by a group of black girls. I had told the principal and a counselor on several occasions, but no one did anything. In my parents' defense, I never told them.

Why not?

My parents consistently told me as I was growing up that they knew everything I was doing and what was going on in my life. So I assumed they knew this was going on and were just allowing it to continue. I grew up very bitter. I was bitter that I was not accepted. And I was bitter because I thought my parents knew I was having a difficult time.

Did you talk to your brother about the experiences you were having at school? I know he's one year older than you.

No. My brother and I are very different. We were raised differently. We aren't close at all.

Explain how you were raised differently than your brother.

I was a hyperactive child, so my parents raised me differently. For me, there was a lot of structure and discipline, whereas my brother, who was intelligent and quiet—and sneaky—would get away with a lot of things.

What was the deeper root of your bitterness? Do you know?

I grew up bitter because I didn't fit anywhere. People would ask me if I'd rather be white. It didn't really matter to me. Whatever my parents looked like, that's what I wanted to look like.

Just to fit in?

Yes. Whether they were white, blue, purple, or yellow, I just wanted to look like them. And because I didn't look like them, I was always defending them. I also felt alienated. Although I had black friends, no one could really understand what I was going through.

Given the scenario you just conveyed, how could this situation have been minimized?

In two ways. First, parents should never tell a child that they know everything that's going on in the child's life. Then the child expects that the parents know the child's in pain. Second, if parents are going to adopt children transracially, it's important that the children have other people in their environment who are like them, whether it be their siblings or the community around them.

By "others," do you mean those who are transracially adopted?

Right, because otherwise there's a feeling of isolation. I'm biracial, and I didn't know other biracial kids growing up. Meeting a black person for the first time when I was eight is incredible. It's accurate, but it's incredible. I think children deserve to be in an environment where they feel safe—and where they feel important, loved, respected. Regardless of whether you are "wholly" black (I use that term in quotes because no black person in this country is entirely black) or biracial, even your black friends can't fully understand your experience.

Did your hair ever enter the picture when it came to your validity as a black American? Was your hair well managed?

My hair is naturally curly and very soft in texture. My mother would cut my hair. I used to be "afro girl" through the 1970s and early 1980s, but I never had a relaxer in my hair. I can blow-dry my hair straight. For me, hair wasn't a big issue with regard to what my mom did with it. But it was definitely an issue in terms of being accepted or not within the black community.

From the accounts I've read, my situation is different from other people's experience in that I was the only black person my family had a relationship with. We never went to such and such a person's home who happened to be black.

You're saying that your parents didn't have black friends?
Correct.
Yet they moved into a mixed neighborhood for you.
Right.
Were you encouraged by your parents to meet people in the black community independent of them?

No. But I don't think it bothered them that I did form relationships with black people to some degree. What made my parents nervous was that I had a few friends in the community who were considerably older than I was, closer to my parents' ages. I think that bothered them.

Why would that bother them?

I think they felt intimidated. My parents were uncomfortable about the possibility that I might discuss what was going on with our family or with me with "outside people."

What did your family bring into the home that embraced part of your black heritage?

Not much. Definitively not much. I went through the Michael Jackson, New Edition phase. But those were things I brought into the home. It was still real hard to find black dolls in the early 1970s. I did have a black Barbie doll. I wanted to look just like her. And I read Maya Angelou's *I Know Why the Caged Bird Sings*. That was the first book written by a black author that I read.

What gave you the insight to embrace the African American heritage if within your own home there were few, if any, imprints of the African American culture?

I'd say it was forced on me. As I grew older, I became more and more inquisitive about this other culture I didn't know anything about. I was trying to understand where I fit in with it. It wasn't until my senior year in high school that I acknowledged to myself that I didn't know anything about this culture and that I needed to do something about that. I was definitely torn and very confused. Even though I wanted to embrace the black community, in so many ways the black community shunned me.

Explain.

On the one hand, if people knew I was biracial, then somehow the black community viewed it as, "Oh, you ain't tryin' to be black?" And then they'd call me really nasty names. On the other hand, if I tried to immerse myself into the black community, my peers would say, "What are you tryin' to be over here with us for?" So I always felt I couldn't win.

That's a point people need to understand. The breakup in communication is not always because the transracial adoptee doesn't take the responsibility to interact in the black community. Often, I believe, we are the ones who seek this opportunity, but the black community's failure to accept us hinders us from making a connection with them.

Exactly. The black community sends me mixed messages. On the one hand, they tell me I'm not really black; on the other hand, if I have white friends, they tell me I'm not trying to make black friends. I could never win. With white people I knew where I stood. The white community either liked black people or they didn't. They'd either accept me or they wouldn't.

And acceptance seems to be based on the shade of your skin or the texture of your hair or the way you speak?

Right. But even though I could deal with the white people better because you knew where you stood, I really didn't want all those white friends. In high school I really wanted to be accepted by the black kids. I carried around a lot of pain trying to understand why I couldn't be one of these black kids.

Could you talk to your parents or your brother about this?

No.

Did your brother sympathize with you?

Never. There was none of that going on. Actually, my brother's best friend was black. His mother was a librarian at the school. And when I was in high school I was close to her. I believe she used to be a Black Panther. Anyway, she was very opposed to transracial adoption and was opposed to how I was being raised. She took me under her wing. It's funny, my brother and I both call her Mom.

Really! Even your brother?

Yes. She's like a second mother.

How did your parents feel about that?

They felt uncomfortable at best. My father passed away a year ago. But my mother might say differently now. I don't believe my parents adopted me in order to go through all this pain. I believe they chose to raise me as if I were their own white, biological child, not because they were insensitive but because they didn't want me to think that they thought of me as being different. The problem was, I was different.

When parents adopt a child of another race, they walk a fine line in deciding how best to raise that child. And I wonder if that can even be done successfully, that is, without the child experiencing a lot of pain. If you raise the child like he or she is your own, you run the risk of the child feeling alienated from his or her black side. But if you raise the child as if she is different—raising her as a black child and taking her to black cultural events—then the child can't help but feel that her parents see me as being different. I'm not saying I disagree with transracial adoption. It's far preferable than leaving a child in the foster care system. If a child has the opportunity to be adopted into a loving, caring family, that far outweighs any pains the child will experience because he or she is different. But you can't ignore the fact that the child will have negative experiences. You have to embrace those experiences and understand your child's frustrations. That's why I think it's so important that the child be raised in a community that also embraces these children.

I agree completely. Speaking about types of communities, what was it like for you living in a diverse community? Did the southern community you were raised in support integration at the time?

I don't think of racism according to regions. Nonetheless, the legacy of wealthy European slave owners still exists in the South. In my hometown, a very affluent all-white community still flourishes today. They have their own police department and their own fire department. There's also "redlining" in the community, so there are no homes there owned by black people.

Even today?

Yes. People have to sign a racial covenant before they move into that community.

Is that legal?

It's not legal but it happens anyway. So the community that was established outside the affluent community is a poor black community. These people were servants to the wealthy Europeans a hundred years ago, and some of these people are servants to those in the affluent community today. My high school is about a quarter of a mile away from that affluent white community. I was on the cross-country team and we used to run through that community. I was the fastest woman on the team so I ran far ahead of the others. Except for me, everyone on the team was white. On several occasions when I was running this route, white people tried to hit me with their cars.

Running through the white community or the black community?

The white community. On several occasions people yelled racial slurs out their windows. Once a police officer from their own police department pulled me over and said that if I didn't stop running there he was going to give me a ticket. This same community illegally searched black people's cars.

So that's the South most people identify with. By the same token, people in the South are much friendlier. It's on a case-by-case basis.

I went to a historically black university in the South, and the Ku Klux Klan would march regularly through downtown, which was right across the street from my college. It's an incredible feeling to be in the 1990s and have the Klan march across the street from your school. By the same token, I still say people in the South are friendlier.

As a child, what was one of your worst experiences?

When I was 12 I spent the summer in the Hamptons, a very plush community on Long Island. Woody Allen, Barbara Streisand, and other celebrities have summer homes there. My aunt's home is there. A lot of the people there are millionaires. The only black people I saw the whole summer were servants.

What did that experience feel like?

I was very bitter. My cousin is six years younger than I am, but because I was tall for my age I looked older and people thought I was her nanny. That hurt and offended me. That whole summer people thought I was her nanny. I'd go places with my parents and people would ask, "Is this on one check or two?" Or, "Little girl, you need to wait in line because this woman is in front of you." So I felt that race was always a part of my life.

That was truly the summer from hell. That's why I felt ugly. I was always on the defensive or under attack. I don't think anyone ever understood how horrible that summer was for me.

How did you deal with the pain and confusion of it all?

Growing up, I spent a lot of time in my room with the door closed. My father, who I was very close with, used to tell me that it hurt my mother's feelings because I spent so much time in my room with the door closed.

Externally how did you deal with the craziness?

I was extremely bitter. Because I was a hyperactive child I couldn't eat artificial flavorings or colorings or I'd go bonkers. So I would get that stuff on purpose as a drug in order to dull what I was feeling. In junior high school these black girls used to beat me up in gym class—it seemed like it happened every day. One day this girl said that she bet my mother was a whore who got pregnant and gave me away. I beat the living shit out of her. They never bothered me again. If I had known that would have been the result, I'd have done it years ago.

My dad used to own an ice cream store, and I worked there every day to earn tuition money for college. In my senior year in high school he sold it but I still worked there. There was a girl who worked there who ignored me when I talked to her. One time I went into the back room and this girl was there and said to me, "You nigger bitch" and yanked my earring out of my ear. I beat the living shit out of her. After that happened, the owner of the store, who had been a friend of my father's for many, many years, told me I shouldn't have hit this girl. I was more hurt by his response than even what she'd said or done to me. This man had known me since I was a baby. I couldn't believe he didn't understand why I reacted as I did.

Did you tell him why you reacted that way?

I said that you can't call people a "nigger" and think nothing's going to happen to you—particularly yanking my earring out of my ear. Another white man who'd been in the store at the time also said I shouldn't have hit her. I remember thinking I didn't fit in anywhere. Black girls never accepted me, and I had wanted so much to be a part of their group. And white folks who were so negative. I was very much in pain.

What helped you get through it?

I've always been in touch with my inner spirit. I know that whatever it is I'm given, I'm strong enough to get through it. Even though it's really hard—and, yes, I'll break down crying in a heartbeat—I know I have the strength that came with me, that I'm going to persevere.

Absolutely!!

I run a lot, and I've always felt like that when I run. Running is the closest to God that I can be. It's the only time I can be immersed in my thoughts and not deal with other people. For me, running is very spiritual.

Despite some of the negative experiences you've had with people in the black community as it related to your identity, why did you still decide to attend a historically black college?

I felt I always had to deal with both communities—black and white—and that I never fit in to either. In high school I was in Advanced Placement classes, and there was an implication that the black students weren't as smart as the white kids. We were constantly being challenged as to whether we deserved to be in the advanced courses. And if any cheating was suspected, it was always the black students who were blamed, as if blacks automatically cheated.

In my last semester of school we had a student teacher for a couple of weeks. At the time we were studying poetry. We had read some Langston Hughes poems. One of them was a poem called *Cross*. The student teacher asked the class, "What do you call a biracial person these days?" So the class starts calling out all these names—real close to the word "nigger." I was so angry. After class I asked her how she would feel if she were the only white person in a class full of black people with a black student teacher and the teacher said, "Hey, what do you call white people these days?" She realized how insensitive she'd been, but it was too late.

So when it came time for me to decide about college, I felt I could only deal with one race. I was tired of constantly being challenged as to whether I was smart, whether I had integrity.

Interestingly enough, during my last semester in high school the school decided to recognize Dr. Martin Luther King Jr.'s birthday as a holiday.

That year we'd missed a lot of school days because of snow, so the school chose not to recognize King's birthday as a holiday. I told my best friend that this was unacceptable. So we wrote a petition about why we should be celebrating the holiday, and almost everybody in the school signed it. After the superintendent told us that we'd be wasting our time if we came and talked to him about it, we called the local news media. We also got the ministers in the area involved. In the end, on that Monday we were out of school for King's Holiday.

I became very active at this point. For me, going to a historically black college was probably the best decision I could have made.

Why do you believe your experience at a historically black college would have been a better experience for you compared to a predominately white university?

Had I gone to a historically white university, I would have remained confused. I would not have known or understood where I fit in. I would not have known about the contributions of many African Americans or biracial Americans. I believe I gained my self-esteem when I went to college. I could not have gotten that from any other place but a historically black university.

For the first time I could sit in the first or second row of a classroom and participate without the professor looking at me like I was stupid or the exception.

It was clearly nurturing for you.

It was very nurturing, and I really needed that. After my first semester there I earned a full academic scholarship, which is something no one thought I would get. And I graduated summa cum laude. I would not have been able to excel at a white university.

You talked earlier about being confused and bitter about life. Once you were in this historically black college, did these feelings fade away?

Oh, no.

So you were still bitter?

Definitely.

What negative experiences did you have at this college to make you feel bitter?

I still looked different. Instead of being this ugly black girl, I was picked on because of my skin color and my hair. I went from being the ugly duckling to an attractive black woman who wasn't accepted because of it.

Now what was the assumption these students had of you?

Because of the way I spoke and the way I looked, they assumed I came from "money." People perceived me as a "snob." Does that mean in order to be black I have to speak broken English?

You're absolutely right! I may get in trouble here but I need to say, does that mean one has to sound "ignorant" to be black? That's an insult to the black community by people in the black community.

Exactly. And it's completely ridiculous. On the one hand, you're upset with people because they think that you are "less than." But then you get upset with your own people when they talk like they have some intelligence.

The university you attended was coed. Did you find you were attracted to the black men there?

Yes. In high school my first boyfriend was white. After that experience, every man I dated happened to be black. I know that one of my ex-boyfriends dated me just because of my external features. My face could have been blank but I'd still look better than someone who was "darker" than me. That was unacceptable to me, to be included in groups of black people just because of what I looked like. Now that I've finished graduate school and am in the professional world, I know that things are easier for me to a degree because of my features and because I'm lighter than other blacks.

Do you think that's because the white community feels more comfortable with lighter-skinned people?

Absolutely. There are two dynamics at work: external features and speech. My looks alone wouldn't be enough. The way I speak is definitely part of it.

I'll never forget when I graduated from college. My whole family came.

Was that uncomfortable for them?!

You think it wasn't? Here you are at a black college and these white folks came to graduation. My mother said that at some point she went to the bathroom and on the way back she kept thinking, "Am I going to be able to find my family? There are so many people here." And then she realized what was she thinking, look at all those pasty white people out there.

I assume she was referring to your family?

I just started laughing because it was true. There's something important I'd like to say. When my husband and I got married, in February, we didn't have a wedding, largely because my father had passed away in September. My husband's parents and grandparents have all passed on as well. So we didn't want to go through all that emotional stuff. Anyway, we bought a home in March and had everyone come up in June. We all had a ball and no one put on "airs." It was so natural. I felt like, wow, maybe this is what it's really all about.

Through transracial adoptions, you pull together communities that would never have come together otherwise. As a biracial child I grew up wishing I was something other than a person of two races. I thought it was a bad thing and that it was alienating. It wasn't bad enough that I was trans-racially adopted but I was also biracial. As I grew older I actually treasured that part of me. I believe no one else can understand race as well as I can or be as objective as I can or as sensitive—toward both groups. I feel per-fectly comfortable now in a group of black people or a group of white peo-ple. Most people don't feel that way.

We've been exposed to both communities and somehow have had to find the humanity in it all and deal with our feelings.

Exactly. People don't understand the kinds of links that transracial adoptees and biracial individuals can provide for people. Someone said to me once that she believed God wanted all the races to get together. That's why you never see an ugly biracial child. I thought to myself, wow, that's true. I've never seen an ugly biracial child—of any two races. That was such a beautiful way to put it.

Based on your life's experience dealing with your identity as a black woman, can you comment on areas within the black com-munity that we need to address?

The black community has bought on to what the European community has taught it—namely, that they are not beautiful in and of themselves and that they need to look a particular way in order to be beautiful.

How do you work through that?

No matter what I look like, whether I'm light-skinned or dark-skinned, I'm just as black as the person sitting next to me. I'm just as black as you are. As a community we need to stop acting as though those who are lighter are "less than." The black community has been complicated not just by race but by class. We need to admit that the things affecting the white com-munity also affect the black community, things like sexism, sexual assault and harassment, homosexuality. We need to stop claiming that those things don't extend to our community.

We need to have a forum where black people, in particular, can speak candidly about these issues. To be fair, several persons come immediately to mind who address these issues responsibly, for example, Susan Taylor of *Essence*.

Right. She's come under fire for that, too. Black people act as if she's divulging this big secret to the white community that we don't all get along. How many black men get killed everyday? Do you really think white people believe that black people all get along? Black people want things both ways. We want people to believe that we all get along but we're angry if white people think we're monolithic.

That's true. If a black person chooses to major in classical music instead of R&B, then that person is white, if a black person chooses to travel abroad, then she is viewed as white, if you try to better yourself, you are white. It's crazy!

The white media point to Jesse Jackson as the leader of the black community. Black people wonder why they have to assign us a leader. White people don't have a particular leader.

There is a place for leaders, and I believe that every individual needs to look at the morals and values he or she holds internally. Ultimately, you have to seek excellence from yourself and not depend solely on a black man or a black woman to lead you out of chaos. For me, the richness of drawing from the experiences of so many great black contributors is that you can learn about their substance and their own struggles. What hero do you pull from?

I admired Langston Hughes. When I was introduced to him in high school, I really identified with his experience.

How so?

He was biracial. It's funny. People say, yes, he was biracial, but he was really black. Anyway, he was very confused about where he fit in the world.

Aaliyah

KENTWOOD, MICHIGAN
APRIL 1998

I think that everybody who is in a transracial situation will have
problems similar to what I had—going this way and that way and
not knowing which way to turn. I'm sure someone has gone through
that at least once in their life. I don't know if someone else's experi-
ence would be as drastic as mine. You just have to get through it.
The struggle will be different for everybody.

Born in Grand Rapids, Michigan, and raised a short distance
from there in the white community of Kentwood, Michigan, Aaliyah has
lived all her life in the Midwest. Adopted in 1972, at a time when transracial adoptions were waning, Aaliyah was indoctrinated in a Christian and
conservative home along with her three other siblings. Her adoptive parents, both currently employed in the health care profession, emphasized
the importance of a college education and strong work ethic.

Aaliyah's story is about a 26-year-old biracial woman who continues to
search for happiness. Appreciative of her adoptive family and childhood
experiences, Aaliyah still has feelings of inadequacy. She believed that finding her black identity and obtaining an African American family of her own
would make her a whole person. After only two years of college, Aaliyah
left school determined to put together the pieces of her life.

Her life diverged into parts of the black community where the culture,
perspective, and lifestyle of those around her clashed with the tranquil and
stable world in which she was raised. Her life evolved around her boyfriend,
Anton, and his family. The realism that came from these experiences forced
her to question more critically than in the past who she wanted to be and
how she wanted to live her life.

Aaliyah is living at home with her parents. She hopes to go back to school
to finish her degree. She still struggles with putting the pieces of her identity and self-esteem together.

You are a young black woman who at the age of 26 has lived a significant part of your life in a white family. In contrast to the physical attributes of your adoptive parents, describe your features.

My skin color is not dark, dark. It's lighter than a full black person, but a lot of people think I'm all black. I have very fine hair—the "good" hair—so you couldn't tell that I'm African American. Growing up, I've heard people say that I'm Hawaiian, Haitian, all kinds of things.

So it was obvious to you that within your family you had dark skin?

Yes.

Within the context of being part of a white family and having to learn to adapt within those parameters, was that reality exaggerated by the community in which you were raised?

I was raised in Kentwood, Michigan, in a house on Curwood all my life. Basically, the community is all white, with maybe one or two black families in the neighborhood.

When I was a child, the fact that I lived in a predominately white community didn't phase me. I found the white kids around here just like any other colored kids. All my friends were white. I didn't have a choice. As I grew up I'd get these smart remarks, people calling me "chocolate chip" or "chocolate cake," stuff like that. White people just trying to be mean.

Growing up in my environment didn't bother me. I felt like I was white because of growing up in this family. I didn't know how black people lived because now, through my experiences, I can tell there's a difference. My family is Christian, and they have morals that are totally different from the families of black individuals I've had relationships with. There are things another person would do that isn't right for me to do because I wasn't raised like that. It gets "deep."

What is an example of something your parents taught you that was wrong to do?

First, no sex before marriage. I lived with my boyfriend, who is black, for a while, and that was wrong. My parents say that is sinful, that it's dirty to be living with somebody and not be married to them. I noticed that with him and his family, people would come to the door at all times of the day. I mean constantly, just knock . . . knock . . . knock.

And this would happen during the day?

Yes. During the day. Late at night they'd get phone calls. My parents don't like phone calls past 10:00 at night. But at his house people would call at 12:00 midnight. People would just come by and visit.

Were both of you living with his parents at the time?

Yes, we lived with my boyfriend's parents for a short time. His sister owned the house we lived in. It had an upstairs and a downstairs. His parents lived downstairs, and we lived with them until the people who lived upstairs moved out so we could move in there. My parents would never allow that either. Let my boyfriend stay with my parents and me? No, that isn't right.

Are the parents of your boyfriend Christian?

I know they know God but they don't go to church like my parents do. They smoke and drink constantly. My parents don't do any of that. It was weird for me to be around that. I'd just sit there and think, "How can she drink all day and survive?"

Was his mother employed outside the home?

She worked at night and babysat her grandchild during the day. But she handled it so well, and she's been doing that forever. So that's just part of her normal day. I didn't grow up around that, you know, seeing my mom with a pint or a fifth by her side all the time . . . and cigarette after cigarette. I smoke but his mom and dad chain-smoke. I wasn't used to that, especially since my parents don't smoke at all. I'm sure they don't like it that I do.

Let's go back. Tell me about your relationships with your siblings.

I'm close to my sister who is 29 years old and also for awhile with my younger brother who is 22. He's changed. My sister and I played together when we were growing up. She was the boss. She'd pull my hair or drink out of my glass, and I couldn't stand that. Then in high school we became closer, especially since we went to the same school. Then she got married, and I was upset. She lives in Battle Creek now. I really miss her. I could talk to her about anything. Partly because she's a social worker, she'd understand me. I knew she could give me advice or at least be an ear to listen to me. I cried at her wedding, not only because I was happy but because I felt like I was losing my best friend.

Your sister was born to your adoptive parents?

Yes.

You have an older brother who was also born to your parents. Are you close to him?

I never really got close to my older brother, who's 30. I wasn't into his life. He's totally different in that he likes country music and that kind of stuff. That's just not me. I don't even see him very much.

Did you play together as kids?

No.

What does he do now?

He sets up computers in businesses. He takes business trips to places like a certain country club that wants computers set up.

Do you find that you got along with your younger brother especially well because he is biracial?

Yes. We understood each other and knew that we were going through the same thing together. When I was younger, I had a few problems getting used to going through this "white thing." My brother took it a little harder than I did. He mostly has white friends and white girlfriends. He's always been the one who got into trouble, the rebellious child. In and out of jail. I was very close to him at one point. I always tried my best to make things better for him, whatever he needed. I was always the one who was at the jail twice a week faithfully. I didn't care about my phone bill when he called and I had to pay for it. When he got out of jail he chose not to live with Mom and Dad. He had nowhere else to go, so I let him move in with me. Anything he wanted to talk about that was bothering him, I would listen.

Did it become more of a struggle for you to live in a white world? A white family?

I knew that there had to be another side.

Before we delve into that, how did you express yourself in your family network?

I buried myself. I spent a lot of time in my bedroom. It reached the point where my parents would tell me that there are other parts to the house besides my bedroom. They'd say, "You can come out! You can talk to us."

The problem is I've never had a lot of friends growing up. I'm talking about the latter part of high school, college, and now. So I spent a lot of time doing things by myself. I'd shop by myself. To occupy my time, I'd go driving and listen to music for hours by myself. That's when I did most of my thinking. Or I'd sit in my room and listen to music. Music is my life. It keeps my attention for hours.

When you listened to music, what would you think about?

About how things would be in the future . . . if I ever survive. Right now I have a relationship problem and a friendship problem. I sit home every night. I'm not an open person. I don't like to show my feelings to anyone unless it's my boyfriend. We've been together for five years and we know each other. I can talk to him. I'll talk to him before I'll talk to my parents. So it was the friendship thing. I also feel like I've been through so many relationships. I've tried so hard to make things work with somebody I cared about but I feel like I'm getting nowhere. I want to get married—that's my goal—and be happy.

While I was growing up, it was always, "I want to be like the other kids. I want to be a white kid." The white kids are happily married. They have successful jobs. My sister has a child. You know, they just seem happy. And I'm still running around looking for somebody. I've been through about five or six relationships. That's one thing I think about a lot and cry about. It's so hurtful.

Why did you feel more comfortable retreating to your room when you were sad instead of talking with your parents about what you were feeling?

I don't know what to say to them. I don't know what kinds of conversations to start up with them. I feel like we're totally different. Since I've grown up from a teenager to an adult, I've changed a lot because I've lived in the city and have seen that side now. I lean toward that. I don't think my parents ever really liked my boyfriend (who's from the city). They thought all the decisions I made were wrong.

Right now I'm trying to get closer with my parents. There was a time I hated them . . . "hate" is a strong word, but it was close to that.

What made you believe there was tension between you and your parents?

When I moved to the city I started getting to know more black people. I never dated white people. I always went for black people. Anyway, I'd bring them home and it seemed like my parents would ask them tons of questions, which I'm sure every parent does. They wanted to know who's taking their daughter out. But I felt like they were easier on the white kids' girlfriends and boyfriends than they were on mine.

Meaning your two older siblings?

Yes. I felt like my parents didn't give my boyfriend a chance. Then when I moved in with him, they met him maybe once or twice and acted as if they didn't like him. Probably because he didn't go to church. They wanted me to find a Christian boyfriend. But in the city . . . I guess I can't say I can't find somebody like that in the city because people like that are everywhere. When I was young I went to church twice every Sunday. Since I grew up I sort of slipped off.

In struggling to find a balance or understanding with your parents and boyfriend, did you end up taking a side?

I pushed my parents to the side and spent as much time with my boyfriend as I could. I didn't even want them to call me on the phone. Every time they called me on the phone, my mom and I would get into an argument. She'd say, "When are you going to go back to school?" My dad would say, "You need to go back to school to get a better job." I was already working two jobs but that wasn't good enough. I felt I was doing the best I could. My parents are well off. I will say. I felt like, "How can you know what struggling is?" They couldn't understand the things I've gone through. And I haven't even told them half the things that have gone on because I know they won't understand and they'll only put me down for it.

Did you view the "attack" your parents made on your boyfriend as an attack on your "blackness"?

No.

Aaliyah, you've mentioned the "city" several times. What attracts you to the city?

I had friends there. It looked so much more exciting to me. Out here we don't get the "souped-up" cars with the booming systems. Cars just don't come by the house like they do in the city. All the people walking down the street. It's just excitement out there. That's what I guess I was headed for. I wanted to be where all the excitement was.

Were your parents linked to the black community?

I don't remember my parents having black friends. They'd try to do what they could to expose me, like taking me to a cultural program. They probably didn't know too much about my cultural heritage, so I accepted what they could do and then I took it from there on my own.

Name several activities you participated in as a family.

When I was growing up we did a lot of camping and outdoor things. My boyfriend's family didn't do things like that, whereas my family had the money to do things with us as we were growing up. All I can remember is camping and doing a lot of traveling. We went to Florida, Disney Land, and other amusement parks. My black friends never experienced those kinds of things with their families.

My friends would call my parents "rich." They'd say I lived in a castle. I didn't like to hear that. I think they were kind of jealous because of how I grew up, as opposed to how they grew up, like in an apartment with one parent.

My friends would say to me, "You talk so proper." I'd get teased by my friends. They called me "a white girl trapped in a black body." It didn't hurt me when they said this. I felt they were jealous because they didn't grow up good like I did, being able to go to Christian schools and not having to talk all that "slang." So it made me feel good that I was raised that way and had the opportunity to get an education.

And then the hair thing. Like I said before, my friends think I have "good hair." But I always wanted the "nappy" stuff. Black people who have "nappy hair" can do so much with it. They can put it in an "up doo" and have it stay that way for three weeks. Put mine up, and it will be a mess in two days because it's so fine. So I go to a hair salon and pay $70.00 to get a French Roll, and it's a mess. I wanted coarse hair ever since I was young.

After the camping and the trips to Florida, when did you see your life begin to diverge from your family?

It probably started in my second year of college. I really got into it after my college years. I stopped going to college because I just didn't want to go any longer. I always had trouble in school. It wasn't easy for me. I had no idea what I wanted to do. I felt like, why go to school and take core classes forever and never know what I want to do. I'm not ready to go. I don't like being tested because I can't remember things. I can remember a song, but I can't remember facts.

What types of music did you like?

I started with rap—not hard rap, the "booty shaking" rap kind of thing. I was into Luke Sky Walker, Quad City, Sixty Nine Boys, and stuff like that. That kind of dance rap. I like how it sounded in my system. All that bass. I had a really nice system with fifteens in the back of my car. Just boomin.' And now I'm into R&B. The love ballads. The slow stuff. The stuff I can sit back and think about what they're actually trying to say.

In addition to listening to rap, what were you doing during this time for a social life?

I was going to the bar every weekend. I was there every Thursday, Friday, and Saturday. I didn't care if anybody came with me. I went there by myself. I got into drinking. I don't think I was to the point of being an alcoholic. But before I went to the bar, I'd begin drinking while I was getting ready so I wouldn't have to buy that much at the bar. I hate to say these things, but it's true. That wild side came out of me when I went to the bar. I didn't care who I took home with me. I took home somebody different every night. Whoever would holler at me, "Oh, Babe, you look good." I wanted what I wanted and that's all I was looking for. I wasn't looking for somebody to care about me because I'd already been through one five-year relationship and that hurt me. After that, I told myself I was going to be single and have fun. And that's what I did. So during that time I was drunk when I came home, and I didn't even know the people I was bringing home. I had money stolen out of my purse, jewelry, my pager. I lost so much stuff because these people would come home with me and they'd think, "She's drunk. She won't even hear anything." They'd get what they wanted, give me what I wanted, then take whatever else they wanted when they left. I'd wake up and my door would be unlocked, sometimes even open.

This went on for how long?

Maybe a year.

What made you stop?

I met my most recent boyfriend, Anton. I've cheated on every boyfriend I've had, which probably didn't help in trying to keep a relationship. But I really cared about Anton, and I wanted to do things right. So I decided I wouldn't cheat on him, and I never did.

I believe that when you do something wrong, it comes back to you. Anton ended up cheating on me. We recently broke up. He's the one I visit in a center, which is an alternative to jail. It's hard for us to completely break up because we've been together for about four years. We lived together most of that time. We're just like "homies," best friends. We can talk about anything.

With him being in a center right now, I'm the only one he has. So I don't want to make things hard for him by breaking up while he's in there, locked up. On the other hand, I feel like I've treated him like a king the whole time we were together, and he stabbed me in the heart. I know it's best if we break things off. My family tells me all the time that I should break it off because he cheated on me. They don't understand. We've shared so many struggles together, so many good times, laughter, memories. I just can't say that if you call me and ask me for $10.00, I'm not going to bring it. I'm not that kind of person. I'm a nice person and will try to do anything to give you what you want. He called me and asked me for money today, and I gave it to him.

Does his family visit him?

When he gets visits, he gets to come home. Either his dad or I pick him up because it has to be a sponsor. Then he'll go to his parents' house and speak with his parents for awhile and then visit friends. I'll come over and spend a couple of hours with him. Even then, I felt stuck in that relationship.

You've made the decision to move back with your parents temporarily. Has this move made your relationship with them closer?

Yes, it has. I feel like they're trying to help me now. When I was living with my boyfriend, so many things happened. When you're young and trying to survive on maybe six or seven dollars an hour, and things may not be going right with one person's job, so one quits and tries to find another job while the other one is supporting you both, it's tough.

I got fired from a job once. I had just bought a 1990 Candy Apple Red Firebird. I financed $10,000 for it and got fired from a job right after I bought it. His income couldn't pay for the apartment and the car.

What happened?

We ran for awhile from the people who were trying to repossess our car. Finally, the car did get repossessed. And it was in my name. So it gets kind of sticky with that, too, when you're living with somebody and the furniture is in both your names and one of the cars is in my name and the other one is in his name. And one gets repossessed. Who's going to pay for it?

Now I'm trying to be honest with my parents, unlike before, when I was going through that hard time. I was going through so much, and I knew they'd never understand. Finally, I did tell them that the car was repossessed and that I went to jail once. Everything came out O.K. I told them, "I'm honest. Now can I move back home?"

Since I've moved back home, it's really been enjoyable. I spend a bit more time speaking with my mom and dad. I ask my mom to go out to lunch with me. My dad has even asked me what he could do to help my situation. While he's a bit leery to lend me money because of other situations, he's decided to pay off my debt and I pay him $200 every paycheck. And I've been faithful. Every time I get my paycheck, he gets paid first. Before, I never thought he'd help me out like this. I could see him helping the other kids before he'd help me.

When you say "other kids," do you mean your two older siblings?

Yes. While I was growing up I'd notice little things, like if I wanted to use the car or if they wanted to use the car. I might have to do a job before I could get to use the car, and they'd just get it. That wasn't fair. Maybe I didn't see that they had to do a job, too. That's just how I saw it. I felt like my parents were harder on me. Growing up, that was hard to deal with. When my parents and I talk about it now, I know it hurts them when I say that. They feel they didn't treat their kids any differently. They were really offended that I thought they had.

Through the ups and downs you've already gone through in discovering your self-identity, what's the next step in that process?

Now that I've seen my "black side," I want to come back. I've lived in the city for quite a few years and now I want to move back to Kentwood. I like living with Mom and Dad.

Using your own definition of "blackness," what do you identify as being black?

For one thing, it's the music I listen to. When I look for a cute man, it's always a black person. When I was growing up, I'm sure my mom didn't know how to give me a black hairstyle, but I've changed that myself. My mom would put barrettes and ponytails in my hair. Since I've grown up, I've headed toward black hair stylists, which was probably hard for them because of my fine hair. I wanted a black hairstyle so I'd look more black, so I'd feel more like a black person.

Are you implying that you didn't feel like a black person?

Yes, because of the way I was raised.

So from your perspective, there's a difference between black and white people in this society?

That's how I see it. As I said, Anton's parents' morals and how they lived were totally different from my parents.' And that's how I see black people as opposed to white people.

Being around Anton's sisters, I've seen how they raise their kids. I'd never think my sister would raise her son like that, letting her child run wild. These kids get whipped with extension cords, telephone cords. I was spanked with a hand or maybe a wooden spoon, never an extension cord. My goodness! And these kids run around dirty all the time, their hair wild. I'd never go out of the house with my hair uncombed. A lot of black people went out in public with their hair standing up on their head . . . they didn't care.

Recently, you met your biological family.

Yes, about four years ago.

Did you know anything about your situation before being adopted?

My birth mother said I was in foster care for a little while. I think it was a time for her to think about whether she wanted me.

How did the decision to locate your biological family come about?

I always wanted to do that. I had to wait until I turned eighteen. Then my brother and I went to Bethany. They pulled our charts to see if our parents wanted contact. Mine did, and his didn't. I think that's another reason why he became more rebellious than I did. He never got a chance to see where he came from. My biological mother lived in Florida so I flew there by myself to see her.

When you arrived at the airport, did you look for someone with similar characteristics as yours? How were you able to recognize her?

She sent pictures. And the agency I went through also told me I had a biological brother. He's two years younger than me. I was 22 or 23 at the time. We look just alike. Just finding out I had a brother was so exciting.

Are there obvious personality traits between the two of you?

Yes. He's very quiet. He's also very smart. I think he got my smarts. I always had a hard time in school, and he's at Cornell University studying to be an aerospace engineer. He's almost a genius.

Did you meet both your biological mother and father?

Yes. I found my father about a year later. My mom told me where he was living and that I could see him if I wanted to. She didn't want to have anything to do with him. She gave me addresses and phone numbers of aunts and uncles. It turned out that my dad lived in Holland, Michigan.

This is such a small world, or else it seems that a lot of people have a connection to Michigan.

For a while I went to Holland once or twice a month to see him. But I've probably not gone in two years. My cousins there say they don't see too much of him anymore. No one can find him. Apparently he was in the war and had some kind of shell shock. I sat and talked with him two or three times. He's also quiet. We didn't know how to start a conversation because we'd never met each other before. He wasn't even there when I was born.

Did he tell you why he wasn't there when you were born?

No. But I know he was an alcoholic and viewed himself then as a pimp.

Were you born out of wedlock?

My mom and dad got married for a short time and divorced because he was an alcoholic and beat her. I think she said they were married for two years. They divorced and then had my brother. I was born first. Then they married, and then they divorced. She also said he was messing around on her and that there were quite a few Robert Jrs. in Chicago—I mean ones I've never met and probably never will. My brother is also named Robert Jr.

So what did you gain from that experience? Did you feel that a void had been filled?

Yes, it helped to know where I was from and why I looked the way I did. I liked meeting my brother. I found out that before I was adopted my name was Rachel. All the people on that side of the family still call me Rachel.

Have you decided to continue your relationship with your biological family?

For a while. I really wanted to spend time with my biological mother, particularly because we were starting to get closer. But then we drifted apart. When I call, her response is, "Oh, here's my long-lost daughter." She wants me to call her Mom and have that mother-daughter relationship. I can't do it. My adoptive parents have raised me for twenty-six years. She wasn't there. I felt she should have decided that before she gave me up for adoption. You can't have it both ways.

Did your biological mother tell you why she released you to be adopted and then kept your brother?

She was about 15 when she had me. Her parents didn't believe it was right to have a black child in the family. I'm sure that times were hard then. I asked her why she gave me up and then had my brother two years later and kept him. And he's spoiled to death. She said that a lot of things could change in two years—which is true, I understand that. I'd rather have been adopted into a good family than to have been there struggling with her.

Would you say that you have a strong sense of identity and that locating your biological family has helped with that?

Yes. I think I do now. I've developed from all the things I've been through and tried.

Has transracial adoption been a positive experience for you?

Yes. In the end it's been a positive thing. I can't speak for being adopted into a black family, whether that would have been better, because being in the stable family I grew up in was a good thing. Like I said, I don't have a problem with white people adopting black kids or blacks adopting white kids as long as they find homes for these kids. I'd rather these kids be adopted into a family whose ethnicity is different than for these kids to sit in foster homes.

Should the adoptive family address the child's ethnicity?

Yes. Otherwise the child will lose out by not knowing about that cultural experience.

Do you feel you lost out because you weren't exposed to the black community early on?

Yes. That might be why I went through so many things, because I didn't grow up in that environment. I tried to expose myself to it later on.

Is this something you want to continue to do?

Yes. I want to be involved in the black community as much as I can. I don't think I'll get that extreme anymore. I've always loved Gospel music. I can see myself singing in a Gospel choir. My goal is to try to get out of the city. I don't want to go back there.

Now that you know what you want and don't want in this area, who is Aaliyah today?

I still think I'm kind of confused. I've always had low self-esteem. Everybody wants to be like somebody else, don't they?

But don't you think there's something you can do about that?

I think I can make things better for myself if I try. I see myself in the mirror as Aaliyah, but I know that Aaliyah can do better. I know I'm capable, it's just doing it that I'm working on.

Do you have mentors or extended family members that are there for you and hold you accountable?

My family pretty much does that. They encourage me to get into Gospel music or a choir, those kinds of things. I also have a few friends.

You mentioned something early on in our conversation that's still in my mind. You said, "I thought about how things would be in the future . . . if I ever survive." What did you mean by that?

I'm just now getting closer to my parents. I want to do things more to their liking. I also want to do things for myself but based on the values I was raised with. I don't want to go through the kinds of struggles I've been through. That's what I mean by "if I survive." I want to survive relationships. I want to reach my goal one day and not go through these merry-go-round relationships. Right now I have a job that I love. But I feel like I'm not doing enough. I can't buy a house with the kind of job I have. And I can't raise a family on this kind of job.

So when I think about the future and what I'm doing and my not liking school and the money I'm making and where I'm at, I hope I survive. Because the world is money-related. If you don't have it, you're not going to survive, that's how I see it. I see the city, and it's a mess. When I lived there, I'd never seen a roach in my life. I saw this bug, and I'm like, "What is that?" Well, I don't live with roaches. We even had mice once. I said to myself, this isn't right. I didn't grow up like this. The most we had was maybe an ant or a spider. I don't want to live like that. I don't want to bring a family up in an environment like that. So I hope I survive and get my act together. I need to decide what I'm going to do with my life. I enjoy cake decorating. I'd like to go to a class on cake decorating.

You'll survive without a doubt. You have to. Do you want to say anything else before we end?

I think that everybody who is in a transracial situation will have problems similar to what I had—going this way and that way and not knowing which way to turn. I'm sure someone has gone through that at least once in their life. I don't know if someone else's experience would be as drastic as mine. You just have to get through it. The struggle will be different for everybody.

And you've learned from what you've gone through and that's a plus.

Rhonda Roorda

Transracial adoption can work. This avenue can give hope to a child and the possibility for the child to develop into a positive, productive, and inspiring person. I've experienced the commitment of white parents to their adopted child; I've also experienced the commitment of those in the black community, such as godparents and mentors, to an African American child who was raised in a white family. And when it happens . . . this joint effort to raise a child . . . it is real and it is powerful for everyone involved!

My name is Rhonda Roorda. I was born into this world as a medium-brown child with kinky hair and a winsome smile. I don't know, and have never met, my biological parents. What I do know from court records is that my birth mother had a son when she was 16. Similar to other African American homes, my biological brother was informally adopted by his maternal grandmother. Ten years later, in 1969, I was born. My birth mother, then 26, decided that what was best for her daughter was to grow up in a stable home and environment. She believed that through formal adoption I would have a better opportunity to make something of my life. And my birth father, what did he think? I'm not certain. He was pretty much out of the picture from day 1.

Not all things happen at a synchronized speed or with much logic. Shortly after my birth, I was placed into an African American foster care home. A match made in heaven, right? No. On the surface it looked almost perfect. I was African American and so was my foster care family. They had the financial resources to provide for me and even another child who I could play with. Perhaps my case history painted a picture that would have made the National Association of Black Social Workers proud. . . . And then, abruptly, my life with my foster family ended. Two years after I'd been living there, I was adopted by a young white couple with a son one year older than me. With my new life, the memories of my foster family were fleeting except the remembrances of bright toys, a play pen, and a feeling of isolation.

How could this happen . . . being placed in a white family? Could this have been what my birth mother wanted for me? Or was this a trick God was playing on me? From two extremes, black and white, I faced an uphill battle, one that I didn't think I could win.

I was raised in a Christian home. My parents emphasized the importance of building good character. They recognized the relevance of culture and ethnicity as a part of that. In 1972 we left East Palmyra, New York, and moved to the Washington, D.C., area. There I attended Christian schools from nursery school to eighth grade. In my classes I was only one of very few black students. But race didn't become an issue for me until I was 13. Or maybe I should say, until then I could push the subject to the periphery of my mind. As I've often heard it said in my life, "Nothing worth achieving is easy." And, I would add, especially if you are trying to hide from something, including yourself. After living in predominantly white neighborhoods, my parents, namely my father, decided that he was going to build a geodesic dome in what was a predominantly black and working-class neighborhood located on the outskirts of Washington, D.C. In addition, as a way to confront a hidden fear that was surfacing, I pushed myself and my parents to allow me to enroll in a large and ethnically and economically diverse public high school. I learned that race and culture were extremely important to people. And somehow, particularly to black students, their perception of me was that I didn't match up to their definition of what being "black" meant.

Fast forwarding to this point, even amid race issues and societal tensions, I believe that God has not played a trick on me. To say that being black in a white family is not complex would not be a true statement. It has been difficult. I think I have gone through every emotion on the spectrum. I've been determined to answer the question, "Who am I?" That question has taken me to urban centers throughout the country, overseas to Central America and Africa, through books about and by black Americans, through the academic doors of higher education, and to the Constitution of the United States. I've come to realize that the crux of who I am is based on my belief in God, the strength of family and friends, and the commitment and viable presence of my godfamily, godfather, and mentors guiding me through my journey. Through the formation of my life, I've seen individuals in black and white America working together for the sake of a child.

First, please provide some background. How many years of schooling have you had, what's the highest degree you hold, where did you go to school, what did you major in? Talk about these things.

I received my high school diploma in Maryland at Northwestern High School. I went on to receive a bachelor's degree in telecommunications with an emphasis in Spanish and sociology at Calvin College, which is a private institution located in Grand Rapids, Michigan. A few years later I completed my master's degree at Michigan State University in communication and urban studies.

Where did you grow up? As you respond tell us where you've lived from the time you were adopted until you left your parents' home. Tell us something about the neighborhoods you've lived in.

With my adoptive family, I believe I lived for a year in East Palmyra, which is near Rochester, New York. East Palmyra at the time was a small, predominately white, and close-knit community. My parents both agreed that it would be beneficial for me and the family to live in a metropolitan area, so we moved to the Washington, D.C., area—Hyattsville, Maryland, to be specific. We stayed in Hyattsville for most of my elementary school years. And then my family moved to Fairfax, Virginia, for a short period. Again the neighborhood I was exposed to was predominately white and middle-class. I would say that that community was a little more bourgeois compared to the neighborhood in Hyattsville.

The transition for me came when I was a teenager getting ready to begin high school. My father built a geodesic dome, in Takoma Park, Maryland. The environment changed literally from white to black. The neighborhood was now predominately black. I'd say the majority of the families on the street were from working-class backgrounds with a few exceptions. The scenery in the area we lived in was beautiful . . . mature trees, hills. We were near jogging trails, basketball courts, playgrounds, alongside a creek. Once I left Takoma Park I headed to college and lived in Grand Rapids, Michigan. Then, after graduation in 1992, I moved back to a suburb of Washington, D.C., and worked on Capitol Hill for a nonprofit organization. Now I live in Lansing, Michigan.

Let's go back even further. How old were you when you were adopted? If you weren't adopted at birth, do you know where you were or with whom until you were adopted? Were there any siblings? Were they adopted? What was the race, age, and sex of the

siblings? If you have siblings, where do you fit into the birth order in the family?

I was adopted at the age of 2. On September 19, 1969, five days after I was born, I was voluntarily placed in a foster home in New York by my biological mother. Approximately one year later, December 2, 1970, the State of New York declared me abandoned.

My understanding from my adoptive parents is that the foster family that initially cared for me was African American and affluent. My foster family's desire, I believe, was to adopt me.

Unfortunately, because of their age and the adoption practices at the time, it couldn't happen. According to my adoption records, I have a biological brother who is ten years older than me who, in 1969, was residing with his maternal grandmother in Florida. My biological father was living in Florida, employed as a teacher, at the time of my birth. He voiced no concern about my adoption.

Did your foster parents think that they might adopt you?

I believe they hoped they would be able to, but realistically knew the odds for that were against them. My adoptive parents indicated to me that I was provided with material things. I looked well-maintained and had plenty of clothes. Based on the information that was relayed by the social service agency, my foster family didn't encourage me to walk or didn't find it important that they bond with me.

My adoptive mother tells a story about why she and my adoptive dad wanted to adopt a child. She explained to me that she didn't want to have another biological child after my brother was born partly because of the painful delivery she went through with him, even though eight years later she gave birth to a baby girl. Also, because my adoptive brother was 3 at the time, my parents thought that having a child close to his age would provide a playmate.

Interestingly, when my adoptive parents began the adoption process, the social worker asked them if they preferred a child of a specific race. My adoptive parents indicated that they simply would like to adopt a child. I came up as a possibility, in addition to an older black male child. The social worker told my parents, "off the record," that she personally was against transracial adoption. Needless to say, my parents adopted me.

I remember the first time race entered into the picture. As I was making the transition from my foster home to my adoptive family's home, my parents placed me into the back seat of our station wagon with my brother,

"Duffy." Now he's called Chris. Duffy was holding an army blanket that I wanted. So I grabbed the army blanket and told him that I get it because I'm red and he's blue. I'm sure I wasn't thinking about what that meant in today's society, but certainly I noticed a difference in our physical traits.

I was very close to my brother Duffy, especially in the early years. I have a picture taken by a *Washington Post* photographer showing my brother and me eating watermelon against a tree on the mall in Washington, D.C. Other pictures I have show him giving me brotherly hugs; he was quite photogenic. I definitely have good memories of us playing together and having a great friendship.

If you ask me whether, during my childhood, my color prevented me from learning to love my family members, I would say no. However, there definitely were occasions when I wished I had hair or skin like my brother. I recall our playing together in the ocean. When it was time for us to get out of the water and wash up, my brother quickly took a shower, shook out his hair, got dressed, and was ready to eat. I tried to mirror this. It seemed so easy. The difference was that, unlike his skin, my skin would dry out faster and look chalky if I didn't put lotion on it. And then my hair would become so brittle from the saltwater, it would literally break off. I think that was difficult for me to understand.

The other issue that bothered me endlessly was getting family pictures taken. My parents will tell you that they had to endure a lot of "attitude" from me leading up to getting family portraits taken. It wasn't that I didn't want to be associated with my family. The problem was that the photographer never seemed to be able to adjust his camera to appreciate a black person amid a mass of whiteness. Instead, the pictures almost always showed just the whites of my eyes and my white teeth. And then my white family members came out true to color. The same thing happened in college when I was having a picture taken for my student I.D. card. I believe that because the majority of the students were white, the cameras were adjusted to address their skin tone—not mine. In the actual photo of me, you honestly couldn't see my face. These are the small things that make a very big difference in a child's psychological development.

What about the schools you attended up through high school? Describe something about the racial composition and your interests and activities in high school. Who were your friends in terms of race and other special characteristics, and who were your closest friends?

My dad supported private schools, Christian schools in particular. Therefore it was natural that he wanted his kids to have the opportunity to attend such schools. Early on, I went to a preschool that was private and then to a private elementary school—kindergarten through eighth grade.

Was it a Christian denomination?

Yes. I think the nursery school I attended was Baptist. The elementary school was Christian Reformed.

Several black kids attended my elementary school. It seemed as though I was the only black person in kindergarten through third grade. Then in sixth grade, there were several black children in my class. I had a crush on a boy named Bobby Johnson; he was African American.

What about your neighborhood?

My neighborhood in Hyattsville was primarily white. A family across the street was black. I'd say that I played regularly with the neighborhood kids and participated in Halloween and other events in the community. Still, during my younger years, I was sheltered both in school and in my family life. While I was free to play and interact with other children my age, I wasn't exposed to many temptations that young kids today are exposed to, like drugs and violence.

Going back to my elementary school years, the students in general had one-on-one interaction with teachers. Parents were very much involved with their children's education and made it a priority to attend student/parent conferences. Academically I was struggling throughout elementary school. Reflecting back on that period in my life, I attribute it to the fact that I wasn't mature and had low self-esteem. It's possible that because of the circumstances of my adoption, my self-esteem could have been impacted. Even though I appeared to be a bubbly and happy child on the surface, a part of me was struggling with self-identity issues. Consequently, my grades suffered: D minuses, D's, and D pluses.

This is in elementary school?

Well, in first and second grades, we had like "satisfactory" and "unsatisfactory," but once the grades started, maybe in third grade, and all the way up, it was one struggle after another. I'd hear, "Rhonda needs to mature," and "She has problems with her reading comprehension, her math skills." Based on the interim reports, my grades noticeably went up when I had the support and encouragement of both teachers and parents.

Early on, I remember having pictures taken and I'd have my hands over my face. I was very shy and guarded when I didn't know a person well.

Through all this, my father was especially supportive and helped me specifically with the academic issues. He went to student conferences with me and spent tireless nights going over and over math problems with me until I figured them out.

What happened when you went to high school? Was that a private, Christian school?

No, I went to a public school. High school was a transitional point in my life. I knew I had to go to a public school in order to confront my fears and explore "who I am" in a different type of setting.

That was near Takoma Park?

Actually the school was near the University of Maryland, about a twenty-minute bus ride away. Northwestern was considered a tough school with an emphasis on basketball. There were close to two thousand students there in the late 1980s. When I was there, more than 50 percent of the students were ethnic minorities, which included African Americans, Hispanics, and Asian groups.

Leading up to my decision to go to Northwestern and overlapping my community/personal life, I was starting to realize that not everyone held my same values and priorities. That was shocking! My person was definitely being tested, and it started in my neighborhood.

As I mentioned earlier, in my neighborhood I was surrounded by substandard homes—culture shock number 1. I saw so many blacks in my neighborhood and in high school that were so different from me—shock number 2. To be honest, it scared me to death.

One story remains vivid in my mind today. When I was about 11, I had a paper route in the adjacent neighborhood. Every morning I had to walk down our street and down a dirt hill to get to where my papers were dropped off. On Saturdays I would routinely collect money. I recall walking down the street and spotting several black males in their teens and early adulthood years. They predictably whistled or blurted out, "Baby, baby, baby . . ." or boldly tried to talk to me. I was so scared of them that I did whatever I could to avoid them. If I saw any of these males approaching me, I was determined to avoid them even if that meant walking half a mile out of my way.

I was angry with my father for moving there and building a house that stuck out. I can only imagine what people thought. Our house looked like it was going to shoot off into space any moment . . . not to mention the visual obviousness of a black child in a white family. I'm sure the people in the neighborhood hadn't seen this form of adoption before. I could tell by their stares and blatant comments. Later on, when I became more comfortable with the community, I found out that there were cousins in our neighborhood who were raised together and, in one situation, the grandmother informally adopted her son's daughter. It was like a family reunion. Anyway, initially it baffled me to see that my white brother and sister enjoyed playing with the neighborhood kids who to me were so different and confrontational.

Back to my story about the black males in the neighborhood who were so rude. On one particular morning I was walking down the hill with my cart and bag. I don't know where he came from, but out of nowhere there was this black male so close to my face that I could feel his breath. This young man said something to me. At the time what he said didn't register but it came to me later on. In pure terror, I dropped my cart and my bag, ran home, stormed into the bathroom, and literally threw up. I was bawling. It felt as though my whole body was shaking. My dad came into the bathroom quite concerned. He said, "Rhonda, what happened!? Did something happen to you?" That's when I told him, between my tears, that someone said . . . "Hi."

That story seems bizarre, but in a very real sense it shows the fear I had toward black males. These weren't fears that my parents instilled in me. Because both my parents supported social and racial justice and worked and interacted regularly with friends from different ethnic and economic backgrounds, I believe they were sensitive to those differences. My siblings seemed to adapt with ease in the community. I, on the other hand, was visibly struggling with the feelings and views I had about the community I was living in. I didn't want to embrace the black community as a whole . . . then. My godfamily and the members of my church who were black were the few I let into my inner circle.

The media also played a significant role in how I viewed black males. The images of black males wearing chains around their necks, smoking drugs, and engaging in malevolent activities portrayed on the nightly news were stored subconsciously in my mind. From the point in which my family moved into the neighborhood in Takoma Park, these same images came crashing out of the TV set and into my world. Going to Northwestern High School was the next step I needed to take in order to continue developing myself—psychologically, socially, and culturally.

Describe your initial experience when you entered Northwestern High School.

When I first entered Northwestern I was devastated. I saw all the stereotypes—kids with big gold chains, boom boxes, picks in their hair, etc.

What year was this?

It was 1984. The school was diverse. There were kids whose families came from different economic and social backgrounds. Some of the students were from different places overseas. The speaking patterns of the students also varied. Some students had thick accents or a "drawl," and other students' voices were "mainstreamed."

Was your brother in the same high school?

He continued in a private school. My dad asked if I wanted to attend that school, but I chose not to. In general, I believe the high school I attended prepared me to go on to college. I certainly did have good times there and memorable experiences. However, to be honest, I went through challenging phases during those four years of high school. Even taking the bus to school was difficult. Some of the black girls and boys who were at the same bus stop were downright cruel. I was called hurtful names, like a "white, rich bitch" and an "oreo." They'd make fun of my hair and the clothes I wore. I remember the dreadful bus rides. I sat in the front of the bus, and they sat in the back. They'd throw wads of paper at the back of my head and be just plain obnoxious.

How did they know that you lived with a white family?

Some of them didn't. I guess they thought that based on my dress, my "hairstyle," and the way I spoke that I thought I was white. Later, people did find out about my situation because of word of mouth. The neighborhood kids saw my family. Being transracially adopted wasn't something I wanted to hide. I just didn't think I had to explain my background unsolicited . . . especially to people who weren't going to use that information responsibly.

Anyway, I continued to "deal with it." I'm almost certain that my parents didn't have a clue about what I was going through emotionally or personally. During my freshman year I tried out for the Pom Pom team. Pom Poms are like cheerleaders. There were at least fifty girls who tried out, and I was one of the girls who made it. I thought being on the team would be fun and a good physical workout. I had no idea that being a cheerleader was such a status symbol.

Right about the time I was going through tryouts, I noticed a small group of black girls who had a serious attitude against me. Once I joined the Pom Pom team, the situation got worse. Those girls made my life hell.

What things did these girls do to you?

I'd be walking down the halls or at my locker and I could hear these girls giggling and mumbling under their breath when they passed me. In class they made mocking statements about my hair or my clothes. Actually, when I made the team they wrote on the chalk board, "Rhonda Roorda made Pom Poms. Can you believe it?" It was done in a very condescending way. Every time I saw them, I felt sick.

Another time I was in the cafeteria. I was holding my tray and looking for a place to sit. I looked straight ahead and happened to make eye contact with these same girls. One of them said, in a loud voice, "What are you looking at, Bitch?" Their words and attitude were so cutting. On top of that, it was hard for me to understand why they were treating me like this, because I didn't feel that I had done anything to hurt them.

But you went through the whole four years? You didn't transfer to a private school?

No, I didn't transfer to another school. I was determined to stay at Northwestern. I have to say that there was definitely drama going on! In my sophomore year in high school I was doing well academically. I had quite a few friends from different ethnic backgrounds and was thinking more about what college I wanted to attend.

My inner struggles were centered around making sense of my self-identity. I became more sensitive about my dark skin and living in a white family. It was unbelievable to me that some black individuals actually categorized other black people according to the tone of their skin and the concentration of African American features. I am confident history can explain this. Needless to say, I was in the category of being dark-skinned and having African features. At the time, looking "African" was not apropos among black students overall.

Please continue talking about your years in high school. What else was going on?

I'm finishing my sophomore year and I'm in a geometry class that's so stressful. I'm pulling my hair out. I just didn't get it. I tried to go to my parents for help. My father couldn't help me because the methods had changed from when he took geometry years ago. My mom was blasé about it. She may not remember this, but she said, "You should just cancel that class and do something else. It's too hard for you anyway." My mom was quite doubtful about a lot of things at that time in her life. I was determined to overcome doubt.

So I took a pre-SAT course offered at the school. The teacher who taught that course was a math teacher as well as the athletic director and basketball coach at the school. He was loved by everyone it seemed, especially by the basketball players who looked to him as their "adoptive father."

Routinely I would attend this class and run out of there to make Pom Pom practice. However, this one particular occasion I stayed after class to complete several geometry problems. I was ready to cry I was so frustrated. Anyway, this teacher helped me and offered his home telephone number to me if I needed additional help with the problems. I was grateful.

Days later there was a lot that hit the fan. I had an argument with my parents about geometry. I was angry because I believed that no one understood completely what I was going through. Basically, I was just so overwhelmed in trying to hold all of it together and making it look easy. Well, I went up to my room and locked the door. I felt safe in my world and believed that everything was going to be all right.

Sitting in my room that evening, I dialed the teacher's number, thinking he could probably solve part of my problem—the geometry. It turned out that he walked me step-by-step through every problem I had questions on . . .

Why do you pause? Did something happen?

The nightmare that lasted shy of a year began as I was getting ready to hang up the phone. He nonchalantly asked me what I was doing and what I was wearing. I was alarmed and immediately thought this was weird. That instinct unfortunately was camouflaged by my thoughts of who he was as an authority figure. Then I thought of how much the community respected him, particularly black males. So, respectfully, I answered his questions and tried to get off the phone as quickly as possible.

Without going into detail, I was sexually molested. The very unhealthy situation that transpired slowly tore me apart inside. My relationships with my friends at school were curtailed. I felt dirty. I blamed myself and was so afraid to go public with it for fear of hurting my parents and letting down the basketball players. To be honest, I looked at the big picture and the dynamics at play and concluded that it looked bad. Who would believe a student over a teacher, let alone a black girl over a white man, someone without power over someone who was powerful?

By the grace of God I was carried through this ordeal and graduated with a strong grade point average that catapulted me into college. It wasn't easy. I think for the first time I saw that I had character, stamina, and a new found faith. If I can say one last thing on this subject: Sexual molestation and rape are such demoralizing acts because both cut at the inner being of a person; it can take the dignity from that person. The sad thing is that family members and surrounding loved ones are affected by this as well.

We haven't talked about your extended family. Did you have grandparents, aunts, uncles, etc., and were you accepted by them? Were you considered a grandchild in the same way your brother and sister were?

My father's family is originally from the Netherlands. He himself came over here as a young boy with his immediate family. My grandfather, who is deceased, and my grandmother raised their four children to respect people for their character and to appreciate people's races and ethnicities.

My father acknowledged the fact that I was black and encouraged conversations about race, class, and history within the home and in public. It certainly was a priority for my parents that their kids be exposed to persons from different ethnic and cultural backgrounds. I'm still in awe how my father, a white man with blonde hair and blue eyes, could understand that as a black individual in this society I had the obligation to myself to participate within the black community. I have to give my mother a lot of credit for this, too.

To answer one of your questions, I was accepted by my extended family on both my parents' sides. However, I think because my parents were raised by parents from completely different cultural orientations and circumstances, race and gender were looked at from different angles. My grandmother from Europe felt comfortable talking with me about race. Her response would always rise to the importance of not judging people because of their color or the way society treats them—and, instead, getting to know people individually. She believed that my race and gender should not be reason to limit my intellectual capacity or degree of ambition, but rather to illuminate my destiny.

That story is a bit different for my mother's side of the family, particularly the generation of folks raised in the thirties and forties. Obviously, these relatives I'm referring to were shaped by the social climate in America at that time. So race and gender played a big role, I believe, in determining the professional and educational limits of an individual in this society. Race was not talked about freely, especially the consequences of slavery on black people in America. Because I entered the family as a young child, my grandparents and their relatives witnessed me growing into a young black woman. I truly believe that my presence within the family was a constant reminder of the need to reconcile, in this case, with themselves and with the black community.

My mom's father is a pastor. As a child I was so amazed with his teaching of the Word. Both he and my grandmother would pray for me and send me cards with words of encouragement. The spiritual foundation, like I said before, was certainly a part of my life from the beginning—as a child I'd get down on my knees and pray to God. In my spiritual journey, God has blessed my life in many ways. In particular, He gave me a godfamily, and then later in my life a godfather, W. Wilson Goode.

Was your godfamily friends with your parents?

Yes. Both my godfamily and my parents went to the same church in Washington, D.C. My godmother, Myrtle, would instinctively clean my nose if she saw it running. If the strap from my dress was slipping down my arm, she'd put it back on my shoulder. Myrtle instilled a great sense of respect in me. Essentially, my godmother opened up her life and family to me so that I had the opportunity to learn about my cultural heritage. I know one thing . . . I began saying, and still do to this day, "Yes Mame" when she calls on me to do something or asks me a question. I have an awesome respect for her. As a teenager, especially, I recognized her commitment to my life, in both good times and bad. Both my families shared in my upbringing.

You were the glue that made the friendship?

In many ways. Because the concern of both my parental families was to raise me so that I'd blossom into my true person. They were willing to accept each other's cultural differences in order to achieve that common goal.

Do you have siblings in your godfamily?

Yes. I have a godbrother named Howard who recently was married to his wife, Jennifer. I call him "Newt." And I have two older godsisters, Ethel and Anita. And I have to mention Anita's husband, Earl, who I consider to be my brother-in-law. They have two beautiful children—Jordan and Cara.

Since Anita and Ethel were in college and away from home when I was in my teen years, I spent most of my time with Myrtle and Newt. My godfamily taught me about an aspect of the African American community through our conversations and laughter together. I was very comfortable around them. I felt at home.

Newt, Duffy (or Chris), and I became close friends. During my teen years Newt and Duffy asserted their "brotherly roles" and were quite protective of me. As far as activities, we went to a lot of movies and to pubs to listen to blues and jazz musicians or we'd just "hang out together." I think, though, that both of them at times thought it was a nuisance to take their little sister places with them.

I also have good memories of going camping with our youth group from church and being in plays. Several of the plays were actually directed by Newt. Some people are raised on the basketball courts. Newt was raised

in the theater. He worked his way in school and college to become quite
a stellar actor. Myrtle brought me to so many of his productions at High
Point High School and at the University of Maryland, College Park campus, which he attended. It reached a point when I knew when to laugh,
cry, and applaud before I was even prompted. We had fun!

What sort of work did your godmother do?

She was an educator. And she is a gifted musician. She did a lot of work
with my godbrother, particularly in his musical productions. She has been
the musical director in our church in Washington for many years. She plays
classical, gospel, and jazz music.

**We've talked about your relationship with your family. Did you
go through any drug or drinking problems in your life?**

There were several things that I promised myself I'd avoid doing, whatever it took. That included getting pregnant out of wedlock, taking street
drugs, and becoming an alcoholic. These factors plague people in all communities. But I think I was especially sensitive to the black community, and
I knew that the combination of these factors was devastating our communities and continues to do so today.

In my own community in the Takoma Park area I had friends and acquaintances who died of drug-related causes. They were either gunned down or
stabbed, or they overdosed on cocaine. That's a traumatic experience. I
can't imagine the pain and agony that the parents of these individuals went
through. I've seen young kids on street corners selling drugs; it's devastating. Len Bias, who I believe was the number 2 pick of the Boston Celtics
in the late 1980s and had graduated from Northwestern High School, died
of a drug overdose. When I first heard about it, I was right down the street
from where it happened, at cheerleading practice. When the team was told
the news, there was a deep sadness. He was family to us. I felt like a sword
had gone through my heart. Four years later his brother, Jay, a friend of
mine, was gunned down senselessly. My heart is still in pain. But I thank
God for the parents of these two young men who held their heads literally
toward heaven and found the strength to educate people about the effects
of drugs and guns on our communities. I truly believe that because of the
many lives they have changed for the better because of these two tragedies,
Len and Jay did not die in vain. Their spirits live on.

**When you had problems it seems that your closest confidants
were your father and your godmother. Is that true?**

Yes. My church was also very supportive; it was like a family. People
cared and were there for me. When I was about 8, there was a lady at the

church I attended who was African American. Daisy Mayo was what everyone called her. She was a grandmother to me. Daisy passed away when I was 8 years old, which was very difficult for me. I had loved her . . . and then she was gone. I think she was an angel that God put in my life for a short period of time. Before she died she gave me a book called *Treasures of Gold: Spiritual Thoughts for Young Minds*. I still have that book.

With all these mothers, substitute mothers, and in some sense father figures, did you ever try to locate your birth mother and father?

No, I've never attempted to locate either of them. But the thought often crosses my mind. I think, though, that it would be overwhelming for me right now, especially working on this book. My adoptive father and mother are very supportive of my finding them, just as they've been about my writing this book. My hope is that I will find my biological parents in the near future, especially my biological brother. I know that my biological mother's birthday is on January 13. Every year at that time I especially yearn for her . . . that word might be a little too strong.

Did your parents purposely join the church in Washington, D.C., because there were African Americans in that church or would that have been their church even if you weren't a member of the family?

I'm not sure. I know they felt at home in that church very early on and have remained members there even when the surrounding neighborhood became predominantly African American. Today, even though my parents are divorced, they still attend that church. Certainly, I think it was beneficial that I was there because it was a diverse church, particularly in its mind-set. I never had the excuse of not addressing who I am because of my geographic location or upbringing.

I learned that the black community is very diverse economically, socially, and ideologically. The same is true of the white community. In Washington, D.C., I was exposed to working-class, middle-class, and upper-class people. I built relationships with black people from many walks of life, including politicians, academicians, public workers, businesspeople, lawyers, and pastors. The lesson to be taught is that stereotypes are just that; they don't necessarily address my world. In fact, many times in my world stereotypes were smashed into pieces.

Let's move to the present for a moment. Do you have close friends in Lansing? What kind of people live there?

I've remained in contact with faculty and mentors at the college and university I have attended here in Michigan. Some of my friends are completing their doctorate degrees in East Lansing. I've met some really neat people through church events in the community here. But most of my intimate friends are scattered throughout the country.

Are you active in a church?

No, because of my load with this project and with my career. But I do attend church regularly. Right now I'm going to a United Church of Christ, a church that is primarily African American and community-based. At times I visit a reformed church, which is predominately white. They are both quite different in structure and style. I feel at home in both, but I think I lean more toward the black church.

Tell me about your parents, their schooling, the kind of work they do or did?

My parents both have their bachelor's degree, and they graduated from Calvin, too. My mother later went on to get her master's degree in gerontology at the University of Maryland, College Park campus.

Where did they meet?

At college. My father was an education major. To be honest, I can't even remember what my mom majored in. Presently, my father works for the *Washington Post*, and my mother has her own business transporting elderly people to special events and taking them on trips.

Did she work as you and your siblings were growing up?

For the most part she stayed home, but she did work part-time as an art teacher at the elementary school I attended.

Has your father remarried?

Yes. He's been married now for more than seven years. My father married a Christian woman who is Vietnamese. They are so much in love with each other . . . it's like they're still on their honeymoon. Le, my father's wife, is very supportive of his children. It's apparent that she has high expectations for herself and us. I've become more sensitive to the Asian culture, the Vietnamese culture specifically. I had to in order to understand Le's perspective on family and social issues.

You have mentors who have helped you through your journey. Tell me about them.

To give you a reference point in my childhood and adolescent years, I think I learned a lot about faith and perseverance. I learned how to set goals and to accomplish them. And I knew there was a God watching over me. I also had an interest in exploring new territory. I loved adventure.

At the end of my sophomore year in college, I wanted to complement my traditional education with more practical experiences. That summer I traveled to Europe to visit my relatives in the Netherlands. I went to Amsterdam, which is notorious for its eccentric environment. I toured the country and learned a lot about the Dutch culture, the food, and the people. There's a museum there, called *Wit Over Zwart* (White on Black), that highlights blacks throughout the world and shows their contributions globally. There was an impressive display there called "Black USA." Included were paintings and other art pieces highlighting African Americans, as well as artwork done by African Americans. Hanging from the arches of the museum was a banner called *Clievers's Assortment Caramels*. Beneath the portraits of three black persons, each in front of different scenery, a caption described the color of their skin—Mocha, Cream, and Chocolate. It was another reminder to me that distinctions are made between the shades of skin color. The museum was definitely distinctive and made me proud to be an African American. I think people in other countries view black Americans with higher regard than Americans do in the states—and not just in Europe but also in other countries and communities throughout the world.

I spent the first semester of my junior year in Central America—Costa Rica, Nicaragua, and Guatemala—on an off-campus program. I was part of a small group of students from various colleges and universities throughout the United States. It became clear to me that in the United States we blacks and whites take so much for granted, like running water, electricity, justice, and for the most part a stable economy. On a practical level, I learned that if I wanted to eat or to get from point A to point B and pass my course work, I needed to interact with the people so I could speak coherent Spanish and also understand their cultural norms. Costa Rica and Guatemala are particularly beautiful countries. The mountains and greenery are breathtaking.

Now about my mentors. The next stop on my journey was to study in Chicago (in another student program) and work as an intern at a TV station. So I moved into an apartment on the north lakeshore with two roommates. I spent a week interviewing at different stations. I ended up going with WLS (an ABC affiliate), which was within walking distance from my apartment. I worked on *Chicagoing with Bill Campbell*, which is a community-oriented program that airs once a week.

I have a lot to say about my experience in Chicago because that experience was pivotal in bringing me to a point where I could begin exploring who I was as an African American woman and a professional. Up to then, I think I had a lot of potential to become the person I'm meant to be, but I was afraid to let myself "blossom." I would purposely dress in baggy clothes, as if I didn't want people to see my body, my personality.

Working at WLS gave me the opportunity to be among professional African Americans in television who also contributed positively to society. When the *Chicagoing* crew was not on location, editing, or in the studio, I walked over to Harpo Studios to watch the *Oprah Winfrey* show. After the show members of the audience normally go down to the stage to shake Oprah's hand, so I did too, of course. When I shook her hand, she told me that my hand was limp and that I should shake someone's hand with confidence. Then she illustrated how. Honesty can be painful at times. That moment changed my life. Something clicked—that the strength within me must exude into my outward behavior, like in a simple handshake.

Talking about honesty, when we were getting ready to finish producing a *Chicagoing* show, Bill Campbell pulled me into his office and had a heart-to-heart talk with me. He asked me if I knew where I was. I looked at him uncertainly. Well, if I had any doubt, he told me I was sitting in the third largest television station in the country, and that if he didn't think I had what it took to be there, he wouldn't have hired me to work at the station. Then he told me, candidly, that I needed to get myself together, basically to get my outer being in sync with my inner being—confidence, hairstyle, clothing, all falling into that category. That was one of the hardest talks I ever had because it was so honest and I knew he was right. I just didn't know at the time if I could do it.

I had another African American mentor, Cyril, who stuck by me and continues to be supportive. Then, he was working in sales at the station. Cyril was successful in his own right. He, too, spoke honestly with me about my potential. He encouraged me to work hard and to stay focused. Now, almost seven years later, I can still pick up the phone and he's on the other end expecting a report on what I'm doing, making sure I'm staying out of trouble.

I could go on talking about people who've touched my life along the way and have made me a stronger person as an African American. From the bottom of my heart I thank Bill Campbell, Cyril, Elsa, Mike, Vernon Jarrett, Franscine, Ray, and Sally Jo Conner. They helped me learn what it meant to be true to myself.

Are you glad that you were transracially adopted?

I'm very thankful I was adopted transracially. I was given a permanent loving home and a solid foundation. It's so easy to harp on the difficulties and hold on to the negative experiences. But I believe that because I was transracially adopted, I had to confront issues about race and identity head on. I didn't have the option of being complacent in my culture. I had to seek out the richness of my ethnic heritage to survive. My parents provided me with the foundation and the opportunities to allow me to do that successfully.

My father told me once, "Rhonda, I'll never know what it's like to be black. I can tell you that, being white and a male in this society, I'm treated differently." He's right. You see that in restaurants, in traveling, in many settings . . . the differences in how you're treated depending on whether you're black or white. But my father and mother provided the means and the freedom necessary for me to grow and function in this society.

With regard to whether transracial adoptees can make it in this society, I believe the potential is there for us to overcome obstacles and be strong and vibrant in our daily lives. We have the ability to bring worlds together, to see both sides of issues confronting black and white people. We have the credibility to do so.

As you know, for years the National Association of Black Social Workers has argued that no white family can teach a black child how to cope in this racist society. Do you think they are right in arguing that transracial adoption doesn't serve the child's best interest?

They aren't talking about my experience. It's important to remember that the situations are going to be different for each child, and that indeed it is the child's best interest that we all should be thinking about. Given that, the question should be, "What can adoption agencies, adoptive parents, the community, and society do to insure that adopted children have rewarding and fruitful experiences?"

If the NABSW or other groups and individuals are concerned about the consequences on black children of transracial adoption, then, first and foremost, they need to contribute to finding permanent and healthy homes for the tens of thousands of abandoned children in this nation, and to help strengthen the experiences of transracial adoptees.

Do you have specific suggestions or advice that you would give to white parents who are now thinking about adopting a black child?

Adoptive parents need to be genuine. They need to understand that there is value in appreciating their children's ethnicity. Another key reality check for white parents to acknowledge is that society will treat their black and biracial children or adolescents differently than themselves— even though these individuals are part of their family.

Years ago, when my family took a cross-country trip, it became clear to me, once we were outside the "chocolate city," that there were white people who didn't appreciate a black girl being with a white family. And they made this known in a nonverbal way. Families must be honest and upfront about the fact that not everybody in this society will accept a "mixed" family.

My plea to adoptive parents is for them to embrace their children, to love them and nurture them. Be tuned into the society we are a part of. Consciously ask yourselves, "What is in the best interest of the child?" You may find that the answer will affect the neighborhood that you move to or the job you take or where you go on vacation. Essentially, the issues black parents face in raising their sons and daughters will be the same issues that white parents will face in raising their black and biracial sons and daughters.

Does that mean having black friends, joining black churches?

Those are good suggestions. Joining black churches. Having black friends. Being in a black or mixed community. Seeking advice. Making partnerships and friendships with the child's ethnic community. You have to make a mental shift. That's when the child's best interest can begin to be served.

All things considered, as you look back now, allowing for stability and love and everything else, would you have preferred to have been adopted by black parents?

No. I look at my life and know that amid pain and difficult situations, I've learned a lot about myself and what is important to me. Ultimately, what has been invested in my life has made me into a strong person, has enabled me to appreciate my essence. I've been blessed to have an African American godfamily and godfather. They have nurtured me spiritually, culturally, and socially, as have my adoptive parents. My godfather impressed upon me the value and strength of humility, integrity, forgiveness, and love. And so, with what God has given me and with my friends and family, I know I'm able to contribute to society and be free!

You know my last question: "What questions of importance have I failed to ask you about your experience with transracial adoption?"

I want to say that transracial adoption can work. This avenue can give hope to a child and the possibility for the child to develop into a positive, productive, and inspiring person. I've experienced the commitment of white parents to their adopted child; I've also experienced the commitment of those in the black community, such as godparents and mentors, to an African American child who was raised in a white family. And when it happens . . . this joint effort to raise a child . . . it is real and it is powerful for everyone involved!

Rev. Keith J. Bigelow

LANSING, MICHIGAN
OCTOBER 1996

You've listened to the Old Negro Spiritual, "Ain't Gonna Let Nobody Turn Me Around"? And you see black people who are on welfare or in a perpetual state of being dependent on somebody and saying that, "because this white person has put me here, I can't get any further." . . . Don't tell me that they are remembering their history. Don't tell me that they are celebrating their "blackness." . . . We need to give our people the knowledge to be successful, not the message that they are in bondage.

Keith J. Bigelow was born in November 1968 into an African American family in Prince George's County, Maryland. He was born into a family that included a mother on public assistance, a father who worked as a mechanic, and an extended family made up of siblings and cousins.

In 1969 Keith's world began to change drastically. His biological mother, no longer able to provide for him, was forced to relinquish him to the state's foster care system. There he lingered for two years, desperately needing a stable family environment. Then, in 1973, the Bigelows, a white couple in their thirties, adopted Keith. They would raise Keith along with their other five children in a Baptist and conservative home in Essex Center, Vermont. After Keith was adopted, the Bigelows interracially adopted two other children: one was Vietnamese, the other Hawaiian.

For Keith, growing up in the Bigelow family was "normal." He enjoyed playing childhood games with his siblings and going on family trips. He did not perceive himself as different, nor did he believe that he was treated any differently because of his skin color. He says, "There was no distinct time that I recall my parents telling me that, one, 'you are adopted,' and, two, 'you're black.'"

According to Keith, his parents handled issues relating to adoption and ethnicity discreetly. Even when Keith needed special products for his hair and skin that could not be purchased in Vermont, Keith's father would go across the lake to Plattsburgh, New York, to the air force base to get the products without bringing unnecessary attention to Keith.

"Room for One More" is a support group for adoptive families. The Bigelows attended this group regularly and found families who adopted black children. The group helped the Bigelows to become more sensitive to issues affecting African American children living in transracial settings. Keith remembers interacting with many of these kids, reinforcing his "normalcy" in his family.

From Washington, D.C., to Vermont, Keith has learned how to adapt to extreme circumstances. He has retained the values his parents instilled in him and strives to do what is right. Now 28 years old, Keith is husband, father, and minister. Interestingly, much of his appreciation for his own ethnic heritage and the plight of others was nurtured by his wife who is Haitian American. In his own understanding of himself and African American communities, Keith has dedicated himself to minister to people living in urban neighborhoods. He continues to "keep the faith" in his journey.

When were you adopted?
I believe it was April 29, 1973, from Washington, D.C.
How old were you when you were adopted?
I was 5.
Tell me about your adoptive family.
I come from a family of eight. Three of the children are adopted and three are biological. One of the adoptees is Hawaiian, the other is Vietnamese, and then there's me, the African American. You could probably say by looking at my family that I'm the one that sticks out, because I don't look like anyone else whereas the others look either like my mother or father. Our family is a Baptist family raised in the Baptist tradition, but we are quiet Baptist as opposed to loud Baptist. My parents were very conservative. My dad worked at IBM. My mother works in the school system as a guidance counselor. My dad has his bachelor's degree, my mother her master's degree. Education was very important to them so naturally that was instilled in all their children.
Where did you grow up?
In the town of Essex Center in Vermont. Some might say Vermont's the whitest state in the Union in terms of race, and Essex is a pretty small town. It's a very quiet place.
Can you tell me why your parents adopted you?

I think they were part of a group called "Room for One More." It's a support group for anybody who adopts a child. So I'd assume that they were just in a group like that and every now and then the group would bring out those catalogues of kids that needed to be adopted. I assume they were looking through the catalogues and saw me and said this would be a good thing to do so let's go ahead and do it. I don't want to say that they had some altruistic type of reasoning for doing what they did. They just said, here's someone who needs a home.

How old were your parents when they adopted you?

I'm guessing. I think they were both in their late thirties.

When they were growing up, was either of your parents connected with persons culturally and ethnically different?

For my mother, the answer is no, only because she was born and raised in Vermont. In the surrounding community where my mother lived, there were very few minorities.

My dad may have been, because he was born in Massachusetts where there was more ethnic diversity. As far as what those associations were, I really couldn't tell you.

I know that neither of their parents ever had an idea that my adoptive parents were trying to adopt a child of a different race. Neither did any of their brothers or sisters.

You said that you were adopted when you were five. Do you remember anything going back to that time in your life?

No.

While you were growing up, can you remember points in time when you felt you were different than your family?

To be honest, Rhonda, I don't recall ever coming to my senses as a child and saying I was different than the people I considered my primary family. I don't think there was ever a time when I said, "Hey, you guys are lighter than me, you guys have different facial features than me, you guys have different hair than me, and you talk differently than me." I don't think I ever consciously did that.

But subconsciously, every now and then, when things weren't going as smoothly as possible, there was a twinge in my mind that said I really hate the situation I'm in. For example, there were times when I would be in school and somebody would scatalogize me and call me inappropriate names or make some comment about my hair or my nose or something else because I was black. It was useless to get frustrated or upset because I'd go home and find myself saying, "Who am I going to tell now?" I couldn't say at this point that I hated white people because of what they've done. To say that would mean that I also hated my family.

How did you feel when you were called names by your peers?

At times I felt frustrated. But my parents always had a special knack of saying, "Yes, you're different, but that's not a bad thing. That's a good thing."

In your childhood, did anyone outside your family notice that you were black and your family was white and verbally communicate that to you?

Yes, on many occasions. My first negative experience was at my first grade open house. I was 6 or 7. My family came to school, and it seemed like everyone was saying, "Keith, where's your mom and dad?" I said that was them, right there. They looked at me and said, "Hold on—your mom and dad are white. What happened to you?" I asked them what they meant by that. To me, that was a strange question, because, as a little kid, my situation wasn't unusual. There were three other white families my family was associated with who also had adopted black children. So for someone to point that out was odd for me because I never really thought about it.

I responded to my classmates by saying, "Yes, my parents are white. And the reason they're white and I'm black is because I like to play with paint and I painted myself brown and it just stayed that way."

Describe the community in Vermont where you lived.

It was predominantly white. In my elementary and junior high school years, I was one of two African American students. Actually, the other person was really from India, so basically I was the only African American for those first eight years of school.

What about in high school? Did you come in contact with African Americans?

There were four African Americans in my high school.

Did they notice anything different about you?

No, because, again, they were in the same situation I was in. They were African Americans adopted by white families. We didn't discuss our situation. We were just black kids in white families.

As a child and adolescent, was television an everyday reality in your household?

No. My parents were very proactive in education. Everything we did was about studying. When we did watch TV, it was *Sesame Street* or the *Electric Company*. These TV shows had a lot of minority kids on them, but, as far as watching everyday TV like the *Brady Bunch*, we didn't do that very often.

During this time did you watch the news?
Yes.

Do you remember seeing violence shown on the newscast?
Yes.

In general, what was the ethnic makeup of the persons committing the violence?
African American.

Do you remember what you saw in these newscasts?
I remember one story about a riot. A group of kids were looting. Another time the power had gone out in some state, and kids were running into stores and taking things.

What went through your mind when you saw this?
I don't honestly think it affected me because I wasn't part of it.

Describe how the kids were dressed?
Baggy jeans, T-shirts. Some had dreads and were wearing baseball hats.

How did you dress?
Like a white person.

How does a white person dress?
You know, well-dressed. Jeans, nice Oxford shirt, boat shoes, argyle socks.

Would you say that you saw a difference between the youths on TV and yourself?
Oh, yes. Definitely.

Describe the difference.
They were dumb and I wasn't. That was plain and simple in my mind. They were dumb because they were doing idiotic stuff that I wouldn't do. Now whether I was saying in my mind that this was a stupid African American and I was smart because I didn't do that, I couldn't tell you that.

When in your life did you come in contact, personally, with someone who looked like the individuals you had seen on the newscasts as a child?
When I went to college in 1987.

About sixteen years later?
Yes. To me some of the African Americans appeared uneducated. They didn't seem to care about themselves, with their dreadlocks, ripped jeans, ripped T-shirts, and sweatshirts hanging half off of them. I saw African American girls wearing very short skirts and jeans with holes in inappropriate areas in the hind area.

Was it important to you to interact with any of these individuals to understand their background and experiences better?

No. I did my best to avoid them.

Why?

I might have been a little apprehensive, fearful of what they might do.

Why would you be fearful?

I thought, are they going to come up to me and decide that here's somebody who looks African American on the outside but in every other way he's not.

Where do you think this fear came from?

I'd use the word *apprehension*. To me, these people looked tough. They looked scary.

Did you have these same feelings about someone who was white and looked the way you described some of the African American students you saw?

Yes. But where I was going to school, white people didn't dress like that.

Then, the difference in dress made you apprehensive?

Yes.

In college, when you were walking toward the African American students in the hallway, what would you do?

Most of the time I just looked down at the ground when I passed them.

Why?

Because I didn't feel like speaking with them.

In the same situation, how did you respond when you were approaching white students in the hallway?

I'd say, "Hi. How are you doing?" I'd give them a cordial greeting.

I guess I felt more comfortable communicating with the white students. Identifying with the white students on campus was normal for me. I could relate to them. I had a pretty good understanding of how white people react and interact.

To understand why it was more comfortable for you to interact with white persons, I need to know the degree of exposure you had to the African American culture. Overall, did your family highlight for you those issues or interests that were embraced by primarily the African American community?

No.

Did your family expose you to the arts, specifically music and cultural experiences that expressed the African American story?

I'd say that my parents gave me literature. I also remember going to one poetry reading by Ozzie Davis. Our family would go quite regularly, with good friends of the family who also had an African American child, to watch the Harlem Globetrotters. Going to see the Harlem Globetrotters used to be a tradition for my family.

What did you think about the Harlem Globetrotters?

They played basketball . . . cool! I always got a free pencil . . . cool! That's about all.

What about going to museums with your family? Did you see African American art?

No. There are not too many museums in Vermont that have African American art.

Did your family or your schoolteachers discuss, within the context of American history, slavery and the literature and political actions that came out of that era?

Not in depth. My family only went to the point of saying that at a specific time slaves had come to America. They were sold, and later, through the Emancipation Proclamation, they were set free. But that was about all they said.

Actually, Rhonda, I'm glad you mentioned that. When I was in seventh grade I had a social studies teacher, Mr. Scott Campotelli, who was a newsman as well as a history teacher. When he was planning a unit about the slaves, he felt compelled to pull me aside because I was the only African American student in the class and in the school. He told me we were going to discuss slavery and that he didn't want me to feel upset or concerned, meaning that I shouldn't be scared. I guess that experience was my greatest lesson about the plight of the African American.

Did you connect yourself with the plight of the African American?

Definitely not.

Why not?

Because African Americans are always depicted on TV as a group in need, a group that is always looking for a handout . . . and I wasn't raised that way. I can never recollect a time—whether I was a youngster dependent on my parents for support or even now—when I begged for a handout. I know that I've never told somebody that I need something just because I'm African American and "you owe me." So no, I wouldn't even group myself with those folks.

Today, what would you say are the major issues for the African American community?

I think there are issues in the area of equality. I think that in general African Americans, when seeking jobs of a higher status, have to work at it ten times harder than the average white person to get the same amount of recognition. In some aspects, as African Americans, we need to address our financial status in a way that supports one another. We need to instill in one another the work ethic, specifically that we should not be lazy and expect a handout but should endeavor to improve our station in life.

Things like welfare don't really concern me at all. I think that at this time welfare impacts people regardless of their ethnicity. One can find, figuratively speaking, ten white people on welfare, ten Koreans, ten Vietnamese, or ten Chinese people all on welfare. So I don't think that it's a situation unique to the African American.

Keith, at what point did you begin to formulate this view?

In 1992, after I married. Before that, I made a conscious effort not to associate with the riff-raff. By that I mean anybody who didn't look pleasant or was in rough situations.

You mention your wife as someone who has helped you address race issues and understands your struggles. She is also someone who takes pride in her Haitian heritage. As a father, is it important that your daughter be raised in the African American community?

It's important that she's exposed to many communities, not just the African American community. We'll do our part to ensure that aspects of the African American culture are there for her to explore herself.

Why is exposing your daughter to the African American culture important?

That's a part of who she is. Cultural influence needs to be positive. I won't let my daughter listen to Snoop Doggie Dogg in my house or Criss Cross and say this is African American. No, that music won't come into my house. But Pattie LaBelle, Diana Ross, Toni Braxton—they might come in here; you know, folks that would consider themselves to be African American and successful.

I want my daughter to look at positive African American people and say that here are people I can be if I just set my mind to it. This applies to any ethnic persons who are positive.

Was there a specific influence in your life that made you acknowledge to yourself that, "Yes, I'm also African American and must invest and take pride in my own community"?

Yes. Again, this had a lot to do with my relationship with my wife. My transformation occurred in part because of what she does. She works in the field of education, specifically with minority affairs. So through daily communications with her and seeing some of the issues she has dealt with,

I've been more willing and open to ask myself if this is something I can learn to identify with. To be able to help and support her, I have to understand at some level that we are all in the same boat . . . we are all going through the same thing. So after I married her I realized that if she was going to help these folks, I needed to support her and understand the people she's trying to help. I need to consider myself a part of them.

Also, since I've been working in the ministry since 1992, reaching out to the African American community, I know that to be an effective minister and for people to lend credibility to what I am teaching, they need to believe that I am an African American pastor who can identify with their struggles.

Looking at your personal struggles, have you knowingly ever experienced discrimination because of your color?

Yes. Right before I moved to Michigan this year, I was applying for an employment opportunity and I called the organization on the phone regarding this particular position. I was introduced to the director of the office I would be working in who also was an African American. He came right out and asked me, not wanting to be rude, if I was white or black. Interestingly, when I heard him speak, he sounded white. Anyway, I told him I was black. He told me that I sounded white. I said, "Isn't that strange, so do you." He continued by saying that I was coming into an office where folks don't like black people, especially "educated black people." This is where the discrimination came in. He said that if I were to call the military base I should only talk with him and that he would interview me over the phone so that the first time people would meet me and actually know I was an African American would be on my first day of work. This director was purposely excluding information so people from the start wouldn't know who I was.

How did that make you feel?

I felt angry. I still feel angry because I couldn't say that, yes, I sound white, but I'm an African American who knows a lot about my job and has innovative ideas.

Was that a lonely experience?

No! Other African American professionals go through the same exact experience, especially if they've been adopted and raised in an all-white family.

Did you think it was unfair that people had this view about you because of your color?

Yes, because they didn't get to know the real me first.

In college you saw African American students. You indicated that you intentionally avoided them. Did you ever think it was wrong that you also had a confined view of these persons without getting to know them first?

At the time I wasn't thinking about how they would feel. I thought about what I needed to do to survive that particular situation and avoid an altercation.

What did family gatherings look like at your house?

Have you ever seen a chocolate chip cookie with only one chip in it? That's what my family looked like.

Did you ever wish there were more chocolate chips in the cookie?

Definitely not. I'm the type of person who loves to stand out and be an individual. I'm different, and therefore I'll have a significant impact on the people I come across.

The National Association of Black Social Workers has taken a strong position against transracial adoption. In most cases they say that transracial adoption does not expose the child to his or her ethnicity. What do you think?

I think that the black social workers who do these studies have been raised in South Carolina or in the heart of Mississippi at a time when an African American was strung up every other day. They ate their "fat backs," their "greens," and their "turkey knuckles." They are saying that this is the African American tradition at its finest. If I, as an African American or as a child raised in a white family, was not privy to that, and therefore am in some ways less than a black person, I totally disagree. For me, my experiences and my family have been exceptionally wonderful.

By the National Association of Black Social Workers saying, "this is what defines an African American child and this is what is going to stand in their way whether they are successful or not," is really simplistic. If they are telling me that because I, as an African American child who wasn't raised in these areas and didn't eat these foods, am going to be a flat-out "numbskull," unable to do anything right, than I'm going to disagree totally. Eating the traditional black food of the South isn't the "end all" and "be all" of being black.

But isn't partaking of these traditional foods a part of what makes up the black community?

It's a part of the black tradition, but it doesn't determine one's success or failure.

What made your family wonderful?

My family encouraged and supported me to achieve goals that were positive and that I thought were important. My parents were willing to sit down with me and listen to what was going on in my life.

What would you change in your adoptive family?

I wish the whole situation was different and that my adoptive parents were my biological parents.

Why?

That's a hard question. I know I was willing to know what my biological parents were like, what their status was. But because I didn't know, there was an assertive effort on my part to make my adoptive parents be the spitting image of my biological parents. I wanted my biological parents to be just as successful as my adoptive parents.

What do you know about your biological parents?

Based on what I've read, my biological mother was a "nondesirable" and had three other kids besides me, all girls. She was on public assistance. My father was a mechanic. I had a lot of cousins. My biological mother decided that she was at a point in her life where she could not handle raising four kids. She decided it was time to put this one, me, up for adoption.

How did that make you feel?

Real angry. How did she decide that she was going to put me up for adoption instead of one of her other children? What was her life like to have had so many kids and not be married? Why didn't my biological father step in and say, "No, don't put him up for adoption." Or if that was her desire, why didn't he say, "Hon, don't put this child up for adoption; let me raise him as my son."

Did you think of yourself as being unwanted after knowing this about your biological parents?

No. I felt angry. There was never a time in my life when I felt unwanted.

Define anger for me.

Anger as in being frustrated. If you watch the *Brady Bunch* or *The Cosby Show*, you see African American families with two parents, being very stable. From what I know about my biological family, it wasn't a stable situation. It wasn't a loving two-parent home environment. It was a struggle. My frustration and my anger came from not being like the families on TV.

Why am I as successful as I am right now having had adoptive parents who are white? Had I been raised in my African American family with just a single mom, I might be on drugs. I might be in jail. Who knows where

I might be? Why couldn't I have been just as successful in the environment I was born into. That's where the frustration and anger come in.

How do you identify yourself? Do you consider yourself black or an African American?

I identify myself as a black person. Were I to identify myself as an African American, I'd be saying that I believe I have current roots in Africa, that that's where my tradition comes from, that's where I was born.

The truth is that I was born in the United States of America and there was no Africa about it. Therefore I don't consider myself to be an African American nor do I use that term to identify myself.

Black is what I am. That's my color. If I say that I'm an African American, then I'm saying that I believe strongly in the history and culture of the African American and that I want to celebrate that and accentuate it in me.

Being African is a wonderful thing. It's just something I choose not to accentuate. It's not that I don't like it. I really don't understand it. Some would argue that our lineage is from Africa. But I don't believe that I have to identify myself as an African American because of it.

In fact, when it comes to the question of history, what do I know about Africa? All I know is what I was told in school. The sum total of the African American history was that way back then, there was a people in Africa, and white people came and brought those people back to the United States as slaves. There's your history.

Have you ever been interested in understanding more about countries in Africa?

Not particularly. It's not something I've missed.

What do you think about this America?

I think America is a wonderful place. I'm glad to be here.

You are—

Black!

Black. You aren't mixed. You cannot cross over. You definitely have African features. What does being black in America mean for you?

Being raised in a white family, being black meant being different. Not different in a negative way, though. I can probably count on one hand the number of times someone looked at me in disgust or said something derogatory because of the way I looked. For me black is simply a color. It happens to be the color of my skin, whereas my parents who raised me, their color is white.

What do you say about black males who live in this country and experience discrimination because of the color of their skin? For example, there are black males who tell of not being able to hail a taxi in Washington, D.C., and are suspiciously followed in stores and asked to present identification just because of their skin color.

Those are experiences I've never had. I've never found it difficult to get a taxi. No one looks at me when I go into a department store. When I've been in the minority as a black person, people have treated me fine. So if you want me to discuss the plight of the African American male, my testimony and perceptions are going to be quite different from other people's. I haven't experienced my blackness like they have.

What does "blackness" mean to you?

It's just a color. If you were to see me and my family walking down the street, the only thing you'd say is that I look different than they do. But in terms of mannerisms and communication and the way we express our feelings, we're one and the same. We're very similar. Folks tell me that even though I'm adopted, I act more like my dad and talk more like my dad than his own biological son.

There is also the concern, in general, that you don't experience the lifestyle that so many black Americans experience. In other words, you've basically been stripped of your culture and your heritage because of the family with whom you live.

Let me ask you this question. When I was the "African American child" who was given up by his mother who slept around town and was "easy as the day is long," when folks were looking for a home for me, why didn't any African Americans step up to the challenge? So, really, the reason I was stripped of my culture was because no one in my culture wanted to give me a home or a chance.

If they are alleging that I was stripped of my culture, it wasn't because a white family was willing to give me a home and the benefits of education and all those things that go into "life, liberty, and the pursuit of happiness." It was because there was no African American family, no black family, that would step up to the plate and say, "Regardless of our situation, we are going to give this young man a chance, just so he can be down home."

And there's another aspect to this. If they are alleging that because I was raised by a white family that I'm not truly black, that gets me fired up, too. I submit to you that I'm probably more black than they'll ever be.

Why?

If you are raised as an "African American" in an "African American" culture, your perceptions and beliefs are never completely challenged. You aren't forced to make your own way in society. But if you're the "black sheep" (pardon the pun) who is placed in a society and culture where you are unique, then you have to confront reality and admit that you are different. Not only am I different from the people around me, but I'm also different from my own family.

The question is: How do I take the darkness of my skin and fit it into my light-colored family. So when you ask me what being black means to me, I say that it means making a way out of no way. This is an education you can't get as a black individual raised in a black family.

Case in point: If a black child comes home from school and says to his black mother, "Johnnie called me a name in school today," she may say, "Oh, he's just a cracker and an uneducated person." Johnnie's white mommy and daddy would handle the situation in the same way. But when I go home to my mom and dad, who are white, and say that somebody at school called me a name, my mom would say, "Well, lets think about this. How did it make you feel?" We'd work through it that way, intellectually, and we'd try to be forgiving. She'd ask me, "Keith, now how are you going to deal with it and work through it and press on toward success?"

Is that how you developed your self-esteem and confidence?

Oh, yes. Here's something the studies may not tell you. At least two of my friends are black and have been raised by black people. In terms of education, these friends of mine were functioning and performing way below me, a black person raised in a white family. So are you going to tell me that I've lost my blackness and my tradition because I've gone on, from an educational point of view, to become very successful? I don't think I'm giving up very much. I refuse to believe that every time someone questions me about something that the only reason is because of the color of my skin. Maybe I had broccoli in my teeth or a scratch on my face. I'm not saying that there aren't people who would look at me and say that because I'm black they don't like me. But that's not everybody. Every time that we're challenged isn't simply because we are black.

You are a black preacher reaching out to the black community. How do you and your ministry connect to people with whom you don't share in their struggles? What is the commonality?

I am a black preacher reaching out to a community. It doesn't matter whether they are black, white, or Asian. I'm just reaching out to the community as God has called me to do. At the church where I work now, the pastor has said that he wants to focus on the African American community. How do I deal with that community? Not very well.

Explain.

I find it difficult to deal with them because, from my perspective, they are very "simple" in their mentality.

What do you mean by "simple"?

I don't believe they have the cognitive ability to understand a situation beyond thinking, "They don't like me because I'm black" or "I'm not successful because a white person had authority over me and has kept me down."

The black community is very diverse. *What type of people within the black community are you reaching out to?*

Most of them are on welfare. Most of them come from "broken homes"—single parents, the father in jail, mom trying to make a home for her children.

In your opinion, are these people trying to better themselves? Are they trying to expand their minds so as to develop both mentally and spiritually?

Based on my own interaction and experiences with them, primarily youths, I would say no. More often than not, these youths are standing with their hands out, saying, "What can you give me for free?" "How can I get out of this situation as easily as possible?"

What do you think fuels this type of behavior?

It's what they've seen their parents and other adults do. The welfare system for blacks is a never-ending cycle of dependency. The system defines their lives. It tells them that based on a certain amount of money, this is where they can live—and it's not going to be the Ritz—and these are the clothes you can afford—and it's not going to be clothes from Bloomingdale's.

So when kids see their parents standing on welfare lines and getting free money and then going home and sitting on their butts all day, not trying to get off welfare, the kids think that if it works for dad and mom, then it will work for me. I believe this is the mentality we are dealing with and it's one I don't understand. One thing my parents always told me was that I had to work.

Clearly there is a difference between the way you were raised and the way the individuals you are speaking about were raised. But I sense there is a deepness to your perspective that allows you to find ways to overcome challenges. How do you convey this to other people, like those you are ministering to?

I work from the perspective that regardless of your color, your socio-economic background, or your current situation, you are lovable and are capable. Old folks used to say, "As long as you put your hand to the plow, you gonna be all right." Since I am a minister and working for a pastor, I hope God is in there somewhere. The bottom line is, I believe we must teach youths that their life is not so much to make themselves happy but to make God happy and honor who He is. The way you live your life down here will have a direct impact on how God will treat you up there.

It's no longer a black or white issue. It's a question of either living saved and free or living sinned and bound and ending up in hell? This is the way we should relate to people.

My education and my success comes from putting my hand to the plow, so to speak. Yes, it turned out that the people who opened their home to me and made a way for me in life were white. But I still could have decided to sit on my butt all day. I said to myself, here's the situation I'm in. Here are all the opportunities and benefits available to me. Let's see how far I can go. Some people may say that the white system perverted me, but I say that I perverted the white system.

We've talked about some challenging issues you've confronted having been adopted into a white family. When the discussion becomes intense, you seem to begin to feel uncomfortable and become angry . . .

If I get angry it means I'm impassioned about an issue. I want people to understand that emotionally, verbally, physically, I am 100 percent involved. That's what anger does for me. And sometimes anger has encouraged me to do a bit of searching, to find my roots, to discover what my environment was like and the place I was taken from.

What would you like to say to opponents and researchers of transracial adoption?

If you see pictures of me and my family, I'm healthy. I'm well adjusted. I look like one of the family. But before you can genuinely write about the experiences of an African American child raised by a white family, you need to talk to some of us first or you need to be in the situation yourself.

Words to potential adoptive parents?

Examine your motivation for adopting a child. Do you want to adopt an "at risk" child because you want to give that child a home? If that's your desire, then adopt the child. But if you are trying to specifically adopt an African American child because you want to make amends with your own community, then don't do it! You would be doing it for the wrong reason, as a way to ease your conscience.

I would especially encourage black families who can afford to adopt black children to do so. I believe that a child needs to have a good quality of life. I mean that parents should have money, provide quality time with their child, and discipline their child appropriately. Showing love to a child is paramount.

Words to children?

Children today need at least a college degree, preferably a higher education. Children need to listen and respect their parents because in that they learn respect for people who are placed in authority over them. Children need to have good communication skills. They need to know how to express their feelings.

About adoption?

Adoption is a good thing whether you are the unique individual in the family or whether you look like everyone else in the family. It means that the good Lord is looking out for you. He has something important He wants you to do. If you are adopted, take advantage of every event that comes into your life. Use these experiences as a learning opportunity.

Unfortunately, some look on adoption as a frustrating experience, because they think, "I was adopted because somebody didn't want me." I know I was adopted because somebody *wanted* me. Out of 150 other kids to choose from, my parents chose me. For me, anger and frustration are important emotions to experience through this whole adoption process. It is the only way people will know that being adopted has had a meaningful impact on me, that I'm not just going through the motions.

Who is Keith?

I am a person who was adopted and has gone on to achieve success. I believe one needs to do his best. As long as you do your best, you'll have no problem with me. But the minute you slack off, there's going to be some hell to pay with Keith Bigelow, Reverend Keith Bigelow, Daddy and Husband.

What makes Keith continue to get up in the morning?

Endeavoring to be a good husband to my wife. Wanting to be the best dad I can be to my daughter by instilling values and discipline in her. I think that knowing that God has a purpose and a call on my life moves me every day, calling me to be the best I can be.

The quintessential thing that gets me up every day is that Keith Bigelow needs to rise up and be the best he can be just for himself.

Keith, but are you black?

Yes, I am black—and make no mistake about it! I can go to the store and get my "greens" and boil 'em. I can go get my chicken and I can barbecue. I can use my euphonics when I need to or my vernacular black English Ebonics when I want to. But I can also assume a businessman's mentality and speak like someone who has an education and wants to be successful. I am someone who has power, and I'm not afraid to use it.

On a spiritual level, how do you define yourself?

I define myself as a child of God who is working hard to honor God—plain and simple. I do the things I do, not solely for the sake of my family or for my career but to fulfill the specific obligations and responsibilities God has given me. If my family is healthy and is getting the things they need to make it in this world then that is just the by-product or benefit of my honoring God.

What does it mean to honor God?

It means doing the best you can with what you have. *Doing your best!* There's no "half-stepping."

You've listened to the old Negro spiritual "Ain't Gonna Let Nobody Turn Me Around"? And you see black people who are on welfare or in a perpetual state of being dependent on somebody and saying that "because this white person has put me here, I can't get any further." Don't tell me that they are remembering their history. Don't tell me that they are celebrating their "blackness."

What they are saying is that not only am I letting someone "turn me around," but I am letting someone keep me down. We need to give our people the knowledge to be successful, not the message that they are in bondage.

Daniel Mennega

AUSTIN, TEXAS
APRIL 1998

At my worst, I resent the community that demands I deny either side. The truth is, the white community has generally done its part to allow me (sometimes forcing me through prejudice) to explore my identity as a black person. It is the black community that resents me for exploring my white ethnic heritage but then turns away because I'm different.

Throughout his life, Daniel Mennega fought against the confines of being labeled "black" or "white." He says that he wants to be identified by what he thinks about and what he likes to do. To him, his identity includes more than his ethnicity and skin color.

Daniel Mennega, a biracial 29 year old raised in Sioux Center, Iowa, was adopted into a Dutch family as an infant. Both of his parents emigrated from the Netherlands and were in their thirties when they adopted Daniel. They wanted to provide a home for a child who otherwise would not have one. Though as a young boy Daniel was not exposed to the African American community or heritage, he believes that the love and consistency his parents showed him gave him the confidence to explore his own ethnic identity and interests later in life.

In the early 1970s Sioux Center, Iowa, where Daniel grew up, had a population of about four thousand people. At that time the community was predominantly white and Protestant. Family and community were cherished. To Daniel, Sioux Center symbolized the value of a small college town atmosphere. It was a place where many of his childhood friends attended the same church and went to the same schools. It was where he felt comfortable.

In his interview, Daniel mentions always being aware of his skin color, particularly during his adolescent years when race issues were introduced in conversations. He refers to a book by William Faulkner, *Go Down Moses,* where a character who is biracial comes to terms with his two different races. In Daniel's own journey, he has come to appreciate that he is mixed, black and white. Paradoxically, he finds that the definition others use to determine the validity of one's "black identity" does not recognize him or his experiences.

Daniel has four sisters, one of whom is adopted and biracial. Born in Grand Rapids, Michigan, in 1969, Daniel earned a bachelor's degree from Dordt College in Iowa and went on to pursue additional course work in graduate school. Currently, he is working as a technical writer for a company in Texas and plans to travel overseas. Daniel maintains close relationships with his father, who is a professor of biology, and his mother, who is a bookstore assistant.

You've been raised in a white family. To draw a picture of what that experience was like for you, let us start by your telling me where you were born and when you were adopted.

According to my birth certificate, in 1969 I was adopted from Grand Rapids, Michigan. The certificate also listed the home of my adoptive parents as being in Sioux Center, Iowa, the northwestern part of the state. So they were living there at the time of my adoption. My parents then took me there, and I grew up in the small town of Sioux Center. My earliest recollection of the population was four thousand, but since then it has increased to about fifty-five hundred people. It is definitely a small town and a rural community.

Do you have any siblings who were also adopted transracially?

Yes. Her name is René. She is biracial. In all I have four sisters. They range in age from 27 to 36. And I'm 29. My sister who is adopted is directly above me. My sister Michelle is younger than me by a year. She and I are the closest, mainly because we played a lot together before going to school while the rest of the kids were at school. And starting in the eighth grade, she was in my class. She skipped the seventh grade. We were in the same crowd in a small school, and we knew each other's friends.

When you were growing up in Sioux Center, were you exposed to African American children?

No.

Describe what it was like for you to grow up in a small, rural, white community?

I found it pretty typical of a small midwestern town. For me, growing up was pretty normal as far as the activities I took part in. I went to school. I hung out with normal kids. I played sports at recess. I got into trouble just like everybody else. I had a lot of friends.

Did you believe at that time that you were accepted by the kids in the community?

I have always been aware that I was adopted. And so my racial heritage was always obvious to me. I don't know, though, if that influenced me all that much in the early years. I certainly didn't feel that my skin color was of any hindrance to my friends.

As a family, what did you do together?

My family is very family-oriented. We have always been big about eating meals together. My father and mother stressed that kind of thing. You come home for supper. You are up for breakfast. Growing up, we had family night on Friday nights. We'd play games. I'd look forward to that quite a bit, especially before I was able to go out. This is before I was 13. We went on family vacations every summer, usually to Michigan because we had family there. The typical vacation was to drive to Michigan in a four-door station wagon.

Regarding family traditions, this is a question that has been asked of me regularly and maybe has some validity. What kinds of foods did your family eat?

My parents emigrated from the Netherlands. So most of the food we ate was traditional European food. That meant a lot of potatoes, a lot of corn, a lot of meat. That kind of stuff. Square-meal type food. "Stick to your ribs" food.

We "got" the meal plan down. Now tell me about the discipline plan within your family.

We had spankings, scoldings, groundings. I don't know if there was much else that deviated from what you might expect. I had my mouth washed out with soap.

Would you agree that you felt you were part of your family?
Definitely.

Did you tend to navigate toward your sister René because she was biracial?

No. During adolescence we had some disagreements because we were close in age. I would also antagonize my sister Annette quite a bit.

How did your classmates treat you? And did you interact well with them?

Yes. And consistently year to year. But the classes above me thought I had an attitude problem, and I got into fights over that.

What caused them to believe you had an attitude problem?

I think I was "lippy." I think I felt at the time that I was being treated a bit differently by them. But at the time I never connected it to race. Occasionally, somebody would call me "nigger" or something like that.

At the school you attended?

Right. In a scuffle or something like that. At the time I never connected that to the possibility of why they may be treating me like that.

When did you notice this? What grade were you in?

I would say early junior high. In fifth, sixth grade.

Would you say that it was during the fifth or sixth grade that you first noticed this type of reaction?

No. That was the first time I realized the tension. There were moments during my childhood when I was aware of some people's negative perceptions of me, of my ethnicity.

Let me ask you this: If I saw you, would I know that you are African American based on your physical features or skin color?

You'd definitely say I was African American. I'm light-skinned. My hair is curly, although now I've cut it short.

Can you pinpoint the approximate time when you noticed that race was an issue for you?

It wasn't until something negative happened that it occurred to me that people made my color an issue. I was always aware of my racial difference. Yet, growing up, if people treated me differently, I never associated that behavior to my skin color. But any time a race discussion would come up, then the racial difference would become a lot more acute. I don't recall any discomfort.

So when you were at home and saw the visual similarities between your parents and their biological children, did you feel different or separated from them because you didn't share their physical traits?

No. I know that may sound strange, but I never have. I think part of the reason is that I have always been aware of my being adopted. So when my sisters would talk about eye color, for example, it wouldn't affect me negatively. We'd talk about how their eye color came from Mom's side, or this or that. And it wouldn't take much effort for us to acknowledge that my eyes are whatever color they are because I was adopted.

What explanation did your parents give you about why they chose to adopt you?

It was put to me this way: Somebody loved me and wanted me to be well taken care of because that person wasn't able to take care of me, and so I was adopted. My adoptive parents told me consistently that they loved me, but they didn't emphasize the fact that I was adopted. I think they mentioned I was adopted as a way to preempt any abandonment ideas I might have and address any concern I might have of why somebody gave me up. My parents' response to why I was placed for adoption was always because my biological parents were not able to take care of me and that they wanted me to have a better place to be raised. I bought it then and I'm happy for it now, no matter what the circumstances were.

That's a beautiful way to phrase it. Essentially, you felt confident within your family.

Very much. I don't know if that was because of the attention I received from my parents, being the only boy in the family.

So the story goes that you are having a "normal" life with your family.

Yes, normal. But even so, I think there were undertones that showed me I was perceived by others as different. My family is also somewhat eccentric. Here you have a family in this all-white, Dutch, middle-class community of Christians, all of whom sort of know one another and do the same things. And then you have this professor, my father, who's come in and is also Dutch and has emigrated from the Netherlands as recently as the mid-1950s, and then all these kids, some of them not so typical. It was my perception that people thought our family was a little odd.

There is a cultural difference between the Dutch influence from the Netherlands and that of the Americans within your community who had Dutch ancestry generations removed. In your own home, then, did you see Dutch influence in addition to the traditional foods?

All the time. I am completely influenced by it and informed by the Dutch tradition.

Was your family open in allowing you to discuss your feelings, particularly if those feelings dealt with race?

Not really. We seldom had discussions about "blackness." I don't think that my parents were politically aware of many contemporary black issues. They weren't interested in schooling me in black history or black pride movements. So it never was a topic I'd bring up to my parents for discussion. Yet, they provided me with the self-awareness I needed to investigate these things for myself.

I want to go back to when you were in fifth grade. You indicated that the older kids thought you had an attitude problem. During that time, was the fact that you were adopted interracially an issue for you?

No, it wasn't an issue or something I struggled with. When I was 18, I was curious to find out what the circumstances were surrounding my adoption. It so happened that my interest in finding my biological parents coincided with a time when my sister, René, who is also interracially adopted, was having difficulty herself with issues that largely related to an identity crisis because of her race. She was struggling with this and went on a big hunt to find her biological parents. Fortunately things worked out, but during that time there was a lot of pain—especially for René and my parents. So at that time I decided I could wait. I didn't want to miscommunicate anything to my adoptive parents suggesting their inadequacies or failings.

As René was going through her struggles, could you relate to her feelings?

Yes, definitely. But I was conflicted. I felt guilty because she was trying to answer questions that I didn't have. Why didn't I have these questions? Was I somehow not thinking intensely enough?

What questions came out of your sister's struggle that you didn't ask yourself?

How does she fit in? How does she fit in in Iowa? Where is her community? Where does she belong? She wanted to identify more with her "blackness," in a community outside herself.

When you look at your own self-confidence, where do you think it came from?

I had plenty of avenues to gain self-confidence. There were a lot of things I could do that made me feel good about myself. I was a swimmer and an athlete. I also had a lot of friends. My parents supported nearly all my interests, socially and academically.

When you chose to attend a predominately white, small liberal arts college in Iowa, did that make you uncomfortable?

No, mainly because I grew up in the town where the college is located. I knew the professors. I was comfortable very early on. And being among a bunch of white Protestant Dutch kids was nothing new to me. That wasn't a difficult transition at all. In fact, I felt a sense of confidence that I knew the campus and knew what was going on.

Standing in the middle of a white Dutch college as an African American man, were you in conflict about where your loyalties were?

Yes. There were times of confusion when I asked myself what was going on? I never felt compelled to struggle with it because I was aware of it.

Let me read something to you that I identified with at that time. This is from William Faulkner. He's describing a character, Lucas, from his book *Go Down Moses*. Lucas is biracial. He has some of the plantation owner's blood in him. Yet it wasn't that Lucas made capital of his white blood, but just the contrary.

> It was as if he were not only impervious to that blood, he was indifferent to it. He didn't even need to strive with it. He didn't even have to bother to defy it. He resisted it simply by being the composite of the two races which made him, simply by possessing it. Instead of being at once the battleground and victim of the two strains, he was a vessel, durable, ancestryless, nonconductive, in which the toxin and its anti stalemated one another seethless, unrumored in the outside air.

That is powerful!

Yes. It is a good passage. I identify with that in a number of ways, especially that he didn't need to struggle with being biracial. I've never been indifferent to it, but I also never felt the need to claim loyalty or to strive to be a part of either community. As it turns out, most of my dealings have been with white communities. People have said to me that I'm not black because I don't "act black." To me, that's completely misguided. Anyone who's been adopted and has lived in a town like mine is going to be aware of his or her race. Growing up in my town, I was considered to be black. Yet, in metropolitan areas such as Washington, D.C., I'm viewed as biracial or even white. In Texas, people sometimes think I'm Latino. When I go to New Orleans, I fit in with the general skin tone there. As far as being "ancestryless," that strikes some truth for me. I don't feel like either race is dominant.

What part of your ethnicity makes you proud?

I'm proud that I'm both black and white. I have a unique vantage.

You say that you take pride in being black and white. Does it concern you that you are separated from or not part of the black community, almost as if part of your identity is missing?

I consider myself part of the black community. I have not separated myself from that community. But I feel that unless I somehow "show" or "prove" that I am part of the black community, the black community doesn't recognize that I am part of it.

Is it legitimate to say that because you've been raised in a white family and a white community that you have been "stripped" from the black community? In other words, has the black community lost you?

Yes, I've been "stripped" from the black community because of my situation. The problem is, I think the idea of what actually defines "blackness" is too narrow a concept.

Maybe the issue is whether you fit within the defined lines of what "blackness" is to a given group of people.

At my worst, I resent the community that demands I deny either side. The truth is, the white community has generally done its part to allow me (sometimes forcing me through prejudice) to explore my identity as a black person. It is the black community that resents me for exploring my white ethnic heritage but then turns away because I'm different.

To what do you attribute that?

I think there are false criteria set up for blackness. It has to do with all sorts of things, like socioeconomic status as well as the political spectrum.

You acknowledge your whiteness and your blackness within yourself. In society these communities are still segregated. How do you then reconcile the two worlds within you and those same black and white worlds outside of you that are so visibly different?

It's not an issue from day to day because of the community I live in, Austin, Texas, a college town. That community encourages individuals to be their own unique person. Or it could be because of the activities I participate in.

What is more important to you, being an individual or making it a priority to fit in within the black community or white community holistically?

Based on how I've been living, my individuality is more important to me. This is generally because I'm not willing to make the sacrifices necessary to be fully accepted by the black community. My individuality also makes the white community view me with confusion. So I'd rather be an individual as far as this issue goes.

What sacrifices do you think you would have to make to be part of the black community?

What I do know is that right now I'm doing what I want to, and it would take something different for me to be included in the black community. It would take a whole different me. My primary focus is not "how can I get in with my own people." I'm drawn to the things I want in life and the things I want to do.

What is it that you want in life?

I want to have done a lot of things by the time I'm dead.

Sounds fair to me.

I believe that I'm good at a lot of different things professionally and socially. So I want to aspire in those areas. I want to travel. I want to get married at some point.

Name some places where you want to travel.

The short list is probably Cairo, Egypt, part of North Africa, different parts of Morocco. Also Spain, Tibet . . .

Why those places?

My parents were risk takers and went off and did things on their own. They immigrated to America when they were 17 and 18. Maybe they passed something on to me in that way. My curiosity, though, is the main factor. I want to travel. How this develops, I don't know.

What were some of the values your parents instilled in you?

My parents are very religious, and I've always been informed by my religious upbringing. Knowing the difference between right and wrong was a central issue. I was instilled with a good work ethic, mostly Christian values including love and kindness.

I think my curiosity came out of a sort of restlessness. But it's a restlessness that I'm comfortable with as opposed to being anxious. The summer after my freshman year in college, three of my friends and I moved for a summer to Massachusetts to work at an amusement park. For me, that didn't come out of the need to leave Sioux Center. It was an opportunity to see what the next place offered. Although now that I live in Austin, I don't plan to leave right away because Austin is an incredible town.

Ethnically, can you "guesstimate" what the makeup of Austin is?

I'd say the town is pretty well-balanced. It has a traditional demarcation, with the black community located east of the highway. As far as the places I'd like to go to, they're about as diverse as I'd like them to be.

Are you implying that there is a ceiling on the number of black people or white people that you want to be around socially?

No. I've always "dug" my uniqueness, the fact that I look different and so on. For me, it's a point of pride. However, the places I go to have plenty of African Americans. That makes me sound like I have a racial quota in mind, but I don't. I go where I like the music, the food. I hang out with people who stimulate me. I don't know what you think that says about me.

That you prefer to be seen as unique, whether in white or black crowds.

Right. Even in high school, if I was feeling lonely, I "trained" myself to think that I was unique.

I believe that I have a lot of unique ideas, that I have a clear connection to my thoughts and a strong sense of self-awareness. That feeling is stimulating.

Why do you use the word "lonely"?

Even though I had childhood friends and friends in high school, I never really clicked with any one specific group. I generally hung out in a number of different circles, like the journalism crowd. I hung out with a lot of athletes. Yet, since childhood, I've never had what you'd call a best friend. I never really opened up to anybody. So there were times I'd feel lonely. And then I'd romanticize that feeling and choose to view it as being unique.

It's almost as if you can have good friends and adapt to different situations but somewhere inside there's a sense that those around you do not see through your lens or understand you completely.

Right. They can't get a handle on me. And I still feel that way.

On the one hand, you embrace that feeling but then, on the other hand, you want somebody to understand the core of who you are?

Yes, absolutely. There are definitely two sides to my feelings. I'd say the dominant one is, "This is what I like." I don't want to be pigeonholed. In fact, sometimes I resist that possibility. But I don't feel like I'm a chameleon just because I'm doing my own thing and it so happens that my thing intersects a number of other people's things.

A hypothetical question. There are two confined boxes. One defines whiteness, the other defines blackness. In your experience, what criteria have others held up to you that defines the box you belong in?

Actually, both white and black people have said the same things to me. A white friend I have at work is pretty open about this and tells me that I'm not black.

What is his reasoning?

Ironically, he says I didn't go to a certain high school like he did in Austin that is predominately black and has a reputation of being "rough-cut."

How did he explain why he went there, being white?

He associated it with his being poor. He has this idea of blackness as those blacks who go to that school and are poor and inarticulate. I find this to be insulting, as it should be to the black community. What's interesting is that I get the same sentiment from African Americans. They also typecast me. Some African Americans say I'm articulate and that I "talk white," and therefore I'm not "down" with anything they are passionate about. They separate me from the black community because, according to them, I don't act black, mainly in my mannerisms and my choices in pop culture—petty stuff—and also because I'm not physically dark enough. I don't know if I could define blackness. The task disarms me.

Is it important to you that the two worlds, black and white, reconcile with each other?

Yes, I definitely think racial harmony is important.

Why?

Let me tackle a few big reasons: first, there'd be fewer deaths; second, a lot of people would have better living conditions; and, third, there'd be generally healthy and benevolent feelings between a lot of good people, where now there is hate.

When you look at the misconceptions whites have toward blacks, and vice versa, would you agree that it is partly because people in these groups tend to put themselves and others in a predefined box?

I see that as the whole problem. I'm not saying people shouldn't have a desire to define themselves and their community. I just don't think it always has to be in terms of differences. Personally, I get mad when someone disputes my blackness. I guess if I extrapolate my feelings of why I get angry, it's because the mind-set of such people is so narrow.

I agree. Narrowness is not a good thing when it prevents you from becoming your own person and becoming an asset to society. Is there a plan that you can propose to minimize the race conflict in this society? I think that's the trillion dollar question.

My route is to travel and explore who I am. I don't have a detailed plan for resolving the race conflict in America.

Through the process of exploring who you are, are you accepting your ethnicities?

Yes.

So you don't feel yourself running away from black folks, given the fact that you spend more of your time interacting with persons in the white community?

No. No. Even though the way my life has taken me hasn't included making decisions that have intentionally moved me drastically closer to a predominately black community. That's never been a high priority for me. Nor do I make choices so I can ingratiate myself into white society.

And you feel good about that?

I feel fine about it. Sometimes I feel guilty, but I know that's false guilt. I don't buy it.

Daniel, based on your experiences living in your adoptive family, what are your views on transracial adoption?

I think it all depends on the parents. But if you're placed in the right situation, the experience is going to be better than ever. I have no regrets of having been adopted into a family whose racial makeup is different than mine.

Out of that experience, your personality and outlook continued to form. Was it easy?

I love my family. I love the way I was brought up. And I also think that the way I am now, my personality, my goals, the way I view life, came out of kind of a struggle—but it was a fun struggle for me.

When in your life did that struggle heighten?

In high school. I'd attribute that to how I positioned myself in school. Essentially, I was in the inside of a lot of circles but never really connected to them. So I started being myself—it was freedom.

Struggle to me brings out a whole lot of honesty in oneself. Would you say that you look at your experience of being adopted into your family as positive overall?

Absolutely.

If you heard someone express the concern that it is a disservice to your community that you were raised in a white family, what would your response be?

A disservice to whom?

The black community.

Oh, because I'm being usurped by the white community?

You got it.

I think that's an invalid fear. If their concerns are that I'll dilute the black talent base because I was adopted into a white family or that now I'll be a white person, too, that's not true.

Are you saying that you, personally, can be black in a white family and that you don't become white or take on a European mind-set?

Yes. At least not predominantly. As I said before, my blackness was made known to me as a positive thing. My sense is that often in the general black community, individuals are first made aware of their blackness as a strike against them. In my early experience, I never had that introduction to my blackness. Therefore, I don't view my blackness as a strike against me. I can see how it might work out that way, but I don't consider my skin color to be an innate disadvantage or an innate inferiority.

I have to confront the reality that I am black in a white family.

How do you interact in both the white and black worlds?

I try to avoid being timid in an all-white crowd. And I try not to be "down" all of a sudden in an all-black crowd. Actually, I don't think about this much.

Do you think you adapt well in both communities?

I have the ability to adapt in both.

How do you adapt, especially in black communities, when you haven't been exposed to those communities regularly?

I definitely feel comfortable in the black community—unless someone tries to make me feel uncomfortable. The way my parents brought me up and the way I've developed as a person enabled me to meet people, like or dislike them, be cordial, interact positively from the time I was 3 years old. So it's not as though all that goes out the window as soon as I meet somebody who doesn't look like my mom. I'm a student of life. I like getting to know other people.

Let's go back to the issue of transracial adoption. Do you think it should be an option to provide children with permanent homes, transracially?

I think it should definitely be an option. It should be up to the parents to decide if that's what they want to do. It's an act of love. But I also think that during the screening process it's important to find out what the potential adopters' perception of race is.

I don't think transracial adoption should be promoted as the solution to a surplus in the foster system. It shouldn't be used politically. Personally, I don't know why my parents chose a biracial child. They wanted a baby and apparently I was available, so they went with me. I don't know if race entered into their motivation or whether it was incidental. I was the only baby available.

Are there any specific factors that potential parents of black or biracial children should be aware of?

I think it would be helpful for parents to know specifically the racial makeup of their child. My parents and I speculate about my racial makeup, but I would like to have known that.

What about adoptive parents being proactive in educating their kids about their ethnic backgrounds?

I think parents should do that. My parents didn't, and I think it would have been interesting to me.

Does that mean it's not essential?

I'd definitely say it's not essential. It might be fun, might make your life more fulfilling and rich.

How do you define yourself?

Along with the race aspect, I define myself by what I like to do and what I like to think about. That's who I am. I change a lot, though.

Looking at it from the viewpoint of your journey thus far, how can others handle the experiences they go through being adopted transracially?

You should take pride in the experiences you have being a transracial adoptee. It is unique. When I encounter things that relate to me in literature and culture, it makes me feel good. That's the reason I reacted so positively to being involved in this study. It legitimates my feelings about who I am, the fact that transracial adoption is an issue that people are talking about. Issues about transracial adoption are relevant to me, and discussion about them gives me a lot of encouragement and pride in being myself.

Tage Larsen

CROFTON, MARYLAND
AUGUST 1997

*As an African American, being adopted into a white family with sib-
lings from different cultures and ethnicities was really wonderful.
The worlds that we were exposed to and the fact that these were our
siblings and we loved one another was truly awesome. I loved my
brother, Peik, who was Vietnamese, and my sister, Siri, who was
Cambodian and beautiful. I loved my sister, Anika, who is my parents' biological daughter. Anika was white and was my sister and I
loved her.*

A classical musician, Tage Larsen plays trumpet in the prestigious *President's Own Marine Band* based in Washington, D.C. His dream is to
play principal trumpet in the Boston Symphony. Tage's professional course
and passion for classical music developed early in his life when he was
exposed to the compositions of Beethoven and Bach. In 1995, Tage earned
his bachelor of music degree at Michigan State University and completed a
master's degree at the Eastman School of Music. His dream and unwavering
discipline to make a contribution to the arts through his endeavors in classical music were inspired by the love and support of his family and friends.

Tage was born in 1970 in Hartford, Connecticut. An African American
male infant, Tage was in need of a permanent home. Separated by race and
circumstance, there was no reason why the life of this child should be united
with a prospering young white couple who had the American dream in
their grasp. As their history shows, the Larsen's redefined that dream. They
began building their family, first by taking in one of society's children and
raising him as their own. And one by one, the Larsen family expanded,
adding nine more children. Four of them were the Larsen's biological children; the rest were chosen from some of the most economically and politically turbulent communities in the world. Truly a mosaic, the Larsens
learned how to appreciate different cultures and ethnicities while each family member learned how to become an individual.

Raised in Cambridge, Massachusetts, Tage lived in a culturally diverse community. He played with both African American and white kids from different economic backgrounds. Many of his parents' friends in the African American community were lawyers, doctors, artists, or musicians and became Tage's mentors, opening his eyes and mind to a life of excellence and unlimited possibilities. Clearly Tage's upbringing gave him the foundation to determine his professional path and social perspective, and ultimately his own identity.

Tage recently located and met his birth mother and biological siblings. He remains close to his adoptive family and returns to Cambridge regularly. Tage and his wife, Amy, live in Maryland.

Tage, where were you born?
In Hartford, Connecticut.
Did you spend time in foster care?
No. I was placed into my adoptive family soon after I was born.
Tell me about your family.
My father is part Norwegian, his father is Norwegian, and his mother and mine are American. I'm one of ten children and the oldest. My parents adopted me first. Soon after that they adopted Peik, Jens . . . and then it seemed like every year a kid would follow. Peik my parents got from Vietnam. Jens is American Indian, Kari is Vietnamese, and Siri is Cambodian. Then my parents had Anika, Britta, Nissa, and Trygve, who is the youngest. And there is Christian from El Salvador.
What was it like living in such a diverse family?
It was really exciting. When a new kid came into the family there would be a huge ordeal. During the months leading up to one of us arriving, my mom would start cooking meals from the country that my siblings came from. When Peik was coming, she cooked Vietnamese food, and so on. She would also introduce us to the culture before the child came. There was definitely a lot of excitement in the house. And of course my parents were just out of their minds thinking another kid, another culture. It was great!
Your parents were able to have biological children, so why do you believe they also chose to adopt interculturally and internationally?
I don't know, but it may have been out of protest. I think they had a lot of pressure from their parents and a lot of societal pressures to do the "right" thing. On the one hand their parents told them they should raise a perfect family—2.3 kids, participate in activities in school, focus on education, and buy your house with a white picket fence. But my parents were

pretty rebellious . . . especially my mom. I think their decision to adopt us was really a statement that here we are basically a middle-class couple who could have this perfect life but we want to do something more, something different . . . Why don't we do something to help society more than just help ourselves? I really think that's why they did it, though I haven't talked with my mom about this.

Do you believe that their initial mind-set of making a statement contrary to societal norms at the time shifted to accepting the reality that their children for life represented people of different races and ethnicities?

Yes. I believe that once they realized how fulfilling it was, once they adopted me and then Jens, and then Peik and Kari, they realized—wow, this is incredible! Not only are we helping children who may not have a chance otherwise, but it's so rewarding for us.

What was the community like in which you were raised?

I was raised in Cambridge, Massachusetts, which at the time was, I think, the most culturally diverse area in Massachusetts.

The time that we are talking about is the early 1970s?

Right. My parents moved to Cambridge because my father was going to Harvard. And it was fortunate given the situation that it was one of the most culturally diverse areas.

Do you believe that your parents intentionally moved into this area because of the children they adopted?

I think so. I think that my father had also planned to go to Harvard to get his master's degree in business.

As an African American, what was it like being adopted into a white family and having siblings from cultures across the cultural and ethnic spectrum?

As an African American, being adopted into a white family with siblings from different cultures and ethnicities was really wonderful. The worlds that we were exposed to and the fact that these were our siblings and we loved each other was truly awesome. I loved my brother, Peik, who was Vietnamese, and my sister, Siri, who was Cambodian and beautiful. I loved my sister, Anika, who is my parents' biological daughter. Anika was white and was my sister and I loved her. At the time my parents didn't force the different cultures on us, but over the years I have come to understand that it was a beautiful thing that we had all of these different cultures and all of these different people.

You have a brother, Peik, who is African American and Vietnamese. Did you feel naturally drawn to him because he is part black?

No. It was pretty much free reign. I would go to whatever sibling was there at the time. I think that what happened naturally was that me, Kari, Peik, and Jens grew up more together because we are the oldest and the closest in age. Anika is a couple years younger than us. Because of age, not because of color or ethnicity, the four of us interacted more closely with each other.

Once you interacted with society outside of your family, did you then feel a certain connection to your brother Peik because of his ethnicity and skin color?

No, not at all. I always considered him to be Vietnamese, American. We were all different. We had our own characteristics. I grew up with people in the Cambridge community who also were diverse culturally so, no, I didn't share a special bond with him because of that.

What were some of the traditions your family celebrated that were representative of your ethnicity?

Our family regularly celebrated, or I should say recognized, Kwanzaa. My mom used that occasion to tell us about the African American heritage.

You mentioned briefly that the neighborhood you were raised in was racially and ethnically diverse. Did you interact with kids in this community?

Yes. In fact my best friends nowadays are the friends I had back when I was a kid. My best man in my wedding, who I have been friends with since second or third grade, is mixed—African American and white. My other best friends are white and I have black friends.

It is really unique and very special. But you know what? I didn't realize it until I moved away. It wasn't until I moved to Michigan to go to school that I noticed how special my experience was.

In a family that reflected a "melting pot" of different races and ethnicities, how did you maintain your blackness, or did you?

I did. I was black. I was African American but I didn't relate so much to the black culture as some of my other African American friends did.

Why?

Because my parents always taught us to know where we came from—to understand our own culture. But we were all basically Americans. My parents also let us experiment and find things out for ourselves. For myself,

I always wanted to become a good person. I didn't relate to the African American culture that much.

Just as your family prepared ethnic foods from the countries in which your siblings came from, did your family cook any traditional African American foods?

Wow. No. I know we didn't.

Did you have black dolls . . .?

Yes. We sure did. My mom had black angels that she would put on the Christmas tree, and black dolls.

Were there artifacts in your home that resembled your complexion and culture?

Yes, my parents made sure of that. They had black friends. My parents made sure that I would hang out with their African American friends. I would get my hair cut at the neighbors next door, who were African American.

Tell me about your schooling. Did you go to a public school or private?

The first school that I went to was a private school, but they didn't want me there because I was black.

Who told you that "they" didn't want you there?

My mom did when I was old enough to understand why I wasn't in school there very long. I was in school there for a month or so. It just got too ridiculous. So my parents enrolled me in a public school and I went there for the rest of my elementary and high school years.

In the public school that you attended, who were the friends you hung out with, racially speaking?

Black, white, Asians, Hispanic. I had all sorts of friends. I had girlfriends of all different races. Since I was raised in a multicultural family, I didn't see the difference until people pointed it out.

Did you ever go to the homes of your black friends? Were these homes different than yours?

Yes, a lot different. Most of my friends who were black came from lower-income families. They lived in projects or apartments. We, on the other hand, had a huge house, a huge garden. We were lucky, very fortunate. But it was shocking to see their houses. They did not live as well as we did. I valued that experience and I think that my parents wanted me to see that people live differently.

Through spending time with the friends you just mentioned in their environment, did you begin to ask yourself what it meant to be African American?

No. I really didn't. I'm an American. I have always been an African American. They were different and they were still African American. I didn't have a problem relating to my African American heritage.

To be an African American, what does that mean to you?

It's the color of my skin. That is why, when you asked me earlier [before we taped], what I identified myself as, I said black, African American. Whatever I have to check on an application I have to check. But I have my own upbringing and I understand my black culture and history as a black person.

As you were going through high school, did you experience any problems because of your skin color?

Anyone who is African American is going to run into racism. Kids are going to tease you, of course. I mean you can be spit on or called a nigger.

How did you handle blatant racism?

I laugh at these people. I get angry for a second and feel sorry for them, really. What else can you do?

When this type of pain surfaced did you have someone you could talk to, like persons in your family?

Yes. I would go to my friends and parents. I'm sure that I asked them why. I have to tell you this funny story. When my family went on vacation—to Bermuda, I think—we went to dinner and there were five or six of us at the time. You can imagine a family with all these different races. We went to dinner and as we walked through the dining area everybody just stopped and stared at us. I asked my mom outloud in a room of silence, why are all these people staring at us? My mother started laughing. When you're a kid, you just don't know.

When you dated in high school, were the parents of your girlfriends offended by a young black man dating their daughter?

No.

What about role models within the black community? Were there any that you idolized or respected?

Oh, yes. My parents were friends with pretty influential people—lawyers, doctors, artists, musicians.

To whom do you attribute your initial interest in becoming a musician?

I attribute it to my father, Rikk. He wasn't a musician but he loved classical music, he still does. Growing up he would play Beethoven, Bach, and many other well known classical musicians. And for some reason I latched on to this and connected to it with a passion. When I was quite young and first playing my instrument I had a real passion for classical music.

What instrument do you play?

The trumpet. I knew very early on that I wanted to play classical trumpet. I think that was because my father had that music around and I loved it.

At what age did you first begin to play?

I began playing at the age of 10 or 11, and I stuck to it.

As you maintained focus in your musical training which would later become your career, did you think about going to college?

Going to college wasn't a choice. I did want to go to college. I knew that if I wanted to play an instrument professionally that I was going to have to get my bachelor's and master's and take auditions. I knew when I was pretty young what I needed to do. I had my course already charted.

In addition to exposing you to classical music, what was it that your parents taught you very early on that you carry with you today?

Work hard and stay focused and determined. Also the values that many people learn—not to steal or lie, to treat people nicely. But as far as my career, it was mostly to work hard and not place too many unreasonable expectations on myself. Everybody has limits and you just have to work as hard as you can and maximize your talent.

Where did you go to college?

Michigan State University.

Why did you choose Michigan State to pursue your additional training in music.

The orchestra conductor, who is actually still there, got me interested in Michigan State. I met him at a musical camp in Maine. He was a great influence on me. He encouraged me to go to the university and the university gave me money to go there, so I went.

Was there ever a point in your college experience where the color of your skin played a dominant role, whether you liked it or not?

Yes, it really did, especially with the relationship I have with my wife. She is white and her parents are white. To this day, things are not cool because of my race.

Were you drawn to black organizations on this predominately white campus for affirmation?

I was not involved in the black caucus or black student groups.

Why not?

I thought that their issues were off kilter. I couldn't relate to them. Like we were talking about earlier, I wasn't seeing things from their point of view. I felt that I'd best serve the black community by doing what I was doing—trying to be the best musician that I could become. Then maybe the example I'd be setting for younger kids and my peers would be my contribution. I didn't think that going out and staging rallies and sit-ins were that beneficial. You can be angry only for so long. Eventually you're going to have to go out there and start proving yourself and assimilating.

Did you participate in musical groups at Michigan State?

I was in the college orchestra and jazz band. I did everything.

Were there other African Americans in these groups or were you the only one?

In the orchestra I was the only one for a couple of years and then a violinist came along I think in the last year I was there. Yes, in all there were only two or three African American musicians.

Did that affect you in any way?

Not in a negative way. I looked at it as a positive thing. At least there was one of us black Americans there and maybe someone would see me and get interested in playing music. Whenever we went out and did school programs for young kids I was always glad when they asked questions.

Why?

I look at myself as being a role model just because I'm doing something that African Americans don't traditionally do.

How does one excite persons in the African American community, young people specifically, about the world of classical music?

First, they have to be exposed to it. There are incredible role models out there like Wynton Marsalis. He has done an immense amount of work going into the community. Wynton Marsalis has probably done more for African Americans and classical music than anybody has, just by people seeing him and hearing classical music. Not everybody has to love it. Letting people be aware of this type of music is the key. I think that nowadays a lot of African American kids are not exposed to it. They don't hear it in school. They don't hear it at home, certainly. It is a whole other world out there that is really exciting and interesting and kids need to be exposed to it.

What is it that attracts you to classical music?

It's the orchestra and the composers and the actual music that they wrote. Full orchestra. There is something about the idea of someone sitting down and composing, for example, Bach's *Brandenburg Concerto Number 2*. It's so complex. Paradoxically, this piece sounds so simple and effortless when actually it's very difficult to play. When you hear that piece, you enjoy it and also realize the incredible mind it takes to write a masterpiece like that. Of course, I went to school and studied it and played it. I understand the theory behind it and it's still breathtaking. For example, in the *Brandenburg Concerto* Bach used the trumpet in a way it had never been used before. It was never written as high as he wrote it, never in such an ornamented way and soloist way. At the time it was unprecedented. Nowadays people listen to it and say it's no big deal. It really is a monumental piece.

How is jazz different, or is it?

I don't think that jazz is much different. You take a composer like Duke Ellington, who is often compared to Bach based on their sheer genius and their works and minds. It really is not that much different. You have composers and you have performers who are extremely talented, incredibly gifted, who can play pieces that are equally difficult and challenging for a classical musician or a jazz musician.

What is it that allows you to be open to classical music and have the discipline to continue in this profession as well as other goals that you have set?

Again, I think that it's my family. It's where it all comes from. That's what gave me an open mind.

Because of your experience not only in school and within your community but in your family you have gained something so beautiful. From that perspective, what do you think about transracial adoption?

I think it is essential and that it not be stopped. I think that every child needs a nurturing, loving family, despite the race of the parents. It definitely should be encouraged.

Reading the article about your family in *Parade* and having this opportunity to speak to you, it is evident that your family has so much love for one another. Is that love enough for you and your siblings to feel confident in searching for your biological parents if you choose to?

Yes. My mom went to Vietnam with my sister and one of my brothers from there about a year ago to try to find their biological parents. They weren't successful. My brother, who is American Indian, has found his birth mother, and I think my sister from Cambodia has tried. At some point we've all tried to find, or have contacted, our birth parents.

And have you found yours?

Yes. I first seriously considered finding my birth parents when I was a freshman or sophomore in college.

What was going on in your life during that time that made finding your biological parents important?

I don't think it was one event. It was a general curiosity that became more pressing. I knew I had to find out.

How did you go about finding your biological parents?

My girlfriend, who's now my wife, and I went back to the agency that helped to adopt me, and that's where the process started.

What followed?

We talked to the social worker. It seemed at the time that the agency didn't have all my records and that it was going to be very difficult to locate my birth mother or my birth family because the records were incomplete. Over a couple of years, we didn't hear much from the social worker. I then put the idea on the back burner. Actually, I was quite discouraged. Who knows what could have happened; I was adopted more than twenty years ago. Then, out of the blue, a couple of months ago, I got a call from the social worker saying that she had important information about my biological family. Then, in a couple of weeks, I was talking with my birth mother. It all happened so fast.

Have you met her?

Yes, I met her. I showed up in Chicago, and she was there with her daughter.

How large is her family?

She has two sons who grew up in the area and another daughter who is in Georgia. I flew out there, too, and met my other brothers and sisters. It was an unbelievable experience.

What was the experience like?

It all happened so fast. I flew out there for one day and flew back.

When you looked at your biological family, did you see any physical resemblance?

I did, but it wasn't as striking as I thought it would be. I wasn't taken aback and I wasn't floored by it. I think I could see a resemblance in my biological mother's smile. Now that I talk to her more, I can see a resemblance in her speech and her mannerisms.

Did you feel a void had been filled, now that you had met your birth mother?

Yes. That was the greatest thing for me. First of all, knowing that she was O.K. And finding out how well she was and how well her family was.

Was the "big question" answered? Did you learn why she gave you up for adoption?

Yes. At the time she already had a son, David, my older brother. She was quite young, I think she was 18 or 19. She couldn't handle it financially and emotionally. And she thought that the best thing for me would be to give me up for adoption. I don't begrudge her at all.

Have your parents met them?

No. We were all going to get together a couple of weeks ago, but it didn't work out. Hopefully it will happen, sooner than later.

Is it your goal to maintain a relationship with your biological family?

Oh, absolutely! They are a lot different than my parents. First of all, they are very religious. I think that that is the greatest difference between my two families. I wasn't raised with religion at all. My parents let us have an open mind about it. But my biological family are devout Christians and they practice it regularly. They are preaching God and blessing me, which is weird because I'm not used to that. But it's cool with me.

What does being black mean to Tage, now that you have had another piece of yourself revealed to you that obviously builds on who you are as a black man?

It means that I am proud to be an African American. I think that as a race we have a lot of responsibility to one another.

What do you think are some of the major issues we face in the black community?

One of the big issues, I think, is our economic standing. I thought about this a lot. What do we do as a race in this country economically? We are probably close to being the lowest wage earners in this society and for the most part we live in low-income housing. The question is, how do we advance up the ladder? I really don't know, but I think that pointing the finger at every other thing as the root of our problems is not going to solve anything. We have to prove that we can be self-sustaining, compete—not only in this country but on the international scene. Until that happens, I don't think that we as a people are going to get that far ahead.

Do you think that as a black community we should depend solely on the direction of so-called leaders within the African American community, or should we also find leaders and direction from within ourselves?

The number one priority is to raise a supportive, loving, strong family. If you are in a situation where you need someone outside your family or community to tell you what to do, that's almost a last resort, when everything else has been tried. Once we've built strong bonds in our families and communities, if we still need someone else to show us the way, so be it.

How do you define yourself? Who is Tage?

I'm still growing. I'm learning more about myself and my family. I have an open mind. I'm trying to work hard at my music and my marriage. I have dreams and I'm trying to accomplish them.

What are some of your dreams?

To play principal trumpet in the Boston Symphony. Right now that's my focus, it's all-consuming.

Right now, what are you doing professionally?

I'm playing in what is called the *President's Own Marine Band* in Washington, D.C.

What opened the door to this opportunity for you?

Before I joined the band I was on the road with a group called the *Dallas Brass*. I was traveling two or three weeks out of a year. Then I auditioned for the band and made it, and it was a chance to stay in one place for awhile. That's what led me to the band.

And before that you received your master's at the Eastman School of Music?

That's right. I studied there for two years focusing on classical literature for the trumpet—learning the repertoire. Today I'm finished with school, but I practice three or four hours every day. It depends on the audition that's coming up.

You mentioned your wife, Amy, several times during our conversation. Where and how did you meet her?

We met at Michigan State about nine years ago. I was a freshman at the time. She plays trumpet, too. Right now she's working for the Washington Opera here in Washington, D.C., and the Baltimore Symphony. She is definitely doing well. At Michigan State, we played in the band together and in the orchestra for three years. Then she went on to Northwestern to get her master's. We've been together ever since.

Amy is white?

Yes.

Has the fact that she is white and you are black created challenges for both of you?

Yes, unfortunately, more so with her family. Our friends are fine with the fact that we married interracially. Her family, especially her mom, has a problem with it.

Why do you think they're uncomfortable with the situation?

I think it has to do with their limited exposure to persons from other cultures and ethnicities. Also, her parents are older than mine, so they're from a different generation.

Have you talked to them about this tension?

No, I haven't. At this point it's not a priority for me to talk to them about it.

Interracial marriage and transracial adoption raise the question of whether it's fair for a person to be forced into living apart from his or her ethnic culture long term. Do you think it's fair?

In my case, having been exposed to so many cultures, it was fair. My parents taught me to love people of all different cultures. I love Amy not because of her color but because of the person she is.

Before marrying Amy, were you naturally attracted to white or black women?

I wasn't attracted to one race in particular. I dated blacks, whites, and persons from other ethnicities. I think people tend to be attracted to those who have mutual interests.

Looking at your life, the lessons, the challenges, and the hard knocks, do you believe you were raised well and are prepared to contribute to society?

Oh, yes. I never had a question in my mind of whether I could make it or not. My parents raised me well enough. For me, it was a matter of what I was going to do and getting on the right course.

It seems to me that because you have lived and participated in your ethnically diverse family, you have had to make a conscious effort to be sensitive to who your siblings are. Being black in a black family or white in a white family, without being exposed to other ethnic groups, in my mind creates a situation where ethnocentrism dominates and one doesn't learn how to cope with the personalities and ethnicities of others.

True. And I think that one of the fears some black people have about having children raised by white parents is that they aren't going to be exposed to their black heritage. I think that's a valid point. You can certainly make the case that a black parent is going to have a better idea of what their black heritage is than a white parent. But I say give them a chance. Because there are so many children out there who need loving families, you've got to give white, Hispanic, Chinese parents a chance—for the child's sake.

From your own experience, do you have any suggestions that would help parents who have adopted transracially?

Move to Cambridge, Massachusetts. It's about having a diverse community that supports it. I would say not to get too discouraged when some difficult times happen and not to be intimidated by people who don't understand your family. What my parents did was to treat transracial adoption like any other situation. Don't treat your biological kids better than your adopted kids. Instill in your child a strong sense of love and family. The child will be a much stronger person if he feels the strength of family. Children will be able to face challenges a lot better if they feel confident that they have a loving family.

Do children lack confidence in this type of situation because their parents do not exhibit the children's physical characteristics? Do you know of any transracial adoptees who feel confused even though they received endless love from their adoptive parents?

I think we all have a certain amount of confusion about our situation. There are different levels of confusion, and it depends on how a person deals with it. I don't really know too many other transracial adoptees and the ones I do know are doing pretty well—at least outwardly.

Finally, based on your personal journey up to this point, what was going on in your soul to deal with your own ethnicity and get beyond racist insults?

I can say that finding my birth mother has completed the circle in this stage of my life. To realize that this is the woman who put me here, this beautiful person—is truly amazing. Before that I experienced hills and valleys spotted with blatant racism. It was painful for me to experience racism, like being spit on because of my skin color. When you're younger and that happens, it's hard. What I've learned is that you need to move on and hold your head high.

David T. Adams

Point Roberts, Washington
September 1997

Growing up I did not feel I could be a black voice living in a white community. I more or less was a showpiece in the white community. If somebody asked me about black issues I would speak my mind, but I didn't feel that I was qualified to speak as a representative of black people.

David T. Adams, screenwriter, educator, husband, and father of two, was born in July 1970 in Hartford, Connecticut. He spent his childhood and adolescent years in a predominantly white and close-knit community. From 1979 to 1992 David attended private Christian institutions in the Midwest. Thrust between the Dutch community, where he was raised, and the black community, to which he was ethnically linked, David grappled with finding harmony within himself.

After remaining in foster care for three months, David was adopted into the Adams family. The couple were in their early twenties and socially compassionate. Largely influenced by the civil rights movement, they believed it was their responsibility, as well as their personal desire, to adopt one of society's abandoned children. Initially they preferred to adopt a black child, but the social worker handling the case encouraged them to consider adopting a biracial child as a way to reduce the awkwardness the child may feel living in a white family. So they adopted a biracial son.

He was raised a middle child in Sioux Center, Iowa, along with his two brothers. The only African American in his family, David grew up protected from the harshness of racial prejudices. As a youth, his interests focused on spending time with friends and having fun. Though he knew he was physically different, David saw his brown skin as a welcome novelty among peers and family members. It wasn't until he was in his late teens when he recognized that the color of his skin merely touched the surface of the African American heritage and experience.

Now, twenty years later, David lives with his wife and two children in Point Roberts, Washington. While Point Roberts is more than a thousand miles away from Sioux Center, David is reminded of the many cultural similarities he experienced as a youth in Iowa. And in the span of time between these two points, David has learned the value of appreciating his ethnic heritage and teaching his children about their heritages. He continues to draw on the rich literary background he gained through his education as a compass in his own life's journey.

Both of David's adoptive parents live in Iowa. They have both earned doctorate degrees and are educators. David remains in contact with his family.

David, it was 1970 when you were adopted. What was happening socially at that time that encouraged your parents to adopt you?

I think it was the civil rights movement. My parents weren't specific about any newsworthy event that made them decide to adopt me. I believe somebody from their church showed them a film about the desperate need for these children to be adopted. This is a sentiment many young families share. Just after my wife and I got married and had our first child, we also thought we should contribute because there are so many children remaining in foster care.

My parents are radical about what they do, especially when they make decisions. They are very extreme. They take specific stances in one direction or another. I thought they might have been trying to make some statement. And when I found out that their adopting me really wasn't a huge statement, that it was more or less a willingness to help, I didn't know if I was disappointed or relieved that I wasn't a statement.

Your parents adopted you in Hartford, Connecticut, where you lived for several years. Then you moved to Sioux Center, Iowa, which is predominately white. Tell me about your experience there.

We lived in northwest Iowa, which is a Dutch community and close-knit. Everybody there was very accepting. The only racial problems I ran into were with little kids my age. In fact, their response was, "Oh, look at the little black kid."

Why do you believe your parents decided to move to the Midwest?

My father had an opportunity to start an engineering program at a college in Iowa.

What was it like living in a white family and being black?

To be honest, from fourth grade, when I moved to Iowa, through eighth grade, I really didn't even notice. On the second or third day after we moved there, my parents arranged for me to meet Dan, who is black and living in a white family, so we could become friends. We remained friends until the end of our junior high school years, when we met up with different friends and fell apart.

Were there any symbols in your home depicting an African American culture?

Not even close. Most of the things in our home were classical reading materials and classical music—nothing cultural in the sense of the African American culture.

Did you notice any physical differences between you and your family, particularly as you were growing up and developing?

Oh yes, I knew I had better skin. By the time I was in eighth grade, I was convinced that everybody wanted to be black because there were all these people getting perms to tighten their hair and getting tan. My mother would say that I have beautiful black skin. My grandmother loved my dark complexion and thought I was handsome. The media has propagated the tan body as being very attractive. Not that I made an issue of my skin color being different from my brothers or that I didn't notice it. I knew I was black. I knew I was adopted. I knew I was different. It just didn't seem to matter at all.

Did your parents tell you why they adopted you?

Never. Not until probably three days ago when I called and asked. That's when they said it was because of the civil rights movement and because of what was going on in their community at the time. They wanted to participate in addressing the needs of the children in our society.

How did you get along with your two brothers—one a year younger than you, the other a year older? Was it challenging for you that they were white and you were black?

It was never an issue between us.

Did they comment on your physical difference?

Never. There were never any negative comments made about the darkness of my skin. If anything, my older brother was jealous that I could darken quickly. He wasn't even white. He was what you might call clear. He was white with freckles. He was annoyed that he sunburned easier. Mike, my younger brother, and I would see who could get the darkest because he could tan. That was more or less the extent of the recognition.

During your family reunions, was there talk about how similar your brothers looked to other persons in the family?

They would say that they were looking more and more like my father.

Did that make you question your relationship with them because you obviously didn't resemble any of your family members physically?

I don't think so. Very typically there were times when I said, like many kids who are adopted, that you aren't my real parents and I should find out who my real parents are. I know I said that to my mother.

Within the context of living in a white family, and also in a white close-knit community, how did you function?

I did everything everybody else did. Nothing set me aside because of my race. If anything, I knew I was a novelty to a town like that. I guess I took advantage of it. Some people took a liking to me because of my racial difference. I was the "cute black kid." I don't think there was any stigma against black people in that community because no one had ever experienced them. Whereas in some white communities where people are exposed to blacks, when a black family moves in with a black kid, then the white people say, "Oh you know those black kids always act that way."

What kind of school did you attend?

I went to a private Christian school of about three hundred students. It was all white except for the occasional exchange student or Asian student. I was there until eighth grade. Then I graduated and went on to Unity Christian High School in Orange City, Iowa, which was also predominately white. Then, in 1988, I went to Dordt College.

In Sioux Center, Iowa, were there any cultural events that your family took part in?

There were big cultural events, but notice the name "Sioux Center." A lot of them were probably Native American.

I knew I wasn't going to be allowed to wear clogs and push brooms, like members of the community did in the Dutch parade, or rather that the community would feel awkward about my doing it. That really didn't matter to me because I didn't want to do that anyway. A lot of people would say, "You're not too Dutch." I still get a lot of that. We just had an open house yesterday. There are many Dutch folks in Point Roberts, Washington, where my family currently lives. My wife introduces me to these people and they say, "What's your last name again?" When we say Adams, they ask if I'm Dutch. I say . . . noooo, I'm quite far from being Dutch.

In the process, did you question race issues? What effects did the media have on your perceptions of race?

I liked the George Jefferson show because I thought George Jefferson was cool. I liked people like him. I also liked Eddie Murphy. I don't think it was because they were black. I had a laugh that was similar to Eddie Murphy's, and people commented on that. On certain days I'd dress like Michael Jackson at school because I could and he was a big hit. Again, I was still cute. I was a cute black kid all the time that I could do these things.

I probably didn't start wondering about things having to do with race until one of my friends who lived near me said something that involved race. I mentioned to him one day that I liked a certain girl in class. He said that I could like her and everything, but that I couldn't marry a white girl.

What was your response?

I wasn't shocked or even taken aback. I laughed and asked him why not. I couldn't comprehend why somebody would think that. He told me that I would have zebra kids. I laughed, and then I thought seriously about it and didn't think that was possible. I was more or less interested with the novelty of that happening—having striped kids.

Did you talk to your parents about race issues, perhaps at the dinner table? Certainly there have been some high-profile cases, like the Rodney King beatings and other incidents of black males beaten at the hands of police officers.

Yes. Most of the discussions occurred when I was already out of high school, so it wasn't so much around the dinner table anymore. I don't recall any conversations around the dinner table about that issue. When it comes to issues about race relations, my family and I don't take one side or the other. I'm more like the devil's advocate. On the one hand, I defend the black community, but, on the other, I'm antagonistic about the way that they act toward certain issues, like the ones you just mentioned. Personally, in relating to the Rodney King beatings, I thought that it was the situation involved. That's what is most important. I try not to make it a black thing, but apparently people do.

What do you mean "it was the situation"?

Well, I believe that Rodney King initially did something wrong and then the act got magnified because of race and then people started losing perspective about the key facts in the situation.

Has race ever intersected in your life where what you've done, be it good or bad, was magnified because of your black skin?

Some people encouraged me to use my color to get certain monies for college. On another occasion, I had a job in Sumas, Washington, working in a grocery store. The management was going to teach us how to run the cash registers, and one kid said, "Oh, don't let him run the registers because you know how black people are." It was mostly small things like that. When I got married, my parents-in-law didn't feel very comfortable about it.

How did your marrying a white woman affect your relationship with her family?

Yes. My wife is white and her parents are both white. My parents-in-law live in a community that is more exposed to Canadians because it's a border town between the states and Canada. Personally, I thought that my wife and her parents were prejudiced when I heard them talk about Canadians and East Indians because of the stigma attached to Canadians in this area. Some Americans don't like Canadians, and some Canadians don't like Americans. My wife's parents were a bit that way. But I never confronted or met with confrontation concerning my in-laws about this issue. My wife did tell me that when she called them to say we were getting married, my mother-in-law told her that she knew how they felt about that. That was all she said at that time. I think it was only a couple of days later when she accepted the fact and accepted me warmly into their family.

Were there any other experiences where race entered the picture?

I was once threatened by a shotgun by some girl's father because the family didn't want her to date me.

When was this?

I was in my freshman year in college, 1989. I went to the girl's house in Sioux Center to pick her up. She was a high school senior. Her dad came out with a shotgun and threatened to shoot me if I didn't get off his property. He didn't call me any names. It could have been that he just didn't like me.

How did you work that out?

I *left*!!!

How did you work it out in your own mind? It's obvious that you were no longer perceived as this cute little black child anymore, that you outgrew your cuteness.

To some people, I'm still cute. I think I tried to be black in college.

Why?

Because it was cool. Especially in a community that was all white. I wanted to shake them up. I got one ear pierced. I actually wore gang colors at one point when the "Cripps" and "Bloods" were getting popular.

Where, in an all-white community, did you get your information about "blackness"?

It started when I took a trip to Roseland, Chicago, in late high school. The people there talked about the intensity of gangs in that community.

Roseland is a black community on the south side of Chicago.

Yes. And it was about at that point that being black started looking cool. I remember seeing *Colors* with my black friend, who was also adopted into a white family. *Colors* was a film that dealt with a lot of racial issues, mostly between the Cripps and the Bloods, but it also had two white police officers who were caught in the middle. We thought it was such a cool movie, so in a way I behaved like that.

Now you have movies like *Menace to Society* or *Boys 'n the Hood*. As a former teacher I saw high school kids react to that the same way as I reacted to *Colors* but it was an uninformed viewpoint.

Was your class trip to Chicago your first experience in a black community?

Yes.

What was that experience like?

I loved it. I loved living in a crammed-up little house with cars parked around it with broken windows and kids sitting in the street—and the guy across the street drinking Colt 45. I found it extremely attractive whereas most of my peers were shaking in their boots.

What color were your peers?

They were all white from Sioux Center.

The white community in Sioux Center saw you as black. Now you are in Chicago. How did the community you were with identify you racially?

They saw me as white. I think it was because I hung out with white peers and I was of a lighter complexion. I know that ginger-colored kids have a lot of problems in the inner cities, too.

Did people there comment on the way you spoke?

Yes. In fact most of them were surprised that I didn't have a black dialect because I was dark-complexioned. I think the way I talked was another thing that contributed to my being considered white. For example, I dated a girl in Massachusetts who was shocked because I didn't talk like most black people. There were times I did and times I didn't.

Contrast your two main experiences, the one where the girl-friend's father threatens you with a shotgun to get off his property and the other, in Chicago, where people shun you because of the company you keep and your dialect.

I'll start with Roseland because that happened first. That made me more aware that I was different. I was proud of that. When we visited that church and that community, a lot of the kids I went with really liked the church and the people and felt that community was closer than even our community in Iowa because of their culture. They thought that was really attractive. I felt kind of cool because I'm a little bit of that and I even acted that way—in dress, speech, and behavior. In Sioux Center, Iowa, I wanted to make people see me as "culture." I was the culture they didn't have. I stood out. There were little children in Chicago who called me "Whitey." That was interesting to me. I was amused. Actually, I liked the idea that I was different in every community. I think I thrive on being different.

Is that a coping mechanism, wanting to be different in many ways?

Very much so. Don't misconstrue that when I say "coping" I can't handle the situation. It's just how I deal with it. It's not like I have a problem with it. It's like when I was little I had to be the center of attention. I think that's why I'm glad that I'm different in the black community and that I'm also different in the white community. I'm glad that when I go places and people are all one particular race, they are curious about me. I like that. It's very narcissistic, I think.

Let me be clear on this. You were fine with children calling you "Whitey"?

I wasn't offended. I was more or less amused. These kids may have even been surprised that they didn't get a rise out of me.

How did you relate to the black people in Chicago? Did you have the skills you needed (whatever they are) to communicate with black people?

Yes. I think many of them actually came up to talk to me because of my skin color. We'd be painting or working on a project and a black kid would come over to me and ask why I was hanging out with them, the white kids, in the group. They actually felt comfortable talking to me—not that I was this open soul that exuded this exceptional sense of welcome, but I think I was the first one they identified with.

I even got that response here in Point Roberts, Washington. Some guy I saw the first month I was here looked at me and asked how it was. I could have misunderstood, but it was almost like, "Hey, here's another black guy."

So you believed you had the skills and preparation needed to talk to black people?

Yes. But not as a black voice. Growing up I did not feel I could be a black voice living in a white community. I more or less was a showpiece in the white community. If somebody asked me about black issues I would speak my mind, but I didn't feel that I was qualified to speak as a representative of black people. I honestly and truly did not.

Why not?

Because I didn't think I was black enough.

What is black enough?

I think it's being a person who understands the community he comes from. I couldn't represent a black community very well because I grew up in a white Christian Reformed community.

But, at the same time, you consider yourself black?

Yes, I do.

What does that mean? Is it what defines the color of your skin or is it your interest in the black community?

It's my skin color. Here's a good example. I'm writing a script on the *Narnia* book and I also want to write a movie script on the *Invisible Man* by Ralph Ellison, which is about a young black man growing up. And I'm thinking, who would I solicit to produce it. Obviously I'd want to talk to producer/director Spike Lee, who is one of my heroes. He's very supportive of black youths in the film industry, but I don't think he'd consider me a black person because of my background. I think a black individual to him, and one he'd support, would have the usual problems and stereotypes that would involve controversy. I didn't experience a lot of that. I am "a privileged black kid who grew up in a very privileged society" and I'd be considered a "stuck-up, 'get-out-of-my-face' kid."

We just talked about the experience you had in Chicago. Let's go back and talk about the other experience you endured in Iowa, at a girlfriend's house. I can't imagine having a shotgun in my face . . .

Well, it wasn't in my face. He held it up. I was, more or less, "good-bye!" I didn't think about it at that point. It wasn't until afterward when she came to me and said that her father didn't like black people.

How did you react?

It made me feel "pissed." I thought he was being an idiot. At that point, I wanted her to go out with me just to tick him off.

Did you talk to your parents about that experience?

No.

Was there anyone you could talk to?

No. When I was in high school I had a friend who asked me a lot of questions because he was curious. He became one of my better friends— a very white farm boy. He was sensitive. My therapy more or less came from him. He thought it was cool that I was "black." Again, that fed into my feeling that being black was cool. In fact, I had another friend in college who even said "God, I wish I was black. I hate being such a white ducky. I want to be black." He talked like it, acted like it, dressed like it. He just wasn't black. And again that feeds into my thinking. The kind of friends I had appreciated me and liked me.

It's hard for me, as someone who is black and was adopted into a white family, to understand why your family didn't demonstrate that it was important for you to be exposed to the black community.

I did go to a black girl's birthday party once, and we saw the movie *Frankenstein*. I don't remember anything else. That was when we were in grade school living in New Jersey.

Then when did you start identifying with persons like Spike Lee or the Jeffersons show or develop an interest in black authors?

It may have started when my mom started to deal with some of these issues for school. She actually said at one point, "Dave, I wish you were more in touch with your black heritage."

The question is, why was this concern articulated then and not some twenty years earlier when you were a child formulating your identity? I know that's an unfair question to ask you; you aren't your parents and, as a child back then, it wasn't your responsibility to figure that out. So let me restate my question: Did it frustrate you in any way when your mother told you that she wished you knew more about your black heritage?

The only reason it frustrated me, especially being in college at the time, was that I wanted to feel informed or know I had a grasp on my African American heritage.

Are you saying that you were severed from your people, the black people in America?

Yes. But I might also say that "my people" were the Dutch community.

That is a valid point.

When I'm asked, "Do you know who your real parents are?" I say that my real parents are the people who raised me all my life. To say that I've been out of contact with my people my whole life is incorrect; I'd say that I've been with my people all my life and I know my Dutch community very well. I know their religious practices, their typical community activities.

You know their "isms."

Yes. But when people look to me to represent the black community, I can't. And I feel embarrassed about that. I'm embarrassed that I don't know a lot about author/poet Maya Angelou or African American history other than what has been obvious in our textbooks.

Apparently, your mother had reason to encourage you to seek out your African American roots. Why was she eventually persuaded to do so?

She definitely didn't say it in a condescending way.

No, from what you initially said, I interpreted your mother's remark as a genuine suggestion.

I may have presented it in a negative way. I think that at the time I was busy with a lot of other things, and she found the African American heritage very interesting and sometimes would talk to me about it. I was so uninformed about it that I'd come across as being uninterested. That's when she said that she wished I knew more about my heritage. It also made me realize that I, too, wished I knew more about my heritage. It's important for me to say that I never blamed my parents for that.

It never occurred to me to wish that my parents did this for me or that for me—although I think I would have appreciated it. My son is very proud that he has African American blood in him, and he is as white as my Dutch wife. One time in the grocery store he went up to the cashier and asserted boldly, "I'm black. I'm African American." The cashier just looked at him with her eyebrows raised.

What about your other son?

He doesn't say much about it. He's only four. He'd rather talk about fire trucks or something like that.

Is his skin dark?

No. My mother and I were talking about that. She said she was hoping that we'd have some cute little dark-skinned kids. Well, our kids are white as white. Most people would think that my wife had children and then married me. My kids don't look like me, but they have my mannerisms and quirks. They look very much like my wife.

In your personal journey, was there a particular time when you tried to connect with your "black" side?

Yes. That happened when I moved to Massachusetts for the summer with some friends. It was after my freshman year in college. My parents didn't want us to go because we'd be on our own and working in an amusement park. I had a lot of black friends then. I started hanging out with them and began to act like them, even talk like them.

How did the black women you met there interact with you?

I met this one black girl who was very beautiful. We went out, and she was so surprised that I didn't act or talk like the black guys she knew. Most of the black girls I met out there were like, "Yo wahtz up!!" That was the way she was when I met her, only to find out that she was much more intelligent than that. When we had normal conversations she didn't talk like that at all. We kind of related the way Arsenio Hall did. When he had a white person on his show, he'd talk normally, but when he had a black person on, he'd change his dialect for that type of conversation.

You say "talk normally." What do you mean by that?

I mean talking without a specific dialect, having no strong accent.

Some people can clearly be distinguished as black or white or Canadian by the way they talk on the phone. Would you sound black?

Yes.

By your conversation, I wouldn't have imagined that.

I haven't kicked in my "Yo Baby," yet.

No, I mean everything—from your regular conversation to your laugh to your comments. I haven't sensed it. Have other people told you that?

Definitely. I've been asked why I talk "white."

Really?

Yes. And the response from people after I answer that question has been anywhere from angry to resentful.

Uppity?

Yes. I am an "uppity rich bitch." It's mostly said by black women. And it was also black women who made most of the comments about my "whiteness." That's why I never went to see the movie *Waiting to Exhale.*

So that means you are still inhaling?

I don't know. I also won't go to see it because I was called to be an extra but my wife failed to tell me. So I refuse to see it because I could have been in it.

I'd like to address several points that have been brought out in this interview. First, your story illustrates the absence of the black community in your daily life, particularly in the early stages. A question people are going to ask is this, "Was it not a selfish act for your parents to adopt a black baby and not make it a priority to expose that child to his ethnic community—and, to take it a step further, then to move to one of the whitest, homogeneous areas in this country?"

When my adoptive parents were going through the adoption process, they said they wanted a black kid. The social worker, who was black, said that maybe it would be better if they had a light-colored kid. My parents sort of shrugged and didn't understand why that was important. Of course they wouldn't understand! They were into this with all their heart. They wanted to take care of a black baby because their community wasn't taking much responsibility. My parents—I'm defending them in a way—didn't understand why they should have a lighter-skinned kid. The social worker thought it might be easier because of the awkwardness both the child and my parents might feel in that situation. She thought it might be easier for everybody all around if there was some mixed blood in the child. So my parents decided she was right and went along with it.

I think you are right. Because of the civil rights movement, my parents selfishly wanted to have black kids without understanding the full ramifications of what it means to have someone of a different culture in your family.

And also not appreciating that person's culture within the family structure.

I think they may have appreciated the black culture but never fully understood how to bring the black culture into the family. I think that's more the case. It's like anyone who has a kid but doesn't know how to take care of their kid until later—and then they realize all the mistakes they made.

What is unfortunate is that you didn't have the opportunity early on to learn about your African American heritage and to decide if that's how you wanted to identify yourself. Consider this scenario: White parents want to give a child a permanent, loving family, but don't understand the value of the child's ethnic identity. The black community fears their future is vanishing. A black child gets removed from his home and enters into the child welfare system— worse, into a white family. The fabric of the black community weakens. The identity of the black child becomes void. What do you do?

Actually, I'm glad you brought this up. It's something I've been thinking about lately. In a way, the black community feels that their children or their men—I'm kind of connecting this to *Waiting to Exhale*—need to be unified and that so many people in the black community have drifted apart. The black community, as an entity, wants to bring it all back.

Why do you believe the black community is threatened by "allowing" white families to raise black children, when indeed these families are giving a child a home?

It could be because it feels a bit like going "back in time" with the racism issue. At one point the black community was asking, "Why can't we mix with the white community?"

That philosophy is being supported by many civil rights leaders and other individuals; people are just getting tired of sitting at the back of the bus and going to segregated schools and movie theaters.

And the white community was saying, "No, we don't want to mix with the black community because we want to preserve our culture. It's bad to integrate races." Soon the white community began to see the light, you might say.

I think that society at large embraced the philosophy and embodied the social conscience that injustice toward human beings is intolerable.

People in the white community understood that it was their responsibility to help children in need. They saw black children being born into families who were unable to take care of them so they chose to step in. They don't quite understand how to take care of these kids, in terms of the child's ethnic culture. So they raise these children, and later the children are saying, "I'm out of touch. I don't know what's going on." This is exactly what I could have done.

Then you go to university campuses and the black people say, "We want to unify. We want our own dormitory." And other people say, "Wait a minute, wasn't the whole civil rights issue against segregation?" Then they say, "Yes, but this is different. We're not being racist. We want to strengthen our culture, and that's why we don't want any whites here." That's the kind of tension going on now.

Well, after voicing this, what are your views on transracial adoption?

I think that it's good. I like the idea mainly because I turned out O.K.

But is your "blackness" intact?

I hear you. I think that if I adopted a black child now, I'd really like to understand the black culture and bring that to my child. But, you know, I think that this concept of understanding the importance of different ethnic backgrounds and cultures is something that just happened within the last ten to fifteen years.

Why do you think it's important to learn about your ethnicity?

Because it's part of who I am. I would love to answer the questions when people ask me about my ethnic background. I worked in a video store for a long time and this guy would come in to watch *Brave Heart* regularly. He watched this movie about ten times a week. When we finally asked him why, he said that he was Scottish and his family was connected to the family that was portrayed in the movie. It was fascinating to him. He couldn't peel himself away from it. I wish I could have that type of background in my life.

I don't want to push this issue too far, but don't you see the mind-set of those who believe that transracial adoption is basically stripping the black child, in this case, away from his community?

Look at it this way. Instead of using the phrase "stripped from their community," consider that those being placed for adoption are now getting homes.

I hear you.

You might even say that their community has basically left them. Their family has left—not intentionally. But no matter what the case might be, the child is in a void, waiting for someone to take care of him. I would say that any responsible, caring family should take that child and raise him in a Christian God-fearing way or in the Jewish tradition if the family is Jewish. Now, if these parents don't fully understand the child's culture, perhaps they should take courses or educate themselves in other ways. Unfortunately such families may not be available, and there might not be any black parents for that child either. So what do you do with the child? Do you keep passing him from foster home to foster home, waiting until a black family opens up? By that time, the kid will probably be really "screwed up." The goal is to get him into a stable environment.

Do you think you are "screwed up" because you are in a white family?

No.

What did your family give you to prevent this from happening?

They gave me confidence in who I am. I can draw. I can read. I can write. I'm a comedian. I can teach. I can do all these things in spite of my race. I would even dare say that I would be this way even if I were in a black family. I probably would have the same strengths and the same interests to a certain degree.

And what do you say to the black community who is saying, with tears running down their faces, "One of our children is gone!!"?

You know what I'd say? I'd say, "Where were you then?!?!"

It's hard to cry over it now. What am I supposed to do? When I'm 16 years old, am I supposed to say to my parents, with great disdain, "You are white! And, doggone it, I'm going to find someone who is black?"

You mean, like divorcing your parents?

Exactly. And I wouldn't be surprised that kids who feel there is a huge void in their life feel they have to find their biological parents. And when they do, either it destroys them or they become so unified with this parent that the other parents feel neglected. That can be very destructive. I've never had that and, personally, can't understand the feeling of having a void in one's life.

I guess what I'm saying is that it's hard living in a white family as an African American individual. The challenges transracial adoptees face—that I face—are very real.

I don't know. I feel ashamed to say that. And it's for the same reason that sometimes I feel I can't speak for the black community because I came from a white community. Maybe I can describe it this way. As a teacher, I taught *Huckleberry Finn*. I'm a black teacher, teaching in an all-white school. We had one black kid in the school. Critically speaking, one of the biggest problems people have with the book is that it mentions "nigger" far too often for comfort. Now, if you're in a predominately white Christian school and you mention the word "nigger" and why it's offensive, to these students there is no offense because they've never had to deal with the meaning of it, the hatred. So these students think it's a good book and write papers on it expressing why everybody should read it. They just don't know how it feels to be called that name.

And conversely?

Now this young Ms. white teacher graduates from college and begins teaching in a black inner-city school. She says the word "nigger" because she's reading *Huckleberry Finn*. Suddenly a little kid stands up and says, loudly, "Who are you to read something like that, you don't even know anything about it?" From her perspective, she says it's great literature and one needn't feel offended by it. Well, I do. How can you tell somebody not to feel offended?

Once I went out with some girl and we were laughing around the bonfire, and she said, "You're so cute, can I call you a 'nigger?'" I asked her if I could call her a "bitch." She said no, that's mean. I said, so is calling me a "nigger." She didn't think so because she liked me and didn't think it would mean anything. She said that she heard black people calling other black people "nigger" all the time.

What was your response?

I said, anybody can call you anything if you're in your own family. If you are in, say, a Dutch community and that community makes Dutch jokes, let them. The same is true in a black community. If that community wants to make black jokes or refer to its people in a certain way, let them.

Where do you draw the line?

If the particular community is offended, then you stop. When I was working in the grocery store, I happened to be on my knees with a brush scrubbing up dirt on the floor. An older gentleman walked by and said, in a scruffy voice, "They got ya where they want ya, hey boy!" I looked up and said, "Excuse me!?" And he said it again. But I don't think he knew what he was saying. I think he was trying to make a joke.

You are criticized by people who say that you aren't black because you were raised by a white family. In other words, you don't have the sensitivities and life experience it takes to be iden-

tified as "black." Now you have made an adult decision to marry someone from a different race. Have you "sold out"?

I married this girl, and it has nothing to do with race.

Before marrying her, did you consider the fact that your wife was white and what the ramifications are in this society?

No, and it's because of my upbringing. All the girls I ever dated were white, except for when I went to Massachusetts. And there I dated two girls who were black. Recently, my wife asked me whether I would have married a black girl. I thought and thought and thought. Then I said, "I don't know. It's hard to answer something like that."

Why?

One of the girls I went out with who was black was gorgeous. So, yes, if I fell in love with the girl, I definitely would have married her.

But given your background, would you have fallen in love with a black girl?

I didn't have the opportunity to fall in love with a black girl, because I didn't have a black community nearby.

As a mixed couple, have you received criticism from society?

Truthfully, it begins to be a novelty, again because I moved into another Dutch community, Lynden, Washington.

Is that similar to the community in Sioux Center, Iowa, where you were raised?

Yes, but magnified a hundred times. To answer your question about being criticized as a mixed couple, no, I never noticed anybody shun me or anything like that.

Does your wife take an interest in learning more about the black culture?

Lately, yes.

Lately?

Because of some of the discussions we've been having lately—ever since the O. J. Simpson trial. My wife and I had a fight one time about race. I can't remember exactly what it was but it had to do with guilt.

Guilt about what?

She thought she shouldn't have to feel guilty because of the way blacks were treated. That's what the fight was about. She believes she accepts people of all races and creeds. She said that she may be prejudiced but that everybody is prejudiced in some way. Her question is, why are black people blaming her for the sins of her forefathers.

Where did the fight come in?

At that point, because I believe in the sins of the fathers. I believe that a lot of the situation the black community is dealing with, like living in the inner city, is partly a result of the acts of our forefathers. People may not necessarily be there if it weren't for what happened in the past. Purebred white girls cannot stand up and say, "It's not my fault, I only want to help you people." Maybe it wasn't your fault, but it was your dad's fault and your dad's dad's fault.

So, in a nutshell, the difference between you is?

I understand how someone can be upset about something like that, whereas she can't.

Why is that, since you were both raised in similar communities?

I think that it's because, again, I am an antagonist. I think I'm very sensitive to the "underdog" regardless of what color or creed he may be. One of my favorite books is *Of Mice and Men* by John Steinbeck. Steinbeck likes the underdog. So in a situation like that, I understand how someone can say, "You owe me something." And if white people can say "your people" to us, then we can say, "your people" to them.

Does your wife understand that some black women might be offended that she married a black man?

No. She has no clue. We haven't even seen the movie *Waiting to Exhale*. I don't think that she's been in any situation that might suggest that she's taken from the black community?

What about the responsibility to her children? Does she understand that they can benefit tremendously from the black community?

Yes. We've done that together. And actually I think she initiated that. My oldest son, Josh, asks a lot of questions about things. One time he asked why we're all different colors. It was during the summer. Josh was darker than his brother. Shari, my wife, is very white and was darker, too. And I think Shari explained to Josh that we're all different races, colors, and creeds, that I have these mixes and she has these mixes . . . and so essentially he has African American blood in him. And she told him to be proud of it. A couple of days later, my son was standing in the grocery store saying that he was proud to be an African American.

So what are we going to do about race relations in America. Can't we all just get along?

Yes. Strange but true, that's really what it comes down to, get the "chip off your shoulder." I turned out fine, but people might say it's because I'm not in touch.

What makes you feel "fine"?

I'm proud of who I am. I'm proud of the family that raised me. I think they raised me well. I think I'm well adjusted. I'm proud of my Christianity and I want to bring that to my kids. My religion is more important to me than the color of my skin. That doesn't mean my ethnicity is not important.

Can we get along?

I think our society thrives on controversy, particularly surrounding race. Society loves to argue about this. I really don't think we're all going to "get along." It just can't be forced—maybe for our children, change can come.

Are there any final words you would like to say?

I worry about the way some people feel about their culture. I think you can have pride in your culture, that you should have pride in your culture. It's important to know as much as you can about your culture. And for someone like me who doesn't know a whole lot about his culture, I want to find out more. At this point in my life I have opportunities to take steps toward that. I have time on my hands, and I'm writing. I think we all need to take that opportunity.

Also, for a black community to feel—to use your phrase—"stripped from his community" I say, thank God there's a family that wants to take care of the child. If these parents fail to bring the child's ethnic background into their family, then, darn, why weren't you there? Why wasn't somebody from our culture, or whatever the particular culture is, there to raise these kids. Don't blame this white family for having the "nerve" to say we want to raise a child. They are doing the best they can. If they've made mistakes, don't blame them for it, because I'm sure they are looking back themselves and saying I wish we had done this or that. I think I'm doing a good job raising my sons right now, but I know there are things I did when my kids were younger that I probably never should have done. That's just part of raising kids.

Dan O'Brien

Moscow, Idaho
February 1998

When you have siblings from different backgrounds you learn we're who we are inside. How we were raised and where we got our traits is what defines us as individuals. It's not about the color of our skin or the way we look or how we're perceived by others.

Known for his accomplishments in the decathlon, Dan O'Brien shoots for excellence: "I want to be the best athlete I can be, and that is the best decathlete in the world." He has already made his mark by winning the decathlon gold medal Title in the 1996 Olympic Games plus many other titles and awards that gave him worldwide recognition. In 1998 he published his book, *The Ultimate Workout*. Dan's dedication to his sport has shown that he is on track to becoming the world's best decathlon athlete ever. Besides excelling in his professional career, Dan is committed to children. Through youth programs like the Dan O'Brien Youth Foundation he has encouraged thousands of kids to capitalize on their potential.

This athlete and child advocate has a big heart and is someone who was given a chance in life. He was born in July 1966 in Portland, Oregon to an African American father and a Finnish mother. His biological parents were young college students ill-prepared to raise a child. Soon after his birth, Dan entered the foster care system and remained there for two years. Then, in 1968, Jim and Virginia O'Brien, a young couple who saw a need to help children, adopted Dan and gave him a loving and stable home.

Much of Dan's personality and outlook on life took root within an ethnically diverse family. He grew up with five of his seven siblings in Klamath Falls, Oregon. Two of Dan's oldest siblings had moved out by the time he was in his teens. The other five siblings with whom he had closer relationships were all interracially adopted. Their ethnic backgrounds include Native American, Korean, Mexican, and African American. Dan's interest in learning about cultures and people developed because of the ethnic diversity within his own family. But he learned from family and peers that the character of an individual is ultimately more important than his or her skin color or ethnic background.

A college graduate and successful athlete, Dan O'Brien has crossed many milestones in his life. His energy, compassion, determination, focus, and discipline have carried him to a new level of self-confidence. Today he continues to reach for the gold.*

We'll go to the early part of your life with the O'Briens. Where were you raised?

I was raised in southern Oregon in a town called Klamath Falls, a community of about thirty thousand people. Definitely a white majority community, a lot of farmers. We lived on the river. My dad worked for the Weyerhauser Company which is one of the largest lumber producers in the world.

Do you have siblings?

When I first moved to Oregon I only had three. My mom had two kids of her own, Kathy and Scott, who were quite a bit older than me. When I was adopted at age 2, Kathy, who was the oldest daughter, was already out of the house. Scott only lived with us for six months before he moved out. Just a short while before adopting me, my parents adopted Karen, a 4-year-old Indian girl.

Of all of your siblings, are you the only African American?

No. I have a younger sister who was adopted right after me—her name is Patricia—when she was 18 months old. She is just like me—mixed, African American and white. We look like we could be biological brothers and sisters.

Do you identify yourself as African American?

Yes, absolutely.

Looking back on your family experiences, what were some of your happiest times?

The Christmases and other big holidays. Because we had so many kids, we had a lot of family around. And a lot of our family lived in Oregon or near Oregon. We had big Sunday dinners. We had huge Christmases with, I would say, a hundred people running around.

Clearly, you were close to your parents and your siblings.

Absolutely.

---

*   [Several months after this interview was completed, Dan competed in the 1998 Goodwill Games and went home with the gold medal in the decathlon.]

As a child, what did you enjoy doing the most by yourself?

I always enjoyed sports. I will never forget the sporting events in my life. I enjoyed going to school, although I wasn't very good at it.

I heard that as a small child you were already running while other children your age were still waddling.

Yes. When I was 4 and 5 years old I was pretty mobile. I could get around real well.

Were you exposed to many African Americans as a child?

Very few, maybe one or two here and there. And where I lived, African American kids were "thugs," bad kids. The kids everybody used to watch out for.

Did that affect your perception of African Americans?

A little bit because you tended to avoid those kids. I went to a school that was out in the country about five miles out of town. When you'd go into town, whether it was for summer camp or the YMCA, and suddenly you came up against these black kids and it was like, "Oh, man, are they going to shake me down here?"

Reflecting on it now, when you looked at these black kids and then at yourself, did you feel somehow that you were connected to them because you were black as well?

Not particularly. I am more connected with people on television. I definitely connected more to people on television.

Black people?

Yes. Some black people. I am mixed racially. On television I really did not see any mixed people. That was an interesting thing for me. I did not really see mixed people on TV, but I did not figure myself really as a black person—just a mixed race person. Like I said, the black kids in my community were a little bit rougher. It was interesting. I really did not see anybody that looked like me for quite a while.

In your own family, did you ask yourself, "Where do I fit in?"

I really didn't ask myself that very much. My brother is Hispanic and I think that once we got into the family we did kid stuff and that was important to me. We lived down on the river and played all of the time. We also had neighbors who came down and played with us. I thought that was cool.

Do you think you did not ask the "belonging" question because it was obvious to you that you were different?

I never asked that question. I think the biggest thing that comes with adoption is you don't have instant role models. You know when you grow up and look like your dad and you kind of got your mom's eyes, or whatever, I think that you fall under the category that you are going to be like them. And I always knew that I was never going to be like my parents.

How did that make you feel?

Well it was interesting because I took other parents on as role models. My friends' parents were people that I more looked at as people that I wanted to be like when I grew up. I had a friend whose father was a pilot. He traveled a lot and told interesting stories. I thought that, "Oh, man, I want to look up to him."

Because of what he did professionally?

Yes.

Was it helpful to you growing up that you had siblings from different ethnic backgrounds?

I think so. When you have siblings from different backgrounds you learn we're who we are inside. How we were raised and where we got our traits is what defines us as individuals. It's not about the color of our skin or the way we look or how we're perceived by others.

What values did your parents instill in you?

Politeness. Kindness. An ability to restrain myself from anger. Self control. And they definitely instilled in me the ability to know right from wrong.

You have a sense of being grounded. Where does that come from?

Being grounded was something that I got from my family growing up. I think that it is about having a certain attitude towards people.

Before being placed with the O'Briens, you were in foster care for two years. Do you have any emotional issues that you may have carried into your current situation?

I don't have one single memory from foster care. The only thing I remember is the day I went home with the O'Briens.

What was that experience like?

It was strange. As I grew up in this family I spent an enormous amount of time alone. I didn't have to. I chose to. Just sitting thinking, doing things by myself. Occupying my time by myself. When I first got adopted by the O'Briens I can remember doing a lot of things by myself or with my sister.

When you were by yourself, what were you thinking?

I don't really remember. I was very independent, even a loner at times. I've always been that way, but I don't care for it now. When I go on a trip to Europe, I have to take somebody with me. I wrote a fitness book and went on a two week tour and took somebody with me. I do that sort of thing a lot, just so I don't have to spend time by myself.

Do you have a desire to find your biological parents in the near future?

Not particularly, though I think about it sometimes. I think that maybe there will be a day when I need to, but I'm a firm believer that we are who we grew up to be, not who our biological parents really are. If my biological parents had a stable life that they were willing to share with me then I would have heard from them by now.

And if you heard from them, would you be willing to connect with them?

Sure. I'd be interested in seeing what they are all about. But the last thing I'd want to do is add stress to my situation right now as an athlete. A lot of things affect your training—and your happiness—from day to day. I don't want to get into a situation where my biological parents are needy people and have needy families. Or they're not nice people. I wouldn't want to burden myself with that sort of thing.

You talked about seeing yourself as mixed and that you did not identify with the black kids in your community when you were younger.

That's right.

Then did it ever hit you that you are an African American connected to a history in this country?

Not really. Not until I was older—when I got into college. When that happened it was a harsh reality. I started hanging out with some black people, wanting to understand and learn about my African American heritage. In general, I think that because I'm adopted, I'm naturally interested in different cultures. When I go to Hawaii, I love it. I see the culture and the roots that people came from. I'm also very interested in the Native Americans and their history. I didn't know anything about the African American history so someone had to take me through it. The people who helped me understand the history better were "hard," angry people. They felt that the white people were keeping the black man down. They were a little militant, I'd have to say. So I got a pretty odd perspective on what it meant to be black living in the state of Idaho.

When you went to school at the University of Idaho, did you know people who informed you that you were black?

A few. I was misunderstood, as well, in the fact that I didn't want to hang out with anybody on the football team or the basketball team. My best friend was a white kid, Canadian golfer. So I got asked about that a couple of times. My response was, who cares what color my friend is? If I want to hang out with black people, I'll find a black friend at some point.

Do you feel comfortable being with a person who happens to be white or black?

Absolutely. But there was a period in my life for maybe a year or two when I had to date only black women. I got hooked there for a little while. I still believe that black women are very beautiful. And if I weren't with somebody now, I'd date a black woman if I was so inclined. Yes, there was a small period where it was like, "Wow!" I was intrigued by black women and I had to go out with only black women for a while.

In your recently released book, *The Ultimate Workout*, you wrote, "There are holes in my past and as a teenager I struggled with my identity." What do you mean by that?

I think that as you grow up you are always trying to find out what arena you are going to fit into. For me to find my place I had to try many things as a kid, especially sportswise. I played all different kinds of sports. I played in the band. I did a lot of group-oriented things. To be honest, I still struggled with feeling like I didn't fit in. By that I mean I wasn't in the "cool" clique in school. I never dated the best looking girls in school. I was kind of skinny and a nerd when I was in school. As I got older and bigger, things changed. I found my niche. I became a very good athlete and suddenly became accepted because of that.

How did your exploration of different interests shape your personality?

When I entered college, I had a wide variety of friends. Some of my friends were white, some were black, some were wealthy, and some weren't. Some were stoners, some were cowboys. I believe that's because I was an open person and still am. I found people I could associate with and who I liked. I could associate with anybody. I used to call myself the chameleon in college because I could fit into any social group that I felt like at the time. I think that's indicative of people who are adopted.

I like that chameleon concept. It rings true.

But I also want to say that when I was growing up and doing a lot of things, I preferred spending time with a good friend to having a girlfriend. Growing up, I didn't have a lot of girlfriends so it seemed like I was a bit of a loner. But as long as I had one good friend I could spend some time with, I was fine. I didn't feel like I had to date or have romances.

You have professional interactions with African Americans—Olympic runner Michael Johnson, for one. Have those experiences helped shape your views about the African American culture?

Michael and I are good friends and I've met his family on a few different occasions. I see a lot of what white America doesn't see. There are black families who are smart and educated. They all don't have "chips" on their shoulders. They are happy where they live. They have a real strong family system. They don't all love rap music. So I think what we are seeing here is the Michael Johnson family who are Americans, rural Americans. They're not inner city. They're not "down." They're not "hype." Michael is kind of a nerd, all in all. He was in school. And I think that when you see a family like that, you think, "that's interesting," especially if they aren't the black individuals you see on a regular basis. I know a lot of black athletes and their families from Los Angeles, and they have a different life. Black Americans in Los Angeles live a different life than, say, black Americans in Texas do. And so, that is what you see. You see a big contrast of individuals. Michael is a track and field guy. And you can see that. He's smart, calculating, and organized. And you have to be that way to be in track and field.

In your book you write about becoming the best athlete as a way of "reaching inside and pushing on to face the moment of truth . . . and quieting your fears." How do you translate that into your own personal journey of discovering who you are?

I think that anytime you are afraid to do things, it holds you back, especially when it comes to meeting new people and going new places. Overcoming fear is hard. I can honestly say that the first time I went to Europe, I hated it.

Where did you go?

The first time I went to Spain. I had that really harsh, out-of-place feeling. I also had jet lag. I'm the type of person, though, who resists change in his life. When I moved out of the house right after high school, it was hard to do. When I went to college away from home, the first month was like, "I'm getting out of here, I'm leaving." But I learned that you have to give things a chance to settle in. But every time I go to Europe for a few days, I get this out-of-place feeling.

So how do you conquer your fear of traveling to the unknown, knowing that your profession is going to take you around the world?

I surround myself with people who can take my mind off of that.

People who identify with the same culture as you do?

That's right. All the time growing up we'd get a new car in the family and I'd say, what about the old one? I like the old one. So here I am, making changes in my life, and it's hard to do. I think it's necessary, though, and I'm thinking more about the future.

Please remind me of what you told me off-tape. What country did you say is second to the United States in the rate of child adoptions?

Sweden. I don't know if more Swedish kids are adopted there, but Sweden is second to the United States in families looking to adopt. When I won my first championship in Gothenberg, Sweden, I did numerous interviews with different adoption agencies.

I'm going now to a time in 1986 when you were struggling for direction in your life. By 1986 you lost your sports scholarship at the university and you had alcohol problems, among other issues. Mentally, what was going on with you at that time?

It was a learning process for me. My life had been very structured in high school. When I was in high school everybody was talking about my potential. I think I just needed to be wild for awhile and get away from all that expectation. And that's exactly what happened. I got crazy in college. That was a time in my life when I thought I needed to spread my wings socially. I was going to get out there and meet people and have fun. You have to realize that the drinking age in Idaho was only 19 at the time. So we were able to go out and act like dopes.

You've found it within yourself to come out of that phase and focus on developing and maintaining your strength, discipline, and determination. How have you been able to do this with so many potential distractions?

A big factor is not wanting anything else. I want to make a living at this. I want to look back when I'm fifty and say, man, I was the best ever in something. And I think my drive comes from just that. It may stem from being adopted. But ultimately to be the best, to be good at something is about creating a myth, a respect, a name for yourself. And I can honestly say that growing up as an adopted person, I had the O'Brien name, but what does that really mean? If I were a Kennedy, that would mean a lot. So all the time I was growing up, I thought, all right, I'm creating my own history, my own legacy, my own name for myself. When my kids look back, they'll be able to say, "I'm an O'Brien, and this is what my family has done."

That's a fulfilling outlook and certainly an incentive to strive toward excellence.

I think the biggest problem in today's society is that there are so many kids out there who are trying to find their way and where they belong. I believe that many of the kids struggling with this are adopted kids. So you get kids hanging out in gangs, kids living on the edge, doing questionable things. And why? Because they just want to fit in. There are a lot of kids out there who look at black and white and ask, "Who am I?" I'm black. I'm white. Well, who cares? I think all of Los Angeles is becoming half-Hispanic. You go to certain parts of LA and everybody looks the same. I was at an art gallery opening in Los Angeles, and I began to feel like it was almost a unisex type of atmosphere. I see it happening all over the world. For people to say that I'm black, I'm white seems odd today; we're all getting so mixed together that I think it's time to be individuals. Individuals are what makes us, not the color of our skin. When we see people on TV we want to be a basketball player or a football player. That's all fine and dandy but you're not going to achieve that because you're black or because you're white or because you're Hispanic. You're going to do it because you're an individual who is doing these things.

This is something I see a lot of. I live in the northwest part of Idaho where there are not many black communities. If you go to Portland, Oregon, or Seattle, you're going to find many black communities. The tri-cities are a few hours away from where I live. It's like three towns all connected and there's about thirty to forty thousand people in each town. There's this kid who comes from Kinnowick. He grew up in a rural community. His father is black and his mom is white. The whole family is mixed, but they're darker than I am. This kid comes to Washington State. What does he do? He joins a black fraternity. He listens to nothing but rap music. He hangs out with kids from LA—and he thinks he's from the "hood." And he's saying, "Well, this is the real me. This is the real black me coming out." I told him, "Dude, you are from rural white America. If I hear you say that you are "down" one more time, I'm going to . . ." What makes me laugh more than anything is the big, tall, white basketball player on the team. He sounds just like the "brothers." How come? Who knows. That's what I'm seeing. It's very strange. For example, I used to go out dancing. I used to think that as soon as I start dancing, the "black" starts coming out of me. I've got great rhythm and I can hear and feel the music. And I agree with stuff like that. But when it comes to rap music and calling women "bitches" and things like that, I don't see it. I've noticed that on a lot of occasions kids from this area who are black try to explore their black history and stuff. And they get drawn in.

What do you say to them, given that they live in a rural area in Idaho?

I say, "You are not from the hood! You haven't struggled like the kids from Compton (California)." A couple of kids from Compton were on our track team. Those kids didn't want to go back there!

What is your take on adopted kids in general? Would you say they are generally similar in their attitudes and outlook on life?

It's funny that you ask that. I met a girl at a restaurant a couple of years ago and we got to talking. I asked her, "You're adopted, aren't you?" She seemed surprised that I knew. I told her I was adopted, too. It was interesting because we had the same idiosyncrasies and the same attitude about stuff. This girl could have been my twin sister. She was of mixed race and had been through the ringer as much as I had. I noticed that she adapted well to different situations, and she was very happy. I think that adopted people are happy—either miserable and on the brink or happy.

Ready to crack or you're happy?

Absolutely. People in my own family have been there and have cracked.

Why?

For a number of different reasons. I have a younger sister who tried to commit suicide. Now she has two kids and she's happy. But for a while during the late part of her high school years, she couldn't deal with who she was and how she fit in, if she was black or white. She couldn't deal with it. And she was a very attractive young girl. When she was 13 she looked like she was 18. She was approached in many different ways by a lot of different people. The bottom line was, she didn't know who was real and who was her friend.

How do you find out where you belong?

I don't think that people find out where they belong. I think you find out who you are and you should be happy with that. Right now I have this notion in my mind that says, "Well, if I could just find the right town to live in, I'd be happy, the town that would give me this and this and this." That town doesn't exist. You might find a place you enjoy living in, but this dream place I think I'm going to find where I'll live happily ever after just doesn't exist. It has to be inside me. I have to be happy inside. So that's what I've been doing for the past few years—creating my own happiness. Then you can live anywhere and be happy. The cool thing is that I have a soulmate now. So as long as we're together, I don't care where we are.

You started a youth foundation to assist children in developing personal, educational, and athletic skills, and you traveled to Sweden, Spain, France, and other countries both to compete athletically and to communicate a message about the value of children. What is your philosophy behind encouraging children to strive for excellence and find their purpose in life?

I think we need to allow kids to make their own decisions. But it's also important to hold kids back. Obviously, if you're exposed to drugs at a young age, you're going to do drugs at a young age. If you're exposed to sex at a young age, you're going to have sex and make bad decisions at a young age. My parents did a really good job holding me back. I had curfews. I had limits on what I was able to do. My parents didn't just ship me off to a friend's house every weekend. I had to go to church at least twice a month. That was just part of the deal. I used to get mad at my mom, and say, "Hey, why can't I do some of this stuff?" Now, I look back at it and think that if I could have stayed out all night when I was 15, I would have made a lot of bad decisions. At the same time it's important that we create an atmosphere where kids can learn to be themselves, not an atmosphere where you're controlling them for the sake of controlling them.

I hear you say it's good to define parameters for a kid to instill a sense of values, ethics, and responsibility but simultaneously allow the child to develop into who he or she is meant to be.

Yes. It's about letting kids create their own identities. Show them that it's not about being black or white. Unfortunately, kids want to fit into a group or a clique. I like to tell kids to try everything (educationally, professionally, and personally rewarding). There's a really cool commercial out right now based on the show *Third Rock from the Sun*. It's a crazy show on NBC about a group of aliens who look like humans and are trying to learn about life on earth. Well, the youngest boy has long hair and is kind of a "nerdy" kid. In this ad on TV, he says, "The neatest kids in school are always the ones who are independent and unique. Be different. Don't be the norm."

He's trying to get kids to quit smoking and doing drugs, that sort of thing. That's the most important message we can give to kids. Be uniquely you. Don't try to wear somebody else's color and act like the group. The mass media makes us want to be Hollywood movie stars or superstar athletes because it portrays that life as the greatest life you could live. I don't agree with that.

You don't agree that being a superstar is the greatest life to live or that mass media should be forming our agendas without us knowing it?

I've been on both ends. I've lived in the fast lane and I've lived a regular life. There's too much of an extreme between Michael Jordan and my accountant. If you asked Michael Jordan what he'd really like to do, he might say that he'd like to be anonymous just for a day, so he could go out and have a nice quiet dinner, go to the movies. The things I like most in my life are the quiet moments where it's just me and my girlfriend or me with some friends or like the time I spent in Hawaii where nobody recognized me. Those things mean more to me than anything else. Obviously, when I get to sit courtside at the Phoenix Suns games and I sign a bunch of autographs, it's fulfilling and kind of fun. A lot of people recognize me. It's neat. But those are not the times I live for.

Since it's February, Black History Month, I think it's fitting to ask you about your views on black history as it relates to youth.

We are trying to create a black history for our youth. The problem is that we don't get beyond the point of telling our children about the struggles and pain that got us this far as black people. We focus mainly on the limitations and boundaries that have been set up for us. So instead of major league baseball players saying, "Look, we've been in major league baseball forever, and this is where we belong." Instead, we keep looking back at Jackie Robinson and saying, "Hey, we've only been in the major leagues for thirty or forty years." So we put up barriers for ourselves because of that. I think we need to learn about black history and understand it but not dwell on it. I think that's what's giving people "chips" on their shoulders. We feel we've been treated unfairly for years and therefore it's O.K. for us to walk around with a bad attitude.

To close our discussion, what are your future goals?

I just want to be the athlete I think I can be. And that's the best decathlete in the world, ever. That purpose is something that really gives me strength in an everyday way. For me, it's about knowing that I'm working hard toward a good goal and providing for myself and my family.

And when it's all over?

And when it's all over, I hope to be associated with some of the best athletes ever.

Seth D. Himrod

EVANSTON, ILLINOIS
MAY 1998

My experiences growing up with my family have helped me not only socially but also in my career choices. I'm able to deal with people in a variety of cultures. I can talk with rich white Americans. I can talk with rich black Americans. I can talk with middle class whites and blacks, and I can talk with poor people.

An advocate for children, Seth D. Himrod speaks publicly about the need to find permanent homes for adoptable children. In 1998 he spoke at the second annual "Chances for Children" event in Chicago sponsored by the Illinois Department of Children and Family Services; Cook County Juvenile Court; One Church, One Child; the Adoption Information Center of Illinois; and the George Halas/Walter Payton Foundation.

Seth was born in Refugio, Texas, in 1971. After waiting in foster care for six months, he was given the gift of a family. The Himrod family adopted Seth and raised him in Evanston, Illinois, where he lives today. During his childhood and adolescent years, he was exposed to a racially and socio-economically diverse community. He saw African Americans who specialized in medicine and law, among other professions.

Growing up in a white family, Seth always knew he was different. Still, he believes he had a normal upbringing. Seth attributes much of his security to the love he received from his parents, their openness to talk with him about personal and social issues, and the opportunities he gained from living in an interracial home. He learned to find balance by accepting the culture of his family and appreciating the value of his African American, white, and Native American heritages.

Currently Seth is a stockbroker and an army reservist. From 1989 to 1992 he was on active duty and spent several months in Kuwait. On returning from Kuwait he settled in Evanston where he excelled as a licensed stockbroker. He recently opened his own firm. In addition to the positions he now holds, Seth plans to become a drill sergeant for the army and work as a firefighter.

Seth Himrod has a 9-year-old son, Timothy, and he maintains close relationships with his parents, both of whom have doctorate degrees. Seth's father is employed as a reference librarian and his mother is a clinical social worker.

As a transracial adoptee and spokesperson for such adoptions, you participated in Chances for Children. Tell me about the event.

It's a sort of big friendly workshop and meeting place for prospective adoptive parents, children available for adoption, foster families—black and white, adoptees, and volunteers. At this place you can get fingerprinted, talk to counselors, ask questions, and start the process of adoption in a more friendly environment than what has gone on before in other situations, I'm sure. You've probably heard the horror stories of people waiting for months, even years, to adopt and never getting a child.

It seems the event went well. I haven't touched base with the followup. Of course there's political discussion about the event. Some people were saying that the kids were on display and all this other "b.s." Regardless, I didn't think the criticism affected the outcome of the event.

What was your role in Chances for Children?

I did two workshops where I talked about an hour with a panel of different people about adoption issues. The black and white combination seems to be the most common in our society and that is what I speak on because I know it best. It seems to me that you need to understand how race affects the way that we live, and how race plays a part in America. Race might not necessarily dive into everybody's life, especially if you're a white family that hasn't experienced this 'ism.' By having a child who is biracial, black, Asian, or Hispanic, you're inevitably going to run into situations in your life that will be different than if you were a traditional white family. That's something I speak on quite a bit. That's not to say that the differences are bad, but if your transracial child comes home and has had a racial slur thrown at him or her, parents need to know how to deal with that. A really good point was brought up at this seminar that if you're a white couple and have grown up in a traditional white family, and you're thinking about adopting a black child, you need to look at your surroundings. Do you associate with black people? Do you have any black friends? Not just at work. Do you have any people in your life that have a cultural background different than your own? If you don't and you're over 30 or

35 years of age, you have to ask yourself, why? Not that that's good, bad, or otherwise, but you have to be aware of it, because as soon as you adopt a child of color you cease to be a white family.

Would you say, then, that it's not O.K. to raise a black child in a rural area, away from his or her ethnic group?

I think that's not O.K. One person on the panel grew up in a rural area in Kansas. She expressed concern or wished that there had been other children of color growing up with her. She said that if there was just one other boy of color in her high school, then she was supposed to date him because there wasn't a lot of flexibility. Whereas myself, I grew up in an integrated community racially and socioeconomically. Where I lived there were great big swings both ways. It was much easier for me to blend in and not feel like I was in the fish bowl. My environment helped me. I don't say this to mean that raising a black child in an all-white community can't work or be positive. But if there are other children and other individuals around you with similar backgrounds, that can help. If as a child or adolescent you can look at a black person who's a doctor, then as a black child of a white family you can say O.K., there's someone I can identify with, instead of only having TV or no black role models at all.

Being a transracial adoptee, you don't deny the culture of the family you're with and you don't deny the culture you were born into. I think you need to have a good balance and a family that is open. You have to have the openness and willingness to communicate your feelings to people.

You mentioned feeling like you were in a fish bowl in reference to being black in a white family. What was it like for you to be raised in a white family?

I think that because I was adopted at such a young age—I was less than a year old—I don't recall any other lifestyle. So I can't say that living in a black family is different. My white family is all I know. As far back as I can remember I knew I was different. It was never a problem. My family, cousins, aunts, uncles were all very open about it. If there were people in my family who had a problem with a child of color in the family, I don't ever remember hearing anything about it. I'm not saying that it wasn't going on behind the scenes, but as a child I don't remember hearing anything about it. My grandfather, who was 80-plus years old, born in 1890, used to read to me on his knee like any grandfather would. So I don't think my skin color was the biggest issue for me being in a white family. My family accepted me. I got presents from my aunts and uncles and cousins, and I played with them. That was great!

You are the only child in your adoptive family?

Yes.

So how did you deal with some of the challenges that transracial adoptees face? Who did you go to, or were you one of those strong ones that didn't need to go to anybody?

I was born a man and I never had any problems. I went to my parents at times for some things and to my friends at other times. I think that growing up in a white culture, with a white family, forced me to deal with people as they are and not just their skin color. So I have friends who are white and friends who are black. And I think that situation made me a person who's a good judge of character.

How so?

I'd watch people. I'd see how they acted and what they did and then judge them on that basis. Instead of saying, O.K., those people are black and are dressed a certain way, so they must be gang bangers. Or that person's white and dresses a certain way, so he must hate black people. To lump all black people, all white people, all Native Americans in their own separate category would be to disrespect my family, as well as myself. I happen to be part white, part black, part Native American.

In other words, you couldn't stop at the stereotypes in determining your friendships and interactions with people.

Right.

That's a good point. I was just talking to my dad about that. I don't assume that all white people are racist and are conspiring to ruin black people, because my own father and mother are white and I know that they love me and have sacrificed so much for me. It's not easy to move past the stereotypes, but you must in order to maintain the integrity of your family.

Right. Like I said, because I grew up not knowing any other way, that seemed to me to be the right way. So now when I talk with people who have cultural biases, I tell them that not everybody is like that. When I listen to some white people talk, they say, these black people are all like that, they just want to "bee bop"—and I say, no, that's not the way it is.

I think my experiences growing up with my family have helped me not only socially but also in my career choices. I'm able to deal with people in a variety of cultures. I can talk with rich white America, rich black America, middle-class whites and blacks, and poor people.

Where were you raised?

In Evanston, Illinois, a suburb touching the north side of Chicago. Northwestern University is there. It's sort of a college town/suburb/northern extension of the city. So, like I said, you have a wide range of people. You have blacks, whites, Asians, Hispanics. You have college students. You have people who moved from the city. In the northern suburbs you have million-dollar homes, doctors and lawyers, etc. So you meet a lot of different people. You either view a certain clique as all being the same because they're rich or you learn to view everybody as an individual.

Did you know other transracial adoptees growing up?

Only on a few occasions. Looking back, it would have been good if I'd gotten to know other kids who were transracially adopted like me. I'm doing that now, as a grown-up, meeting other transracial adoptees and asking, "Did that happen to you, too?"

Looking at it from the eyes of a grown-up, I'm much more critical. I look at a lot more things. As a kid I was concerned with playing baseball, footfall, basketball, and watching cartoons.

Kids don't seem overly concerned about race issues. As a kid, I just wanted to play with other kids my own age and have fun.

Right! The race issue came into play in junior high school. I did have some racial slurs thrown at me and had problems as a child, but that happens because you're a child. That's going to happen no matter where you live, whatever your upbringing. Kids are going to be kids.

Did your parents intentionally live in an integrated community, or did they just happen to live in Evanston?

I think it was just that they happened to be there and Evanston was the right fit. My dad got a job working at the seminary while he was finishing his Ph.D. and my mom was a social worker in a suburb a little farther north from here. I don't know if they made a conscious decision, I didn't really ask them. It might have been some blind luck, seeing that I was born in Texas. Neither one of my parents are from Texas. My dad is from Minneapolis and my mom is from Long Beach, California. They had to come into this sort of triangle, geographically, to find me. Divine intervention.

Did your parents explain to you why they adopted you?

I don't know if it was infertility problems, and I don't know if I ever really asked. I just assumed that if they wanted to have kids, they would have had them.

Do you think it affected you in some way that you were the only dark-skinned person in your family?

Probably. When you're a teenager, you start looking at yourself more. And you wonder how other people perceive you. I always knew I was different, but that that was O.K. My parents never said, you're different so here are the rules for you. I was just part of the family.

How did your parents show you that you were part of their family?

They showed me love, compassion, understanding. Just the way all good parents do. They support you, they're open, they talk with you, they give you opportunities. They put food on the table, help you with your homework, tuck you in at night, read you stories. All that stuff. In that sense I had a very normal, healthy childhood. I had a great time. I went to church. I sang in the choir until my voice changed. I was an altar boy—it's called an acolyte at my church. I played sports from the time I was 5 until I left for the army. So my parents supported me in what I wanted to do—cub scouts, baseball. They set limits. You can't do this, you can't run the streets at night. You're not going to join a gang and all this other stuff. I needed that direction, and they gave it to me.

At what age did somebody make derogatory statements to you because of your skin color, and do you remember discussing the incident with your parents?

I was probably in first grade, 6 or 7 years old. I was just thinking about that the other day. I think we were in a snowball fight, white kids and black kids. One of the white kids said a racial slur, and one of the black kids got mad and started crying. Well, I got mad and started crying, too. At 6 you really don't understand. I told my dad that I was upset. And he was upset and talked with me about it. From then on, whenever those situations erupted, I believed I could go to him and tell him how I felt. And that became more important when the situation got worse.

In your own transition from a child to a man, how has society treated you because you're black?

As I got older, I stopped being this cute little boy and others perceived me as this black teenager and a menace to society. Apparently, I was liable to rape, kill, or whatever. I got pulled over by the cops, I got slammed against the wall with a flashlight up in my face. Questions were thrown at me, like what am I doing? Where am I going? You fit the description; come over here, we got to talk to you. Those things are what anger me. The fact that I was able to go to my dad and see his pain and outrage, the same way as I was feeling even though he never experienced it, was a support system for me. He never had a cop do that to him. Instead of asking me what I was doing, he'd tell me I should be upset about what happened.

How do you make sense of that kind of indoctrination, going from a cute black boy to a menace to society?

I think that's a difficult issue black males have in general. Whether you're biracial or very dark, you're going to have those problems.

It's clear that as a black individual raised in a white family you're not exempt from the reality of being a black male in America.

That's right. In fact, you may be more so if you lived in a community that was 99 percent white and you're the only black person living there. And if somebody robs a store, the residents are going to be, like, "Well, there you go." Because that's what people are taught. They watch the news and see black kids on TV killing each other, and they assume, "Well, hey, he must be doing that." At 15 or 16, I wasn't doing anything like that.

When I do public speaking before parents who have dark-skinned sons, I tell them to prepare for the fact that their sons will be treated unfairly because of the color of their skin.

I can't even imagine what my relationship would be like with my family if they weren't close to me. I live next door to them now. I don't ever want to move. I'd like to stay as close to them as possible.

It sounds like you have a good relationship with your parents.

I think I do, now more so than when I was a teenager. As a teenager, you don't want to be close with your parents just because they're your parents. From 14 to 18 you want to pretend that you're on your own. But I have a great relationship with them and I can go to my dad and say, "It happened again, Dad." I was sitting outside my house and a cop stopped me and asked me what I was doing there. I told him, "I live here. I pay taxes that pay your salary. That's what I'm doing here." "Well, you have a smart mouth," he says. I'm tired of that. I can't sit on my front porch and enjoy a summer night because that's "probable cause." And I'm in the suburbs. If you're in a more isolated area, where you're the only one, you stick out like a sore thumb. If anything goes wrong, you're the one who is going to get caught. I think parents need to know that their young men are going to go through that.

You're a professional and a contributor to this society, and yet you are still a victim of injustice.

Absolutely. I can be wearing a suit and tie and carrying a briefcase on my way to talk with some guy about hundreds of thousands of dollars of investments. But when I'm driving in a car, I'm just a black guy. I'm one of "them." Apparently I'm part of the problem, not the solution. Maybe I think that way because I've been pulled over so often for no apparent reason. To be fair, I was pulled over the other day and I think I was speeding, I had my military uniform on, and I was coming home from weekend duties. And I got a warning, believe it or not. The cop looked to be mixed, either Hispanic or mixed black and white. He said I was speeding. I don't know if I was or not. Another car passed me, so I wasn't the only one. It was the first time I only got a warning. I thought that was pretty cool. I've been stopped when I was wearing my uniform and taken out of the car. It's a problem.

What do you do professionally?

I'm a stockbroker. I run my own small firm. In the building I live in there's a one-bedroom apartment. I live upstairs. When my tenant moved out, I turned the one-bedroom apartment into an office and moved my business in there last fall. I've been a stockbroker since 1994. So I'm closing in on about four years. I started when I was 23, right when I was a trainee for five or six months. I got my license in the beginning of 1995 and left the company I was at. Then I worked at a black-owned firm, which was very nice. I did pretty well early on and rose to vice president in about ten months. Close to a year after that I was the president. I was 24 and managing guys who were 15 to 20 years my senior. It was a great experience. I passed up offers downtown that, looking back, would have made me more money, but I had a good rapport with the owner and he was a friend and mentor at the time. But then, as with all business relationships, sometimes it's time to take a different direction, so I decided to be on my own.

How is that going for you?

It's going O.K. I make O.K. money. I sometimes need to make more. Because I work on my own, I can have months when I work very hard and make lots of money. And I have months when I work very hard and make no money. I don't have a large clientele. I keep my business small. I purposely do that. I don't want to be a slave to my job. If I worked downtown, the money would be better but the lifestyle would be twelve-hour days at the office plus an hour commute each way. I wouldn't have any time for my son, for TV, or for a social life and doing other things I like to do. Being my own boss gives me some control. It lets me do what I want and set my own hours somewhat. However, I do need to watch the stock market on the screens during the day. Besides that, I do some part time security work at the hospital every now and then, hardly worth mentioning. And then my other job is working in the army reserve. I was in the active army for three years—joined when I was 17 and finishing up high school. I had the grades to go to college. My parents very much wanted me to go. But college wasn't calling me. I like to learn what I want to learn, like being a stockbroker. I grasped everything there is to know about becoming a stockbroker in a very short time. I have never failed an exam to get my stockbroker and manager licenses.

Let me go back to the army reserve. I did active duty from 1989 to 1992 and spent about seven months in Desert Storm. I jumped out of planes and fired weapons. I was a paratrooper. I liked all that high-speed stuff.

I've been doing that for a while. I just recently got back in the reserves to be an instructor. I want to be a drill sergeant and teach the young men the things I learned in my brief stint in combat and just other things that I learned in the military that can help make it a better place. I'd like to show that there are other people out there who aren't making the same mistakes as some of these drill sergeants you may have read about in the press. A lot of it is blown out of proportion, but a lot of it is certainly out of control. So you need to have people with integrity teaching young soldiers how to defend our country, because it's very important.

How have you maintained your focus and integrity in all of this?

I think my family taught me a lot of that. I think that because I'm a male I identify with dad on a lot of things. He's a small guy. I've been as big as him since I was 14 or 15 and definitely as strong as he is. Professionally, my dad is a librarian. He taught me a sense of right and wrong and gave me a religious background. He taught me that a man is only as good as his word, no matter what. A lot of things can be taken away from you—your dignity, your humanity, your life—but my word is mine. So when I say something, I mean it. I'm going to be there for you. That's important to me. I think one principle here guides all the other things. So if I say I'm going to show up to work on time, then I'll be at work on time. If I say I'm going to work hard and support my son, then that's what I'm going to do. I think if you look at it that way, it's easier to maintain the straight and narrow path. Yes, along the way there are temptations and you can make a quick buck here and there. But if you know it's wrong, you don't do it.

Another thing, by having a child at a young age—I was barely 18—I have to look at things from the standpoint of what I'm going to tell my child about right and wrong. I can't very well tell my son not to do drugs if I do drugs or tell him not to drink and drive if I drink. He never sees me drinking a beer. Now he may decide to drink when he grows up, and that's fine. I choose not to. That's my choice. What am I going to do, rob banks for a living and tell him he shouldn't steal? So I think my dad and mom instilled in me things that are acceptable behavior. These are the values our society is based on. Not everyone will follow those things, but my parents said to me, "You can make sure you do what you know is right and do your best."

I don't want to come off as some sort of saint. Nothing can be farther from the truth. I've strayed from the beaten path as much as the next guy. I was a teenage father, so obviously I'm not perfect. However, I wouldn't be ashamed to put my life on the table to be scrutinized. I'm not proud of everything I've done, but I've owned up to everything I've done up to this point. We'll see what next week brings.

Why did you choose to be a stockbroker?

All the jobs I have are important to me because, through them, I can affect people's lives. That might sound kind of sappy. Another thing I'm trying to do is become a fireman two days a week—forty-eight hours on and seventy-two hours off. That will allow me to run my business and spend time with my family. If I have that, I'm Superman, I'm happy. That and a big-screen TV and watching the Minnesota Vikings in the Super Bowl. I don't have to be a Hollywood movie star. My athletic dreams have turned into recreational activities. I understand reality. Anyway, a fireman can save people's property and their lives and really make a difference. As a drill sergeant, I can help teach young men to stay alive. That's the bottom line— to stay alive and do their jobs. If I can do that, I can help families avoid the grief of having their sons come home dead. And as a stockbroker I affect not only their lives but their family's future. I can help a family invest so they can buy a house later on. Fifteen years from now their child is getting ready to go to college and they've saved a college fund because we invested wisely. And then, when they're getting ready to retire at 45 or 55 or 65, they have enough money to make the decision. If they want to work they can, and if they don't they don't have to. So those three activities kind of define who I am. I'm not *totally* giving. I want to be paid for my services. But I don't think I ever take more than I give—I think there's a balance there, and that's what I like.

How does a conversation differ when you're discussing long-term investment with white individuals as opposed to black individuals?

The major difference is that in the black community investments are never talked about. The topic of investment was not discussed with us as children or as grown-ups. We're not educating ourselves to make a conscious decision to put something aside for later. It can't all be about the present. I know that when I was 24, 25, I bought a house. I sacrificed buying a brand new car. And believe me, I fought with that decision for a long while because I drive an old, beat-up Chevy station wagon. Some of my friends drive a Lexus or a new Toyota or Blazer. That's all well and fine, but you have to talk about investing for the future.

My biggest challenge when I'm talking with black people is that they've never seen an investment. Or the only investment knowledge they have is that investment is too risky and you'll lose all your money. It seems everybody has a friend who lost $50,000.

What is the makeup of your clientele?

Probably the top four or five are white and one or two are black. I don't care anything about color. The color that matters most to me is green. A lot of my clients grew up rather affluent or they've been investing for years and they have large portfolios. They're interested in the bottom line. How much money can I make? They understand the risks, and are willing to take certain risks. They understand that tax laws are encouraging you to take certain risks in the stock market because you can recoup some of your losses.

In the black community, on the other hand, I often see a mind-set of, "I don't want to pay that much, and I really don't want to risk any money." That mentality is understandable because the information hasn't flown in our area. It's not taught in the high schools. Whereas in my high school we had classes where we did little stock market games and pretended to invest money in the stock market. So I was already investing when I was 15.

Did you go to college? Where did you learn so much about this?

I didn't go to college. I don't know if that's the right image to project. Education is good. But, for me, I knew what I wanted to do. I wanted to manage money. I just had to find a way to learn how to do it. And I did. And the kids really like hearing that. I like seeing their faces light up whether I'm talking about transracial adoption or finance.

You have a passion to contribute to society.

I think that's something we have to do as professionals in the black community. We need to go back to the community and tell kids that there are lots of opportunities out here. Yes, everybody wants to be a professional athlete. When I was in high school, that's what I wanted to be. But you realize somewhere along the way that you're not the best kid on the team, and so you're not going to be the best in the world, ever. When that reality sets in, you have to decide what you're going to do with your life.

I always knew I was going to wear a suit and tie. I just didn't know exactly what I was going to work at. I was always into money. Despite the rumor, not all white families are rich. I grew up very middle-class. For example, I didn't get my first car until I was 21. But the food was on the table. I think I had a nice upbringing, and I feel blessed.

I want to go back to the issue of providing children permanent homes. What do you believe we as a society need to do to encourage the placement of children in permanent and stable homes?

I think adoption agencies need to recruit prospective adoptive parents. They're out there; you just need to find them. They want to adopt a child, but they may be a little gun shy or afraid of the process because of the horror stories that get in the news. There was the baby Richard case not too long ago where a child was taken back from a family after being in their care for several years. And there's the recurring problem of terminating parental rights.

I think it's important that we have more events like Chances for Children. Every little bit helps. Every opportunity these kids have to get prospective adoptive families, every time we can qualify a family, is a step that needs to be taken. I'm not suggesting we just ignore basic requirements in the process. There needs to be a background check done on parents. But I think those security measures can be done in a matter of months, not years. I'm not a social worker and haven't gone through the adoption process myself so I don't know all the details that go into solidifying homes for kids. Still, I think there are so many kids out there who want the opportunity to have a home and there are so many parents out there who want to give a child the opportunity to have a home—yet somehow they pass like ships in the night. And why? Because we get mired in this bureaucracy that believes that kids need to be with this or that race of parents. *And caught in the middle are the kids.*

Children are the greatest asset in the world, yet we treat hundreds and thousands of our children like a poor investment.

I couldn't have said it better myself. What can an abandoned 15-year-old boy do, living in the city, a kid who hasn't been raised with any sort of moral background or rules to follow and without stability or love? Then all of a sudden he's released into society at 16. What's he going to do?

Look at the background of some of the strongest people in society. I bet very few grew up on the streets with no parents or guidelines. It takes a strong person to be great. Look at the heroes and the great people we have. Many of them came from a strong family environment, even if they only had a single parent, male or female. I overheard this argument the other day where someone said, women raise children better. I'll argue against that opinion all day. I'm a single dad and I think I'm doing all right. What better role model for a young boy than a dad? Or what better role model than a mom? It's about someone who's going to be there all the time. Not this XYZ family for the first nine years and this other ABC family for the next seven years. Somebody you can belong to is what's important. Take pride in your last name, and in who you are, and that you belong to this family. Families have pluses and minuses, and you get both. That's a good thing.

A very good thing. What are the values you instill in your son, Timothy? He just turned nine?

Yes. I'll be the first to admit that I'm not nearly the parenting team my parents were, because I'm doing it on my own. The two-parent family is a great way to go but I'm a single parent. I just try to teach him to be respectful of others. Right now he goes to church more than I do, because I work into the middle of the night sometimes. That's not an excuse, though. I expect him to do his chores and to be part of this family. He understands that and takes pride in being part of our family. When he makes a mistake or gets into trouble, as all children do, he understands that he not only let himself down but that he also let the family down. Again, he's part of the family. It goes beyond just me and him. Even though we're not Himrods by blood, we're Himrods by family. My mother is no more a blood relative to my father than I am. Yet, they love each other the same way they love me and the same way I love my son. So that's what I teach him, that the family unit can have many different shapes. There's no one correct way. A lot of blood-related people can't stand each other. But our family is small, and I think we're close-knit. I even feel good about the cousins, aunts, and uncles who I don't often see. I get cards from them for my birthday and we talk once in a while, and that's because we all lead very busy lives and live in distant parts of the country. But we're still family.

Lester Smith Sr.

HYATTSVILLE, MARYLAND
JULY 1997

*Transracial adoptees and the parents involved should be granted
the same respect as any person who would adopt someone of
their own race. We're looking to the best interests of those
needing to be adopted. We're not looking for any glory in that
process.*

Lester Smith Sr. grew up during the time of segregation in the
small southern community of Arrington, Virginia. His parents separated
when Smith was in his early teens. Smith's mother supported her family
by cleaning homes and washing clothes. Smith contributed to his family's
well-being by working at a general store in town. In 1953 his mother moved
her family to Washington, D.C. Soon after, Smith, upon invitation, decided
to return to Arrington and live with the owners of the general store where
he worked. At the age of 13, Smith was informally adopted into the Jones's
home as their son. From 1954 through 1959 Smith resided with the Joneses and was employed in their store. In 1958 the Joneses adopted an infant
daughter, Sandra, who is Caucasian.

During the period with the Jones family, Smith made concessions to the
social laws and practices of the mid 1950s. He says that because of his skin
color, he had to attend a black church while his "adoptive" parents attended
a white Baptist church. When the family went on social outings, such as
to the movie theater, Smith sat in the "black" section and the Joneses sat
in the "white" section. In his family environment, racial divisiveness was
also apparent. Smith refers to "living in a small room in the back of the
house and the Joneses occupying the 'big house.'" The family ate at the
living room table, but he ate separately.

The racial ironies Smith encountered in the 1950s were not so different than the racial discrimination he battled as an African American in the
workplace in the 1970s and 1980s. Yet, in spite of the black and white
paradoxes, which in the South took on social and economic implications,

he was able to realize the opportunities, knowledge, and love the Jones family bestowed on him.

Lester Smith Sr. is a retired civilian employee of the Department of the Army and lives in the Washington, D.C., area with his wife, Portia, their son, Lester Smith Jr., and their four grandchildren, Cierra, Porchia, Lester III, and Briana. He still maintains close ties with the Jones family.

Although you haven't been legally adopted into a white family, for a significant period in your life you've identified with a white "extended family."

Yes.

To understand how this relationship evolved, I think we need to go back to the time it first began. When did you start living with your extended family?

In about 1953 or 1954 through 1959.

How old were you at the time?

I was 13 or 14.

Where did this happen?

In Arrington, a small town in Virginia. Arrington is about forty-five minutes south of Charlottesville, Virginia.

What events brought you and your extended family together? And what led to your biological mother leaving Virginia?

Mr. and Mrs. William L. Jones owned a general store in Arrington. At the time my mother and father separated I was working at their store. To help support my family I worked after school and on Saturdays, making $3.00 a week. I used that money to help my younger sisters buy their school lunches.

When my mother decided to move to Washington, D.C., the Joneses told me that if I wanted to stay with them, they'd be glad to have me. At that point I wanted to go to Washington with my mother. But after being in Washington for a short time, I wrote to the Joneses that I had reconsidered, and, if they'd allow me, I'd come back to live with them. They responded positively, and that's when I moved in with them.

The Joneses are white?

Yes.

Why did they choose to take you in?

Mrs. and Mr. Jones both realized I had special talents and that I wanted to have a quality education. So they decided they could help me to do that by letting me live with them in Virginia where I could complete my high school education and learn other values. Not that my mother didn't teach me values, because she did.

In the 1950s and 1960s what was going on socially in your community?

Everything was segregated at the time. I went to an all-black school. Even when I went to the movies with the Joneses they'd be seated in the white section of the theater and I'd have to sit in the black section. If we went to a restaurant, the same principle applied. They'd eat in the white section, and I'd have to sit in the black section. A white person was always addressed as "Mr." or "Mrs." but a black person, regardless of age, was always called by his or her first name. For example, my mother called Mr. Jones, "Mr." Jones, even though she was older than he was. But he referred to her as "Annie."

At this time, did you identify the Joneses as your adoptive parents?

No. I realized my mother and father were my biological parents, but I respected the Joneses as if they were my parents for the values and guidance they gave me during that time.

When you interacted with the Joneses at a time segregation was legally enforced, did the reality of segregation pose a threat to your extended family or break the family up?

It didn't break up the family, per se, because I knew they loved me, that the problem wasn't because of them but was because of the law of the land. So even though I had to sit in a separate section when we went out, I didn't view that as the Joneses discriminating against me. Those were just the facts of life. You had to be separated, even though people knew who I was and knew who the Joneses were. Had it been possible, I believe the Joneses would have allowed me to sit with them whenever the occasion arose.

How did your extended family show you love?

They were very supportive of what I was doing. They encouraged me to do what was right. When I was growing up I was encouraged to do other work, like pick peaches during the summer to earn my own money and to buy my own clothes. And when it came to studying for school, even though I was working in the store at night, they always gave me the opportunity to do my homework.

Were the Joneses religious?

Yes, they were Baptist.

Did religion play a role in the family dynamic?

They made sure I attended Sunday School, and I also attended church. They'd go to their church, and I'd go to mine.

Would your family drop you off for church and then pick you up after they were done worshiping at their church?

No. My church was within walking distance from where I lived. Their church was in the opposite direction. So they'd drive to their church, and I'd walk to mine.

Within the confines of your home you had a relatively close-knit family, but then in the outside world you had to live differently because of segregation?

That's correct.

Can you talk about what your world was like during this time, being black in a white family?

I experienced mixed emotions, as far as my being accepted by other white people. While I was working in the store, I wasn't allowed to operate the cash register. The Joneses would bring in white people to help out part-time to operate the register.

Why this blatant difference?

I really don't understand it. I don't know whether the Joneses felt I was incompetent or didn't trust me. I can't say why.

Could it be because customers might have wanted to see someone other than a black person handling money?

I'm not sure.

What were your responsibilities in the store?

I worked as a stock boy and a clean-up person. I also delivered groceries.

Regarding your relationship with your extended family, what was your daily routine within your family?

I'd get up in the morning, go to school, return from school, and work in the store. When dinner was served, the Joneses would sit at the table and I'd be seated somewhere else in the house. I'd eat the same meal as they ate, but I didn't sit at the table with them. The Joneses lived in the "big house" and I lived in a one-room place outside the house.

It seems that segregation was also occurring within your own family?

Yes, it was.

Were you able to visit within the home?

I could go into the house for a visit and to eat. But I wasn't allowed to sleep in the house. On Sundays, when I'd get back from church, there'd be a plate in the room where I was living. Occasionally they'd go out for a drive or to a movie. But they made sure I had my meal in my room.

Were you able to bring friends into the house?
No, only into my little room.
Were your friends black or white?
Black.
Were the friends of the Joneses primarily black or white?
White.
Would your family have friends at the house?
Sometimes. The friends who'd come over were mostly their family members.
Were you invited into the home when their relatives visited?
No.
Was that a strict rule?
I don't know if the term "strict" would apply. I knew I was permitted into the house at certain times or to do certain things. So I realized that if family members or friends were visiting that I wasn't to be there. It was an unwritten rule. I think "not allowed" may be too strong a term. I knew with the situation being the way it was that I *shouldn't* go into the house.

Please clarify this for me. You've said that you thought of the Joneses as your family. What made this so, considering that you and your extended family were visibly divided because of race? You lived in a small room in the back of the house, and they lived in the house. They ate at the living room table, and you had to eat elsewhere.

That's a good question. I guess I was very naive and didn't make any particular distinction. I believe I was so grateful for the things they were doing for me that I didn't see any difference.

Those things really didn't come into my mind until later on in life when I questioned why I had to do this versus that. It's hard to answer that question.

When you had your friends over in your little room, what was the conversation like?

Well, being teenagers, we basically talked about girls. Once in awhile we'd talk about why I was living out here and they were living in there. But that didn't come up frequently.

Was it odd that your friends had to visit you in this room? What I'm getting at is, did you visit your friends in their homes?

Yes, I'd visit them in their homes.

And your friends would live in the same home as their parents?

Yes.

They'd also eat at the same table as their parents?

Yes.

Was that odd, from your perspective?

Well, again, I was naive and didn't give it much thought. Like I said earlier, I was grateful for what they were doing for me that I thought it was natural. When I visited my friends and ate with them at their homes, it did go through my mind as to why it was different for me with my family. Sometimes my friends even asked me why.

And how did you respond?

I honestly don't know what I said or what my reaction was. I remember that when I went to school, some people would say, "Oh you live with the Joneses," and for some that was a positive thing.

Why?

Because you were the big kid on the block.

Because you were with white people?

Yes.

Let's talk about your schooling. Did you go to an all-black school?

Yes.

Are you light-skinned or dark-skinned?

Medium.

Were there kids in your school who were light-skinned?

Yes.

At that time were kids being treated differently just because of the shade of their skin?

Oh, absolutely! In those days we used the phrase, "If you're brown, stick around; if you're white, you're right; and if you're black, get back."

And what category were you in?

I'd say I was "brown, stick around."

Did you have friends that fit into the "black, get back" category?

Yes. The color of your skin determined how you were treated.

How were you treated?

Among the blacks, because of my status living with the Joneses, I was treated a little differently than a dark-skinned black person who was viewed as something "less than." If you were light-skinned, you'd be treated a little differently than the way I was treated. It all depended on the color of your skin as to how the blacks would treat you.

How did the blacks, who didn't know you were living with a white family, treat you?

As a black. In other words, wherever I went, people who didn't know my status would treat me like a black.

By black people?

Yes. By both blacks and whites.

How did blacks treat you like a "black"?

Typically, you're a young black male and have no status. If you want something, the money has to be up front.

I don't understand that term. What does "money up front" mean?

It means that you pay cash before "we" sell you anything. Typically, after coming from a movie with my black friends, we'd go to one of the black restaurants—that's the only place we could go to as a group—and order a sandwich. The staff would want to make sure you had the means to pay for it before they'd even prepare the food for you.

How did white people treat you?

When I went to a business establishment to buy something, white people would treat me the same way they'd treat other blacks. To them, I was viewed as not having the means to pay for what I wanted to buy solely because of the color of my skin. If I walked into a drug store, I'd be watched from the time I walked into the store until the time I left to make sure I didn't do any shop-lifting. That happened to black people who entered any establishment.

A white person could go into a restaurant, and immediately the question would be, "Can I help you?" But if a waiter was serving me, a black person, even though I showed him that I had the money to pay for what I wanted, he'd leave me to take a white customer's order and then come back to me. They'd even interrupt my order to turn to the white customer.

If a black person had money at that time, was that person given prestige because of his material wealth?

No. The assumption was that if you were black you were poor, particularly living in that area. Therefore you had no means to pay for what you wanted. So even though you may have had the money, the white people assumed you had nothing, and that was often the case. The blacks had very little money. Most of the time, when a black person purchased something it was on credit.

What did credit mean at that time?

It meant that if someone wanted to buy food or other necessities he'd go into one of the general stores and would establish credit. For example, you'd say that you couldn't pay today for some bread, meat, and potatoes, but that you'd pay at the end of the week. The store owners would then establish a book to account for the transactions.

You made fifty cents a day. It would take approximately two months to pay off your credit just for basic necessities.

Roughly. I was using my money at that point to buy lunches at school for my two sisters. They were living at home with my mother.

What period are we talking about?

This would be before my mother left to go to Washington, D.C., before 1954.

And what was your biological mother's occupation in Arrington?

She did day work—washing clothes, cleaning houses, etc.

Was there a difference in your living conditions between the home of your biological mother and that of the Joneses?

Yes. My biological mother had to work every day to support the family. I also had to do certain things to support the family.

You were with the Joneses from age 13 to 18. What was going on socially at that time? First, let me back up and ask you to compare the neighborhood you lived in with the Joneses to the one where you lived with your biological mother.

The Joneses lived in what was considered a middle-income environment. My mother lived in a very poor neighborhood. My mother's house had electricity but no telephone or television. We had a battery-operated radio. The Jones's home, on the other hand, had total electricity, a telephone service, and a television, which at the time was a premium.

Did you have the opportunity to watch television?

Once in awhile I'd get the chance to watch television. I'd be permitted to come in and watch things like a major fight. But other than that, no. By the time the store closed at night, it was already 9:00. And because I had to get up the next morning for school could have been why I wasn't permitted to watch television.

The Joneses disciplined you?

Yes.

They also legally adopted a daughter?

Yes.

And she was living in the house. How old was she?

I believe she was about 2 or 3 months old when they adopted her.

So you really didn't interact with her as a peer?

Absolutely not.

Did they let you hold her?

No.

Did they let you sit next to her?

No. I don't know if that was planned, but I didn't get involved with Sandra at all. The only time we ever talked was after she was grown. I've met her about twice, maybe three times, since then.

By now, you were about 19. You're less naive. What was going on in your mind about race?

Martin Luther King Jr. was beginning to establish the civil rights movement. I began to realize something was wrong and had to be fixed, including my situation. By him coming out and talking about these issues, I began to realize I should have equality—in the places I went, the schools I attended, and so on. I knew then there was a problem.

You must have been undergoing an internal struggle, especially because you were living in a white family and segregation was still a reality. What was that inner journey like for you?

During the time Martin Luther King Jr. began to expand the civil rights movement, Mr. and Mrs. Jones made comments that this man was out to start trouble. And I'm thinking that if he's saying we should no longer have a black and white section and that when you go to a water cooler there shouldn't be one for colored and one for white and when you go to a bus station you shouldn't have separate places on the bus, then I began to think about my situation.

How did you hear about Dr. King? You weren't watching television regularly.

Right.

Were you reading?

I heard about what Martin Luther King was doing in talking with Mr. and Mrs. Jones. They'd be telling me about what was going on. Or there'd be a general conversation in the store and I'd overhear.

Did other white people in the community, and especially the Joneses, see any good qualities or strengths in what Dr. King was envisioning?

I honestly thought that my relationship with the Joneses was something every American should be entitled to, that blacks and whites should get along together and live in harmony.

The Joneses believed this?

Yes. They truly believed it, and Mrs. Jones told me that on many occasions. They saw no need for such a movement. They thought such a movement would only cause trouble among the blacks and the whites who were in harmony with each other.

Clearly, the definition of "harmony" is relative.

Let me clarify that point for you, if I may. Mrs. Jones taught me from the time I was living with them that if you were to treat other people the way that you would like to be treated, then there would be no need for a civil rights movement.

What do you believe the civil rights movement symbolized for them?

They felt that the civil rights movement would create chaos among the blacks and the whites, for those people who were getting along together. You have to remember that this was a small town I was raised in and everybody knew everybody. Even though there was segregation, there was respect for those people who respected each other. They felt that what Martin Luther King Jr. was doing would cause a division among those feelings. Other than the segregation, we in the community did not have any other racial disturbances. There were occasions when I was approached as a "nigger" among certain white people.

And they would call you this?

Oh, yes. They made it clear that I was only living with the Joneses and that I was *not* part of their family. There were times when I got into fights. I recall one time, in particular, when this white boy wanted to fight me just because I was living with the Joneses. He indicated to me that I wasn't part of the family. We got into a fight because of that. Then he told his parents about the fight, and they told the Joneses that Lester beat up on their son. Mrs. Jones called me in to ask me what happened. I explained to her what led up to the fight. She immediately went back to this boy's parents to inform them that I'd done nothing wrong and that I had been provoked.

When you looked in the mirror who did you see? Was there a sense of loneliness?

I didn't see loneliness at that time. Again, I thought and felt and still believe now that what I saw in the mirror was the fact that I was a blessed individual. I told myself that the Joneses were doing everything they could for me and I would disregard whatever other people, black or white, would say negative about my situation.

What were your goals at that time?

I wanted to graduate from high school and leave the county. The Joneses didn't realize that was my goal. They were very disappointed when I decided to leave them and move to Washington, D.C. They felt that what they had done for me and what my future could have been would be something they could cherish. I think I really disappointed them by not staying there and helping them run the business.

We've talked quite a bit about Mrs. Jones's relationship with you. How did Mr. Jones treat you?

He treated me fantastically. In fact, when I turned 16, I went to get my driver's permit. Mr. Jones coached me and did everything a father would do to have me qualify for my permit. He took me to the testing station and stayed there with me. Once I got my permit, he allowed me to use the truck to deliver groceries. Once in awhile I could use the truck to go to school. He treated me like his own son.

What did it mean to be black at that time?

To be black meant, as I said earlier, to "get back." That meant you took a back-row seat to anyone who wasn't black. If you were a black person, you were inferior. You weren't able to move up in society. You'd always be what you are because that was the perception of a lot of black people and white people at that time. To be born black meant that you were to be raised on the farm, working from sunrise to sunset, for a couple of dollars a week. You were born not to succeed in any category. I think black women especially believed that all they could do was have children, stay in the house, cook, clean, and work in white people's homes. The whites, on the other hand, were born to be prosperous in life, to do the things that all the white people, who felt they were superior to blacks, could achieve.

This was only forty years ago. And this was the mind-set within the black community?

Yes.

From the 1950s to the present, how, in your opinion, has the race issue changed or evolved, and has the mentality of black people on the whole changed with the times?

Things really haven't changed in the 1990s. Some black people feel they're in this twilight zone and can't succeed because the white man, who has the power, is prohibiting them from moving forward. So I think that from the earlier years until now, some of those speculations and perceptions are still there, that in the 1990s we still can't move forward because the white man has the power.

Do you think that is a mind-set or a reality?

I think it's a reality. I believe that many white people who have power are afraid they could lose that power if a person of color or with other national origins were to be given the opportunity to succeed. Racism and prejudices are still alive and well. They, the white people/management, are trying to do certain things to give a sugar-coated perception that they are there to assist you. But they only give you a certain amount of rope, and once you get to the end of it, they jerk the rope away from you. They won't let you excel.

Has the civil rights movement had any impact on addressing the inequalities and injustices that have exploited segments of humanity?

On paper, yes. But in reality, no. It's there. It's being practiced. If you look around communities you'll see that that's the reality, but you can't determine how it's being done because of the covert operation being directed toward minorities and blacks.

Even though the Clinton administration is doing all it can, it's not enough. I know that President Clinton can't do it all by himself. We have to change the mentality that blacks and minorities, including women, aren't capable of serving certain functions in the workforce because of their gender and race.

What are your views on Affirmative Action? Is Affirmative Action a positive policy?

The intent of Affirmative Action was great when it was established. The problem is in the application of the program. There are now rules, within the Affirmative Action program, that are bent and favor white people. Anytime a black person or a minority files a complaint of discrimination, the rules are changed to deny that racism is a blatant factor preventing minorities from excelling in the workforce, regardless of their accomplishments and education. To me, the Affirmative Action program is a piece of paper. It doesn't confer equal opportunity to anyone other than a white person.

You have a son who is black. Given the social and political climate in today's society, what values and work ethic are you teaching him?

I'm teaching my son that he should work hard, be honest, and accept the responsibilities that are his. He should treat other people the way he wants to be treated. I tell him to get a good education, so that when he applies for a position he can prove that he's just as qualified as other applicants.

I stress that instant gratification is not the way to live. The way to get real gratification is to work hard and earn it. Once you do that, you can say, "I did it my way." I also try to instill these values in my grandkids.

Without question, there's a racial divide in this country. Transracial adoptees, I believe, have the potential of bringing these two worlds together with a candid and heartfelt discourse about race. Given that, what are your views on transracial adoption?

I think transracial adoption is outstanding. I have no problem with a couple adopting a person outside their race, if it's out of love. For example, if I were to adopt a child, I'd adopt that child for love, not because I want to send a statement to the world.

There are groups that are completely opposed to transracial adoption because of many of the issues you raised in your experiences with the Joneses in the mid-1950s, at a time of blatant segregation. Can a black child be raised and affirmed in the society we live in?

Transracial adoptees and the parents involved should be granted the same respect as any person who would adopt someone of their own race. We're looking to the best interests of those needing to be adopted. We're not looking for any glory in that process. And I think that relates back to my case. I was allowed to live with the Joneses because of my need for certain things and because of their love for me and their desire for me to do whatever I wanted to do in life.

Are you presently in contact with the Joneses?

Yes, absolutely.

Do the Joneses allow you to visit regularly in their home and eat with them at their dining room table?

Yes. In fact, every time I go to the country to visit them, I'm welcomed. Mrs. Jones makes the best upside-down cake. Whenever I let them know I'm coming for a visit, she makes that cake for me. I can't explain the love between them and myself, but it's there. It's very deep. Yes, I can sit down at the table with them and eat.

The Joneses are lovable people. When they celebrated their fiftieth anniversary I was unable to attend. It broke my heart because they wanted me to be there to showcase me.

I stay in contact with them. I call Mrs. Jones on Mother's Day and Mr. Jones on Father's Day. I call them on Christmas, on New Year's, and so on.

What imprint does Lester Smith Sr. want to leave on society?

The importance of treating people the way you would want to be treated, and also that being a black person doesn't mean you have to "get back." Being black means you can do anything you want to if you put your heart to it. Move ahead regardless of the stumbling blocks before you and stay committed to yourself!

And to all people I say, try your best to excel. And once you try that, everything else comes into focus. If you don't try and if you don't apply, then these things will never come to closure.

Ned

GRAND RAPIDS, MICHIGAN
JUNE 1997

*In my workplace I can associate and fit in to a degree but it only
goes so far . . . I still feel too black for my coworkers and yet with
some of my students, I'm too white. They say: "He talks too white,
he's a sellout." I guess I have a lifelong challenge of trying to figure
out where I fit in, who I am, and how I can find happiness in my
particular life circumstances.*

When asked how he defines himself, racially and ethnically, Ned
says "as an African American black man." Ned was born and raised in Grand
Rapids, Michigan. He earned his bachelor of arts degree at Calvin College
and is pursuing his master's degree at Western Michigan University. In the
past several years Ned has devoted his time to teaching. He believes teaching is a way for him to give back to his community and to have the most
impact on kids. In 1992, during Ned's last year in college, he married his
wife, Sharon, who is African American and also an educator. Both Ned and
Sharon planned to have children early in their marriage. After a number of
failed attempts to have biological children, they agreed that adoption was the
best alternative for beginning their family. In December 1996 Ned and
Sharon adopted an African American baby boy, Gabrielle Lewis Olawasean.
   Ned's identity has been influenced by the African American culture and
struggle. He has learned from the philosophies of people like Marcus Garvey, Martin Luther King Jr., and Malcolm X. For Ned, in many respects
history paved a path to understanding his African American heritage and
his own multi-ethnic experience.
   While Ned's interests focus on African American history and the black
experience, his perspective is informed by a larger and more integrated
vision. While growing up, Ned lived in a racially and ethnically mixed
neighborhood. It was normal for him to play with both black and white
children. Through his eyes, he did not see skin color as a factor in judging

the character of his peers. As an adult looking back on this experience, Ned believes that his perspective broadened, dispelling myths about both black and white people. Another significant phenomenon in his life that shaped his perspective was living in a white family. Adopted in 1968 with his twin sister by a Dutch Christian Reformed family in their late twenties, Ned learned to love and trust persons outside his ethnic background. He also gained an understanding of the Dutch tradition and realized the value of Christian education. Ned's interview elucidates the strength of an integrated vision and the pain of "not fitting in" completely in either world.

Do you remember the community you were raised in at that time?

When our parents adopted us they were living in Rockford, Michigan. My dad is a schoolteacher in Rockford. So we lived there for about nine months to a year and then moved to the southeast side of Grand Rapids.

Unlike Rockford, was the southeast side of Grand Rapids a diverse community?

At the time we moved there it was predominately white with some African Americans, but then within ten years it became predominately African American.

Do you remember some of the children you played with as a child?

Yes. I had a good variety of friends on the street. My next-door neighbor was white, but most of the other children in the neighborhood were African American, with a mix of boys and girls.

Did you get along well with your sister?

Very well. She's my biological twin, so when there was no one else to play with we had each other. We were good friends.

Was your relationship with your parents as good?

I think I had a very good relationship with my parents growing up. They were committed to raising my sister and I as effectively as they could. My parents knew that when they adopted us there would be challenges facing them as white parents with interracial children—although most of society would perceive us as African American. They were committed to trying to overcome a lot of those hurdles. Part of their commitment led them to live in the neighborhood we lived in. And when the neighborhood changed and became predominately African American, we stayed. Even my aunts and uncles couldn't understand why my parents would stay in a neighborhood like that. So my parents had a pretty good understanding of our situation, and they made some conscious decisions to make things better for us.

Were your parents comfortable talking to you about why they adopted you and issues that might surface because of your ethnicity?

Yes. They let us know that we were adopted from birth. As young as I can remember, we knew we were adopted. Then, when we got older, my mom and dad told us why. Apparently they had tried to have their own children but weren't successful—I believe my mom had three or four miscarriages—so they sought adoption and wanted the first children available. When our names came up on the list, my sister and I were actually placed in separate foster homes. Few people were interested in adopting twins. When my parents found out we were twins, they wanted to keep us together.

Can you recall the values that your parents tried to instill in you as a child?

My parents are strong Christians, so they tried to instill in me the whole Christian value set: honesty, integrity, commitment, hard work.

We spent quite a bit of time with our extended family. On all the major holidays we visited with both my mother's and father's families. The family was pretty close-knit.

Did you get along with your aunts and uncles, and was race ever an issue with them, that you can recall?

I wasn't aware of a lot of things that went on in the background, especially as a child. I felt that I got along with my aunts, uncles, cousins, and grandparents. But I do remember feeling a bit tentative, a little awkward about where I fit in. But we never had any problems. Then as I got older and talked to my parents, they shared with us some of the fears and trepidations that my grandparents, aunts, and uncles had had in my parents' adopting black children.

What were some of those trepidations?

They worried about how society would see us, what people would think, and how we, as kids, would get along in that situation. They were wondering whether adopting biracial kids was really worth all the hassles.

Starting elementary school, can you recall some of your experiences?

I went to preschool in a special setting. It was more clinical, not just a run-of-the-mill preschool. I think my parents were interested in observing us to see that we were developing normally in this particular situation.

From there we went on to Alexander Public School for a year and then transferred in first grade to Oakdale Christian School where I obtained most of my elementary education. Oakdale is a small Christian school, interestingly, of all the Christian schools in the Christian Reformed tradition, it has an ethnically diverse population.

While you were in this diverse school, did your parents develop relationships with persons outside their own cultural background?

Most of our neighbors were black, but outside of that I didn't see my parents seeking out black friends. They did always try to be a part of the community, interacting with the neighbors, block parties, neighborhood organizations, that type of thing.

Did you feel comfortable interacting with the neighbors, particularly the black neighbors?

Very comfortable. Of course children don't have all the preconceived notions and stereotypes, all the things society places on adults. So as a child I didn't feel different from anybody else.

When did you realize, if at all, that race in this society plays a part in the formation of your perceptions and stereotypes?

I think I first realized that when I entered the school system, in first or second grade. Before that, my parents, although they did decide to stay in a mixed community, were definitely white, Dutch, Christian Reformed people with all the values, ideas, and conceptions that go along with that. I really believe that my sister and I were both raised as if we were white.

What does that mean, being raised like you were white?

My parents were white, my extended family was white, and we went to a predominately white church, so my way of speaking, my behavior, my ideas and values—all those things were white.

I especially think what was most noticeable for the people around me was the way I spoke, very proper; my diction and annunciation reflected what our society would call "talking white." When I first walked into a classroom, everybody turned and looked at me. They had an image in their minds of how this little black boy was going to talk, how I was going to behave. Then when they saw how I behaved and talked, I got a lot of questions. Why do you talk white? Why do you talk so proper? Do you think you're better than us?

Did black people say this?

Both black and white people. I wasn't what they expected; I didn't fit their preconceived notions. I couldn't really put my finger on it back then, but I knew somehow I was different from my classmates.

How did you handle that difference?

I mainly tried to ignore it. I smiled and laughed it off. Today I realize it caused me pain, but back then I didn't know how to deal with it.

When you went home and looked in the mirror, what did you see?

Even though, like I said, I grew up like a white boy, I definitely knew I was black. In the mirror I saw a little black boy and had no negative associations with that.

As you were growing up, were there any black Americans who contributed to your life?

I always could talk with my parents, but a really important part of my childhood were the neighbors across the street. The family moved in when I was in middle school, and they had a boy about my age and a girl a couple of years younger. I became good friends with the son. His family took me in, particularly his mother. So for many years they were like a surrogate family. That helped me a lot in terms of getting inside a black family and seeing that they were just an ordinary family, like my own. I was exposed to black culture in depth.

In your white family, were you affirmed by objects having to do with your black heritage?

No. My mom and dad didn't emphasize that. There was no Kinti clothes, none of that. Our artifacts were mostly Dutch, from my parents' heritage, like Dutch teapots, blue and white Delftware. We also ate Dutch treats and cookies—Ollebollen, etc. Occasionally we'd go to the Dutch store, and my mom would buy Dutch food.

How did you feel about that? Did you feel like you were going into another culture and learning about other people?

At that point I just looked at it as regular food.

Regarding your adolescent years, can you think of a major challenge you confronted in high school? Did the race issue become harder to deal with?

Yes, the race issue got harder to deal with. I went to Grand Rapids Christian High—a very homogeneous group of students, Dutch Christian Reformed, all white. So that really intensified the conflict. Again, when I walked into the classroom, everybody had a preconceived notion of how I'd behave and talk. I never fit into the stereotypes.

Did the media have an impact on your perception of the black community and black males in general?

No.

Did you feel that because of your color you could not succeed?

No. The media didn't affect me and I didn't see my color as a setback. I never thought my color would hold me back in life or that I couldn't do this or that. My parents gave us very high self-esteem.

So then in high school you were realizing you were different.

Right. A lot of this I've realized only later in my life. Because of the particular situation I was raised in, I was afraid people wouldn't love me, that they wouldn't like me.

Why?

That's how I see it now. I don't think I was aware of it when I was young. Just being a black person in a white environment made me afraid that somehow people wouldn't like me. I always felt different so I became a politician or a diplomat. I wanted to keep people happy, to please them. I never wanted any conflict, any strife. Because I so wanted to be loved, I was timid and passive in any kind of confrontation. I rolled with the punches. Along with that, I tried to like everybody. In high school I was seen as one of the nicest guys. I talked with everybody. I didn't fall into cliques or exclude the nerds or the jocks. I ran with everybody and put on a shell to protect myself.

At this point, did you seek to identify with other black adolescents?

To some extent, primarily through culture and music. I listened to a lot of black music, rap in particular, and that was one of the ways I tried to identify with the black community. At Oakdale I developed a set of friends who were predominately white, and I ran with those guys. I had a lot of black acquaintances but they weren't my close friends. In high school I pulled away from the black family in my neighborhood I was telling you about. In general, I didn't associate with many minorities.

Did you feel you were missing out on something?

No.

Venturing into your adulthood, when you went to college what were some of the issues you dealt with?

Again I followed the expected program. From Oakdale Christian to Grand Rapids Christian High and then to Calvin College, the next logical step in the Dutch Christian Reformed tradition. I survived high school because of my personality, my diplomatic side. Everybody saw me as popular. For example, in my senior year I was Homecoming King. I was also captain of the wrestling team. But when I went to college it was different. The environment was much larger and the setting much different. The feelings I had in high school changed. I got tired of playing the game I'd been playing. I looked back at my high school days with regret thinking that my winning Homecoming King, the whole thing, was meaningless.

What became meaningful to you in college?

I began to seek out other minority students. At Calvin we had a group called Harambe Jahard, which means "living together." Harambe Jahard was a club where minority students congregated. That's where I reached out specifically to African American students.

Within Harambe Jahard did anyone find out you were adopted into a white family?

Oh, yes. Most people did. Even in college I had this need to explain why I acted and talked the way I did. Again, whenever I opened my mouth, somebody would say, "Why is he talking like that?" It's like if you broke your arm and you're wearing a cast. People automatically ask, "What happened to your arm?" At first you're willing to explain but then you get really sick of explaining. That's how my experience in college was. Invariably within the first week or two of meeting someone, I'd get the question, "Where are you from?" Then they'd start probing to find out why I acted and talked the way I did.

What were your responses?

I was very open about it. I told them I was adopted into a Dutch Christian Reformed family. I gave them a little shpiel and moved on.

Did you think that affected your relationship with them?

I think that sometimes who I was as a person was challenging and threatening to them. I was perceived as the "Golden Boy"—having the best of both worlds. I had lighter skin and proper speech. Because of my cross-cultural background I didn't face the severe challenges that black males were facing at Calvin—the total culture shock and inability to relate to the Dutch Christian Reformed culture. I felt comfortable socializing in the coffee shop and hanging out with white people.

I can imagine that your classes were primarily white. Was it challenging for you to interact within these class settings?

I was used to being the only black person at that time. At church, I was the only black person. In class at Christian High, I was the only black. That was something I'd learned to tune out a long time ago so it wasn't uncomfortable for me.

Was it especially important to you to reach out to the black community, particularly acknowledging the homogeneous population at Calvin?

I never really reached out to the black community, although I did encounter a black pastor who was taking courses at Calvin Seminary. I attended his church several times. He and I had a brief but important relationship. Attending that church gave me a lot of new insight and perspective on issues.

How do you racially and ethnically identify yourself now?

As an African American man. I always have. Looking in a mirror, there's no way I could say I'm white. I never felt comfortable saying I'm mixed because most people don't perceive me that way, whites in particular. If I tell someone who's white that I'm 50 percent white, they say, "Whaaaat??" But most African Americans aren't surprised because they see the color of my skin and my facial features.

What does it mean to you to be an African American in today's society?

I face unique challenges in today's society. Our society has a lot of negative stereotypes and pessimistic views about black men, like we all play basketball, we all smoke pot, we're all criminals and gangsters and into rap, we're all dangerous.

In your last year of college you married a black woman. Has your wife helped affirm who you are as Ned?

Yes. I started dating in high school, and I dated a lot of white and black girls. It always seemed like there was this interracial barrier when I dated white girls. Either her parents struggled with their daughter dating a black man, or the girl was embarrassed to tell her grandparents she was dating a black man. I felt that some of the girls I was dating just dated me to be rebellious or to experience another side of life. I didn't face that when I dated black girls, although they still had some adjustment to make since I had a different background from theirs.

When I started dating Sharon and thinking about getting married, I made a conscious decision that I wanted to marry an African American woman. I was tired of that whole hassle. I did have a serious relationship in college with a girl who was white. She came from a racist family. I think she was into black men as a way to rebel against her family. Anyway, for whatever reason, she couldn't tell her parents she was dating a black man. In fact, at first she told them I was white. They'd call and I'd answer the phone and talk to her parents. Because of my diction and elocution, they were convinced I was white.

Did her parents ever meet you?

No. I guess I just got tired of playing those games in a relationship. I knew I could probably find a white woman who's family would accept me, but I got tired of all that. Being black in a white family all my life and always getting stared at, always getting funny looks in restaurants and stores, I just decided I'd marry a black woman and not have to deal with that whole aspect of who I am.

Recently, you and your wife adopted a child. Can you tell me about that?

We've been trying to have kids, but we couldn't. All my life I've said that somebody adopted me and did me a favor, maybe saved my life. I've always intended to adopt children and have some of my own. So when we couldn't have children, it was natural for us to adopt.

Did you decide specifically to adopt a black child?

We preferred to adopt a black child, but we would have been open to any child who needed to be adopted. I didn't want to press that issue because I doubt any adoption agency in America would place a white baby with a black family, not even an Asian baby with a black family. I can't see that happening in our society even though there's no formal rule. I bet it almost never happens. I find myself resenting that, that a white couple can adopt a black baby but a black couple can't adopt a white baby.

Tell me about your son, Gabrielle.

His name is Gabrielle Lewis Olawasean. He's six and a half months old. He was in foster care for about six weeks.

In the process of getting your son, did you become aware of the state of welfare in America or in the state of Michigan?

I didn't learn anything new. Sometime in college I learned that a lot of black children needed to be adopted but that there weren't enough black families seeking to adopt. A friend of ours, who was in this field, told us that blacks had always adopted their own, informally. A girl gets pregnant and can't afford the baby so she gives the baby to someone in her family, like her grandparents. Now, because of our society and the way it's changed, a lot more black children are making their way into the welfare system, but the black community isn't educated about these children.

What are your views on transracial adoption?

A big part of me says it's fantastic. I know for a fact that my parents love me and raised me to the best of their ability and that I had fabulous opportunities. I love my parents and get along well with them. I also feel confident that this same kind of situation could happen for countless others, yet I have reservations because of the difficulties that do arise.

When I was adopted in the late 1960s I think that there were other Christian Reformed families adopting in this grand social experiment. The civil rights movement had ended. Dr. Martin Luther King Jr. had given his

"I Have a Dream" speech. People believed that much of the prejudices, hatred, and discrimination would soon be over. I don't think these people dreamed of a utopia, but I think they expected it to be easier than it was, never realizing that twenty years later the whole civil rights movement may even have regressed. So I'd say I support transracial adoption if parents are educated and willing to make the necessary effort to give their kids their own racial identity. It was easier for my parents because my sister and I both chose to live very much according to their values. I have friends, though, who ultimately chose to speak more like an African American than a white American, and that caused trouble in those homes. Parents have to be willing to deal with that kind of choice. I don't think many parents are aware that that kind of thing can happen.

As a transracial adoptee myself, I've been called names like "Oreo," "Whitey"—the list goes on. Minimally these names communicate to me a disapproval of blacks being raised in white families. What do you think?

I've been called those names, too. It's very very painful because it cuts to the core of your being. There's no defense against those things. It's part of society, man's inhumanity to man. It doesn't matter what race you identify with. There are names to hurt everyone out there. We've all been hurt by people in society.

Groups like the National Association of Black Social Workers talk about the difficulty of a black child being raised in a white home. Do you support their view that transracial adoption is not in the best interest of the black child, that indeed it is cultural genocide?

A part of me affiliates strongly with that. I understand that argument and even agree with it. But in my own particular situation, my parents and I were able to overcome a lot of those dilemmas and difficulties. And today I'm an African American male and have an African American wife and child.

Another argument of those who oppose transracial adoption is that black children who live in these kinds of families are not prepared to deal with societal barriers and achieve success in the future. Do you believe this is true?

I agree to some extent, but here's my dilemma. Growing up as a transracial adoptee, I've always felt that I'm on a fence, half-white and half-black, somewhere in-between everyone else. Or in school I'd feel like I was too black for the white kids and too white for the black kids. To this day I have similar feelings. Even in my workplace, where I can fit in to a degree, it only goes so far. I still feel too black for my coworkers. At the same time I'm too white for some of my students. They say: "He talks too white, he's a sellout." I guess I have a lifelong challenge of trying to figure out where I fit in, who I am, and how I can find happiness in my particular life circumstances.

What motivated you to become a teacher?

As I grew up and thought about different careers, I believed I could do anything I wanted to. Somehow I always wanted to reach out and give back to my community.

Your community being?

African American. I was really inspired by Dr. Martin Luther King Jr., Malcolm X, Marcus Garvey, the black civil rights leaders, and all the black activists who were trying to empower and improve life conditions for African Americans. I wanted to make a contribution and decided that in teaching I could have a powerful impact on a great number of students.

How did the civil rights leaders, like the ones you mentioned, contribute to making the movement so successful?

They'd reached a point where enough was enough. And had gained political maturity to the point where they were ready to stand up and fight for their rights.

Can this same mentality be applied to what is going on today, especially with regard to the crisis facing black America? For example, drugs are running rampant in our communities, and young black males, at an alarming rate, are being gunned down or incarcerated.

We face a unique challenge today. Back then, most of the challenges were explicit, "in your face." There was something concrete to stand up and fight against, like the right to vote. Whereas today, after the civil rights movement, a lot of the challenges have become implicit, behind the scenes, so it's harder to figure out the remedies. It appears today that the path of success is wide open to us, yet we hinder ourselves in so many ways because of our frame of mind, our perspective. Our greatest challenge now is for us to fix our own problems and not to rely on the government or other people to fix them for us.

What do you think are issues facing both black and white students in your classroom?

In my particular setting, Kentwood, Michigan, a suburb of Grand Rapids, a tremendous number of the white students are middle-class. They've been superbly equipped for school. They're intelligent. They have a good work ethic. So they don't face many challenges. But most of my poor white students haven't been very well-equipped throughout their whole school experience, and a lot of my minority students also struggle, but not all. The difference between the kids has more to do with their socioeconomic status than with race. My affluent middle-class African American students are on a par with any other kid in the school system. It's the kids who come from a lower socioeconomic status who aren't as well prepared to handle the challenges of school.

What is going on federally in K-12 education that is impacting your teaching?

There's a push for national standards, although what affects us more are the state standards. For example, the Michigan framework for social studies has set a standard that all Michigan students must meet. So our school has had to restructure its program to meet those standards.

Do you think the minority kids can realistically meet the standards?

They'll have some difficulty. Many of my minority students, specifically my African American students, are not as well equipped as the others. They don't read or write as well. Their thinking skills aren't as effective. I'm not certain why that is.

You earned a good educational foundation and clearly have proven your competency in achieving high educational goals. To what do you attribute this?

The middle-class values of my parents. Like I said, kids from middle-class and upper-middle-class families do better, regardless of their ethnic background. Their parents start educating them before they go to school. These kids know how to read and write. Their thought processes, their natural inquisitiveness, their ability to ask questions—all these things are developed before they go to school. I can't prove this, of course, but I think their parents prepare them more effectively for the school system. My parents prepared me very effectively. I could read and do math before I went to school.

And there are those who have access to the Internet, to current books and resources, and those who do not. Do you believe it's important to bring these worlds together?

Definitely. The further behind blacks fall, the worse things will get for us. We'll continue to be undereducated, underemployed. We'll continue to make up a disproportionate number of the prison population and the welfare population. We have a tremendous challenge ahead of us.

What do you say to black children who are living in a white family? How might they overcome some of the challenges that you had as a child?

There's a dilemma I faced as a child, and it's one that many children may face. White parents will go to their black child and ask, "How can you fix your situation" or "How can you deal with your situation?" I think it's inappropriate to ask children such questions because they're only children. My dad asked me a lot of questions when I was young about what he and my mom could do to make transracial adoption better for me. I thought to myself, I don't know. I'm a kid. How am I supposed to know?

When I talk to people who may be in this situation, I put the burden squarely on the adult. I say, you're the parent, you figure out how to improve the situation for the child. My parents' approach was to live in an African American neighborhood. That's not practical for all people adopting transracially. But I encourage such parents to go to a black church, not for a week or two but for a year. That's not much of a sacrifice. Not only should they go to a black church, but they should get involved in activities, like joining the choir. By doing that, white parents will finally get an inkling of how their child feels every day in an all-white school, an all-white church, an all-white family reunion. Parents need to identify with what their children are going through.

What about people in the black community who are very critical about black children in a white family but haven't done anything themselves to minimize the concerns they express?

That's probably a hard situation for them. If I were an outsider and there was a white family across the street who had adopted a black child, it would be difficult for me, as an outsider, to help fix that situation. That white family may not welcome my suggestions. Again, the burden falls squarely on the parents' shoulders. If they don't want help or can't even recognize the problem, there's nothing an outsider can do.

As we spoke of earlier, most children in foster care are black. How can these children make it in today's world?

I think the responsibility lies with the parents, with the system. The adults in a child's life have to love and provide for that child as best as they can. Children can't handle these problems themselves. They come up with self-defense mechanisms. For me, it was to laugh, smile, deny everything and push away all the pain, the sorrow, the suffering, pretend everything was wonderful. Other kids act out. They rebel and do drugs.

Wrapping up the interview, what values do you want to instill in your own son?

Certainly my religious beliefs, my Christianity. Also honesty, integrity, willingness, a good work ethic. I want my son to have high self-esteem, to shoot for the stars, to live a better life than I did, to achieve greater things than I achieved. I also don't want to remove all the challenges in his life. I want to teach him to be a problem solver, to overcome the challenges he'll face in life.

So who are you today?

I'm pretty happy about who I am today. I'm a fairly successful teacher. I have a happy marriage. I'm very happy with my wife and my family. I'm still close with my mother and father and sister and my extended family. I've fit in well with my wife's family. At first they didn't know quite how to deal with me, having been raised by white parents. But I think they love me and I love them. For the most part I have a sense of peace about who I am as an African American. Yet I have a lingering feeling at work that I don't quite fit in with my colleagues and all my students. Right now I attend a black church, the Messiah Missionary Baptist Church, and I don't quite fit in with the congregation. So I still feel that I'm somewhere in the middle, in limbo, on the fence, not fully in one world, not fully in the other. But I've learned to be happy with that.

Pete

FREEVILLE, NEW YORK
SEPTEMBER 1997

*I've gone through the struggles that every other black person
has gone through in this society, just because of the color of my
skin.*

Born in Ithaca, New York, during the late 1960s, to a Nigerian father and a Scottish mother, Pete was placed for adoption because of racial pressures forced on interracial couples and their offspring. In Nigeria, where Pete's biological father would return home as a physician, interracial relationships of this kind were not tolerated within his own family. Six weeks after being in foster care, Pete was adopted into a white Protestant family with three biological children, two daughters and one son several years older than him. They were raised in Brooktondale, a small town near Ithaca.

Pete attended predominantly white high schools in New York from 1982 to 1986. In his sophomore year of high school his adoptive parents divorced. Pete moved with his mother to Ithaca where he completed his junior year. With his grades dropping, Pete knew his opportunities were dwindling. In 1987, after graduating, he pursued what he thought was his only option and joined the army. It was there, in a segregated setting, that he was forced to decide with which group, white or black, he would associate. In 1990, after returning home from the army, he took the civil service test and ranked in the top 3 percent.

Now a police officer in Ithaca and a volunteer with the local fire department, Pete appreciates his experience living not only with his adoptive family but with an African American family who opened their home to him during his adolescent years. Struck by the clear distinctions between the black and white cultures, Pete believes that his background has helped him to interact comfortably with both groups. Nevertheless, he deals with misperceptions from both communities because of the color of his skin. Race,

Pete says, is always the baseline, whether he is dressed in plain clothes, just walking in a store, or doing his job as a police officer.

In the summer of 1995 Pete was profiled in *American Demographics*. He is interracially married. Pete stays in contact with his adoptive father, who is a businessperson in the printing profession, and his adoptive mother, who is a librarian at the University of Central Florida. Contacts with his siblings are rare. Soon after the taping of this interview, Pete was reunited with his birth father, who visited him in the United States. Pete has biological siblings living in the Washington, D.C., area.

I was born in Ithaca, New York. I was adopted approximately six weeks after my birth. Then I was raised in Brooktondale, New York.

What kind of community was Brooktondale?

A small area located about seven miles from Ithaca. When I lived there, the community was very rural, the houses spaced about one-eighth of a mile apart. My dad has a hundred acres of property there. It's pretty spread out.

Were there any black people who lived near you?

No.

In your immediate family, are you the only one who is adopted?

Yes. I have two sisters and a brother. I've never been super close to my siblings. My brother is 34, obviously much older than me, and has vastly different interests. I keep in touch with him only when I bump into him or see him at family outings. I've lost touch with my older sister, too, over time. She moved south to North Carolina. I'm in touch with her about every six months. My younger sister, who is 30, is mentally retarded. I see her occasionally when I visit my parents, again, usually during family gatherings such as Thanksgiving and Christmas.

What was it like growing up black in a white family?

It was strained at times basically because the hobbies I was interested in were quite different from the activities my siblings participated in. For example, my brother and sisters were into their schoolwork and didn't play a lot of sports. I hung out with my friends and played sports.

What did you play?

Baseball, football, basketball, everything. Schoolwork at the time, even though I did well, was not my number-one priority—as it was for the rest of my family.

So you believe that the struggles you confronted within your own family were related mostly to personality differences?

Yes.

Did the fact that you were physically different from the members of your family affect you?

It never became an issue for me. I'm a very outgoing person. I think it would be more of an issue if I wasn't. I had loads of friends, and they never made my color an issue.

Would your friends comment on the obvious physical differences between you and them?

Occasionally some kids, as kids do, would say something upsetting, but other than that, no, my friends never said anything.

In the schools you attended, were there other black people?

There were two or three African American kids in my high school class out of a graduating class of fewer than a hundred.

Were you particularly drawn to those two or three students because they were African American?

No, they were my friends. The school was good in that people treated everybody the same, for the most part. I wasn't drawn to them or pushed away because of the color of their skin. I considered them friends as I did anybody else.

In your childhood years, did race impact your perception of life?

No, not until I got older. I didn't understand prejudice. At times something uncomfortable would happen, like somebody making a racial slur, forgetting I was there.

Did your parents tell you why they adopted a black child?

When I got older, my parents told me that after they'd had their third child, who turned out to be mentally retarded, they wanted to have a fourth, but, after much discussion, they decided they didn't want to risk having another disabled child. So they opted for adoption. Once they started the process, they were told that African American male children were the hardest to place. So they chose to adopt a black male child. Plus, I was a really cute kid!

Did you discuss your adoption with your family?

I don't remember any conversations about that. My conversations with my siblings were vague. I was very independent and spent a lot of time inventing games to keep myself occupied. I also had friends outside the family to keep me busy. Growing up, I think I was closest to my brother because he played a lot of the games I did and was good at keeping me entertained.

Looking back on your experiences now, do you know why you tended to be independent?

That's just who I am. I don't have a problem with being alone. Maybe then it was because I wasn't close with my family members. So when my friends weren't around, I spent time doing things by myself.

From your childhood to your adolescent years, what were some of the hardest issues you had to deal with?

Probably being so different, not that I'm a different color but that my personality is so different from my parents. Looking back, I wish my father had been more a part of my life. As a kid, my father didn't understand the activities I wanted to do or my professional goals, like a sports career. I miss that my father wasn't around for me like the other kids' fathers. He didn't go to my school games or generally take an interest in the things I was doing.

Most of my other friends' parents were vastly more involved, like being at the games, whereas my parents weren't. They had more of a laid-back attitude, like, "Tell me what the score was when you get home." In fact, I'd stay at a friend's house on game nights since school was twelve miles from my home.

Did your parents take more interest in their other children's activities?

My parents focused more on studying. They wanted us to study a lot. And that's basically what my brother and sister were doing anyway. I was the one singled out because of that. "Why aren't you doing your homework?" That type of thing. My siblings were already upstairs doing theirs or else it was already done.

What is your parents' background?

They met when they were going to school. They're both Ivy League. I guess they fell in love and got married. My dad got a job at Cornell University in New York. They then decided to move to Brooktondale.

We actually moved to Hawaii for three years when he got a job there.

How old were you when you moved to Hawaii?

I was 2, and we lived there until I was 5. Then we moved back to Brooktondale.

Do you remember Hawaii?

I remember being stung by a Portuguese Man-of-War. I didn't particularly like Hawaii. I remember a lot of the bad things, like how big the slugs were after it rained or the twelve-inch centipedes that were poisonous.

As a family, what did you do together?

We had picnics on the back lawn. I remember cooking s'mores. I remember holidays and some of the wacky traditions we followed, like wrapping gifts in paper bags.

That's a new one. What was the meaning behind that?

To save money. We also cut down our own Christmas tree. We had a wood stove. I hated going out and chopping wood with my dad. My feet would get cold. We had assigned chores that we had to do before we could go out and play with our friends.

I'm telling you a lot of the negative things because they stick in my mind. We're not a very visual family. We didn't have a television. So many of the things you remember other families doing, like watching cartoons in the morning, was virtually nonexistent unless I went to another person's house.

Did you read a lot?

Quite a bit, often for no other reason than I was bored. But I did take an interest in reading. My dad used to read Greek mythology to me, and I was very interested in that.

Growing up, were you familiar with African American leaders or African American literary persons?

No, that was never stressed in my home. They never made a connection. They never said this is your heritage.

How did your life unfold after you graduated from high school?

I have to take a step back. In my sophomore year my parents separated. I was given the choice of staying with my dad in the "fun house," moving in with my mom, who now lived in Ithaca, or moving in with my best friend, John, who lived up the street from my dad.

And you chose?

I hemmed and hawed for a while. I was intrigued about moving to Ithaca because it's a bigger city and I'd hung out there on several occasions. That's when I started interacting more with African Americans. But I decided to move in with my friend's family.

Why did you choose to live with your friend's family rather than with one of your parents?

My dad and I weren't getting a long at the time. The last summer before I moved, my parents had put a lot of restrictions on me that I didn't think were fair. My friend's family was upper middle class. They ate better food. They gave me more freedom. They had a colored TV. I think that intrigued me. And John and I were such great friends that I thought I'd have the best of both worlds.

Did they offer their home to you? How did that happen?

They had already talked to my parents about it. They knew the separation was hard on us. They also knew about the problems my father and I were having. John's mother told me that I was considered part of the family.

Are you still close with them today?

Yes, I consider them a second family. In my growing up, they had a big impact on my life. John's father was my coach in several sports. Unlike my father, he was into sports and followed John and myself and helped me out practicing.

So I lived with them my sophomore year in high school. After that, I decided I wanted to move to Ithaca with my mom. I spent my junior year with my mom, who was going through an adjustment herself. She gave me more freedom than should be allowed by law. I met a whole set of new friends. I was meeting more black friends and finding out their vast differences, cultures, and habits.

What types of friends were you hanging out with there?

Sports friends. They were white, mixed, and African American.

How did these friends respond to you? Is this where color comes into the picture?

Yes. This was when I began to realize that I was different and that it was going to be difficult to fit in with some of these classes of people. This was when I wondered who I was.

That question often hits at the age of sixteen.

The African Americans I was around often let me know I was different. They said I talked differently, listened to different music, and had white friends they didn't necessarily get along with.

What kind of music were you listening to?

Mostly rock. In Ithaca people listened mostly to R&B and Rap. It wasn't that I didn't like it. I didn't understand it.

Forgive me for asking you this question, but can you dance?

To be honest, I had to learn. I started learning ahead of time at the roller skating rink. But, yes, dancing took some learning.

Who taught you?

That was when "break dancing" started. A friend, Kevin, taught me. He had an Ethiopian heritage, but he could easily pass for white. I'd classify him as a "wanna be."

"Wanna be" white or "wanna be" black?

A "wanna be" black. But he was from the city. He knew everybody. Some of his flair was his genuine personality, but some of it was the "wanna be" air he had. To him, I was a student. The whole gambit of body language, speech, dancing, it all came into play at that point. It was often frustrating and took a lot of work.

The dancing?

Not specifically the dancing. The whole scenario was frustrating, trying

to reach down into myself and figure out who I was, what I wanted to be—
and I had nobody in my life who could tell me these things.

Who could you talk to about these things?

I had a very close friend back then, Jennifer, who is mixed. She had a
white mother and a black father. As far as my getting connected, Jennifer
probably had the greatest influence. She was very proud of her black heritage. Through her, I met a lot of black people. Because we were friends,
I was just accepted for that reason.

Were you comfortable meeting black people?

That depended on who the person was and how he responded to me. I
treated them openly. At times there was tension, but I was never afraid.

My mom always told me that I was great at adjusting to new situations,
and I still am. I don't care what anybody says unless they're in my shoes.
I went through this over and over with my wife. When you're in different crowds, you need to adapt. But that's hard for my wife to understand
since she comes from a strong family background and was never in that situation. It's hard for her to understand.

**I understand what you're saying. Adapting into different situa-
tions doesn't mean you necessarily change your inner being. Sometimes you have to adapt to minimize the tension between other
people.**

I also think that playing sports in high school and doing well at it gained
me respect tenfold from peers who might not have accepted me if, say, I
played the violin. Sports was one way I could prove myself.

**The girls in high school who were attracted to you, were they
black or white?**

Both. And that was another thing I had to go through, being the new
face in town. So I had girls asking about me. Then a lot of other guys were
jealous.

**Did you seek out people in the black community you could turn
to with the questions you were asking yourself, like who you were,
where you fit in?**

I talked primarily to Jennifer.

**What did you realize about yourself, being black in a white
family?**

That social concerns, like a person's upbringing and culture, affect your
life. I felt I was at a disadvantage because of my situation, because I didn't
know who I was. It took time to decide what my priorities were. It was a
confusing time. It was tough.

You had an experience that turned your world 180 degrees. Tell me what it was like living in a white family for most of your life and then living in a black family for a year.

My mom decided to move in with this guy she'd been seeing for sometime. So here I am, a newly transplanted person from "hicktown." The question was, do I go back to Candor?

Did you decide to go back to the town where you were raised?

No, I'd just made new friends where I was. I didn't want to go back and see myself as a failure. That's what I thought at the time.

So where did the black family come in ?

I had a black friend, Tony. He asked his mom if I could stay with them. So, low and behold, here I am.

You've had wonderful friends helping you along the way.

Yes. And this family was truly black. There were no whites in the family. I ended up moving in with them my senior year of high school. That was the most important year of my life. If I'd had any doubts about cultural differences, I soon found out the score.

What were some obvious differences between your family and theirs?

Everything—from dress to eating to talking. Everything was different.

It's a different world.

Yes, it is.

Did you notice a change in social views between this family and your own?

I learned there was prejudice on both sides. The conversations were different, even the TV shows they watched. In the black family a lot of debates came up about affirmative action and their views were just the opposite of what my white friends believed.

Living in this black family, did you feel affirmed?

I felt at ease about myself. I knew there were a lot of things I needed to learn about their culture and lifestyle. Tony had four sisters and a younger brother. The house was huge, three stories, and we shared the room upstairs. Tony and I talked a lot. He helped me adjust, to fit in with the family. After awhile I felt like I belonged there.

How would you summarize your experience with Tony and his family?

It enabled me to see the differences between white and black. It helped me round myself out, see things from a different angle.

Did you make a conscious decision at that time about what world you wanted to be in? Or did you choose to walk the line between both worlds?

I chose both worlds. The experience evened me out. I understood both sides of the spectrum because I'd lived both sides. I was "culture-ized." And I'm becoming more and more comfortable with that. Where I live now I go down to the community center, which is all black, and play basketball every night. I'm comfortable going to parties. Everybody knows who I am and nobody has a problem with me. I'm a well-rounded person now.

Let's fast-forward to the present. What are you doing now?

Professionally I'm a police officer with the Ithaca Police Department, on the level of patrol. I also work part-time for a small village police department. For nine years I've been a volunteer fire fighter. Currently I'm a captain at the Ithaca Fire Department. I'm also an emergency medical technician and I do mutual aid with a small department that's right down the road from where we live.

You appeared on the cover of *American Demographics*, a nationally distributed business magazine out of Ithaca. From my understanding, this magazine showcases segments of society and the issues they confront for the purpose of identifying trends in this country. You were profiled specifically because of your profession. How were you chosen to be featured in the magazine?

The magazine wanted to feature a police officer. Since the magazine is based in Ithaca, obviously they started with the Ithaca Police Department. The head guy at *American Demographics* had seen me a couple of times when I was walking the beat. Apparently I had the "look" he was looking for. My chief gave me permission to be on the cover, so off I went for my photo shoot. A couple of rolls later I was on the cover.

As a police officer patrolling a relatively small city, what are some of the major crimes you see?

A lot of domestic violence, a lot of armed robberies. There's also a lot of larceny, shoplifting and things of that nature. We investigate everything from burglaries to stolen cars. The population of the city I patrol is thirty thousand, not counting the students at Cornell, and about sixty thousand counting the students. You can draw a line right through the middle of the city—on one side are the students and on the other side is the working class, crack-addicted people. When I'm working in one beat it's a totally different environment than when I'm assigned to the other.

Have you arrested black youths?

Yes, quite a lot. In the territory I patrol there's a big crack problem with younger African Americans, dealers and users. There's a lot of crack-related crimes whether it be armed robberies or thefts to get money for cocaine.

What led you to becoming a police officer?

I've never been a person who's overly comfortable in an office, wearing a suit and tie. I'm more of an outdoors, outgoing type of person. So my personality fits that of a police officer.

You also have a unique reference point, having lived in both a white and a black family.

Having such a diverse background, I can understand things from both a white and black point of view. That's been an advantage for me as a police officer. The job's tailored to my personality.

Within the territory you patrol, what is the black community's perception of the police department?

I'd say there's mistrust of the police department and its inner workings.

What problems is the black community combating in particular?

There's a huge problem with education. The black kids don't have the same opportunities to go to college as other kids because of money. A lot of younger kids still in high school are frustrated after years and years of being discriminated against, so they decide to turn to easier money-making schemes. It starts from there and only gets worse.

I could easily have gotten into trouble when I was growing up in that environment. That's one of the reasons why I joined the army. I decided to make a positive move since things weren't going well for me here.

What activities had you experimented with?

I experimented with drugs. I hung around people who were fighting and stealing. I had more and more involvement with the police.

Looking back to that time, what do you think drew you to that behavior?

Being in that setting and wanting to fit in with the crowd. I interacted with people who were doing those things. If I was living in Candor, where I'd been raised, many of the situations I experienced here in Ithaca would never have presented themselves.

You had the opportunity to get out of the neighborhood and away from the individuals you hung around with.

I take a lot of pride in having realized that if I continued what I was doing I would fail.

What small steps did you take to alter your lifestyle from doing drugs and getting into trouble with the law to being a law enforcer?

I knew I wanted to do something positive with my life. At that point, at the end of my high school years, I didn't have many opportunities. My grades had gone down. I even failed a couple of courses. My friend Jeff and I ended up joining the army.

What led you to join the army?

Tony had family members who had joined the army. He told me that things were working out for them. Six months later, Jeff and I joined the army. It changed my life.

Did you find your niche in that new setting?

I went through an adjustment phase wondering, "Who do I become friends with, whites or blacks?" I resorted to making friends with blacks and whites. It was like starting over again in a social setting, thinking where do you fit in? And many times the two groups don't mix, especially in an army setting.

How so?

Many people are coming and going, either being stationed somewhere or being shipped off to somewhere else. People don't have time to form long-lasting friendships, so the white people go here, the black people go there and the mixed crowds go somewhere else.

Have you befriended any of the black youths you come in contact with on your beat?

Not really. Many of the kids we deal with don't like the police. The calls I make now are rushed. I get one call done, I go to the next. I'm not a community police officer and don't have the time to reach out and try to make a difference.

Do you do certain tasks to help the community?

Yes. By being a fire fighter I believe I'm helping the community. But then this question springs its ugly head: "What am I, as a black male and a police officer, going to do for the black community?"

How have you dealt with that?

It's rather complicated. Within the last six months we've had a selection committee for the job of narcotics investigator. In the past the procedure was to select people based on job performance. But certain people added pressure, people who believe that the "good-ol'-boy" network was in place. That's when the police department thought it necessary to create a selection committee, and I was the one selected as the investigator. One of the more vocal committee members complained that the selection steered away from minority members, even though I'd been selected. Supposedly this person made a comment that she didn't consider that I was "black" because I was adopted into a white family. That infuriated me and many of the other officers.

Do you consider yourself to be black?

Yes. I base my "blackness" on the way society sees me. Because of my color, I have to go through the hardships and struggles brought on by racism. For example, as a young black kid going into a store, I'm the one people watch to see if I'm going to steal anything. I'm the one who's called names in different situations. I'm the one who's going to have problems dating a white woman. So I've gone through the struggles that every other black person has gone through in this society, just because of the color of my skin.

Once you take off your police uniform and walk into a store, you're treated like a black man off the street.

Right. And that would be my argument to that committee member.

Were you able to talk with the woman who made the comments?

Yes, I spoke to her about it. She wouldn't comment on what she'd said, but she did remark that it was important to have somebody from the community in that position. When I asked her what she knew about me, she said, "Not much."

There's a misconception in the black community that I haven't done enough for the black community as a police officer, such as going to community centers and doing things with the young kids there, doing my part as an African American. I know I could be doing more. I told this woman that if this was important to her she should have talked to me about it.

I have a friend, Marlon, who's black and from the community. Because Marlon is a community police officer, he's able to take the time to make connections with the kids. That's his job. So people compare the things Marlon has done to the things I've done. And according to the black community, I don't fit the profile.

That's unfortunate. Does it affect you personally to arrest a black male?

It did when I first started. When Marlon and I started working for the police department, the community definitely was testing us. Some of the guys in the community looked at it as having two brothers out on the street. They wanted to find out if that meant they could get a break.

How did you establish yourselves?

As good police officers. The people we deal with most of the time know what we're about. I think I'm known as a fair officer. In terms of giving breaks, I don't differentiate between black or white.

Does that line become gray at times?

Sometimes I get involved in situations where I feel another officer is being too tough on a black person. Most of my officers are white. There might not be blatant racism within the police department, but at times one picks up subtle nuances.

Within the territory you are policing, is police brutality a reality that black males should be concerned about?

Not at all. But that's the first thing you'll hear in any incident, and I've been through so many. The number-one catch phrase is, "You're only messing with me because I'm black." On the flip side, I get frustrated hearing officers get defensive and say that that's the excuse blacks always use when they're in trouble or feel cheated. Of course, when issues about affirmative action come up, the setting gets more uncomfortable for me.

As a black male, what do you fear?

Professionally I think I'm caught in a "Catch-22." If I do well in my career, I'm viewed as a token. If I don't do well, then I hear, "We knew you wouldn't anyway."

According to statistics, African American males are the highest demographic group incarcerated in this country. Do these statistics scare you because you are a black male?

No, because of where I am now.

And where are you now?

I'm a working professional who's gotten a bit lucky and has worked hard to get where I am. Most of the "stats" pertain to kids locked up for drug use, black-on-black crime, that type of thing. If you were to examine police officers killed in the line of duty, it wouldn't read 80 percent black, 20 percent white. I don't even think about those statistics. Regarding the problems society faces, I look at the big picture.

What do you see as the major issues facing society today?

Society is plagued with racism. If we're all going to be on the same level, everybody should be entitled to a quality education. Money talks too much these days. Look at O. J. Simpson. If he'd been a black bus driver, he'd be waiting his turn for the chair. Even in American history classes, we're taught that the cowboys were right and the Indians wrong. For the most part, everything is taught from a white point of view. Only in the last several years are we seeing black studies introduced in the classroom.

What do you need in this society to succeed?

You need to work hard and strive to be the best. But, realistically, that can only take you so far. You need love. You need connections. You need to understand the other person's point of view.

What is your opinion of transracial adoption?

For the most part, I think I turned out fine. The older I get, the more I think there are problems with it. What is most important in making transracial adoption work is for the adopted family to understand that there are cultural differences. They have to be responsible in making sure that the child has an identity.

Why do you believe that cultural exposure is so important for the child, since we live in a diverse family?

Because society sees you by the color of your skin. It's that simple.

How can learning about your background help you?

It allows a person to take everything in and decide what he or she is more comfortable being. It allows a person to make choices.

As black adopted children, we already started out with advantages and disadvantages, being ethnically different from our adoptive parents. So it's not something that's going to surprise us down the road. I think transracial adoption offers a child an opportunity. For one thing, the child has a family. My own experience has taught me to look at issues from different angles.

Your wife, Brenda, is white. Was race an issue in your decision to marry her?

Not at all. At first it was physical attraction, and then getting to know each other. Our relationship is interesting at times. I feel she needs to "be brought up to speed" regarding certain points of view, especially in her understanding differences between groups.

Has Brenda been exposed to black people outside of her relationship with you?

I was the first person she dated who was black.

When she dated you, was there a mutual understanding that she would learn about the African American culture and interact with people within that community?

No.

Now that you're married, does she recognize the value in building relationships with persons in the black community?

To her credit, she's understanding the differences in social views.

You recently located your biological mother and uncovered detailed information about your biological father. Tell me about that.

I've been in contact with my biological mother, who's white, from Scotland, for about a year and a half. She came to my wedding.

How did you get the ball rolling, and then finally meet her?

I wrote to the Family and Children's Center I was working with. Through this center, my biological mother sent me pictures of my biological father and all the information she had on him.

Did you find physical similarities between you and your biological father?

Others think so, but I don't.

You discovered that your biological father is Nigerian and is a doctor. How did you respond to the fact that he is in a high-status profession, so to speak, as opposed to the image many of us have about our biological parents, namely, that they didn't have the means to support us?

I was happy I even knew what he looked like. I had a sense of finally. Finally I was beginning to understand who I was. He was very athletic. He played soccer, what they call football in Nigeria. Finding that piece of my life helped me find out the origins of my heritage. That my biological father is Nigerian was a strong statement against all the people who told me I was white.

Do you feel connected more to Africa?

Yes. I definitely have an interest in Africa and want to do more research on it. When I visited my biological mother for the first time, she gave me a plant with flags of all my different ethnic backgrounds. I'm part Scottish, part English, part Nigerian. There were at least six different flags.

What is the family composition of your biological parents' side of the family?

I have a half-brother on my biological mother's side. On my biological father's side I have a couple of brothers and sisters, and one of my sisters lives in Washington, D.C. My biological father is coming to the states in 1998, and I'm going to meet him then.

The small tribulations my wife and I experience as an interracial couple are nothing compared to what my biological parents went through back in the late 1960s.

Does it make you feel "better" in any way that your biological parents are from different ethnic groups?

It makes me feel more at ease. I don't have to feel ashamed, like I'm letting my family down because I married a white woman. It's kind of neat.

Are you planning a trip to Nigeria to visit your biological father?

He lives and works in Saudi Arabia, mainly because of the political climate in Nigeria. His whole family lives in Nigeria and goes to see him now and then, or he flies back to see them.

Did your biological mother tell you why she gave you up for adoption?

Yes. She and my biological father went through a lot of stuff because he was black and she was white. When she became pregnant, they knew at the time that they couldn't publicly get together as a couple. It was more evident to him since he came from a Nigerian family who was set against him seeing a white woman. My biological mother would have moved to Nigeria with him, but he knew it wouldn't work out, given the reality. Ultimately they broke up. My biological mother wasn't with him when she had me.

Did your biological father have the opportunity to see you being born?

He knew I was being born, but I don't believe he ever saw me.

What did your biological mother do once you were born?

She moved to Ithaca for a while and stayed with her brother.

And who is Pete today?

I am a well-diversed and culturally enriched person. Having come from different ethnic backgrounds, I've experienced both sides, black and white, and that has given me a special perspective on life.

Does race matter?

Not to me. Race is a part of my life, however, that I deal with every day as different issues surface. And I deal with it the best I can.

Britton Perry

ROSLINDALE, MASSACHUSETTS
DECEMBER 1996

This is going to sound phony, like a cliché, but it's true. You have to recognize, find, and maintain your inner strength. No matter what it is, no matter where you get it from, because, when it comes down to it, you are all you have. You have to love yourself for who and what you are. From there you can go on to idolize, to have mentors, to find support. But most important is to have a firm belief in yourself and the strength that keeps you going from within.

Britton Perry has a brilliant career as an actor and teacher. He was born in Boston, Massachusetts, and was raised in Rochester, New York. He attended Brockport University and Emerson College. Britton enjoyed learning the acting trade. It was through this medium that he could express his feelings and when he was the happiest.

Britton grew up in an upper-middle-class family. His parents adopted him in 1970, shortly after he was born. Uncertain whether they could have children of their own, they were eager to adopt. Race was not an issue for them. According to Britton, they simply wanted a child.

He was taught that there was value in learning about different cultural histories. In spite of that, Britton's cultural orientation was in a predominantly white environment. Britton found that in order for him to make sense of his physical differences within a white setting and understand the African American experience, he would have to pursue those issues on his own.

His life so far has been one of great privilege and opportunity. He has accepted the challenge of exploring more about his ethnicity and contributing his time and his talents to communities. It is through the struggle that he is refining who he is.

How old were you when you were adopted?
Only a few months old.

Where were you raised?

Different places: Boston, Philadelphia, and Rochester (New York).

Do you have siblings?

Yes. I have two brothers and one sister. They're all my parents' biological children.

Did your parents tell you that you were adopted?

Yes. They told me when I was younger. But it was easy for me to figure out. I was black; they were white. It was also helpful that I had black friends at the time who were also adopted into white families.

What made you realize there were differences between you and your family?

People they emulated were different from people I'd emulate.

As you were growing up, what physical differences did you notice about yourself compared to your siblings?

I noticed that my body developed differently from the bodies of my white male counterparts—lips, butt, hair, etc. My hair's more wavy than an Afro, though.

Did your parents talk to you about race?

No. Both my parents are well-educated, but they never explained what it was like to be black because they really didn't know. At the same time they were able to explain to me what was important for me to learn. They were there to support me.

Did your parents tell you why they chose to adopt you as opposed to a child who was of their same ethnic or racial background?

They didn't think they could have children, so they were looking to adopt a baby. The baby's color really didn't matter. They were just overjoyed to have a child. My parents told me that when they saw me I was so cute that they just had to have me. My mom did tell me, though, that they were concerned that color and other physical differences would come into play later in my life.

How did you feel when your parents told you that their reasons for adopting you included the fact that you were cute and lovable?

Part of me thought that the main reason to want a child would be to have someone to love and take care of. Overall, I thought that by choosing me they were not discriminating. They just wanted to love me.

As a child, did you go to cultural events with your family?

No. There was not a lot of African American influences for me growing up. Anything I did for my own cultural reinforcement was on my own.

But I was exposed to other cultural history. My parents made it known *very early* that exposure to other cultures is crucial and exciting!

So your family did not intentionally try to expose you to the African American heritage?

No.

Were any of your parents' friends African American?

When I was a child, they had a few African American friends who'd come over to the house. But for most of my life, there were very few African Americans in my life.

Within the professional arena, did your parents work with African Americans?

Yes. My dad is currently a librarian and he works with a variety of ethnic minorities.

Do you know if your parents consulted with persons in the African American community about how to raise you?

No, I don't think they did.

Tell me about the community you grew up in.

My community was in the suburbs and was primarily white.

In the elementary grades in school, were you exposed to any African American children?

Some, but not many.

Did you spend time with them?

Yes. Playing.

Were you curious about your black classmates—their dress, why some may have behaved a certain way? And then did you talk to your parents about any questions you might have had?

Occasionally I'd ask questions. I asked why some people are darker than others, why people's hair is different, things like that.

What did your parents say?

I could sense that they didn't have the answers, but they tried to explain as best as they could.

Were there other African Americans in your high school?

Yes. Yes, my high school was predominately African American.

What high school did you go to?

A school for the arts, in Rochester, New York.

Was that when you had your first orientation to the African American community?

Yes. I'd definitely say that it started in junior high.

How did you respond to this experience?

I wasn't surprised or shocked. It wasn't like I opened the door and then there were black people there. It was almost refreshing because now I had more friends that I could talk to and hang out with. I had black friends growing up, but now I had more. So more questions could be answered. I could feel more comfortable and mingle.

How did the black students treat you?

The same as my other friends. I do think that at times they felt a little animosity when they found out I was adopted into a white family. At times they were a little skeptical of me.

Why skeptical?

They were wondering what my values were, where I was coming from, whether I was an Uncle Tom or "being down" with them.

How did you handle their reaction?

It was difficult at times. I probably showed signs of "Whatz up with you?" I think I more or less did the best I could at the time. There wasn't much I could do. I just rolled with it.

Have you been called names because of the way you look?

Some kids called me "bloody zebra" in my earlier years.

I never heard that term before.

It's because I'm mixed—white, black, and Indian. The zebra is for the black and white, the red for the Indians. I felt pretty hurt. That was my first racial slur.

When was that?

In fifth or sixth grade. It was tough at times growing up in neighbor-hoods with mostly white people. I was called other names. For instance, when you drink out of a bottle and wrap your lips around the bottle, they say you "nigger lip it." Basically they're pointing out that black people have big lips.

Did you talk to your parents about this type of ignorance?

At times I would, at other times I'd keep it to myself. If I was really devastated about something or had a lot of questions, I'd talk to my par-ents. But I tend to keep things to myself, hold my feelings in. I know this isn't the best coping method but I've always tried to control my feelings. I become more open with people I trust.

Were there mentors or friends available to you?

Yes, my best friend, Steve, from junior high school. He's also adopted, and his dad is black and his mom white. They grew up in a very exclusive community, very suburban, upper-class white. His father is a principal in the school. We bonded instantly when we first met.

Going back to your high school years, tell me about your relationship with black and white students.

I formed equal relationships. I think I was more comfortable with my white friends because of my upbringing. I did hang out with black kids, but it was harder for me because I'd hold back, always wondering what they were thinking about me.

Did you ever ask them?

Sometimes. But sometimes I'd just pretend and wouldn't tell them my situation so that I wouldn't be judged.

At that time were you proud to be living in a white family?

Sometimes I was, sometimes I wasn't. There were times that I felt ashamed and other times that I felt privileged.

When did you feel ashamed, and why?

When I couldn't relate to other people's experiences and felt there'd been something missing. I thought I'd understand more about my black friends' situation if I'd been raised in a black family. And that's when a lot of questions came up about cultural things.

But then there were times when I was glad I was with my family. I knew my family was safe, secure, and I knew I'd be supported and have the opportunity to do things. My feelings definitely fluctuated.

You spoke of keeping your feelings inside as a way of coping with your emotions. Do you have a lot of pain inside you? Today, what are those emotions?

Sadness, a sense of emptiness. I honestly think I'll always have questions, feelings of sadness. I don't think that will ever go away. That's a hard thing for me to say, but I think it's true. I think that deep down inside, anybody in a similar situation would probably also have questions and a sense of emptiness. I speak for myself, but I hope other people will look to fill that void, too.

I sense the emotions you are experiencing are deep. What do these emotions feel like?

It's not anger. I know I was given a great family with incredible opportunities. I've been happy. I've been provided for. Looking back at my life, things certainly could have been worse. But I don't mean to avoid your question. The feeling I get is like right before you go on stage, a feeling of butterflies in the pit of your stomach. It's an infinite feeling of butterflies that you know you're always going to feel in the pit of your stomach. You know exactly how it's going to feel, so you try to suppress it.

What happens if you don't suppress that feeling?

I get depressed and feel the urge to call somebody and talk to them, to vent. Or I write down how I'm feeling just at that minute. It makes me study more, pick up a book, try to find answers.

What makes you cry?

Where I'm at right now in my life, my major question is, will I ever find my biological father or mother?

Do you want to?

Yes, but all the legalities are holding me back. My birth mother can't be told where I am until I sign certain papers, and vice versa. And to initiate the search is taking me a long time because I'm wondering if she's looking for me anyway. If I initiate the search and find out she hasn't been looking for me, I'll be devastated. But then if I never start to look for her and she's been looking for me, then she's probably devastated right now and I'll never know who she is. Then there are a lot of people telling me that I'll never find my dad, my original father, that makes me really sad.

Why do you want to find your biological parents?

I think it's important. It would bring closure for me. I'd know where I came from, and I'd be able to look into the faces of the people who created me. I think everybody needs to have a sense of who they are and where they came from. A lot of people take that for granted. When it comes to religion, people look to their creator, the person who's responsible for them. For me, my creator is my biological parents. I'm trying to gather the strength to find them.

At a point in your life, you spent quality time in the arts. What made you develop an interest in drama?

When I was real young I always liked to perform. I had a lot of energy and was quite outspoken. I'd say I was animated. I enjoyed putting on a show. It just became a natural path that my parents steered me into. And that's when I was the happiest, when I was performing.

Why?

I admired actors and actresses. It was such a great way to express oneself. Acting was the epitome of expression.

When you acted, did you ever touch those feelings deep within, the pain you felt at having being adopted, not knowing your biological parents?

That question brings up a lot of memories. When I was at Emerson College, one of my drama teachers was trying to get some emotion out of me. He said, "Britton, why can't you feel this emotion. I want you to feel sadness." He told me that everybody has anger, frustration, and sadness within them and that when I'm on stage I need to bring these feelings out. I was having difficulty tapping into those feelings. My teacher helped me explore those feelings by asking me about my childhood, like what made me angry, what made me frustrated. I was supposed to act these feelings out. All of a sudden the feelings erupted. I started yelling and screaming and crying. I felt the biggest rush of satisfaction I'd felt in a long time. Even though a lot of people were staring at me, it didn't matter because I felt successful, that I'd done it. I also felt relieved that those emotions had finally come out. That I remember distinctly.

Being transracially adopted into a white family creates interesting dynamics in every aspect of an adoptee's life, especially when dealing with relationships across the color line. When it comes to dating, are you attracted to black or white women?

Unlike many of my black friends who are adopted into white families, I've always been attracted to black women, ever since I first started dating. I've dated more black women than white women. Growing up in the community that I did and being exposed primarily to white people, I've never been able to figure out why I was particularly attracted to black women. It wasn't because of the fascination or the curiosity. Those were factors, but, to me, dating women of color was something real and sincere.

Did the women you dated ask you questions about your family?

Yes. Usually when they heard my voice for the first time they'd ask me where I was from and whether I was mixed. When they realized that both my parents are white, they began to understand why I act and talk the way I do. It comes full circle for them. Some either choose to discriminate and break up for that reason or stick with me regardless of my living in a white family.

With most of the women I dated, I found they were very curious and supportive, and my living in a white family wasn't a factor to them in having a relationship with me. But as soon as someone hears my voice, that immediately brings about questions. It always has and always will.

Did you meet the families of the women you dated?

Yes. I had one very serious relationship with an African American woman in college. I met her family. I fell in love with her and thought I wanted to marry her. She was beautiful, intelligent, dark-skinned, etc. Unfortunately our relationship didn't work out, but it had nothing to do with our families or with color. That was probably one of the greatest relationships I ever had.

Let's talk about intimacy. When you are in an intimate relationship with a person who cares a lot about you and wants to be with you, both emotionally and physically, does it scare you to be vulnerable? I ask that because somewhere along the line, in a genuinely truthful relationship, you have to expose the sadness, the laughter, the pain, the joy, the complexity of your life.

It's very hard. In the relationship I was just in, my girlfriend was continuously encouraging me to explore myself more, talk with my parents, challenge them about issues pertaining to me, and dive more into the African American community. While my former girlfriend was supportive and understood where I was coming from, it's always been hard for me to adjust to people from different cultures. It's difficult to come forth and say that I can't relate to certain issues because my orientation is different. For me, showing my true feelings has been a very high mountain to get over in every relationship. Every relationship has problems, but this is the hardest problem I confront.

I imagine that eventually you're going to have children. Would teaching your children about their cultural heritage, as well as discussing with them issues on race and culture, be an important part of their foundation?

Unequivocally. That's why right now I'm trying to conquer as many battles as I can with myself, to find my birth parents, to come to a sense of closure, so I can explain to my children what I did and why I did it. It's important for them to know who they are and who their grandparents are.

My parents weren't outspoken about my identity and race and culture. Unlike my parents, I'll be outspoken to my children because that's what I wanted from my own parents—to become more knowledgeable about the issues pertaining to me and to talk about these issues more openly.

Black or mixed people living in an affluent society where they're stereotyped as being an Uncle Tom are going to find that people will discriminate against them, no matter what family structure they come from. I've seen blacks who come from a strong nuclear black family, but because they are articulate and successful, they're still called white, an Uncle Tom, or a "wanna be." So it seems that success and intelligence is frowned on by some who consider that to be crossing over.

Thinking back to your childhood, did the media play a role in defining your views about black people?

I've been disappointed all my life with the way the media personifies us. I think it's a crime.

Did you believe the television images were true?

Frankly, I'd take a look at myself and say those images are all bullshit. Excuse me for swearing, but it "pisses me off." I'd look at my black friends and think that what the media was saying about us was wrong! I think Hollywood has had a field day stereotyping us.

What were some of the stereotypes?

In movie after movie the black guy would die first. The black guy would be the one stealing cars, the racist, the pimp, the pusher. Being an actor I've studied this for a long time and have gotten involved with issues like this. If you look back at the history, many of today's great black actors all played stereotypical roles to get where they are now. For example, Morgan Freeman played a pusher, a pimp, etc.

Robert Townsend has struck me as both an individual and a director with great integrity. He's been genuine and professional in addressing this issue. He should be applauded for publicly denouncing the stereotypical roles that blacks have been type-casted to play.

I agree. There have been black actors who have never accepted negative roles because they were smart and knew it would take them into the wrong avenues of their life. And it's hard to turn jobs down.

I think America has never really accepted blacks as having a complete family. The media and Hollywood usually doesn't present blacks as having solid families like whites do. Americans didn't grow up with a black *Leave It to Beaver* or a black *Andy Griffith Show* or a black *Jetsons*. I can go on and on. What people see in the media shape the nation's thinking. It influences me as well and what I think.

Staying on the subject of the media and what it communicates to this nation, what was your view of O. J. Simpson?

It's difficult for me to talk about this. Once again, I'm a victim of media bombardment, like we all are, shaping our decisions by what the media hands us. It's hard for me to decide what happened in the Simpson trial because nobody really knows. Whether he's innocent or guilty, I will say that this case was by far one of the greatest things that could have happened to the morale of the African Americans, and that's because O. J. Simpson, the "Juice," was being represented by some of the most powerful lawyers in America, like Johnnie Cochran, and then he was found innocent of the criminal charge. So we have a case of a black man who was represented to the fullest because he had the income to do it. That doesn't happen often when blacks are on trial for murder. Yes, he may have committed a civil wrong, but more power to him for building himself from having nothing to having everything and being able to provide for himself.

That's why I try to leave the element of guilt out of it. Instead I look at what he did in life, what he came out of, who he is, and what message that sends to the African American community.

The Rodney King case, of course, was different than that of O. J. Simpson, but it still divided the nation and caused bitter feelings, particularly in the African American community, that the Los Angeles Police Department could brutalize a black man as they did. What do you think about that case?

Thank God for video cameras. I'm glad it was caught on film. There are a lot of racist cops that should be discharged from the force permanently. Unfortunately Rodney King was a victim, but he stands for so many people who have been brutalized.

I'm sorry Rodney King was brutalized, but I'm glad that people were actually able to see what happened. Then, of course, the media tried to tell the flip side of the story, showing Reginald Denny, who is white, being beaten by a crowd of bystanders, conveying that black people were taking revenge. Those were two isolated incidents but the media tried to merge them.

In your opinion, what issues are facing the African American community, and how do you think you can help in providing social solutions?

I would commit myself to my children to wipe out the ignorance young people have. I'd be honest, explain things, and be there to support them at all times. I felt at times that I was let loose, and that's where my mistakes and questions came up. I want to be there for the young people who are going to shape the future. I want to make sure they have the strongest foundation available by connecting them to people who can give them the answers.

We, as African Americans, need to get more black children into school. They need to graduate from high school and college. I believe there are ways the African American community can be stronger than it is now. Do you think that public policy issues, like the Affirmative Action Program, make the black community stronger?

Yes, definitely. I think it would be a crime if they did away with affirmative action. Because of all the disadvantages the African American community endured, colleges should continue to accept ethnic students and to help them in special ways. People try to write the whole program off as laziness. After years and years of generation after generation not having opportunities, I think these opportunities should be provided. The funds are there, but the government doesn't want to use the money for this. Ways have to be found to help these communities succeed. It's the government's responsibility to help.

What are the advantages and disadvantages of being adopted into a white family?

Since an early age, I've always been told that I should see the advantages of growing up in a white community and being black, and thus able to understand both sides. I believe I've appreciated the benefits of both worlds. I have a unique way of looking at things, and I'm grateful for that.

But there are definitely negatives. I feel that I'm not really accepted or acclimated to one culture or the other. Would I consider adoption in the future? That's hard to say because of all the questions and difficulties I've gone through. Do I want to subject somebody else to that, or do I want to succeed in doing what my biological parents were not able to do? I hope I'll be able to make that decision and be satisfied with it by the time I have a wife. It's not that I don't support adoption, I just need more time to consider it carefully.

What message would you give to thousands of children who don't have homes? These children are black and white, from all different backgrounds.

This is going to sound phony, like a cliché, but it's true. You have to recognize, find, and maintain your inner strength. No matter what it is, no matter where you get it from, because, when it comes down to it, *you* are all you have. You have to love yourself for who and what you are. From there you can go on to idolize, to have mentors, to find support. But most important is to have a firm belief in yourself and the strength that keeps you going from within.

To those white parents who are looking to adopt black children, what would you say?

I'd say here's a brochure for college; you'd better take some courses in the African American culture. I think there's honesty in that. Parents shouldn't fake it, go out and try to make friends who aren't really your friends. You have to be true to yourself, but at the same time you have to learn with your child. Don't try to conquer the African American community by making all these friends. Don't be afraid to say, "I don't know." There's nothing wrong with admitting that. But then you have to say, "I want to know. Can we find out together?" Sometimes children need to realize that parents don't have all the answers, that they are learning as well.

Who is Britton? And what can you say to your biological parents in answering this question?

I'll have to get back to you on that. That's one of the most perplexing questions I'll face, if I ever meet them. I'll probably be speechless.

What would you want them to know?

I'd want them to know what my life was like. I'd try to tell them the high points, the low points, what I've done, and what I intend to do.

What single words describe you today?

Energetic, outgoing, intelligent, fair, informed, African American, mixed. I'm happy with who I am, but I think I'll always be searching. I don't think I'm the end all and be all, but I am confident and secure about who I am.

Taalib

Parents who adopt transracially need to plan how they're going to raise their children. A parent can't allow mere circumstance to determine a child's life. A transracial child needs someone who can see what he or she sees, someone the child can identify with. History has shown us that black children in interracial homes have issues that children in same-race homes don't have to deal with. Regardless of what color the foster or adoptive parents are, if they're committed to being good parents, they must pursue and maintain cultural bonds for their adopted child.

Born in Massachusetts, Taalib was soon adopted in 1968. He was raised Roman Catholic. Most of his childhood was spent on a farm in Vermont where his adoptive parents fostered hundreds of children with special needs and adopted sixteen children from different ethnic backgrounds. His experiences growing up included going fishing with his family, taking camping trips in the wilderness, and especially listening to the stories endured by the foster kids who fell victim to abuse and neglect in their biological homes.

When Taalib was in elementary and high school, he battled racist attacks by neighborhood friends who, as he says, eventually turned into "new enemies." No longer could he interact with his peers on a social level. Race became the decisive factor in determining his legitimacy. During this period, his feelings of isolation were exacerbated by being black in a white family and a white community.

Taalib used his pain to better himself athletically and academically. In 1986, with the support of his parents, he attended Syracuse University and, later, Northeastern University School of Law.

In college, Taalib identified with the black groups on campus. He made it a priority to gain knowledge about the history and struggle of black people in order to strengthen his own self-identity. But it was through the relationships he built in the African American community that made him aware of the crisis facing African American males and compelled him to pursue his law degree.

Taalib's life has been full of successes and challenges. In his journey thus far, he's seen one of society's nightmares—children abandoned, abused, and neglected. He has realized the necessity of knowing one's ethnic heritage. And he has recognized the investment of a stable and loving family.

Tell me about your adoptive parents.

My adoptive father passed away two years ago. He was the oldest of three boys and came from a small town in Kentucky. He came from a family of military men. He enlisted in the navy in his sophomore year of high school. He was also an All-American football player. While in the navy he was a cook. He was a big man, and after the war he became a coal miner and then a foreman in a steel mill. He was also into hunting, the environment, country living. This is one reason why we lived in Vermont, a place where you could go fishing and camping. When I was 5, we bought the property we live on. We own three hundred acres. The population is about five thousand.

Is the population predominately white?

Yes. It's like a Norman Rockwell painting. There are farms, expensive houses, but also shacks and trailers. Each property has an average of five acres.

Tell me about your adoptive mother's background.

She's first-generation Polish and Irish, the oldest of three. She has a sister about five years younger and a brother about ten years younger than she is.

Your parents met and got married in their late teens. In 1968 they adopted you as an infant. What was it like when you entered the picture?

They bought a hotel in 1965 in western Massachusetts and converted it into a home. It's three stories and has ten bedrooms and three bathrooms. The first floor was once a furniture store and warehouse. My family lived on the second and third floors. We were the only family that lived in the building.

What was your town like?

It was a small industrial town. It has an air force base and many factories. My father worked at one of the factories that made tools for Sears.

What were the people like who lived there?

Because there was an air force base in the town, quite a few military families lived in the area. Most of my neighbors were Portuguese, French,

Polish, Puerto Rican, Irish, or Italian. They were very much into their cultures, so it made for an interesting melting pot. All the men worked in the same factories so they knew one another and interacted. The women were primarily housewives. Every house had a mother, a father, and a child.

Professionally, your father worked in a factory. What did your mother do?

She was at home taking care of us. In 1968 there were about fifteen kids living in our home.

Fifteen kids. Were they foster kids or adopted?

Except for two, they were all foster kids.

So she was a foster care mother?

Yes. She spent her life doing that. Her career was to take care of us. She spent her time making sure we received all the things we needed—food, clothing, shelter.

What led your father and mother to become foster parents, as well as adoptive parents?

My mother was in an accident when she was young that left her unable to have children.

By your thirteenth birthday, you saw more than four hundred foster kids come through your home.

Yes, more than four hundred. We lived in this huge building with a lot of bedrooms. Many of my adoptive mother's friends were either foster parents or social workers. They encouraged her to make use of the space and help kids who needed shelter.

When I was younger, around 5 or 6, a lot of kids would come and stay for only a couple of weeks, a couple of days, a couple of months, and then they'd be gone.

Why were these kids removed from their biological homes?

Mainly because of neglect and abuse. Sometimes the court would decide that further investigation was needed in certain custody cases, causing kids to be displaced from their homes. My house was a holding cell for wayward children.

How does one go about "parenting" four hundred foster kids, particularly kids who have special needs or need physical assistance? Is it feasible to provide stability for children who may only be in the foster home for two weeks?

Most definitely. A lot of kids who came through stayed in contact with my adoptive mother. They let her know how much they appreciated her being in their life and giving them the opportunity to do something with themselves.

The term *special needs* **is used broadly in reference to children. I've heard the term used to describe healthy black children as well as children with disabilities. What were the characteristics of some of the special-needs children who were in your mother's care?**

In the 1970s the special needs kids at the Wilsons were mostly white and were reared in poor households that were unfit. In some cases the parents were divorced or alcoholics. Many of the kids came from the same home. The Wilsons would take six kids who were all brothers and sisters. Whatever the problem was, it would usually be resolved so the kids could go back home.

So your mother's home served as a safe place for these kids until they could be returned safely to their biological homes?

Yes.

Is that why you said it can be a positive thing for kids to be housed in foster care homes?

Yes. The experience can give someone stability, if only for a short time. When you're young and taken from your home, for whatever reason, or if the conditions in your home are unstable, you're scared, confused, upset. Your confidence and self-esteem are destroyed. The experience impacts your outlook on the future and what you aspire to be.

When social service agents put you back into the situation they took you from in the first place but never properly address the root of the problem, it really screws up a child. Ultimately it affects the way a child behaves in society. It also affects the way a child treats himself.

What was it like for you and the other kids in the home? How were you treated by your parents and what activities did you participate in as a family?

When the kids came into the house, the Wilsons treated them with dignity and respect. They gave them clothes, food, shelter, and love. We had many toys. Mr. Wilson was into nature and the wilderness, so we all had a chance to explore the outdoors. Nature is very humbling; it can't be replaced by toys or television. For entertainment, we had squirrels, goats, cows, deer, rabbits, chickens, frogs, dogs, cats, birds, orchards, streams, and gardens.

Summer at the Wilsons was like camp for a lot of my brothers and sisters coming through. Not only was the house big, there were always fifteen to twenty youths in the house. We always traveled together and did things together, things we'd never done before. Kids who were returned to their biological families missed the experience they had with the Wilsons. They remember it. Some of them, although they live with their biological parents, still consider Mrs. Wilson their real mother.

Just hearing your description of your home underscores for me the urgency to expose children to positive influences.

There are situations where the biological families can't take proper care of their children. The children are neglected, abused. If that is all they know in life, they're going to self-destruct and be destructive to society.

Families are out there who are willing to provide a loving and stable home for abused and neglected children. Children need order to grow up and become productive citizens—spiritually in touch and psychologically sound. It doesn't matter to me what reasons people have for not being supportive of foster care. The pain I've seen my brothers and sisters go through, the things that have been done to them, are nothing less than cruel, inhumane, horrific. Some of their stories would give you nightmares for years. There have been many nights when I couldn't sleep after hearing what had been done to them.

How many siblings do you actually have?

I have fifteen who are adopted and twelve who are foster children. A total of twelve foster and adopted children currently live with Mrs. Wilson, as well as seven dogs, a bird, and two cats.

Do your siblings come from different backgrounds?

Yes. Black, Puerto Rican, and white. When I was younger, most of my brothers and sisters were white. When I was a teenager, most of my siblings were black or Puerto Rican. One of my brothers has cerebral palsy.

So the pattern seems to have changed in the mid-1980s, when black and Puerto Rican kids were coming into your family?

Right. Crack and drug abuse were the major factors. Most of my brothers and sisters, in the 1980s, were born either alcohol addicted or crack addicted or both. When I was a child, the kids who were coming in were older, 10 through 15. In the 1980s, the kids were coming in a lot younger, 2, 3, and 4 years old.

The children born alcohol- or crack-addicted are currently on medication. Adrenaline is popular in my family. At school most of my brothers and sisters are labeled as children "at risk" or with "special needs." They're in the Special Olympics. But if you were to talk to them, you'd never guess it. They're very bright.

What is the age range of the kids now living at home?

I'd say between 5 and 45. There are eight kids in school right now, fourth through eleventh grades. They're black, white, and Latino. The younger ones are black, and the older ones are white.

Two of my brothers were forced to live in a closet for months while their biological father starved them to the point where they began eating their feces in their effort to survive. They were 5 and 6 years old. They were both born perfectly normal. Now they're 15 and 16. Neither of them will ever be able to function without a primary care provider, medication, and direct supervision.

Clearly many of the kids your parents adopted or fostered came from painful backgrounds. I think it's wonderful that even as a kid you were able to listen to their stories and still do what kids do, have fun with one another.

We raised one another. Fortunately I was adopted at an early age and was never abused. I learned so much from my brothers and sisters who were going through really tough times. Mrs. Wilson allowed them to speak and live freely, whatever their form of expression. The foster kids who were there for only a short time appreciated that. They could be kids and have fun.

Did the fact that you were black and adopted into a white family have any relevance for you in the situation you were in?

I was the first black child they adopted (or even brought into foster care). There were four others who came before me who are foster children. They were older. They were my sister's boyfriends. They were either black or Puerto Rican. They had afros and dreadlocks. They were my first introduction to the black community. When I was young, they were the ones who helped me. They taught me a lot. They were always around.

Your mother has been fostering children for a long time.

Yes. She's in her late sixties, and she's been a foster parent for more than forty years.

By the time you were a teenager, you had clearly gone through a lot and had seen the consequences of children addicted to crack. You probably had more than a hundred good reasons why you should blame society, be angry and close-minded. What made you realize the importance of a college education, particularly if neither of your adoptive parents had gone to college?

Mr. Wilson realized the value of education. He always stressed to all the kids that we had to do well in school. He'd reward us for our academic achievements. A lot of the camping and fishing trips were rewards for trying hard in school and staying out of trouble.

Was it a given, then, that you would pursue a higher degree?

I knew I had to be educated. He reminded us every day, as long as I can remember, about the need to obtain an education. He'd talk about the men he was working for. They were a lot younger than he was but they had their college degrees. He told us that they were the ones getting promoted and getting higher salaries, even though Mr. Wilson knew more about the shop than they did and had more experience.

How did you do in school?

I did well in high school. I didn't do so well in grammar school. At that time I really was affected by having been adopted into a white home. When I was around 5, I remember wanting my biological mother. The other kids in the house were white, and so were Mr. and Mrs. Wilson. I was the only black child in grammar school. Everybody else was white.

Is it apparent physically that you are African American?

Yes. I have a medium-brown complexion with kinky hair.

Were you noticing a difference in the way kids in your neighborhood played with you?

I noticed a difference in their attitudes. I was in second grade the first time I was called a nigger.

Was it white people who called you this name?

Yes. And it was the kids' parents who were teaching them to call me these names.

The parents?

Yes, they were teaching their kids the words. The kids were really young, and at that age skin color means nothing to you. In fifth grade I wanted to hang out with them, go bike riding. But whenever I got to their houses, the parents would ask, "Why did you bring him here? I don't want you to hang out with niggers." They'd always say something mean, and they'd say it right in front of me. Sometimes they'd pull their kids aside, but I knew what they meant. And I was doing nothing to nobody.

This was all going on in the early 1980s?

In the late seventies and early eighties.

So when these kids and their parents called you these names, did you feel that they were negative terms?

Yes. Because the parents didn't want me to play with their kids. I just wanted to have fun. As the years went on, old friends became new enemies.

I largely attribute racism to why I did poorly in elementary and junior high school. I never wanted to go to school. I always pretended to be sick. I'd cry every night because I hated the situation I was in. I wanted out. I thought that only my biological mother could get me out. I prayed all the time for her to come and rescue me. Of course she never came.

What values did your adoptive family instill in you that helped you survive?

I realized at an early age that a kid respects his mother and father when they're stern. The Wilsons taught me to be passionate about who I am and whatever I choose to do. I knew I had to survive, so I got into martial arts. I started seeing education differently. I no longer saw it as a way to get a trip or a new jacket. I saw it more as a way to beat racists at their own game, to really get under their skin. I focused on what Mr. Wilson was saying about education and also the experiences of my foster brothers and sisters.

What made you change your way of thinking?

It bothered me that I couldn't hang out and have fun with the other kids because of my color. I realized there was nothing I could do to appease them. I also realized there was no way I could stop my pain or stop them from ridiculing me other than by bettering myself. I promised myself when I was 12 that I'd never get beaten up again. That's when I really got into physical fitness and exercise. I was continuously working out. In my freshman year of high school I joined the track team. I was running fifteen miles a day, all year 'round. In high school nobody called me names. Some of my best friends in high school were white girls. There were no black girls in my school. In high school I stayed away from dating and concentrated on education and athletics. I did well in high school. I graduated with a 3.8 grade-point average (GPA). About ten of my classmates in my homeroom, all through high school, were the top-ten scholars in the school, and I was competing with them on tests. They all were basketball players or soccer players, and they were representatives in the school government offices. I was the one who kept them sharp. I'd do better on a project, and they'd be so upset about it that they'd study harder so they'd get better grades than me.

What type of high school did you attend?

It was a small Catholic high school. There were 140 students in my graduating class, and approximately 600 in the school.

When you graduated in 1986, where did you go to college?

Syracuse University. My first semester I had a 2.5 GPA. In my second semester I started getting into partying and drinking. I was running with three different crews.

What did you do in these groups?

We drank, smoked, played basketball, and partied. We never took an early-morning class. We had classes on Tuesdays, Wednesdays, and Thursdays, and had Fridays off. Our weekends started on Thursday and ended on Monday. My grades started going down. That's about the time I got interested in joining a fraternity.

In the news lately, attention has been drawn to the dark side of fraternities. Young men have died trying to get inducted into these groups. Students destroy property, get drunk, and hurt themselves just so they can be accepted. Is it necessary that students who pledge a fraternity go through these forms of activities in order to be included?

No, you don't have to go through it. It's something brothers do because they can't handle the freedom, the power, the authority of being a member of such a group. Many brothers who join fraternities are guys who are looking to belong to a support network. It allows them to do some of the things and live some of the dreams that they value.

You received your bachelor's degree in history?

Yes, in black studies. I wanted to be a professor. I had planned to go on to get my master's and my Ph.D. At the time I was really into teaching people about history.

What led you to law school?

I saw too many black men with great potential side-tracked and destroyed by criminal activity or the criminal justice system. That was my main motivation.

I discovered Afrocentrism in 1989, and I started thinking about what that meant. I thought about all the problems I could help to solve or prevent by being proactive. Being a lawyer gave me the power and ability to intervene in people's lives, to keep them from going to jail or provide resources that would help them. I felt I could make a difference.

What are your views on transracial adoption?

My opinions are mixed. I think foster homes are definitely the key. We need foster homes to give abused or neglected kids the opportunity to succeed in life. If they're placed in good foster homes, they'll be much happier children and more stable adults. They'll have the opportunity to enjoy healthy relationships, maybe even help their biological family out when they get older.

To answer your question, I think children who are adopted transracially need more than just love; their parents need to have a multicultural plan.

What do you mean by a "multicultural plan"?

Parents who adopt transracially need to plan how they're going to raise their children. A parent can't allow mere circumstance to determine a child's life. A transracial child needs someone who can see what he or she sees, someone the child can identify with. History has shown us that black children in interracial homes have issues that children in same-race homes don't have to deal with. Regardless of what color the foster or adoptive parents are, if they're committed to being good parents, they must pursue and maintain cultural bonds for their adopted child.

What do you think are the key elements that transracially adopted children need?

Complete knowledge of self. Giving a child self-knowledge is more than just accepting the child as a human being. That child must know who he is as a black person and what his ancestors endured. The adoptive parents must give him an opportunity to get involved and participate effectively in cultural activities. Regardless of how loving an adoptive parent is, a transracial child is in a hostile environment. A black child goes through many things that white parents don't see. The parents must make a real effort to see what's going on and do something about it. Sadly, I'm not certain adoptive parents are being trained to think like that. In those cases I'm against interracial adoption. Adoptive parents cannot raise black children in a bubble.

So the bottom line is . . .?

Once a black child has self-knowledge, that child will be able to love the adoptive parents more. The child will also be able to love him- or herself more.

What shaped your views on transracial adoption?

My opinion comes mostly from seeing traditional families succeed or fail, seeing blacks, whites, and Puerto Ricans succeed or fail. My values transcend race. Appreciating transracial adoption means being honest with oneself and putting the child's needs and best interests above everything else.

On a spectrum ranging from being confused to being comfortable with who you are, where would you fall at this point in your life?

If 1 is "confused" and 10 is "understanding myself," then I'm a 6.

What do you think needs to change on a policy level regarding the care of our nation's children?

Without resources, education, or funds to make the necessary changes in children's situations, we're helpless. There's very little any single policy can do. It just serves as a Band-Aid for the welfare system or the Department of Social Services. Without investing resources in the children's future, the craziness isn't going to stop.

What about the view that social agencies are set up in such a way that they actually discourage black families from adopting or fostering black children?

If more black people would become foster parents, there wouldn't be a need for white people to adopt black children. I don't think most white people purposely adopt black children. They end up adopting them simply because most foster children are black.

Do you think that that's a bad thing?

Some white parents I know who have adopted a black child have good hearts and are really nice people, but they're a little naive. They're caught up in a life that isn't productive for a black child. The environment they live in may not be safe for a black child. The black child may be learning to accept, even like, certain things that are actually destroying that child's people, that child's race. Is it worth it? That all depends on the adoptive home. What are the parents like? How are they raising their child? Are they in touch with the child's ethnic community? It's very subjective.

Returning to the issues facing children in this nation, I think there are many contributing factors. There are more black kids in foster care than white kids, so more black kids need permanent homes. But there are more white foster homes than black foster homes. So the bottom line is that something needs to be done with these kids. Society can't just lock them up or let them bounce from home to home until they're 18 and then incarcerate them. Therefore, if a good white family is available for a child, then I say put the child in their home. I believe, though, that each situation should be considered case by case.

What are you involved with now, and why did you return to Vermont?

When Mr. Wilson died two years ago, I thought about moving back to help out. As I mentioned, we have three hundred acres. There are now five houses on the property. One has eight bedrooms and is where my younger brothers and sisters live. Most of the kids are between 5 and 17. So with all this property and all these kids, it's easy for a house to fall apart and for my brothers and sisters to get out of control. I decided to leave Boston and return to Vermont in order to save money and help my mother out.

Of all of your siblings, how many went to college?

Three. I have my JD, one sister has her bachelor's from Boston University, and my oldest brother has an MBA from Holy Cross College.

What are some of your other siblings doing?

One sister is married and lives in Massachusetts with her husband and two kids. One brother is a vice president of an exchange firm.

How many of your siblings are professionally working?

Seven, I believe.

Where are the other ones?

I don't know. Mrs. Wilson stays in contact with them. They're all over the country. Some are in jail, some are strung out on drugs. The ones who are disabled still live in Vermont with Mrs. Wilson.

Chip

GRAND RAPIDS, MICHIGAN
JANUARY 1997

*I did the white boy thing, and I did the hard-core black dude
thing. . . . I just took each side to the extreme so now I know how
each side works. . . . Relating to people is like learning another person's language.*

Each individual's journey to self-discovery is unique, and its
course takes many converging and diverging roads. Chip's journey centers
on finding answers to questions about who he is and where he belongs. His
journey began in a secure home with loving parents and three older siblings and stretched to the streets of urban Grand Rapids, Michigan.

Born in Ann Arbor, Michigan, in 1973, Chip spent the first five years
of his life moving from family to family. For him, those five years were
marked with painful memories of mental abuse and abandonment. He
remembers not looking "black enough" to be placed with African American foster families. On one occasion, his hair was dyed black to make him
physically appropriate to be placed with an African American family.

In 1978, after going through ten different foster families, Chip found a
permanent home with a family that had three other children, one of whom
was adopted and white. The family believed that, in addition to raising their
two biological children, they had a responsibility to adopt needy children.
During the 1970s Chip's adoptive mother was a homemaker, and her husband, who had earned his master's degree in communication, worked outside the home. When Chip was 8 years old, the family moved into a mul-
tiethnic community in Grand Rapids.

Throughout his childhood, Chip grew to love and trust his family. He
enjoyed playing with his siblings and going on family trips. But he found
in his adolescent years that the memories he tried so hard to forget before
being placed permanently propelled him to take extreme and at times dangerous measures to find a niche within the black community. For a time,
race and rage determined his attitude and behavior toward other people
and toward himself.

Now 23, Chip recognizes the opportunities he gained from his adoptive family. He says that because of his family he has the foundation "to do something good in his life." He believes that his interracial experiences have allowed him to interact genuinely with persons from different ethnic and cultural backgrounds. Chip is still finding answers to questions about who he is and where he belongs, but he's recognized that the truth about who he is stems from accepting his past and moving ahead to accomplish what his heart tells him to do.

Do you remember life before you became a part of your adoptive family, at the age of 5?

I have flashes of being in different families.

Were you in foster care?

I moved around to different families, but I don't remember being in foster homes.

What is your first memory of meeting your adoptive family?

I remember coming up to the house with the social worker and with my little brown paper bag, and there I was.

Describe your family.

Middle-class, white, open-minded, really cool. I wasn't forced to go to church; I could do what I wanted. There were rules and everything, but my parents let me be myself. I have a brother, Chad, who's 26—we call him "Big Bird"—and two sisters. One of my sisters, Melodie, who's 27, is also adopted but from a different family. She's white. My other sister, Kim, is 28.

Was it challenging for you, being black and growing up in a white family?

I didn't have a problem with it until I was 11 or 12, when I started getting into girls. Before then I didn't have a problem. I had a really good childhood. I got everything I wanted, took trips to Disney World, all that fun stuff, family stuff.

Did you notice physical differences between you and your family?

My hair. We lived in Hawaii for awhile. You know how black people's hair sometimes turns red? Well, the sunlight turns my hair bleached white, really blonde. So I had white curly hair, and that was different. I always knew I was different but I never knew why. The visible difference between me and my family is obvious. When I was smaller I had kinky hair, and I have wide hips, a wide nose, and full lips.

Did you believe you could pretend you were white, especially when it was convenient?

Yes. I had white friends. I was different, but white people accepted me. They liked me and treated me like I was special.

Did your friends know you were black?

Nobody ever said anything about it—until I got older. We were just kids, playing.

What happened when you got older?

Like I said, when I was 12 or 13, I started getting into my black side, hanging out with black people.

You talk about getting to know your " black side." Why was this important to you?

It was a way to find myself. I realized, hey, I'm black; I can't get my hair like Billy Idol's, like I tried to, because my hair's too curly. So I just tried to find myself and started making a lot of black friends.

My mom and the rest of the family moved to Heritage Hill in Grand Rapids, Michigan, which is a mixed area. She said she moved there because she wanted me to see another side of me, to get to know the African American community. I was around 8 at the time.

How did you get along with the people in that community?

Fine. I had friends, I was just chillin.' Like I said, I didn't have a problem when I was younger. It only hit me when I got older.

Explain that feeling.

It didn't hit me like, "Oh, man!" I just started changing, like a Tiger starts out as a cub and then changes and gets meaner. He can't help it; he's a tiger.

Did you get meaner?

Yes. For a couple of years I went through a real mean stage. I was rebellious and wild. A lot of that was because I wasn't in Catholic school anymore.

How did you explore, as you say, your "black side"?

I did my hair in black styles; you know, like the Philly fade. I stopped dressing "preppy," like I did when I went to Catholic Central. I started wearing big, saggy clothes, Adidas.

What's the story behind the saggy clothes?

It comes from New York, from "B-Boy." Have you ever heard of a B-Boy?

No.

Have you seen the graffiti on the walls in New York?

Yes.

There'd be a cartoon character next to the graffiti who'd be chillin' or break dancing with the goggles—that's B-Boy.

First it was break dancing and the next step was Wu-Wear. The Wu-Tang Clan has a video out on BET (Black Entertainment Television) and rap videos about their baggy clothes, dickies, Wu-Wear. They're from New York, too. It's the same as B-Boy's, but for 1996 and 1997. It's just like clothes lookin' good.

Is the saggy clothes a "black thing"?

It's an everybody thing now, but, yeah, it started out as a black thing. I noticed something about black people; they like to look good. Like I said, it started from a black thing.

Earlier you brought up an interesting point about the need to find out who you are as an individual—getting to know your "black side," as you put it. I'm wondering if that need made you identify with a particular kind of dress. But were there other signals that told you there was more to Chip than you knew?

Yeah. All of a sudden I asked myself why all these black girls were attracted to me. Something was different about me. It was like a piece was missing from what I knew about myself, so I went out to find it. For a while I thought that being black meant being hard-core, so I got off on the wrong track, with the wrong kind of friends. I wore my hat to the left and wore red, like the Vice Lords, a gang in Grand Rapids. There are also the BGDs, the Black Gangster Disciples from Chicago. Anyway I got into that stuff. And I was skipping school.

I got shot—that's what that scar is near my eye—with a .22. It blew a hole near my eye, messing around with that stuff, being around the wrong people. The bullet ricocheted off my head. I was lucky. That's what I mean by my "black side." I was just exploring.

And what did you find?

I found out that I can get along in both worlds. I can talk with a black person and relate. I can talk the same language, the same slang.

A debate is now going on about Ebonics. The term combines the words *ebony* and phonetics. It's about schools using slang terminology so that teachers can be more sensitive to students who communicate primarily in slang. What do you think?

Teaching slang isn't going to work. Slang is slang. You can't put it in a dictionary. It changes just like that [snap, snap, snap]. I can see teaching Spanish. But you can't teach slang. Everybody's got their own slang, you know. It's just your own Wu-Tang style.

How did you learn to speak slang?

Being around people. Have you heard the word *chill*?

Yes.

That's slang. You just pick up on it.

I hung out with mostly black people because I went through my anti-white stage, even though my adoptive parents are white. I guess it was something I had to go through because of all the anger that was built up in me. Before I was adopted I went through a lot of mental abuse, and the abuse was from different families. It seems that I wasn't black enough to be in some black foster families. So they dyed my hair so I'd look more black in this one family I was with. I guess my anger got built up. And toward my teenage years, I went through a wild, crazy phase. Everybody goes through a crazy phase growing up.

I realized I was black, but I went overboard with it and tried to be too black, too hard-core. I was getting into fights, attracting attention. I was wearing African medallions. I took what I represent to the extreme. I have to realize that I'm lucky because I'm part of both sides of the world. That's my life, and I have to accept it. I don't look at it as a disadvantage.

My mom knows how to be a really good mom. She's the best mom, she's so cool. But she didn't understand me and couldn't because she's not black and wasn't raised in the "hood." You don't necessarily have to be raised in the "hood," but there's something about being black. I'm not saying black is better, but there's a difference between black and white. It's like putting two different species of fish in the same tank. They're all fish but they're different.

It was hard for my mom to understand what was going on with me, so she got me a counselor. Of course she was a white counselor, and she didn't understand *what* I was talking about. Finally my mom got this black dude counselor, and he was real cool. He helped me out. I just needed to be on my own.

After being kicked out by my adoptive mother and her husband, I got to live out all my adventures and see what life was all about. Now that I'm grown and see that life is hard, I realize I had to get myself together.

You referred to being anti-white at one time.

I don't know why really. Me and my boys would get drunk and go out and jump some white dudes. Dumb stuff like that. I guess I was trying to prove something.

What were you feeling when you jumped these guys? Did you get satisfaction?

No, I felt bad. I don't know how my friends felt. But deep down I knew it was wrong because that stuff comes back to you. Plus, that's probably why I got shot, messing around like that.

I just felt bad 'cause you're a part of everything whether you like it or not and everybody is a part of you. I figured that out. So if I'm out jumping a white dude, I'm jumping myself, because he's a part of myself. I'm just hurting myself, and I got feelings, you know.

What was one of the most painful memories you can remember as a child?

The abuse and stuff I went through with different families before I was adopted. I don't remember specific events, but it had an effect on me. It's those hurt feelings inside me that have been tucked away. I think that's why I went into my wild stage, because of all that stuff that had been packed away for years and needed to come out.

How do you relate to blacks and whites now? Is there a difference in your style of communication?

Yes, there's a difference, but I feel more comfortable around blacks. It's like this: If I get pulled over for a ticket and the cop is on his radio, he always says, "I got a black male here." They always say that.

When I was in high school, they had me down as white. I don't know why. But one day the principal, who's black, pulled me aside and told me they had me down as white. I told him to go ahead and change it to say that I'm black. I get along better with blacks. I feel more comfortable.

You can cross over?

Ru Paul?

What's Ru Paul?

You never heard of Ru Paul, cross-dressing? I could carry myself as white. I did that once. I put a relaxer in my hair. My friend Chris did it for me. It looked like lightening just hit me. And I wore the tight Guess jeans. Yeah, I can carry myself like that and get away with it.

Why haven't you?

Because that's not me. It could be, and that's what my parents would probably want me to do just because it's a white world. You can get better jobs. Your appearance, that first impression, counts. That's why my hair is cut. I had dreads. I used to get my hair braided every week. But its time to get clean-cut.

Now I stay at home with my adoptive mother and her husband, so I got to follow their rules. I guess I don't choose to cross over because I don't feel like that. I don't feel like a normal American person, because I'm not. My life's been so twisted and different.

Now that you're home, after having been through some difficult experiences, what have you learned about some of life's twists and turns?

I look at my life in a good way. I've experienced stuff that others haven't, from both sides, black and white. I "dissed" all my "homies" and stuff because they're not doing anything with their lives. They're still cool and all that, but they're not doing anything . . . bad news to hang around them. They bring me down, bring my attitude down. So all of a sudden I'm back home, living this middle-class life. And some people don't even get a chance to get out of their neighborhoods, neighborhoods that are filled with guns and drugs and stuff. So I got a chance to do something for myself.

I was talking with my mom the other day about going to film school. She said I could go and she'd pay for it. I tell myself, take advantage of that! I didn't see it like that back when I was 16 or 17, when I thought I knew everything.

Do you ever think about love?

It feels good to know that you're wanted and loved. The reason I mentioned the brown paper bag earlier in our conversation, when I first met my adoptive parents, is because my mom told me that when I walked up the driveway with that little brown paper bag, she immediately fell in love with me. Then we made chocolate chip cookies. That's why she calls me Chip. It feels good to be loved.

I'm real cool with animals. We always had pets, cats and dogs. I guess I'm real cool with them because they don't hurt you back. They don't talk about you and say you're ugly. A cat will come up to you and purr when you pet him.

I didn't have a lot of friends before I got adopted. I was still bouncing around. When I came to my adoptive family I found love—toys for Christmas, people caring about you. It's a good feeling. I'm not trying to sound like the late rapper Tupac (Shakur), but I'd like to put my shout out to other people too, my love.

Society puts a lot of emphasis on race. Blacks and whites have been polarized in this country. How do you find a balance between both worlds?

I've lived both lives. I did the white boy thing, and I did the hard-core black dude thing. I don't mean hard-core black dude like it's always got to be hard-core. I just took each side to the extreme so now I know how each side works. I put myself in the middle, not just being adopted but also being mixed. Relating to people is like learning another person's language.

What would you say to white parents who adopt black children?

I think it's good, but you have to understand the kid. You, the parents, can't force him to be white. That's where the problems come in. Read a book. Don't give me the book to read. Read about Martin Luther King Jr. and learn something about who I am.

If I adopted a kid who's a different race from me, I'd try to get where he's at. You gotta be more than a parent these days. Instead of saying to the child, "You're grounded," you gotta be able to understand the kid because he'll talk to his friends before he'll talk to his parents. It's wild with drugs and guns out there. I'd try to learn about his background, whether he was Asian or Chinese, and find out about his biological parents. I'd do whatever I could.

What do you want in life?

I want to be happy, straight-up. Straight-up grin on my face because I'm that damn happy. Happiness to me is feeling confident, feeling secure, not worrying. I guess happiness is feeling that you're not so different. It's like feeling you got it under control—even if it's for a minute or half a second . . . feeling like, "Boom! That test, I passed it. Boom!"

What are the advantages of being adopted into a white family?

You got the inside track. You can learn the way a person operates. With black people, same thing, you learn both sides. It's knowledge. A lot of people don't get that because they're prejudiced or they don't want to learn about other people. They get stuck on the "no, man, I'm black not white" mentality.

Do you think that society in general should work to overcome racial and ethnic barriers, or do you believe that the white and black worlds should remain divided?

I think it's cool if everybody gets along. Your spirit is a part of everything. A black person and a Chinese person are a part of each other. I believe there are people who want division. They want black people to kill each other in the 'hood' and put drugs in the 'hood.'

Malcolm X realized that everybody was the same. He found out that there were white Muslims and black Muslims. He was trying to bring people together. That's why I believe he got killed. He was getting too powerful. People are insecure. People are scared to be real.

Are you real?

I try to be. It's hard. When you're doing something good or doing the right thing, man, people try to bring you down for some reason. It's like you wanted to do this interview. I was nervous. I could have easily done something else. But you're trying to do something, so I wanted to support you. I've learned you need people like that. I've had "home boys" who I thought were my friends totally 'diss' me. At times I reach the point where I'm by myself, can't trust anybody.

We talked briefly about the advantages of being black in a white family. What are some of the disadvantages?

I see things differently. Black people like the heat. They like the house hot. A white person keeps their house so damn cold. Like at my mom's house, I got sweaters on. I tell them they've got to turn up the heat. They tell me, "Put a sweater on." You know, stuff like that. Eating. Music. It's in your genes. That goes back to the beginning of time.

You are who you are. Just because you're black in a white family doesn't mean you have to act different than who you are. You're still going to be who you are. Have you ever seen the movie *Brave Heart*? He was raised by his uncle because his dad got killed, but he was still Brave Heart. He didn't try to be like his uncle. It's that simple. It doesn't have to be complicated.

Do you want to have kids?

Yes.

What will you teach them?

I'll teach them from what I learned, so they don't make the same mistakes I did. I'm going to make sure I understand my kids.

One of my biggest problems as a child was that my mom didn't understand me because she couldn't, even though she tried her hardest. It's like you talking to me about algebra when I haven't had an algebra class. It's another language and I can't "hit" it. That's another disadvantage of being black in a white family—the communication barrier. My brother, Chad, never had serious problems. The only time I remember him getting into trouble was when he tried to light a fire in the fireplace and didn't open the hatch and the room got smoky. That's just him.

Are you still in contact with your sisters?

I talk with them at Christmas time. I don't get a long very well with Melodie. She has a lot of problems.

You said earlier that Melodie is also adopted?

Yes. She's the one who lives in Detroit. Anyway, I don't know about her. It's a bad scene.

My sister Kim lives in Colorado and she's the one I talk to at Christmas. We're real tight. Melodie is in her own world. She's getting into that wild stuff.

Reflecting on your own life experience, particularly the impact of being in foster homes for five years, do you think it's important for children to have permanent homes?

Yes. Kids need to have permanent homes so they can start their lives. It's like a job. Are you going to change a job every two weeks? Pretty soon you'll stay at one job and start making a future for yourself. That's when you start progressing. You want to stay in one place so you can "veg out." The point is, you're trying to grow like a plant.

It's good to have somebody to trust. The first five years of a child's life are the most important. A baby needs to be held or needs a pacifier for security. If a child is in a foster home with a bunch of other kids, they don't get the tender care they need. These kids are treated like patients. It's not good, man, it is a bad scene!

You need somebody to tell you they love you. If you're in a foster home with fifty other kids, I'm sure the person on duty isn't going to tell everybody that he or she loves them, every night, before the kid goes to bed.

What have you learned about yourself and your adoptive family in living with them?

I'm always learning. Now I know I'm not alone.

What do you mean, you're not alone?

Rhonda, you're going through the same stuff. So it's not like you're looking at me like I'm strange because I'm adopted. With adopted kids, parents have to watch what they say or don't say about their kids because they're fragile. They've already been wounded in battle.

PART III

In Their Own Voices:
Summary and Concluding Remarks

Twenty-four men and women participated in this study. The twelve women range in age from 22 to 28. Eight of them were adopted when they were 3 months old or younger. The other four were 1 year, 18 months, 2 years, and 6 years old. But the 6 year old had been living with the family as a foster child since her birth. The respondent who was adopted when she was 2 had been in foster care with an African American couple, who may have wanted to adopt her but were not allowed to because of their age. Rhonda had been abandoned by her birth mother and was taken directly from the hospital to the black family. Five of the twelve describe themselves as "mixed," the others as black. Kimberly, one of the five who describes herself as mixed is married to a white man and is the mother of two sons. Two of the mixed respondents are married to black men, another is unmarried but has a son who is two and a half, and the fifth is unmarried and has recently moved back to her parents' home. Eight of the women have at least a bachelor's degree, one is working on her Ph.D., one has an M.S. in speech communications, and one is working toward a master's degree in social work. Three are currently working toward completing their B.A. degrees, and one graduated from high school and has taken college courses but is not currently working toward a degree.

Among the women, Donna Francis, the 26 year old who is working on her Ph.D. on the history of American education, has the strongest black identity. She describes herself as having had only black friends from the time she entered college. She says, "Not only is my pigment black, but my thoughts, the way I relate to other people, and the way I talk and dance and socialize are black. I consider the issues facing the black community, my issues." But Donna Francis is just as empathetic about the positive relationship and the strong ties she has to her white parents, who adopted her when she was 4 weeks old, and to her sister, who is a year younger than she. "I've never felt out of place or uncomfortable in my house and have never doubted that I was fully their daughter." Both Donna Francis's parents are teachers. Donna Francis goes on to say,

> I really like the person I am, and I attribute that to my parents. They have helped to make me very independent, strong-willed and determined, compassionate and loving, accepting and understanding, all the things parents hope to pass on to their kids. Their "whiteness" had less to do with it than that they were Mom and Dad and loved me completely. I know my parents would do anything for me and my sister. . . . They never worried about whether I would doubt my love for them or turn on them because they are white. They stepped back and let me do what I had to do to understand who I was as a black woman living in America in 1997. They listened to me when I talked, and we talked about race and gender.

Donna Francis is quick to say that "just because you're pro-black doesn't make you anti-white."

Donna Francis is generally supportive of transracial adoption but believes that white families who live in isolated communities should not be allowed to adopt black children. Of all the interviews with the young women who have been transracially adopted, Donna Francis is the most strident and most empathetic about her black identity and her commitment to the black community and black issues.

Jessica, the senior at a traditional black college, also states that she loves and is completely happy with her adopted family but that her family could not help her forge her black identity. For that, Jessica claims, she had to go outside her family and, in her words, create "a family of black friends." She, too, reports that her own experience with transracial adoption has been positive but, again, in Jessica's words, "I don't look fondly upon white people adopting nonwhite children." While Jessica, like Donna Francis, feels strongly about her black identity, she doesn't focus on a desire to work on black issues, nor does she express a commitment to the black community. But then, Donna Francis is working on her Ph.D. and Jessica is in her senior year of college.

Four of the respondents, two of whom describe themselves as mixed, do not place their racial identities at the top of the list. Andrea, who is 23 and has a son, two and a half, states clearly, "Race wasn't an issue." She cites her parents, who adopted three children who were mixed, of black and white races, "because they wanted three babies. Race and sex weren't issues." She goes on to say that for any adoptee, whether adopted within the same race or transracially, the "most important thing is growing up in a family that loves and supports you."

Kimberly also comes from a family that adopted across racial lines. She was one of six adopted children, all mixed, black and white. At 27, Kimberly, a graduate student in social work, married to a white man and the mother of two sons, describes her family as expressive and loving, and her mother as her advocate. For example, Kimberly reports that when she was having trouble with a teacher in junior high, her mother went to the school and told this teacher, in effect, that her daughter was having a problem with him, and that "I thought he was racist, and, according to what I'd told her, it seemed he was having a problem with the black kids in his class."

Kimberly lived in a socially mixed neighborhood. Her mother's closest friend was of mixed race (black and white), and she was married to a black man. They had an African American babysitter. Their church, which was, and is, an important part of the family's and Kimberly's life has black and white members. Kimberly is a strong supporter of transracial adoption. As a professional social worker, she stated, "I'll never join the National Association of Black Social Workers because of how strongly I oppose their position. I believe that their very strong voice has divided people and society on this issue." On a positive note, she urges the NABSW to focus their efforts, money, and knowledge on educating people about how to raise children from different cultures "so we can do the best for the child."

Shecara, a 28-year-old nurse who describes herself as biracial, is the mother of two children, a 7-year-old daughter and an 11-month-old son. Shecara had ten siblings, all of whom were born to her adoptive parents. After a complicated adolescence in which she moved away from her family, both literally and emotionally, she had a difficult relationship with her daughter's father, who was in and out of jail during much of their relationship. Shecara moved back to her parents' community and began putting her life in order. This involved working out a better, more open relationship with her parents and siblings, working at a day care center, going back to school, and, finally, obtaining a degree in nursing of which she is justly proud. In December 1996 she married her current husband, who is the father of her eleven month old son. The fathers of both her children are black. On the issue of transracial adoption, Shecara places family above race. Although there were times when she felt no one understood her journey of racial discovery, Shecara considers herself blessed that she was adopted by her caring family.

Laurie, the most "cosmopolitan" of the interviewees, who, before entering high school, had lived in Sierra Leone, the Ivory Coast, Panama, Bangladesh, and Thailand, also does not put her black identity at the top of her list. Laurie's world travels were the result of her parents having joined the Peace Corps when she was 18 months old, and then later the Diplomatic Corps of the State Department. The family (her parents and two birth brothers who were 3 and 6 when she was adopted) lived in Sierra Leone for about five years. They returned to their hometown of Seattle for two years and then, when Laurie was about 9, the family went off to the Ivory Coast. Laurie and her family returned to the United States, settling in Washington, D.C., in time for her to start high school. Laurie believes that a child's best interests are met by being adopted into a supportive and loving family. She feels "incredibly lucky" to have been adopted into a family that "adores and loves me. They picked me." Her Jewish identity is also important to her.

Laurie's mother died about a year before Laurie was interviewed. In her interview she tells us that when her mother was diagnosed with cancer of the colon, Laurie asked her for a copy of her health records. Laurie explained that she was not doing this in order to find her "real" parents. Both Laurie and her adoptive parents agreed that they, indeed, were her real parents.

Regarding a problem she has with the black community, Laurie said that spokespersons for the black community do not accept the fact that "some of us who have dark skin are multiracial." In Laurie's words, "the black community puts us in a little box. . . . You have to be black." Her final words to transracial adoptees are these: "Feel lucky because so many children out there don't have a family . . . and don't let other people depress you by saying it's bad to be adopted by white people. Saying that is evil and wrong."

Like Laurie, Chantel is also unequivocally comfortable with her racial identity and with having been adopted by white parents. She credits her family for her accomplishments, her outgoing personality, and her ability to look past racial prejudices. Chantel has put her beliefs into action by founding an adoption program, Assist One, in Sacramento, California. In her words, "the bottom line in adoption is the kids." Chantel urges black and white families to adopt black children, white children, children of any race or background.

Growing up in the same family, Nicolle, Chantel's sister, describes their family as a living experiment proving that race does not have to be a negative issue unless one allows it to be. Even though Nicolle states, early on in her interview, that "love transcends all racial barriers," regarding her own racial identity she reports that while her parents can sympathize with her they cannot empathize because of the difference in the color of their skin. She also reports that while she is clear about her black identity, she gained that clarity on her own. While Nicolle disagrees with the NABSW, she nevertheless views transracial adoption as a second choice to placing a black child in a permanent black home. She does believe, however, that a permanent white home is better for a black child than foster care.

Another respondent, Rachel, is a 22-year-old black woman currently living with her family in a small community in Illinois. She attends a community college and works as a teacher at a child development center. Rachel identifies herself as "just a woman who happens to have darker skin. People would classify me as an African American, but I don't see myself as being African American." Rachel also told us that she feels no connection to the black community. Unlike most of the other families described by the participants in this study, Rachel's parents were older (in their late forties when they adopted her), working-class, and high school educated. She believes her parents did nothing to help her learn about her history or background. She also believes that her mother held her back by always referring to Rachel's "hip problem" and warning her that she was trying to do too much. Her father contends, and continues to express it, that "college isn't for everybody." Rachel feels that transracial adoption can be rewarding for a child if the parents are willing to expose the child to his or her background and history. Unfortunately that has not been Rachel's experience.

Iris, 27 years old, college-educated, married to a black man, and employed as a professional negotiator, reports that her parents "chose to raise me as if I were their own white, biological child, not because they were insensitive but because they didn't want me to think that they thought of me as being different." The family moved to a Southern community when she was 7 because they wanted her to live in a more diverse community. Unfortunately her experiences in junior high and high school were difficult. Iris reports that she was "beat up every day by a group of black girls." It wasn't until she attended a historically black college that she gained her self-esteem. It was at this college, Iris claims, that for the first time she could sit in the first or second row of a classroom and participate in the class discussion, not feeling that the professor assumed she was stupid. It was in college that she learned about the contributions of blacks and biracial Americans.

Iris believes that the black community still makes too much of skin shade, that they need to stop acting as though those who are lighter-skinned are less black. She recognizes and urges others in the black community to admit that the black community also has problems with class issues and sexism.

Aaliyah, a 26-year-old employee at an insurance agency, is the outlier in this group. She has recently moved back into her upper-middle-class parents' home after a tumultuous relationship with her lower-status black boyfriend, who is currently in jail, and his family, whom she described as constantly smoking and drinking. About four years ago Aaliyah sought and located her birth parents. Her white mother was 15 when Aaliyah was born. She had married and then divorced Aaliyah's father because he abused her. Aaliyah found her father a year later, but no relationship developed. Today, Aaliyah reports that she likes living with her mom and dad, she is learning how to spend more time talking with them and going out to lunch with her mom. Aaliyah wants to survive and get her act together.

The coauthor of this volume, who is 27, is also one of the participants in the study. Rhonda was 2 years old when she was adopted by a white family in upper New York state. Her parents divorced when she was 21. Her black godmother, whom she met at her church, and her father were her significant others during the years she was growing up. Regarding her feelings as a transracial adoptee, Rhonda says, "We have the ability to bring worlds together, to see both sides of issues confronting black and white people. We have the credibility to do so." She makes specific suggestions to white families who want to or have adopted a child of a different race: join a black church, have black friends, live in a racially mixed community.

Of the twelve male participants, eight were adopted before they were 6 months old, one was adopted when he was 2, two were adopted when they were 5, and one lived with a white family in a southern, rural Virginia community from 1954 to 1959 when he was between 13 and 18 years of age. Four were born and raised in Iowa, Michigan, Illinois, and Oregon. The other eight were born and reared on the East Coast in Connecticut, Vermont, Massachusetts, New York, Maryland, and Virginia. Eleven of them range in age from 23 to 31. Lester is 57. Six are married, three to white women, one to a Haitian woman, and two to American black women. Four of them have children; one adopted a black child when the child was 6 months old. One is a single father.

The work lives of our respondents show a good deal of variety. There's a professional athlete and Olympic gold medal winner, a minister, a property manager, a ninth-grade teacher, an aspiring screenwriter, a student, a stockbroker, an actor, a police officer, a technical writer, and a retiree from the Department of the Army. Eight of the participants hold at least bachelor's degrees. At the time the interviews were conducted most of the respondents lived in small or medium-sized cities.

Seven of the respondents (the professional musician, the minister, the stockbroker, the professional athlete, the two writers, and the retiree) are very positive about their experiences as transracial adoptees. Keith, the minister, was adopted at the age of 5. In addition, his family had five birth children and two adopted children, one from Hawaii and the other from Vietnam. He characterizes his family as "exceptionally wonderful," and his advice to families who are considering transracial adoption is to "adopt because you want to give a child a good home." Keith identifies himself as a black, not an African American. He says, "I was born in the United States of America and there was no Africa about it. Therefore, I don't consider myself to be an African American. . . . Black is what I am." Keith also claims that he has not suffered from discrimination. He emphasizes hard work: "We need to give our people the knowledge to be successful, not the message that they are in bondage."

Daniel, the 29-year old technical writer, is entirely comfortable and happy about his relationship with his family and about his social identity. He feels at ease in both black and white communities. He describes his black identity in these words: "My blackness was made known to me as a positive thing. My sense is that often in the general black community, individuals are first made aware of their blackness as a strike against them. In my early experience, I never had that introduction to my blackness. Therefore, I don't view my blackness as a strike against me."

Daniel is proud of his parents who emigrated from Holland when they were 17 and 18 years old and whom he describes as risk takers. The values they instilled in him—a strong work ethic, knowing the difference between right and wrong, and love and kindness—are ones he wants to hold on to and follow all his life. He views transracial adoption as "an act of love."

Tage is a 27-year-old African American professional musician who was adopted at birth in Hartford, Connecticut. Tage plays with the President's Own Marine Band in Washington, D.C. His dream is to play principal trumpet with the Boston Symphony. The family moved to Cambridge,

Massachusetts, in the early 1970s because his father was going to Harvard University. In addition to having four birth children, Tage's parents adopted six children: two from Vietnam, one from Cambodia, one from El Salvador, and one Native American. Tage is the oldest of all the children in the family. He is married to a white woman whom he met at Michigan State when he was a freshman. She is also a musician. He describes the neighborhood where he grew up as diverse. He and his siblings had black friends. About transracial adoption, Tage recommends that the adoptive family "live in a diverse community and instill in your child a strong sense of love and family."

David, an aspiring screenwriter, is 27, married to a white woman, and the father of two sons, aged 7 and 4. David was adopted when he was 3 months old. Both his parents hold Ph.D.'s—his father in engineering, his mother in elementary education. He has two birth brothers. When he was 9 David's family moved from Hartford, Connecticut, to Sioux Center, Iowa, because his father was offered the opportunity of starting an engineering program at the university. David reports that the civil rights movement was probably an important factor in his parents' decision to adopt a black child. The schools David attended—elementary, high school, and college—were private Christian (Dutch Reformed) institutions. His wife is white and a member of the Dutch Reformed Church.

As an adult David feels he has confidence in himself. He tells us that he's "never had a void" in his life. David points out that the goal of adoption is to get the child into a stable environment. If a child is passed from one foster home to another, just waiting until a black family comes along, "the kid will probably be really 'screwed up.'" David is proud of who he is, proud of his family, and proud of his Christianity. He thinks of the Dutch community as his people. In David's words, "My religion is more important to me than the color of my skin."

The Olympian gold medalist reports that his happiest memories are holiday dinners with his family, which include seven siblings, several of whom have been transracially adopted. He credits his family with instilling in him values that allow him to be the best at what he does, which at this time in his life is professional athletics. Dan believes that family environment, not biology, largely determines "who you are." Like the other professional athlete we interviewed, Dan has also established a foundation. His is primarily to help children develop their social and athletic skills. Dan identifies himself as mixed race, but he urges everyone to be individuals and not to focus on race.

Seth, the stockbroker and a single father of a 9-year-old son, lives next door to his parents. He is their only child. Seth plays an active role in describing the positive aspects of transracial adoption. The major themes in Seth's interview are his enthusiasm for his work as a stockbroker, his ties to his parents, his desire to be a positive role model for his son, and his positive views of transracial adoption.

Lester, the 57-year-old retiree from the Department of the Army, was informally adopted by a white family and lived with them for only five years, during his adolescence. Growing up during the time of segregation in a small southern community, the circumstances under which he lived hardly fits that of an adopted child. For example, he was not allowed to have his meals with the family or sleep in the main part of the house. But Lester's feelings about the Joneses are extraordinarily positive. He describes them in the most generous and positive terms and has maintained ties with them for more than forty years.

The next group of participants offer a more complicated profile of the adult male transracial adoptee. Ned, a 29-year-old ninth-grade school-teacher who is married to a black woman and the father of a 6-month-old adopted black son, sympathizes with the NABSW position. Ned and his biological twin sister were adopted when they were 6 weeks old by strong Christian schoolteachers. About his own experiences, he explains, "I feel too black for my coworkers and yet with some of my students, I'm too white." He believes that he and his parents were able to overcome many difficulties. Today he describes himself as an African American male with an African American wife and child. In working out his racial identity, Ned decided that teaching would enable him to give back to his community and also to make an impact in the community. He ends his interview on a poignant note, describing a lingering, uncomfortable situation at work where he doesn't quite fit in with his colleagues or his students; nor does he quite fit in with the congregation of his black Baptist Church. He is in limbo, but has learned to be happy with that. Regarding his relationship with his parents, he unquestionably loves them and gets along well with them. He knows they love him. Ned is not unaware of the role social class plays in his dilemma. Any middle-class African American, he recognizes, may have identity problems similar to his.

Pete found his way into this study because his picture was on the cover of *American Demographics*, and we learned he was a police officer in Ithaca, New York, who had been transracially adopted. Adopted at 6 weeks of age into a family that had three birth children, today Pete serves as a police officer in a community near the area where he grew up. He is married to a white woman. Pete characterizes his major differences with his family as those of personality and interests. Pete's passion was sports, whereas school and studies, and their three birth children, were his parents' priorities (his father was a librarian at Cornell University and both his father and mother held master's degrees). When his parents separated during Pete's sophomore year in high school, he moved into a friend's home, the father being Pete's coach in several sports. The family was white. A year later Pete moved in with his adoptive mother, but in his senior year, when his mother moved in with her boyfriend, Pete went to live with a friend's family who was black. After finishing high school he joined the army. Upon getting out of the army he took the fire fighter's exam (his first choice as a career) but didn't do well enough to be offered a job. He then took the police officer's exam and scored highest among the applicants.

Like Ned, Pete finds that he is not "black enough" for some members of the black community. Professionally he feels caught in a "Catch 22." If he does well in his career, he's viewed as a token; if he doesn't do well, the explanation is obvious—he's black. Pete supports transracial adoption but believes it's very important that the adoptive family understand the cultural differences between blacks and whites and help the black child learn about those differences and acquire a black identity. Pete claims he learned a lot about those differences by living with a black family. Recently, Pete discovered that his birth father is a Nigerian doctor, and someone who is very athletic. They've made contact and plan to meet soon, when his birth father comes to the United States.

Britton is one of the respondents who is ambivalent about who he is. He was adopted when he was a few months old because his parents didn't think they could have children. But subsequently, after adopting Britton, they had three children. Britton attended a special high school for the arts in Rochester, New York, where the majority of students were black. Before transferring to that school, Britton had a hard time with blacks, who, he tells us, made his life "hell." A major goal in Britton's life is to find his birth parents. He needs to know where he came from. He feels that he is not really accepted or acclimated into one culture or the other.

Taalib was adopted into a family where the mother was a full-time foster mother. By the time he was 13, Taalib estimates that more than 400 children had come through their home. His parents also adopted 16 children of Hispanic, black, and white backgrounds. Taalib's father died shortly before we interviewed him; his mother is in her seventies. Taalib's adolescence and his college years show a great deal of turbulence, with wide emotional and behavioral swings. Taalib reports that he did well in high school, but when he got to Syracuse University he began to party and drink heavily, and his grades suffered. His weekends began on Thursdays and ended on Mondays. After six years he graduated from Syracuse, straightened himself out, and went on to law school. Over the years Taalib became involved in black power activities. He reports that he decided to go to law school because, as a lawyer, he thought he could help his black brothers.

Regarding his attitude toward transracial adoption, Taalib strongly believes that love is not enough and that white parents who adopt a black child should have a multicultural plan. That plan should include a soulmate for the child, someone the child can identify with because they are both of the same race.

The last participant, Chip, is 23 years old, was adopted when he was 5, and currently lives with his adoptive mother and her husband near the community where he was raised, Grand Rapids, Michigan. Chip describes his background as Irish, Indian, and black. He tells us that, in the first five years of his life, he experienced mental abuse from black families who would not accept him because he wasn't black enough. His adoptive family consisted of two birth children and an adopted sister who was white. When Chip was 8, his mother and siblings (his parents had separated) moved to a diversely populated area of Grand Rapids. At this point, Chip claims, he began to explore what he calls his "black side." He did his hair in black styles, wore saggy clothes and African medallions, skipped school, and joined a gang. He narrowly missed losing an eye from a gunshot wound.

About his mother, he says, "She's the best mom, she's so cool. But she didn't understand me and couldn't because she's not black and wasn't raised in the 'hood.'" Not until his mother sought out a black counselor did the situation start to improve.

At the time Chip was interviewed he was living with his adoptive mother, who told him she would pay for him to go to film school, if that's what he wanted to do. Chip blames many of his problems on his experiences before his adoption. Foster care was a "bad scene." Chip supports transracial adoption but emphasizes that the parents have to understand their child, read about black history, and not force the child to be white.

What messages emerge from these interviews? Clearly, these adult children believe that their adoptive parents loved them, cared for them, and tried to do right by them. Do they believe their parents always succeeded? No! The major complaint from those who are critical is that their parents did not know how or did not understand that they needed to rear their black or mixed-race child differently than they reared a child of their own race. They should have worked harder at finding out how to raise a black child. They should have learned more about the history of the black community in this country; they should have associated more with black families, lived in mixed neighborhoods, joined black churches. They should have attended public events with black families. Four of the women and five of the men make these points. But they, too, emphasize how much their parents loved them.

While all the participants believe they benefited by having been adopted, they offer advice to white families about how to make life easier for the black child they adopt. This they do without questioning the good will and sincerity of white families who choose to adopt black and mixed-race children. For Donna Francis and Jessica, and to some extent Taalib and Chip, their black identity is all-important. But for the others, the more salient definition of who they are is not their racial identity but rather their work, their talents, their family attachments, and their religious commitments.

Finally, when we compare the responses from the 1991 Simon-Altstein survey data to the reflections and opinions expressed by the participants in this study, we find a good deal of consensus. All the participants believe that transracial adoption served them well; all of them feel connected to their adoptive parents; and all, except one, support transracial adoption, but with the strong recommendation that agencies and prospective parents recognize the importance of learning about their child's racial history and culture and make that history and culture part of both their child's life and their family life...